The Origins of
the Anglo-Saxons

Don Henson FSA, MIFA

Anglo-Saxon Books

By the same author

A Guide to Late Anglo-Saxon England
The English Elite in 1066

Published 2006 by
Anglo-Saxon Books
Frithgarth
Thetford Forest Park
Hockwold-cum-Wilton
Norfolk   England

P.L.

British Library Cataloguing-in-Publication Data. A catalogue record for this book is available from the British Library.

ISBN 1–898281–40-8

The Author

Don Henson is an archaeologist with a passion for British prehistory, and for early medieval history and literature. After studying archaeology and researching prehistoric stone tools at Sheffield University he worked as a museum education officer, before his current job as Education and Outreach Co-ordinator of the Council for British Archaeology. He believes the past has a vital role to play in people's lives today, and is equally passionate about public archaeology. His fascination for the Anglo-Saxons began with an attempt to read Beowulf in Old English when he was 15; a task he hopes to complete one day after 35 years of trying!

Tum omnes consiliarii una cum superbo tyranno caecantur, adinvenientes tale praesidium, immo excidium patriae ut ferocissimi illi nefandi nominis Saxones deo hominibusque invisi, quasi in caulas lupi, in insulam ad retundendas aquilonales gentes intromitterentur.

Then all the members of the council, together with the proud tyrant, were struck blind; the guard – or rather the method of destruction – they devised for our land was that the ferocious Saxons (name not to be spoken!), hated by man and God, should be let into the island like wolves into the fold, to beat back the peoples of the north.

Gildas *De Excidio Britanniae*, chapter 23 (Winterbottom 1978: 26 & 97)

Contents

Contents

Contents

Contents

Contents

Foreword

This book has come about through a growing frustration with scholarly analysis and debate about the beginnings of Anglo-Saxon England. Much of what has been written is excellent, yet leaves me unsatisfied. One reason for this is the fragmentation of academic disciplines so that scholars often have only a vague acquaintance with fields outside their own specialism. The result is a partial examination of the evidence and an incomplete understanding or explanation of the period. My own field of expertise is archaeology. The growth and increasing dominance of archaeological evidence for the period has been accompanied by what I regard as an unhealthy enthusiasm for models of social change imported from prehistory (my own area of specialism). Put simply, many archaeologists have developed a complete unwillingness to consider movements of population as a factor in social, economic or political change. All change (e.g. the adoption of agriculture) becomes a result of indigenous development, and all historically recorded migrations become merely the movement of a few aristocrats or soldiers numbered at most a few hundred. This has never seemed to me to be credible. A further source of discontent for me is the polarised nature of debate about the period. Scholars' views are often based on particular beliefs and biases, and yet these are seldom made explicit. One of the positive gains in the humanistic sciences in recent decades has been the recognition that our interpretations and analyses are determined as much by the present day context in which we work and by our own biases, rather than by an objective and neutral examination of the evidence.

My own fascination with the 5th and 6th centuries began many years ago with a chance encounter in a children's encyclopaedia when I was a teenager. What I came across was a piece of Old English, a quotation from King Alfred's translation of *De Consolatione Philosophiae* of Beothius. This led me to *Beowulf* and then to Sir Frank Stenton's magisterial *Anglo-Saxon England*. My academic education and research headed off towards prehistory but Anglo-Saxon history, literature and culture remained an abiding interest. In my career, I moved into heritage education, in which I needed a broad overview of all periods of human history. Understanding the interplay between all forms of evidence became part of my outlook on the past. I also became aware of just how marginal the Anglo-Saxon period was in education in England. Yet, I also saw how important an understanding of that period was to very real debates about the nature of identity and citizenship in 21st century Britain. False assertions of English racial homogeneity became a real possibility, running counter to our understanding of the realities of English history. False embarrassment about asserting an English cultural identity as being somehow politically incorrect were equally in evidence. Neither of these respects the reality of England's origins, nor allows a proper appreciation for the importance of the 5th and 6th centuries in understanding much of our nation's later history

This book is an attempt to satisfy my own dissatisfactions. It attempts to address a serious issue: what are the origins of the Anglo-Saxons. In doing this, I hope I have not been guilty of what I decry in others. I make plain and openly declare my own standpoint and biases. I attempt to cover a wide range of evidence and pay due account to all. I have no doubt that this work has faults, not least of which is my own vague acquaintance with fields outside my own area of expertise. I hope the reader will accept that it is better to sin through enthusiasm that to sin through omission.

Don Henson

York, December 2004

Introduction

In common with nations that have dominated empires or states for a long time, and whose junior partners have achieved a level of national consciousness, the English are beginning to wake up to the problem of their identity. With the advent of devolution for Scotland and Wales within the United Kingdom, the increasing incorporation of the United Kingdom into a European Union, and perhaps in the face of increasing monolithic globalisation of the world in an American image, the English have begun to ask a simple question: who are we? There has been an explosion of writings about English identity and nationhood. These are just some of them: Ackroyd 2004, Barnes 1999, Baucom 1999, Colls 2002, Davies 1998, Duffy 2001, Easthope 1998, Fox 2004, Haseler 1996, Hitchens 2003, Jones 1998, Kumar 2003, Langford 2000, Linsell 2000, Matless 1998, Paxman 1999, Scruton 2001, Smith 1996, Vansittart 1998, Weight 2002, Wood 1999, 2000. The question may be simple: who are the English? Yet, as is the way with simple questions, they lead to complex answers and debates.

Part of the exploration of Englishness has to be the investigation of the origins of the English identity, and this must involve the study of what is sometimes called the migration period. This was the time when the collapsing Roman Empire in western Europe coincided with the migration of ruling elites and peoples. It saw the foundation in principle of what would become, much later, the nation states of this part of Europe. For Britain, it was the time when Germanic peoples from across the North Sea came and eventually took over political control in the south and east, creating the new identity of the Anglo-Saxons. Thus began the process that would lead in the early 10th century to the creation of the Kingdom of England. We can learn much about how aspects of the later English identity began in the events of the 5th and 6th centuries, but we can also learn how to distinguish between cultural identity and genetics, and avoid simplistic equations of Englishness with racial homogeneity.

This book is not a history of the 5th and 6th centuries. There are plenty of these already. Nor is it a detailed account of the evidence and the period. It is rather an exploration of the nature of the creation of Anglo-Saxon identity. Such an exploration can only take place with an understanding of the formation of group identities like ethnicity as derived from sociology and anthropology. Any use of social theories inevitably entails the adoption of a political stance since our attitudes towards forms and processes of society in the past must reflect our attitudes towards the same in the present. I begin by examining the social anthropology of ethnicity, and make explicit my own philosophical stance towards social issues. This is followed by an exploration of how ethnicity is defined and works in practice. To be useful in a historical or archaeological study, ethnicity as a concept needs to be broken down into its component characteristics. These markers of ethnicity allow ethnicity to be explored in societies for which we cannot directly interrogate living informants. Some markers are primary, inherent in the nature of ethnicity itself, and some are secondary – either behavioural or cultural – and are capable of greater manipulation with a more uncertain relationship to ethnic identity.

The period of the 5th and 6th centuries was characterised by the twin processes of migration and conquest. Rather than present a narrative of events of this period, I have opted to explore the period thematically, using the markers of ethnicity as chapter headings. The discussions range over history, archaeology, language and literature. They also aim to stimulate debate and will sometimes include divergent points of view. Some aspects of the period are far from certain due to the imperfect nature of the evidence, and consensus in our understanding of these will always be unlikely. In the end, I present my own interpretation of the period. This is not the same as that of others, and I expect that many will disagree with it. This is only proper given the nature of the period and the current state of historical and archaeological theory. It is possible that developments in archaeological methodology may well help us to resolve some of the questions about this period of Britain's past, but much will remain the subject of debate; often impassioned and fierce.

In conclusion, we can provide a summary of the creation and manipulation of ethnicities during the period. We can see the roots of Englishness and what we owe to the generations of both migrants and natives of these two hundred years.

A more detailed consideration of selected aspects of the period is given in the appendices. The importance of the Empire and the kingdom of the Franks to the events in Britain may be obscured when reading more widely about the period. Few will be familiar with the succession of Roman Emperors, nor the complex succession of Frankish kings. Both are given for reference in appendix 1. As already stated, this work is not meant to be a detailed political narrative of the period. The political context is left to appendix 2, which contains details of each of the Anglo-Saxon kingdoms established before 634, along with what is known about their royal families (whether factual or legendary). An account of the Tribal Hidage, an early medieval listing of kingdoms and provinces, can be found in appendix 3. Details of the features that the Old English language shares with other Germanic languages are given in appendix 4. This serves to show how close the language of the Anglo-Saxons was to its cousins in its earliest recorded forms, and how much more alike it was during the migration to Britain. The material culture of the Anglo-Saxons, as revealed by archaeology, is described in appendix 5. This will help when reading about the archaeology of the period, when a reader's knowledge about such culture is often assumed. Place-names are an important category of evidence for the period. Summary information about the distribution of Germanic, British and Latin place-names can be found in appendix 6, where the distribution of these names provides important clues to the different experiences of different parts of Britain in the post-Roman era. The dominant figure in the literature about that era is undoubtedly the figure of Arthur, possibly the most contentious subject of debate in the whole of the early medieval period. Sources for the identity and existence of Arthur are provided in appendix 7. Finally, a detailed chronological narrative is hesitantly given in the timeline. Providing a well dated chronology for the 5th and 6th centuries is fraught with problems, and will be the subject of lively debate and disagreement. Nevertheless, not to do so is to avoid many interesting issues, and does little to help the reader place the discussions within the text in their proper context. While a conventional bibliography is useful for further reading, there is much to be said for engaging with the primary sources, and a list of the most important of these, with references, is given in the section on sources before providing the bibliography itself.

Writing this book has been an interesting exercise in grappling with a wide variety of materials. With some of these I have been familiar, and have the necessary expertise as an archaeologist to investigate. Others have been more unfamiliar, and have necessitated stepping into new territory, for which my qualifications are uncertain. I have no doubt that my discussion of some of these areas will have been inadequate. However, it is my strong belief that the study of the past must involve using all the evidence in a holistic way and not simply cherry-picking evidence with which you are familiar or which supports your own case. I cannot pretend that my conclusions and understanding of the period are either new or right. I have arrived at an interpretation of the period and of ethnicity which I am comfortable with, and which I feel respects the evidence. This is not to say that other interpretations could not also respect the same fragmentary and inadequate evidence. What I hope is that I have encouraged the reader to think about issues of importance, to question all interpretations of this period, and to explore the evidence for themselves to arrive at their own conclusions. If that helps them to understand better the notion of Englishness in the modern world then I will be well satisfied.

Constructing Ethnicity

"We must accept that people belong to many communities, for instance, their family, their neighbourhood, their profession or work, clubs, associations, etc. Not only must we accept this fact but welcome it. We must welcome too that people move from community to community."

Grimond 1978: 213

A model of ethnicity

This book is an exploration of the earliest events and developments in the origins of the English people. Making such a simple statement as this begs several questions. To talk of 'the English people' is set up a category and to assume it has a historical reality. There are people now who will describe themselves as English. There has been in the past (from perhaps 927 until 1707) an English state. There are ancient writers who have identified themselves as English by language or 'culture' (e.g. Bede in the 8th century). How far are we are justified in assuming continuity over 1,300 years, and more, in what was meant by the term English? The historian Geary has written persuasively, and with passion, about the distorted view of national identities made possible by the study of history (Geary 2002: 15):

> As a tool of nationalist ideology, the history of Europe's nations was a great success, but it has turned our understanding of the past into a toxic waste dump, filled with the poison of ethnic nationalism, and the poison has seeped deep into the popular consciousness.

However, he has also made clear that the work of 'modern' nationalists from the 19th century onwards was only possible because it could build upon genuine ethnic identities existing for many hundreds of years. The nature of these identities was very different to the ethnic identification with nationalism that we have become used to. It is my purpose not to trace and describe the identity of the English 1,600 years ago but to explore the characteristics of people living in Britain at that time and to see how the features which we now take to be 'English' or 'Anglo-Saxon' were created, used, manipulated and distributed.

I will, therefore, explore the concept of ethnicity as applied to the English in the early years of their existence. To look at ethnicity is to examine the nature of society: how it is composed, how it operates and its purpose. My interest in the period and the topic comes from being an archaeologist. Archaeology as the study of human behaviour shares much with disciplines like sociology or anthropology (and even political philosophy). As Geary and others have shown, disciplines like history and archaeology often developed within a specifically political context.

The abuse of history and archaeology in the mid-20th century (e.g. in Nazi Germany, the Soviet Union or Fascist Italy) has led to a desire since then to see both subjects as somehow neutral and objective studies of the past. Apart from Marxism, modern archaeology has been slow to make use of ideas about the individual and society developed in its sister fields. Thus, ideas about the individual have only recently found their way into archaeology, e.g. Thomas's rejection of modernism and the tradition inaugurated by Descartes. Indeed, Thomas has stated "I have hoped to emphasise the way in which the formation of personal identity is contingent upon the existence of social context and cultural tradition." (Thomas 1996: 54).

Everyone who studies past societies will necessarily have views on how this should be approached, and most adopt particular standpoints that have been previously explored by sociologists, anthropologists, philosophers or politicians. Archaeologists have shared fully in the major intellectual currents of the social sciences over the last 200 years (Johnson 1999, Gamble 2001). The original, and for many still the main, approach used by archaeologists in studying the past is culture history. This involves identifying the unique features of the physical record being studied. The result is the definition of archaeological cultures; that is, the attributes of the material record of artefacts and sites belonging to particular places and times. Inevitably, this led to the equation of these cultures with named groups of peoples from the historical record, and by extension, the equation of cultures with peoples in the prehistoric past, e.g. 'the Beaker folk' associated with a material culture of the Early Bronze Age in western Europe. Change in culture and the replacement of one culture by another was mostly ascribed to movements of peoples (migration, colonisation, conquest), or occasionally through trading contacts. More sophisticated analyses and interpretations were developed in the 1960s as part of the so-called 'new archaeology', nowadays known as 'processualism'. This was an attempt to understand the social and economic processes underlying material culture. Changes in the archaeological record were explained by processes of internal change, removing the need for movements of peoples, and by extension cutting the assumed connection between cultures and ethnic groups. An alternative to the new archaeology was provided by Marxist archaeologists. These preferred to analyse contradiction and conflict between socio-economic groups as the prime cause of change in the past. This provides a necessary corrective to seeing ethnic groups as unified entities, but has often led to problems recognising non-economic motives for social structures or change. It is the Marxists who have quite rightly pointed out that all archaeological analyses and ideas are conditioned by the society and the time in which they are produced. Our interpretations of the archaeological record are as much a reflection of the present as they are an accurate description of the past. It is fitting therefore that archaeology now shares the post-modern condition of intellectual life characteristic of today. That is to say, many archaeologists accept that there is no objective, absolute interpretation of the past. We cannot analyse our data and come up with the explanation for why it is the way it is. This dominant form of archaeology in Britain is sometimes called interpretive archaeology, or post-processual archaeology; not so much a single school as a set of shared attitudes. Archaeologists are now much more aware of their role in actively constructing their interpretations in the present, including an acceptance of personal bias. Many would now accept that material culture is consciously manipulated by individuals and that it can symbolise more than simply utilitarian functions. This differs from the dominant mode of thought among archaeologists in North America, which is often described as neo-Darwinian. This sees human culture as subject to processes of selection and placed on an evolutionary trajectory. There is a greater tendency to deal with whole cultures than with individuals, and to see cultures as having an inexorable life-cycle. It has much in common with culture history, whereas interpretive archaeology has more in common with modern sociology and social anthropology.

We must accept that archaeological analyses are affected by the present-day context of the archaeologist and his or her personal biases. These may reflect background, upbringing, education, character or simply personal interest. Seldom however do authors make clear what their particular standpoint is. This is often known by their colleagues, or is evident to the reader who is aware of different points of view. I must be honest and make plain that my particular standpoint is that of a Liberal. In other words, I share many of my views with a particular political and philosophical tradition. The origins of this tradition may be found in the debates during the Civil War in the 17th century, e.g. Milton's defence of free speech in his *Areopagitica* of 1644. Much of the intellectual turmoil of the Civil War revolved around the problem of how to build a political community in which everyone could feel that they belonged; in other words, what is the proper relationship between the individual and the wider group. Is this relationship based on consent or on obligation? The debate was taken further by John Locke (1632-1704) in his *Two Treatises of Government* in 1690. For Locke, every individual had needs that could not be satisfied alone. Every man, woman and child needs to be part of a society whose members agree to surrender some their independence for their own good. Thus, Locke anticipated by some 300 years the current trend in archaeological theory towards understanding the individual in relation to their social context, so-called interpretive archaeology (Thomas 1996). Locke stated the aim of society as being the preservation of property, by which he meant the life and liberty of the individual, and the products of that person's labours, their estates. As society was set up to benefit the individual, it was based on a form of consent, which could be withdrawn if that society failed in its purpose. Here was Locke's justification for the Glorious Revolution of 1688. Here also is the germ of the idea that people form voluntary communities and that any group can last only for as long as it meets the needs of its members. In the context of the time, belonging to the group involved accepting a common identity and set of cultural norms. Deviation from these norms may be allowed, but the 'deviants' would thereby forfeit part of their rights in the group as a whole. A major feature of identity at the time was religion and while toleration of religious minorities was a feature of the Glorious Revolution, full engagement with the political institutions of the state was allowed only to communicant members of the Church of England. The next key figure in the development of Liberal ideas was John Stuart Mill (1806-1873). In his book *On Liberty* in 1859, his focus was on the limits of social interference in the life of the individual. Accepting that no person is an island, he sought to limit the degree of social control on that person's freedom. For Mill, a healthy society was one that accepted the variability of its members and so respected individual freedom, up to the point at which the individual did harm to others. He realised that all people would seek their own form of fulfilment and would therefore differ in their tastes and activities, but that no society could function if it allowed any individual to do harm. Any society would therefore be a variable patchwork quilt of behaviour rather than a cohesive set of norms obeyed by all. In some senses then, Mill can be compared with the so-called 'new archaeology' of the 1960s which broke down the monolithic cultures of early archaeology into interacting and overlapping areas of study. Mill was engaged in the mid-19th century debates between conflicting ideas about how to interpret the past (Parker 1990). The influence of the French 'inventor' of sociology, Auguste Comte, had led to a school of Positivists, who took a deterministic view of history in which historical events were subject to broad currents of thought or development pulling along individuals in their wake. Their opponents preferred to focus on individual choice and action as the motive force for historical events. Mill strove to reconcile the role of the individual with the role of forces beyond individual control. Not only would society be a patchwork of individual choices in behaviour and culture, it would also be subject to individual consent. To deny the right to do harm to others, has the corollary that the group is expected to satisfy the needs and wants of its members (to remove the incentive to do harm). A social group can therefore exist only so long as it meets the needs of the individuals who are members of it. These individuals act in various spheres throughout their lives, such as religion, economy, the family, politics. Each sphere would have its own norms, created and replicated on an individual basis rather than set down from outside as a standardised package to be adopted or not. This is the basis for the more modern syntheses of the Liberal view of society. Jo Grimond (1913-1993) in *The Common Welfare* of 1978 shifted the focus of action away from the state, as too remote from the individual, to the social networks within which individuals lived out their daily lives; what he called communities. A key feature of Grimond's perspective is that the individual did not have only one social persona but several; taking part in various communities at the same time or throughout their life. Each person became a self-conscious social actor, entering into and leaving social networks, and finding fulfilment through them. This has much in common with recent trends in archaeological thought which have sought to bring the individual into explanations of the past, seeing the cultural features of a society as stemming from multiple sets of individual choices. Depending on the context, the same individual could express their identities in different ways and would choose to belong to groups that offered him or her the greatest sense of fulfilment of their needs or wants. In practice, such choice is often limited and the individual's ability to choose can only operate in a restricted range of social arenas or through enhanced choices at times of great social instability.

For the Liberal, the fundamental unit of human society is the individual. This individual is an independent person with the capability to make his or her own choices in both thought and action. As a result, everyone seeks to express their individuality and achieve some sort of self fulfilment. However, our ability to do this is constrained by various internal and external factors. Internal factors include the values, interests and beliefs of the person concerned and which guide their life into certain areas of activity or ways of behaving. The external factors stem from the fact that all individuals exist within social networks. It is through these networks that individual choice is acted out. The networks themselves overlap, and may or may not share some of their members. They exist to provide the individual with either support or the means to achieve his or her chosen path in life. In the modern world, there are many networks for a person to take part in: the family, the residential neighbourhood, the workplace, the school parents' group, the local pub, the amateur society or evening class, the football supporters' group, the pressure group or political party etc. Some of these networks are active in the sense of being constituted on a regular basis and having accepted norms of behaviour, dress etc. To some extent, an individual will take on a different persona in each of the networks that he or she belongs to; behaving in different ways and adopting different codes of dress. Some networks are passive, in that they only come into being under special circumstances and have latent norms which everyone can recognise but do not necessarily act out in everyday life. A group of unrelated travellers, previously unknown to each other, will discover a shared sense of relationship with their fellows at times of stress, often based on mutually recognised myths, e.g. the British, normally reserved and unwilling to talk with strangers, find that they will readily pull together with others and engage in a lively sense of shared comradeship in the face of a common difficulty or disaster. This will be attributed to the so-called spirit of the Blitz, or the Dunkirk spirit, experiences not shared by other nations (and seldom directly by the people involved). Apart from family, an individual today (perhaps unlike in the past) belongs to most of their active networks by choice. Separating the individual from the network is very difficult. An individual's identity is shaped by how they see themselves but also by how others see them. The network is shaped by the behaviour of its members. The collective effect of social interaction between them creates a group dynamic that in turn helps to shape the behaviour of the individuals joining the network.

There are various implications in this for ethnicity. Ethnic ties can be seen as one example of community, linking individuals with each other for mutual support and advantage. Like other kinds of community, ethnic units are not immutable. They are formed with explicit or tacit consent of their members. Should the members decide that the unit is no longer working to their advantage, they are in theory free to switch to another ethnic group. In practice of course, this will only be possible in exceptional circumstances. The ethnic unit must deliver what its members need - security, material and emotional well-being, and avenues of social advancement. Belonging to such a community involves obeying its rules and norms. At the same time, there must be ways of expressing individual identity, tastes and desires, while also expressing other community identities that exist alongside the ethnic unit. Units of residence, kinship, religious orientation, age, gender, profession or political organisation can all form part of the series of networks or communities which are contained within, or sometimes cross ethnic boundaries. Ethnic cohesion is achieved through interaction between members of intimate networks like close family and friends, effective networks such as kinship or occupation, and the extended networks of neighbourhood or social group (cf. Gamble 2001: 82). Individuals may have choice about what groups they belong to within a society, and may have choice in expressing themselves through behaviour or culture, yet they belong to societies with a past. The existence of that past guarantees the existence of traditions which members of that society are encouraged to respect. Even the individualist John Stuart Mill accepted that it was the force of tradition that often acted as the binding cement of social groups (Parker 1990: 46). Expression of ethnic identity will therefore vary from person to person, from area to area and from social group to social group. We should expect to find a great deal of variability underlying emblems of ethnic identity, and yet we should also expect to see elements of continuity based on ancestral culture and behaviour.

Ethnicity in practice

Definitions of ethnicity vary greatly and there has been much academic debate about the nature of ethnicity and its usefulness (or even its reality) as a concept (Jones 1997). Here I will create my own definition. Readers may wish to share my definition and analysis of ethnicity or they may not. Either way, by being open about my particular standpoint, readers can evaluate for themselves the conclusions I reach in this book.

Ethnic identity is the sum total of largely accepted norms arising from the various active networks which share a self perceived view of themselves as members of an overall, usually passive, network, based around a notion of difference between themselves and some other group. This overall network is the ethnic group. The nature of the ethnic network for most people is that it is given at birth, rather than adopted by choice; although choice may be exercised later during adult life. The commonest expressions of ethnicity are based on language and/or religion, two aspects of daily behaviour that underpin individuals' relations with others.

Although acceptance of an ethnic identity is usually a given condition, choice still exists in how that identity should be expressed. The precise form of language, the system of writing adopted for it, codes of dress, styles of material culture, even modes of behaviour can all be 'chosen' by the ethnic community. In reality of course, it is the individuals within the network who do the choosing and precise forms of ethnic expression are often negotiated between individuals through their active social networks. Individuals vary in their personalities and physical abilities. There will inevitably be differences within the cultural expression of ethnicity, both geographically and over time. Individuals will either express their identity through making a statement (e.g. adopting particular dress or speaking in a particular way) or through particular actions that are shared by others within the same overall ethnic network (e.g. supporting a sports team or defending the nation in war). Some actions or experiences can be seen in retrospect as defining or reinforcing a sense of ethnic identity, either in reality or in myth, e.g. the spirit of the Blitz or the Jewish sufferings at the hands of the Nazis.

It is the actions of the individuals within the social networks that define ethnicity. As individuals have the capacity to exercise choice, then expressions of ethnicity can be changed over time, and even manipulated by individuals for their own ends. Learning a second language may ease someone's acceptance into a new group or a change in religious affiliation may do likewise. Ethnicity is therefore not

20

unchanging for all time. Changes in ethnic identity can and do happen. Migration from one society/culture to another can result in the second and third generations adopting a different ethnic identity from the first migrants. Marriage can result in the adoption of a new identity by the spouse (most commonly the woman). For various reasons, people may deliberately reject their old identity in favour of a new one. Nevertheless, for most people an ethnic identity is inherited and given at birth. To consciously adopt a new identity is therefore an act of choice. Social networks exist to serve the individual by providing physical and psychological security, avenues of advancement and fulfilment, and the provision of the physical necessities of life. If a network fails to do any of these things then it will cease to recruit new members and die, or it will be changed from within as its members accommodate their actions and statements to new realities. The reasons for changing one's ethnic expression should be a fascinating topic of study for those who look at the development of Englishness over the last 1,600 years.

This view of ethnicity has much in common with the ideas of Jenkins and others who take a social constructionist approach to the subject (Jenkins 1997). This approach has recently begun to find favour among some archaeologists who study the early medieval period (Moreland 2000). Key elements of this approach are that ethnic identities emphasise cultural differentiation between groups, that the cultural forms of ethnic groups arise through the social interaction of individuals, that ethnic forms can be manipulated and vary over time, and that ethnicity is defined both collectively through social interaction and through individual self-perception. Jenkins (1997) refined this approach by adding further features of ethnicity that allow more in-depth analysis of how ethnic groups function. Ethnic groups can be subject to a process of categorisation by others as well as self-definition. Such categorisation can become part of how the group sees itself, even though originating in often negative perceptions by others. The process of categorisation can often be part of wider power relations between groups and individuals, which can form an important context for the working out of ethnic relations. The practical consequences of being part of a named group will depend partly on the nature of the political and social ties between groups. As these are always changing, the nature of a group may change, even though the name remains the same, and likewise names may change but the nature of the group can remain the same. The nature of groups and their differentiation is expressed through what Jenkins calls the cultural content. Jenkins feels that while those who study ethnicity have tended to look at boundaries and relationships between groups, time also needs to be devoted to studying the cultural content - what it means to be part of one group or the other.

The final feature that needs to be incorporated into a social constructionist model of ethnicity is historical tradition. This is an important corrective to the reliance of the model mainly on individual choice. Ethnic groups have a past, and that past can lay down powerful traditions that can govern how ethnicity is expressed in the present. In other words, the articulation of ethnicity is contingent on local historical circumstances (Jenkins 1997: 110). In this way Jenkins answers the criticism of the social constructionists levelled by Smith (2000) that the persistence of ethnic groups over time cannot be understood solely by regarding them as artificial entities manipulated in the present for personal advantage. We must be clear that ethnicity and the historical persistence of ethnic units are divorced from genetics. To say an ethnic group persists over long periods of time is not to say that a people can trace blood kinship with each other or with descent from biological ancestors. While this might be true, it seems to me that where modern thinking on ethnicity has still to progress is in exploring the links between group genetics and ethnicity. Some sort of genetic basis may well be involved in the creation of ethnic identity in many cases; in some cases in the form of an elite carrier of group values who may or may not form the majority of the group and who are responsible for the beginning of the group's historical tradition.

A particular advantage of the social constructionist model is that it allows us to refine which elements of ethnicity can be subject to personal choice and which are fixed in particular historical traditions. Choice is exercised as the act of moving from one ethnic identity to another. Such movement may be neutral but is more likely to involve a move from one identity seen as disadvantageous to another that confers greater advantages to the individual. Particular advantages may be status, sense of solidarity, wealth or social/political position. The disadvantages being escaped from may be low status, poverty, alienation, feelings of isolation, low self-esteem or the disparaging categorisation of others. Escape from these is possible through social or geographical mobility. Migration might well offer such opportunities. The lack of ability to move from one identity to another is more likely in long-established and geographically stable groups with well defined hierarchies and rules. Alternatively, new identities might even be imposed against personal choice through capture in war, being enslaved or being obliged to follow the dictates of social superiors. The precise configuration of choice will depend on the particular circumstances of the time.

Pinning down an ethnic identity is an exercise in futility, like trying to grab a bar of soap in the shower. Expressions of ethnicity are always changing, using various modes of expression and incorporating earlier expressions within a complex, multi-layered structure. What is easier to study is how ethnicity changes over time - watching where the bar of soap is moving is easier that trying to pick it up! In this book, I accept that the nature of being Anglo-Saxon changes through time and it is the nature of the change that I wish to explore. In the process, we will gain an understanding of what it meant to be Anglo-Saxon at particular times, and of the origins of part of our ethnic expression at the present day. It may be that we can also reclaim something from earlier expressions of being Anglo-Saxon and enliven our consciousness of our own English ethnicity now.

The study of ethnicity

Versions of ethnicity

The idea of ethnicity has been much debated by scholars. Ethnicity has been seen as either primordial or instrumental; as either something innate in the human condition, or as an artificial construct design to serve a particular social purpose (Hutchinson & Smith 1996: 8-9). A primordial view of ethnic units sees ties of kinship, religion, race, language, place or custom as a persistent marker of identity lying outside the notion of citizenship and viewed by people as a given condition of their identity. It is perhaps truer to say that ethnicity could be seen as a set of primordial sentiments inherent in people's view of themselves. A person's emotional attachment to an ethnic identity can be extremely strong, leading to a sense of ethnic superiority over others, what Weber called *ethnic honour* (Weber in Hutchinson & Smith 1996: 37). In an instrumentalist view, ethnicity is something to be manipulated consciously by status or interest groups, or even individuals, in their own interest, and so cannot be primordial. In reality, elements of both views may be right. Primordial views of ethnicity fail to account for change in ethnic expression and for movement of people between ethnic groups, while instrumental views cannot properly deal with the emotive passions aroused by ethnicity and with the durability of ethnic identities (Hutchinson & Smith 1996: 32-34). A Liberal model of ethnicity will obviously have more in common with the instrumentalist view (social constructionism), although we can allow that the desire for ethnic identification may well be an innate part of being human. It is the precise expression of that identity that is subject to choice and the test of social utility.

Certain characteristics are taken by many writers as more important for defining ethnic identity than others. As early as the 10th century, Abbot Regino of Prüm defined nations in terms of descent, customs, language and law, while ancient authors often concentrated on language and costume/weapons as distinguishing features (Pohl & Reimitz 1998: 17-18). In more modern times, Geertz in 1963 put forward six ethnic sentiments: kinship, race, language, region, religion and custom (Geertz in Hutchinson & Smith 1996: 43-44). Nash proposed a trinity of primary markers: kinship, commensality (eating together), a common cult (Nash in Hutchinson & Smith 1996: 25). For Nash, dress, language and physical features were only secondary markers; surface expressions of a deeper feeling of difference. Similar views were put forward by Weber, who saw ethnicity as based primarily on kinship and physical similarity, common customs or experience of migration/colonisation, with language and religion as especially conducive to ethnic feelings but not necessarily coincident with them (Weber in Hutchinson & Smith 1996: 35-36). The problem for historians and archaeologists is to identify which cultural markers were significant for the ethnic identities of people in the past. Markers which the academic of today may take as being of prime importance might not be the ones taken by people in the period under study. In the medieval period, it is clear that language could be taken to be a primary marker of ethnicity in an abstract sense (Bartlett in Hutchinson & Smith 1996: 127-132), something that few scholars would nowadays accept. However, the idea of ethnicity in the medieval world was linked more usually to the notion of social or political communities, in which there seem to have been five main elements of ethnicity (James 1989): tradition, custom or manners, language, law and descent.

A recent and authoritative study of ethnicity (Smith 1986: 22-31) used six characteristics as the basis for defining ethnic groups:

1. a common proper name (to name something is to give it an identity)

2. a feeling of common ancestry (the most basic element of ethnicity)

3. shared historical memories (myths and actual events)

4. one or more elements of a common culture (e.g. language, religion, culture)

5. a link with a homeland (either lived in or in exile from)

6. a sense of solidarity (an emotional bond of togetherness)

This is an encompassing definition that provides a useful analytical framework for studies of ethnicity in the remote past. As noted by Hines (1994), some of these attributes can be seen in early medieval writings, e.g. Bede whose notion of group identity was bound up with notions of name, territory, traditions and language. Smith's definition is one that will be explored further during the course of this book. However, in order that ethnicity can be investigated using the evidence available it may be necessary to revise and classify these characteristics (see below under *Ethnic markers*).

Ethnicity, race and minorities

Using kinship as a key feature of ethnicity does not involve a necessary connection with race. Ethnic kinship need not be real; it is often presumed without any basis in reality. Moreland (2000) has pointed out that early medieval ethnic groups can clearly be shown not to have been based on blood relationship between all their members, even though they were seen as such by those involved. The important point about kinship is that the kin accept one another as somehow biologically related at a theoretical level. It is clear that ethnicity is a cultural phenomenon. Ethnicity is not the same as race; the physical characteristics derived from a population's genetic make-up. While racial characteristics can often be used to mark different ethnic groups, many ethnic units occur within racial types, and some ethnic units can contain a wide variation of racial characteristics.

It needs to be stressed that ethnicity is a characteristic of all human societies. Too often the term has been restricted to minority groups. A good example of this is Clarke, who largely redefined British archaeology in the 1960s and provided the theoretical foundations for the so-called New Archaeology. Clarke referred to ethnic sub-cultures as marginal groups within larger cultural entities (Clarke 1968: 251). Ethnicity was clearly something that marked off minority populations from some sort of larger entity. Such a view says more about the author's perceptions of ethnicity in the 1960s than it does about ethnicity itself. In the modern world, it is true that minority groups may emphasise their own cultural markers, while majority groups may be unaware of their own, cf. the modern English with the Scots and Welsh in the United Kingdom. However, all groups, whether majority or minority, have ethnic characteristics. It may be that minorities feel the need to defensively emphasise their cultural differences more than others and so are more visible, but this does not mean that only minorities have ethnicity. To a majority group, it is the minorities that regularly stick out as being different in their behaviour or appearance, and so at the present day we are used to the expression 'ethnic minority'. The majority group itself can only see its own difference from others by reference to groups of a similar or greater size. This is an infrequent occurrence for most people, who are thereby less aware of their own characteristics and so less determined to stress their own ethnic identity. Nevertheless, that identity can soon be activated when people come into contact with other majority groups, e.g. on holiday or in the sporting arena.

Ethnic intensity

Feelings of ethnicity, of belonging to a group bound by blood, are extremely strong and emotive. They can be characterised as non-rational, incapable of explanation (Connor in Hutchinson & Smith 1996: 69-75). Ethnicity is often a matter of belief, articulated through potent symbols and self-consciously expressed through literature and music.

The strength of attachment to an ethnic identity is fundamentally an emotional bond. A good example of this is Linsell (2000) who defines the highest level of nationalism (ethnic identity) as the 'communal world of the imagination', consisting of empathy, identity, loyalty and emotion. These are intangible but powerful qualities. Ethnicity is above all a subjective state of being. For those who are actively involved in ethnic politics, the dry language of academia cannot adequately express how they feel. Where academic scholars use the term nation to refer to modern states and import the word *ethnie* from French to describe ethnic units, the activist will use the term state for political entities and the more emotive term of nation for the ethnic group, and will wear with pride the badge of nationalist.

A key to the nature of the emotional bond is provided by Scheff (1994). He notes that the urge to belong is one of the most powerful of human emotions (Scheff 1994: 277). Absorption of the self into the group is to displace feelings about one's self into feeling for an idealised wider entity. The individual's attachment to the group is in an inverse relation to their feeling for themselves. The psychological explanation for this is based on the notion of self-esteem and feelings of pride or shame in one's own status relative to others (Scheff 1994: 285). Overtly acknowledged shame is part of inferiority complexes, which can be overcome by a feeling of belonging to a wider group with the status that is lacking in oneself. Bypassed, unacknowledged shame is translated into anger, either at the self or at others. Anger towards others can be mobilised by becoming part of the group and striving for superiority and aggression against other such groups that may be deemed responsible for perceived injuries towards one's own society.

Strength of ethnic feeling then should be greatest in minority groups and for groups whose members are in inferior social, economic or political positions. Majority groups and those enjoying the benefits of society will be less emotionally attached to their ethnic identity.

The clearest expression of ethnic intensity is found where a people feel themselves to be especially chosen by their god or gods for a special mission. The idea of being a chosen people is very common (Smith in Hutchinson & Smith 1996: 189-197) and imposes on the whole people an obligation to live according to the customs laid down by the gods. While the Jews are the most well known example of a chosen people, they are not the only such people, e.g. the Armenians, ancient Egyptians or Pilgrim Fathers. Smith (1999: 130) has noted that intensity of ethnic feeling often depends on a sense of uniqueness and of mission, both essential aspects of being a chosen people. This can be crucial for long-term ethnic survival since it imposes on the people a duty to observe a particular life-style. Among the ancient Egyptians, this sense of being chosen was expressed through the Pharaoh while among Jews it was vested in the whole community. Both had in common a religious basis for their ethnicity. Smith has put forward a classification of four ways in which being chosen can manifest itself:

- imperial-dynastic - based on kingship, often with the ethos of warrior leadership of society and acted out through warfare;
- communal-demotic - based on the people and their link with the land, often in revolt against larger political units or more powerful enemies;
- emigrant-colonist - a people migrating to a new land, and feeling that divine providence is helping them establish a new order;
- diaspora-restoration - returning exiles achieving regeneration and spiritual renewal.

None of these is mutually exclusive and aspects of some of these may be found at different periods in the same ethnic group. We should expect the first and third of Smith's schemes to be especially evident during the early medieval period in western Europe.

A key feature of ethnicity is that ethnic groups define themselves in relation to others. Belonging to one group implies not belonging to another. It is the boundaries between groups that in a major way define those groups (Barth in Hutchinson & Smith 1996: 79). It may be that the intensity of ethnic feeling is related to the degree of psychological distance between one's own ethnic identity and that of others. This can involve either feelings of inferiority, leading to intense nationalism among minority groups, or feelings of superiority, common in imperial overlords or majority groups. On the other hand, relations between ethnic groups that are in regular contact and are competing for physical space, economic resources or political advantage are often categorised by mutual dislike or distrust. Such relations may be expressed through elevating ones own ethnic group above that of the rival group. Hence ethnicity is often a problem for majority populations within modern democratic, multi-ethnic nation states.

Democracy involves competition for political office and the rewards of power. To elevate one's own ethnicity by projecting the idea of others as being less than cultured or civilised - the barbaric identification of others - lies outside the accepted norms of democratic life. A majority group will often suppress its own ethnicity out of concern for the feeling of minority groups. For instance, assertions of Englishness would be frowned upon as offensively racist in many quarters through being associated with a white Anglo-Saxon heritage, and therefore excluding many modern English people with different origins.

In pre-modern societies, assertions of ethnicity by dominant groups need not be a problem. Smith (1986: 79-87) has put forward a model of two types of ethnic group in pre-modern societies: the aristocratic and the demotic. The latter involves the whole population in expressing ethnic identity, but usually in a specific context or in small scale groups (e.g. city states or immigrant groups). It is the former, the aristocratic model, which formed the basis for most political units of the ancient world. To an aristocratic ethnic group, the ethnicity of subject peoples is of no concern provided the power and privileges of the group are not challenged. Multi-ethnic empires were thus common and racism was less of an issue. In practice, I would contend that the aristocratic and demotic modes of ethnicity are not so sharply differentiated as Smith suggests, especially in the early medieval period, in which there were determined attempts to align aristocratic groups with the 'nation' they governed. In particular, the example of Anglo-Saxon England shows how a concern for racial identity of governors and the governed could develop over time. The clash between demotic and aristocratic modes of ethnicity would become acute in the 11th century, when an alien aristocracy was imposed upon the country. By the Norman conquest, England was given a minority dominant group and a majority subject group, the ethnic implications of which are fascinating to explore.

Changing ethnicity

Ethnic units are not unchanging but are always adapting to changing circumstances; being updated to adopt new poses. Ethnic identity is reinterpreted by each new generation, although the past constrains the expression of identity in the present. This is the paradox of ethnicity. The identity of an ethnic group is often marked by reverence for symbols and structures inherited from the past. We can almost define an ethnic group as a social network that shares a common heritage, and wishing to keep that heritage alive for future generations, as stated eloquently by Fishman (in Hutchinson & Smith 1996: 65):

"The physical heritage of ethnicity creates expressive obligations and opportunities for behaving as the ancestors behaved and preserving their great heritage by transmitting it to generation after generation."

Each generation will interpret its heritage in its own way, adapting it where necessary to changing circumstances. However, some ethnic groups have been more conservative than others. Minority and diaspora groups in particular often cling tenaciously to traditional practices in the absence of political institutions or territory. Most ethnic groups however will change their expressions of ethnicity over time. In some cases, the ethnic group itself may even disappear.

Smith (1986: 95) has put forward an optimal model of changing ethnicity which is particularly apt for the study of the early English. A population emerges in a given area sharing common characteristics. At first, the population is only loosely organised politically and only gradually achieves unity. This unity is often achieved through warfare and leads to increasing centralisation and a formative period of cultural achievement to which later generations can look back as a model for the future. If this state endures long enough, it will infuse the whole population with its ethnic ethos and so ensure its survival beyond any future political eclipse of its leaders.

The key element for Smith in ensuring the survival of ethnic majority groups is the development of state bureaucracy through which the values and culture of the dominant group can permeate down to all levels of the population. England is particularly cited as one of the best examples of this process (Smith 1986: 109). For some authors, the development of modern industrial 'nation' states has been the prerequisite for the emergence of ethnicity (Shennan 1989: 14-16). However, it is clear that ethnicity has existed before the advent of modern states. For the medieval period, the link between ethnicity and kingship has been seen as explicit (James 1989). The growth of kingship allowed a new 'national' feeling to emerge that overrode the more local loyalties of the tribe. However, to follow a purely politically deterministic model would be to deny any biological content to ethnicity at all, and thus revert to a purely instrumentalist view of the subject.

Primary ethnic markers

I take ethnicity to have primary and secondary markers. Primary markers are those characteristics of ethnic groups that define them as ethnic rather other types of social group (e.g. class). The chief of these is kinship - a feeling of shared biological relationship, which may or may not be real. It follows from this that there will be some sort of origin myth that sets out the putative ancestry of the group, a history of shared experiences that link the ancestors with the present members of the 'family', and a name or names by which the group is identified to others. Transmission of origin and experience to later generations will take the form of oral tales and written 'histories'. Whether these tales and histories are real or constructed is neither here nor there. Their function is to bind the group; not to produce a historical analysis. The name of the group must be a primary marker. To have a name is to have an identity in the first place, yet, as we shall see, names can be misleading and although a name can stay the same, what it denotes can change. Secondary markers are the signs by which an ethnic group can be identified and can take various forms in different groups, each marker being subject to the possibility of change over time. These secondary markers, the culture of ethnicity, may be behavioural - involving the acting out of set patterns of behaviour (e.g. language, religion, social customs or political structures) - or material expressions of such behaviour (e.g. dress, body decoration, building styles, artefact forms). All ethnic groups have a material heritage that is a fundamental part of their identity. Attempts to eradicate, defeat or expel an ethnic group will often involve attacks on their physical heritage (as seen in the wars in the former Yugoslavia in the 1990s).

Kinship

It is accepted by many that ethnic feeling is similar in kind to feelings of kinship. Behaviour that is appropriate to one's ethnic community will be that expected within a family setting (Eller & Coughlan in Hutchinson & Smith 1996: 49). The metaphor of blood is applied to both race and family. We speak of the blood-line to denote genetic ancestry. We also say that blood is thicker than water. The notorious misuse of ethnicity by the Nazis in Germany was often phrased in terms of blood. The 1935 Nuremberg Laws stated in Article 2. (1) that "A citizen of the Reich may be only one who is of German or kindred blood". It then went on to define German citizenship in terms of kinship. However, the identification of ethnicity with kinship is not as simple as many writers have made it seem. Feelings of kinship in early medieval groups have been said to result from common social and political solidarity. In other words, political action cemented by social contact produces a feeling of shared kinship. Social contact in pre-modern societies, and indeed political association, was often the result of both blood relationship and kinship by marriage. This is not the same as saying that all ethnic groups must be the biological descendants of a common ancestor or that they share racial characteristics. Anthropologists have long known that kinship is not necessarily based on genetic relationships (Hendry 1999: 184). It is however necessary to accept that many ethnic groups feel a bond of kinship as part of their identity, although how this is actually organised and expressed varies greatly from one society to another. There is no common model of human marriage and kinship. The precise organisation of kinship depends on how inheritance is recognised, patterns of residence and rules concerning marriage. These in turn vary according to the economic basis of the society and other factors.

The importance of kinship is seen most clearly in so-called 'primitive' societies. These are, of course, anything but primitive, having complex social and economic systems, and rich material cultures. They are only primitive in the sense of not being industrialised urban economies with the social and political structures that go with this. In such societies, kinship is a major organising principle. In many cases to be non-kin is to be an enemy or stranger; that is foreign to the ethnic community (e.g. Sahlins 1972: 196-197). Economic relations will often follow social relationships, such that close kin are more likely to be generous and more distant kin are likely to be more exploitative. Sahlins (1972: 200) noted that inter-tribal relations are marked by the fading out of positive morality up to a point at which it becomes intergroup hostility. In other words, while the relationship between economic behaviour with kinship distance can be described along a continuum, there is a discontinuity in economic behaviour at the boundaries between ethnic groups which suggests that kinship is thought of as having been broken. A positive trading environment between groups often depends on the creation of marriage ties between individuals who can then restore some sort of kinship across the ethnic border; using kinship by marriage as a substitute for kinship by blood.

Ethnicity is aided by the existence of bounded kinship networks, unilineal systems such as matri- or patrilineal clans. These are units with established boundaries covering several generations, in which the individual is subsumed into the wider group. Such networks are not the only form of social organisation however. Bilateral groups are just as important and very different in their characteristics (Pehrson 1971). A major feature of bilateral groups is that they are based on the individual, rather than the group. The small family of a person, their parents and siblings and children reckoned in both the male and female line is the basis of the system. A person does not belong to a clan and their identity is not ascribed to them at birth (although in practice the father's identity may cover that of the children until they can forge their own). Bilateral systems offer greater flexibility in forging wider social networks and for this reason, ethnicity based on such systems will be relatively fluid. Individuals are freer to move with their spouse and join other social units than the one they were born in. Rather than stability over successive generations, bilateral kinship emphasises relationships between siblings and alliance between families through marriage.

In a society based on patrilineal inheritance (the reckoning of descent through the father), a common form of organisation is into lineages or clans sharing a common male ancestor. The clans will be widely spread and intermixed with each other, and any particular political unit - kingdom or tribe - may consist of several clans. There will also be strict rules about marriage such that a man may marry only outside his clan. It may also be the rule that the brothers of a husband or the sisters of a wife are regarded in some way as equivalent, a form of polyandry or polygamy. In this way, different clans within the tribe are bound together through ties of marriage. The ethnic unit may be the same as the kingdom or tribe, or may itself be a larger grouping of independent political units. In ancient Rome, society was organised into clans, these into larger curia and these in turn into three tribes, together comprising the Roman people (Morgan 1877). By the time of the Roman Empire this organisation had long been superseded by a political, territorial organisation. The existence of organisation by kinship among the Germanic peoples is attested by Tacitus, who noted that the fighting units of the army were made up of men from one family or clan (Mattingly & Handford 1970: 107). Unfortunately, the precise words used by Tacitus, *sed familiae et propinquitates*, are ambiguous and can be translated as either household and neighbours or family and relations. Even in the latter sense they do not necessarily imply the existence of bounded unilineal kinship units (reckoning their descent from only one of their parents). Early Germanic society has traditionally been assumed to conform to a unilineal pattern (Murray 1983: 31). However, even the evidence from linguistics to support an ancestral Indo-European unilineal kinship system is very weak and could just as likely fit a bilateral system (Murray 1983: 37). Unfortunately, evidence for early Germanic social structures is scarce and hard to interpret. Writers like Todd (1992: 30-33) paint a portrait of society based on charismatic individuals attracting retinues in a kaleidoscope of political units. The evidence of Roman and Greek 'ethnography' of *Germania* from the time of Tacitus onwards shows that tribal units were being combined, divided and reformed throughout the period. They also contain no certain evidence for bounded unilineal kindreds (the evidence of Julius Caesar is regarded as ethnographic myth by Murray 1983). Todd though does note the existence of tribal assemblies and some units did maintain their existence over many hundreds of years. It may be that bounded social organisations were in the process of breaking up during the migration period and that retinues of warrior leaders played a part in this. It could be argued that the existence of polygamy and the special relationship that existed with maternal relations may be remnants of unilineal descent groups that were a feature of the earliest Germanic societies. However, it is likely that the Frankish evidence for bilateral kindreds containing up to 2nd or 3rd cousins at the widest was not new and reflects a long-standing Germanic system (Murray 1983).

Bounded kinship groups like clans can only be maintained through rules of exogamy. Individuals are allowed to marry only members of other clans, never within the clan. On the other hand, the larger grouping of the tribe may be bound by endogamy, individuals having to marry only from other clans within the tribe itself. Marriage rules are effective in terms of boundary maintenance. They are less important where bounded kinship groups do not exist, e.g. in bilateral systems, and often have to be imposed through elaborate legal and moral mechanisms, such as the incest rules of Christianity.

Germanic society as portrayed in the historical sources from the 5th century onwards is certainly bilateral. It may be that the opportunities presented by contact with the Roman Empire had promoted the rise of warrior elites, who were able to support a bilateral system of kinship. This does not preclude groups not in contact with Rome or outside the orbit of western Europe from maintaining earlier forms of organisation. However, the evidence from later heroic literature would suggest that a widespread bilateral kinship system was the norm throughout the Germanic area. The earliest documentary evidence certainly suggests that this is the case (Lancaster 1958). Alliance and rivalry between families is the very stuff of heroic poetry. Much of this is centred on the role of women, often placed in tragic situations through marriage. The social focus is not on descent but on alliance between generations. In two Old English poems (Greenfield 1975, Tolkien 1982), we have an old feud between the Frisians and the Danes, in which Hildeburh, the sister of the Danish King Hnæf, is married to the Frisian King Finn. The feud breaks out once more and Hildeburh is faced with the true tragedy of losing kin by blood or kin by marriage. Bilateral systems of kinship are ideal for a period of migration with warrior-adventurers carving out new polities and retinues. They also allow flexible marriage patterns that can break the bounds of ethnicity. On the other hand, unilineal systems would be ideal for providing stability and could be the basis for settlement by families in need of mutual support. Of course, a bilateral aristocracy could coexist with a unilineal dependent population. However, it is only really the bilateral systems that would gain notice in most historical sources since these would be the ones most active under individual leaders. There are sometimes notices of groups without kings or leaders, e.g. the continental Saxons, which might signify unilineal societies. In such cases, it is noteworthy that these groups tended to be more tenacious in their identity over time.

Origins

Various elements can be incorporated into ethnic myths (Smith 1986: 192), including notions of when, where and how the 'nation' was born, along with some idea of who the ancestors were - including a hero or heroes to be venerated. Origin myths can be of several types. In some cases, a people may believe itself to have divine origins; to be the chosen people of a particular god (Smith 1986: 35). Origins can also involve transformation, that is the change in lifestyle of a people, e.g. from nomadic pastoralist to sedentary cultivator. In these cases, looking back to origins can involve a nostalgia for the lifestyle and its associated values that have been lost but are often seen as purer than the somehow soiled values of the present. Where the people's origin involved migration or exile, this nostalgia may be for a former territory or homeland. Conscious manipulation of past myths has been part of the raising or controlling of ethnicity throughout history. This often takes the form of exalting a hero who exemplifies all that is deemed good and whose life forms a model to be followed in the present. Even modern nations are not immune to this, e.g. the mythical status of the founding fathers of the United States of America.

Ethnic myths often bring together historical fact and legendary elaboration (Smith 1999: 57). Smith suggests that there are two types of myth: the genealogical and the ideological. In myth based on genealogy, there will be a divine, noble or heroic ancestor linked to the present by ties of blood. An ideological myth refers back to the virtues of a golden age which it is the duty of present day generations to recapture. It is suggested that both are opposed to each other in a creative tension in modern ethnic units, which helps to unite the whole group. In earlier times, we may say that genealogical myth is the basis of status for many ruling or aristocratic families, while ideological myths have a wider application in drawing people around the royal or aristocratic core. For example, the Arthurian golden age helped portray an idealised western European society based on kingship and nobility which could highlight ideals that everyone could share.

There are several components of fully fledged ethnic myth:
- when - an origin set within a particular historical situation or context;
- whence - a homeland from which the group has come;
- how - the act of moving from the homeland to the present area of settlement;
- who - the ancestor or exemplar;
- action - models of conduct which the members of the group are expected to follow.

Myth provides a unique identity, a claim to territory, a status and claim to political autonomy. Smith (1990) suggests that ethnic myths emerge at particular times. This include episodes of conflict between groups or periods of profound socio-economic change. In the modern world, ethnic myths are the creation of intellectuals (writers and artists), who thereby become the guardians of ethnicity and enhance their own status. The myths are taken up by rootless middle classes who need a cultural identity to make their own, and from whom the intellectuals are usually drawn. The myths are then used by the middle classes to mobilise the workers and peasants behind their own leadership to satisfy their political aspirations. In this way, ideological myths are particularly powerful tools for the aspiring groups to use to oppose the genealogical myths of ruling groups. The uses of nationalism in the break up of Communist Yugoslavia might well be a good example of this. In earlier times, the intellectuals would have been the clerics of the church. The audience for their writings would be the patrons on whom they relied for their living; royalty, nobility and gentry. It may be that we can see a reversal of Smith's relations between the two types of myth in the early medieval period whereby genealogical myth was a powerful force for breaking up the ideologically based Roman Empire by newly established Germanic kings.

Experience

Shared experience can take many forms. Migration, natural disaster, warfare and genocide are perhaps the four most intense experiences any people can undergo. Of these, it is warfare that is the most ubiquitous in the historical record. Migration to be effective in creating a sense of separate identity must transport a people from one homeland to another in which they can maintain their exclusive identity. Such situations are rare in the history of any one people (although there are exceptions, e.g. the Romany or Gipsies). Natural disasters are uncommon and genocide has thankfully not been the fate of most ethnic groups (although sadly the fate of all too many). It is warfare that is the commonest experience creating shared experience, memories and myths that can bind a people together (Smith 1986: 37-41). War is also a crucial means whereby a ruling dynasty can rally ethnic support around itself and cement its place as the heart of the 'nation'. As Balandier (1986: 507) notes "war becomes a living system for maintaining society as a whole". War enables those in power to strengthen their position. By waging war against an external enemy, the cohesion of the social unit is reinforced. Success in war brings lands and wealth that can be distributed to further enhance the prestige of the elite and the identity of the group with their rulers.

> We few, we happy few, we band of brothers;
> For he to-day that sheds his blood with me
> Shall be my brother; be he ne'er so vile,
> This day shall gentle his condition;
> And gentlemen in England now-a-bed
> Shall think themselves accurs'd they were not here,
> And hold their manhoods cheap whiles any speaks
> That fought with us upon Saint Crispin's day.
>
> William Shakespeare *Henry V*

In many cases, in addition to notions of origin and historical experience, there exists also an idea of the golden age - a time when the community reached its full potential and existed as a free nation with an identity that no other can share. For a golden age to have existed, there must have been a decline in the group's fortunes and there may also be myths of decline, liberation and rebirth. Past and present are thus linked. To look forward to a renewed future necessarily involves invoking the models of the past, reviving the heritage of the group as a source of pride, identity and a model for the future. Smith (1986: 209) suggests that heritage and myths of the golden age are an important part of modern nationalist attempts to resist "the assimilating pressures of modernity". I will suggest below that they are equally part of pre-modern political agendas, and that earlier elites were just as conscious of ethnicity and capable of manipulating symbols to provide a sense of community for themselves and their people.

Name

In these days of legislation and bureaucracy, we are accustomed to the idea that a people have a distinctive name by which they are known. We may also acknowledge that their name for themselves, in their own language, may be different from the name we use for them in our language. In English, we say *Germans* but Germans say *Deutsche*. Our word that is the equivalent of the German word, *Dutch*, is reserved in English to describe the people of the Netherlands. In earlier times, it may be that we need to accept a variety of names being in use, belonging to different contexts and liable to different interpretations. The name of a people could even change over time. The Gutones of the 1st century, had split with part becoming the Tervingi by the 4th century, becoming in turn the Vesi and then the Visigoths (Wolfram 1988: 20-24). It has often been pointed out that many of the Germanic tribes identified by Tacitus no longer appeared in historical sources of the 5th and later centuries, but had been replaced by other names and configurations of peoples. Equally, a name may be long lived but be applied to a variety of ethnic or political units. Perhaps the best example is that of Burgundy. The Burgundians were originally an east Germanic speaking people located between the Oder and Vistula, and later also on the central Rhine, who made their way inside the Roman Empire and were settled as *foederati* around Worms in 411. This first Burgundian kingdom was destroyed by the Huns and the survivors were moved to a new kingdom farther south, to the north and east of the Alps, in 443. This second kingdom was conquered by the Franks and absorbed into the Merovingian state in 534. However, it maintained an identity and re-emerged in 888, split between an independent Kingdom and a Duchy inside France. By this time, there was no longer any ethnic identity as east Germanic Burgundians, the whole of the area speaking Romance dialects. The kingdom was absorbed into the Holy Roman Empire in 1032. The revival of Burgundy as a separate power began in 1384 with the union of the French Duchy of Burgundy with the Imperial Free County of Burgundy. This formed the nucleus of a power which spread over the next 100 years to cover almost all the land northwards, including Luxemburg and Flanders, as far as the County of Holland. The aim of the last Duke, Charles the Bold, was to create a new middle Kingdom between France and Germany; an aim that perished with his death in 1477 trying to annexe Lorraine. This new Burgundy straddled the linguistic divide to include both French and German speakers and would have had a curious ethnic identity, far removed from that of its earlier 5th century namesake.

The case of Burgundy may raise in our minds the question – did medieval people have a view of ethnicity as opposed to lordship? Medieval writings about ethnicity tended to view language rather than political organisation as a key marker of identity (Bartlett in Hutchinson & Smith 1996: 127-132). For example, Bede in his *Ecclesiastical History of the English People* in 731, mentioned five languages of Britain in his day and then went on to treat each language as a separate people (Colgrave & Mynors 1969: 17). These did not equate with five states or kingdoms. In practice, attitudes towards language and ethnicity were deeply ambiguous. Many writers realised that ethnic groups need not equate directly with language (Pohl & Reimitz 1998). The reality of the medieval world was that many people could be bilingual and that their ethnic identities were expressed using a complex mix of characteristics, of which political structures were often key components. Political structures will identify themselves with a name, but as we have seen what is meant by that name may change over time.

A further complication arises when we as modern scholars use names for people in the past. We often do so with a cavalier disregard for the meanings of the names we find as used in the historical record. Reynolds (1985) has demonstrated admirably that our modern usage of the term Anglo-Saxon is deeply flawed and ambiguous. The term Anglo-Saxon arose on the continent in the 8th century as a way of describing the Germanic inhabitants of Britain: the English Saxons as opposed to the Saxons still in Germany. In Britain itself, the terms *Angli* and *Saxones* were to some extent interchangeable, but were usually used to signify one or other subgroup by the Germanic inhabitants themselves, while the Britons and Irish regarded them all alike as Saxons (and still do). It was only in the 9th century that the compound term 'Anglo-Saxon' was used within England, and this was soon replaced in the 10th century by the simple term English. Nevertheless, scholars today refer to the Anglo-Saxons in both a cultural and chronological sense to cover the Germanic inhabitants of Britain from the 5th century to the Norman conquest. This signifies a great deal more uniformity and ethnicity than actually existed at the time. Likewise, the use of the term Celt to describe the pre-Germanic inhabitants of Britain has been attacked as deeply unhistorical, saying more about modern ethnic attitudes and nationalism than ancient reality (Collis 1994).

Land

Having a separate territory to call your own is not a necessary part of ethnicity but for most groups is an essential part of their self-definition. Smith (1999: 150) has used the term ethnoscapes to describe the relationship of a people with their land. Making the land an integral part of one's identity is more than simply marking it out physically. It is a process of identification with the land, whereby the landscape itself becomes a cultural artefact. The naming of places and the placing of events, often sanctified by religious association, creates powerful emotional bonds between people and their land. The landscape itself may be felt to influence the character of the group living in it. It becomes an active participant in shaping ethnic character. Perhaps, the best known embodiment of this is the nationalism of Elizabethan England as described in a speech of John of Gaunt in Shakespeare's *Richard II* (first folio edition):

This royall Throne of Kings, this sceptred Isle,

This earth of Maiesty, this seate of Mars,

This other Eden, demy paradise,

This Fortresse built by Nature for her selfe,

Against infection, and the hand of warre:

This happy breed of men, this little world,

This precious stone, set in the siluer sea,

Which serues it in the office of a wall,

Or as a Moate defensiue to a house,

Against the enuy of lesse happier Lands,

This blessed plot, this earth, this Realme, this England,

Any landscape consists of discrete places, each of which is named and has associations in the mind which govern how we feel about them. Figures of importance to the wider community like saints, gods, mythical or legendary heroes can be ascribed to particular places to locate them in a wider web of communal recognition and belonging. In this way, a group lays claim to a landscape. The land and the people become one. Ancestors can fulfil a powerful role in validating claims to connection with particular lands. Group cemeteries or graves of individuals can be used in this way. The graves need not be real however. Legendary resting places of heroes like Arthur can fulfil the same function. Religious sanction can often tie people together through bonds over wide areas. For example, Canterbury as a centre of pilgrimage in medieval England would have helped integrate many into a shared feeling of nationhood.

Such identification of land and people takes time to achieve. For migrating groups, there may be a concern to establish identification very early on. The very naming of the landscape may serve this function. The use of popular etymology to ascribe place names to people belonging to one's own group can achieve the same purpose and may perhaps lie behind the use of such etymologies in the early medieval period in England. An instance of this may be seen in the ascription of the name Portsmouth in the Anglo-Saxon Chronicle to an eponymous founder Port arriving in Britain in 501 with his two sons Bieda and Mægla, rather than Latin *portus* (Sims-Williams 1983: 29). Renaming the landscape is perhaps more important than establishing boundaries since boundaries will already exist and cannot be nationalised in the same way as names.

Behavioural culture markers

Language

Language has often been taken as a key symbol of ethnicity, even as a fundamental definition of ethnicity. To be a separate people almost demands having a separate language (e.g. the attempt by Norway to legislate for a national standard in language since independence). However, serious study of language, especially in the discipline of sociolinguistics has shown without doubt that language as a marker of identity can be manipulated through individual choice (Trudgill 2000). Medieval authors were perhaps more sensitive to the realities of the relationship between language and people. Various medieval writers noted that a single language could be possessed by more than one people (Pohl & Reimitz 1998: 23). Unfortunately, attitudes by scholars who are not linguists remain rather simplistic and still tend to equate language with biological groups. Work on the development of Indo-European languages is often couched in terms of the spread of Indo-European peoples, and attempts to find archaeological evidence for the spread of these languages often reinforces this view, even in spite of denials to the contrary (Mallory 1989). Languages are pictured as moving from one area to another like armies marching across the landscape. The origins of various Indo-European languages are often linked to changes in archaeological evidence, in turn linked to movements of peoples, e.g. the supposed advent of the Greeks into modern day Greece at around 2200 BC (Mallory 1989: 70-71). In practice, language is an act of speech. It is a type of behaviour which can be passed on from one person to another by teaching or copying and more closely resembles traded artefacts moving through and across ethnic groups. Nevertheless, all peoples are conscious of the high visibility of the speech they use as a marker of their identity in social, gender or ethnic terms. Many groups do in practice make an identification of their language with their ethnic identity, in the same way that they may adopt particular styles of dress as ethnic markers. Yorke (2000) has noted that early medieval writers often equated the notion of an ethnic group, the *gens*, with having a separate language. She points out that in Old English the word for language, *geþeode*, is clearly derived from the word for people, *þeod*. Trudgill (2000: 44-45) notes that language may be the most important criterion for ethnic group membership. It has been shown that language can play a highly symbolic role in ethnic identification, especially in multi-ethnic societies with unequal access to status and economic or political power (Horowitz in Hutchinson & Smith 1996: 285-291).

Different dialects of the same language may also serve to identify someone as belonging to a particular ethnic group, which begs the question - what do we mean by language? It may be thought that a separate language is one that cannot be understood by the speaker of another language. In the modern world of legally defined standard languages in the service of nation states this may be the case. However, in earlier times (and in practice still today) many separate languages will be mutually intelligible because languages vary in a continuous way between different geographical areas. Speakers either side of a political border may speak very similar dialects and yet have quite different standard languages laid down by their particular nation state. In earlier times, the standard would be that of the prestige ruling group, perhaps centred around a royal court or commercial capital. Rather than think of languages and dialects, it may be more sensible to think of autonomous and heteronomous varieties of speech (Trudgill 2000: 4). Autonomous languages are those which develop independently according to set norms determined by the centres of power. Heteronomous languages are those varieties actually spoken by the people and show continuous variation geographically or socially, often evaluated in relation to the supposed norms of the autonomous standard. This distinction is more useful than that between language and dialect since all varieties of language (including standard varieties) vary in grammar, vocabulary and pronunciation and can be considered dialects. Dialects may be mutually intelligible versions of the same language, but subjective attitudes to language as an ethnic marker may lead some speakers to elevate their dialects into separate languages, e.g. Serb and Croat, Urdu and Hindi, Swedish and Danish. When this happens, they become autonomous varieties of speech, with the possibility of separate future paths of development.

Varieties of speech, whether language or dialect, are a cultural trait, and are open to being manipulated by their speakers. While use of speech can signal or reinforce ethnic identity, a deliberate change of speech can be a useful method of integration into social networks and power structures, resulting in the ethnic assimilation of individuals and groups. There needs to be some perceived advantage for the individual in pursuing this strategy, perhaps related to political or economic structures. An understanding of such processes has been tentatively applied to such problems as the linguistic expansion and differentiation of Indo-European speech (Mallory 1989: 258-261). It could equally as well be applied to much later examples of linguistic change, e.g. early medieval Europe.

Religion

A functionalist interpretation of religion would see it as a way of promoting and affirming existing social structures and so maintaining group cohesion (Hendry 1999: 122). While this is not the only reason behind religious belief and practice, this aspect of its role means that religion can be a particularly powerful marker and shaper of ethnic identity. The tenets and rituals of religion deal with the eternal verities of life and have a moral force that few other types of human behaviour can match. The social power of religion lies in setting norms based on moral or divine sanction. Furthermore, some religions have an organised and select priesthood; a specialist group of people with skills not possessed by the majority. The skills of the priesthood enable them to act as the shapers and transmitters of ethnic tradition (Smith 1986: 36-37 & 42-43). Ethnic boundaries will often be marked by subtle differences between expressions of the same religion that may mystify outsiders and yet be potent symbols of identity to those involved. A religious convert may be fully accepted into his or her new community but the nature of conversion is accepted as a deeply personal act, viewed with suspicion and often seen as a betrayal by those left behind. It is unlikely to be an act undertaken lightly if religion is part of the accepted ethnic norm. Only if religion ceases to play the role of identifier does the ease of conversion increase. Sectarianism is often a cover for ethnicity as the complicated splits within Christianity over the last 1,000 years have often shown. The role of religion can be especially important in ensuring the survival of minority ethnic groups (Smith 1986: 109-114). In the absence of political leaders, it is the religious organisation through its priesthood, body of law and religious practices that can give shape to everyday ethnicity. A modern example would be the role of the chapel in maintaining Welsh identity in opposition to the Anglican church in Wales during the 18th, 19th and 20th centuries.

Religious practice takes place at times of celebration, stress or during episodes of transition (Hendry 1999: 145). Birth, coming of age, marriage and death are notable transitions for the individual. Religious rites can be very personal when based around these and yet also take place in communal settings whereby the individual is integrated into the community through the transition. The precise theology underlying religious practice is perhaps of less importance than the binding together of individuals through commonly recognised rites.

As Smith (1986: 120) points out, for religion to be effective as a guardian and renewer of communal identity it needs to be both adaptable and inclusive. It has to adapt itself to political, social and economic change, and it must bring all levels of society within its orbit if it is to integrate the whole of the people into one identity. Religions which today may seem dogmatic and fixed were not always so. The early history of Christianity shows a great deal of flux in dogma and practice. The adaptability of the Papacy to changing political circumstances in the early medieval period has long been well known (e.g. Previté-Orton 1971: 289-294). Its ability to compromise with, and adopt, pagan practices is a sign of its realism and a key to its success. In the case of Britain, the adoption of Christianity by the Anglo-Saxon kings might in some cases be a case of them seeking integration through religious unity by converting to the religion of the majority of their subjects, rather than an imposition of new and alien religion from above.

Action

We all conduct various actions in our daily life and throughout the year that involve cooperation with other people. We build up sets of customary ways of doing things with the tacit agreement of our social networks which serve to reinforce the social bonds. These actions may be as simple and common as forms of greeting or methods of eating. They may also be special actions reserved for particular times of the year or particular activities, such as sporting occasions or religious festivals. In some cases, these actions may have ethnic overtones. A mundane example from the modern world which shows the differences in behaviour which to most people are unconscious is the British habit of eating with a knife and fork, contrasting with the American way of using these same items.

In most cases, variation in behaviour is acted out within the immediate social networks of the individual and detailed variation will be local or regional in extent. The term 'customs' captures the nature of such actions. In modern

English, the compound term often used is 'folk customs', which brings out the local and small scale nature of these kinds of actions. Folk customs serve to demarcate areas from each other at the level of the village, the shire or region. None of these is necessarily ethnic. To be an ethnic signifier, the custom must be more widely shared. Perhaps a particular festival is celebrated only by one group, albeit with many local variations, e.g. Guy Fawkes Night in Britain. However, even this can be seen as a particular adaptation of a wider festival, known in Ireland as the Celtic Samhain festival of the 1st November.

Variation in behaviour is more difficult to identify in early medieval contexts. One example is the national handwriting styles that emerged from late Roman handwriting. National minuscule hands developed in Lombard Italy, Visigothic Spain, Merovingian France and a common insular minuscule in Britain and Ireland (Drogin 1980). Variation at a more local scale or among the majority of the population rather than learned elites is harder to find given the fragmentary nature of our evidence for the period.

Social and political structures

For some writers, ethnicity is associated with the rise of state level organisation of political units in modern times. However, Smith (1999) has pointed out that ethnic consciousness has existed since the beginning of recorded history. Some states in the ancient world, were run by dominant ethnic groups, e.g. Persia, or could be predominantly of one ethnicity, e.g. Israel or Egypt. Some ethnic groups however were not mobilised in states of their own but might be split between several smaller units, e.g. the Greeks or Sumerians, whose unity was maintained through cultural or religious means rather than politics (Smith 1999: 106). To understand the link between politics and ethnicity we need a greater understanding of how society is structured and the link between social organisation and authority.

Society is commonly structured in two ways: through horizontal relations of kinship and through vertical relations of authority. The link between the two is often intimate and strongly related to notions of ethnicity. For some writers, e.g. Moreland (2000), ethnicity cannot be understood unless it is considered as an expression of power relations between individuals and groups. The use of ethnic labels in early medieval documents is most usual in reference to kings and warfare, suggesting that political context had an important part to play in the mobilisation of ethnic feeling at that period (Moreland 2000). This raises the question as to the extent of the political community that shared this feeling. Before the modern era and the advent of democratic politics, the term people or nation was usually only applied to the politically active part of the population. If ethnic labels applied to the elite of a society, discussions about the ethnic characteristics of the whole population will be fruitless since this would be to talk at cross purposes.

The link between authority and horizontal social relations can be seen in the terms used for kinship and authority in many languages. Old English is especially revealing. A selection of words is presented in Table 1 which shows how words for ruler or authority figure are related to words for group or family, and both in turn related to some notion of activity that semantically links the two.

Authority	Group	Related words	Related verbs
cyning (king)	*cynn* (kin, family) *cynd* (kind)	*cyðð* (kith)	*cennan* (bear) *cunnan* (know)
dryhten (ruler)	*dryht* (nation, army)		*dréogan* (suffer, take part in)
folgoð (office)	*folc* (folk)		*folgian* (follow)
frigea (lord)	*fréond* (kinsman)	*fréo* (free) *fríge* (love)	*fréogan* (love, free)
léod (king, man)	*léode* (people) *geléod* (compatriot)		*léodan* (grow from) *lǽdan* (lead, grow)
magu (warrior)	*mæg* (kin, family) *mægð* (race)	*mága* (man) *mægð* (woman) *mægen* (strength)	*magan* (be able)
ríca (ruler)	*ríce* (kingdom)	*ríce* (strong, rich)	*ricsian* (rule)
þéoden (ruler)	*þéod* (people) *þéodnes* (society)	*geþéode* (speech)	*þéodan* (associate)
wealdend (ruler)		*weald* (power) *onweald* (authority)	*wealdan* (wield)

Table 1: Related words for authority and group in Old English.

A useful perspective on the link between political integration and ethnicity for the early medieval period has been put forward by Woolf (2000). He points out that different geographical scales of integration progressively involve less and less of a proportion of the population. At the level of the township or parish, most active adults will know, or know of, each other and will be able to meet together regularly since they live no more than about one hour's journey away from a central point. The higher level of the province or shire would involve a full day's journey for assembly and most people will not be in day-to-day contact. This would make necessary some sort of magistrate to mediate in disputes and coordinate communal action and decision-making. The higher level still of the nation would involve more sporadic contact for those who could afford to travel and spend time away for an extended period. The effective group of adult males at this level would spend most of their time apart and not be in familiar day-to-day contact. The group would beheld together by intermarriage and ritual activity. As the nation in arms it would need war leaders on an occasional basis. Ethnic marking through symbols of identity to signal co-membership of the group would be most important at this higher level.

Material culture markers

Wiessner (1983, 1989) has put forward a view of material culture as a way of transmitting messages. There are two important aspects of material culture, both of which are involved in the term 'style'. Emblemic style carries information about group identity while assertive style symbolises the identity of the individual. Both these aspects of variation in material culture differ from the unconscious variation in patterning of artefacts due to human action within varying social situations (Sackett 1982, Shennan 1989:18-20). Emblemic stylistic traits need not relate to ethnic group identity; they can refer to various other aspects of group identity, including sex, status or age. As Shennan notes, the problem for the archaeologist is to recognise emblemic style apart from other aspects of style and also to isolate which aspects of it are ethnically determined.

Material culture areas have often been equated with particular peoples, although there is also an appreciation that some cultures do seem to have covered more than one language or ethnic group, e.g. the Chernyakovo group of the 2nd to 5th centuries AD in south east Europe, which seems to have included Goths, Sarmatians and Slavs (Mallory 1989: 79). Perceived links between material culture and ethnicity underlay much of early 20th century archaeology, which identified cultures in the archaeological record and treated them as though they were separate peoples migrating across Europe, or even the world. Thus, a particular style of pottery in use in Britain around 4,500 to 3,700 years ago was identified as the cultural marker of 'the Beaker folk', an aristocratic group bringing bronze metallurgy to less civilised natives. More recent interpretations would see Beaker pottery as part of package of prestige items adopted during a time of social change to signify a particular elite ideology (Clarke 1970, Case 1977, Harrison 1980). A good account of this culture-historical approach is to be found in Jones (1997), who described the growth of culture history in archaeology from the 1860s to its heyday in the 1920s. She noted the link between the culture concept in archaeology with ethnic groups that was a fundamental part of this approach. However, she also noted that one of the approach's key exponents was Gordon Childe who, while accepting an ethnic connotation for cultures, explicitly rejected a linkage with notions of race (Jones 1997: 17).

More recently, archaeologists have taken a more sophisticated and sceptical view of the link between material culture and ethnicity, recognising that cultural patterns owe a great deal to various types of social action, not just ethnic identification (Shennan 1989, Jones 1997). They have accepted that ethnicity can be seen as a subjective state of self-description by individuals. As Amory (1997) notes, "It is not easy to determine subjective ethnic identity from objectively visible culture". The link between material culture and ethnicity is thus complex. We should note that a nation like England has not had a single culture history shared by all its people (Moreland 2000). It would be truer to say that there are multiple culture histories intertwining in a way that resembles a particularly complex piece of interlace ornament, only certain strands of which will be shared by particular individuals at any one time.

The use of material culture to symbolise, shape and manipulate identity will become more important at times or places of social stress, e.g. at boundaries or in times of severe competition for resources (Hodder 1982). One such time of stress might well be migration with its disruption of family ties, removal from familiar economic and social patterns, and the insertion into (or creation of) new patterns of behaviour and relations. Competition between groups might also lead to a greater emphasis on material culture to signal identity. Both of these stresses have been invoked by scholars studying the 5th and 6th centuries in Britain. For the Anglo-Saxon period, Richards (1992) has noted that material culture seems to have held a variety of meanings for society at the time, only some of which were related to ethnicity. Patterns of association can be seen in various artefacts in early Anglo-Saxon burials, e.g. applied bosses on cremation urns and cows as burial offerings with adult males, incised hanging arches with young girls or applied decoration with tweezers, crystal beads and playing pieces (Richards 1992: 143-145). Richards (1992: 147) has also suggested that stress from migration and competition might be a reason for the weapon burials, pottery and metalwork in early Anglo-Saxon communities, reflecting an overseas migrant warrior origin myth. We might expect that competition between emerging elite families might be signalled by stressing their power and status in burial (Hedeager 1992). Securely established elites on the other hand will tend not to make such a great show of stressing identity in burial but will instead make their display of wealth and power in religious observance, e.g. making offerings to the gods. The archaeological near invisibility of British elites in the 5th and 6th centuries can be contrasted with the very obvious Germanic identities being displayed in the east of Britain. Such an emphasis on marking identity could have arisen if the Germanic migrants were a marginalised minority defensively stating their ethnicity. The decline in the habit of placing grave goods in burials during the 7th century might then signify that the Germanic migrants had raised themselves in power and status forming an elite feeling more firmly entrenched and secure, rather than the adoption of Christianity (which, as has been noted many times, has no strictures against grave goods).

A particularly important part of material culture is dress. The clothes we wear and the attachments and fittings we use with them are an outward and unavoidable expression of ourselves. Hendry (1999: 86) notes the symbolic use of dress to make statements, such as fitting into the group and signalling personal identity/status. The signalling of dress is towards outsiders and to others of the same group. We might expect that competition between individuals or groups will lead to an inflation of symbols; ever more exaggerated forms of dress, or rapid replacement of dress items by newer forms. Some items of dress are highly portable and would be of greatest symbolic effect in face-to-face encounters between people who are of different groups, or who do not come into frequent contact with one another. In these situations lack of personal knowledge of the person can be compensated for by the artefactual signalling of status and identity. Germanic brooches seem to fall into this category, as highly visible and malleable forms, capable of variation within an overall type and of a potentially infinite variety of shape and decoration.

It is not only dress that can be used to signal to others. The body itself may be so used. We are used to seeing body piercing and tattoos at the present in western European society, or the dreadlocks of Rastafarians, but these are not new phenomena. Wherever we look, we find bodily adornment or even mutilation as badges of status, ethnicity or rebellion, e.g. African scarification or Maori tattoos. The most well known example in the early Germanic world is probably the Swabian knot, a way of tying the hair that distinguished both hierarchical status and ethnicity among the Swabians (Tacitus 1970:133).

Even variation in building styles can reflect ethnicity. The post-Roman period in Europe saw the emergence of 'national' traditions of architecture (Altet 1997: 75-76). For example, Visigothic churches developed in a distinctive way from the 7th century having very compartmentalised internal plans, large well hewn stones, an upper floor to the apse and other features. English churches of the same date seem to be mainly simple naves with *portici* (singular *porticus*), usually without apses. However, not all variation in building design will reflect ethnic traditions. Some building traditions will be regional, e.g. in English medieval timber framed houses, while some variation in design will result from the use of different building materials or for protection against particular climatic features.

From all that has been said above, it is clear that there is no simple link between ethnic identity and material or behavioural culture. Ethnicity can be seen as a particular example of a social network in action. The idea of networks now underlies much of modern archaeological analysis (Gamble 2001: 81-82). Such analysis is close to the ideas of the politician Grimond (1974) and the archaeologist Clarke (1968), who put forward ideas that a person or artefact lies at the centre of an overlapping pattern of communities or distribution patterns. Ethnicity is only one of a number of networks that will be used to define an individual's persona. Archaeology is now much more sophisticated in its analysis of archaeological evidence and such equations of material culture with people are no longer made without a great deal of qualification. However, we should not imagine that the notion of ethnicity has no utility or reality. It is clear that once we have historical records to illuminate the past that there were groups of people who identified themselves as ethnic groups, and that much of the period of early recorded history is taken up by the movements and migrations of many of these peoples. One such migration was that of the Angles, Saxons and others from northern Germany to the shores of Britain in the 5th and 6th centuries AD. This book seeks to analyse that migration and the following creation of England in terms of ethnicity. In the process, it should shed much light on the nature of the links between ethnic identity and behavioural and material culture.

History and archaeology

The migration period, the 5th and 6th centuries, is rich in ethnic complexity. Yet, it is a remote time with little in the way of personal testimony. We can only study the ethnicity of the time through the disciplines of history and archaeology. We need to understand how these two have developed to see how their views of ethnicity and of early medieval Britain have changed over the years.

The beginnings of serious historical and archaeological study of the Anglo-Saxons lie in the early part of the 19th century. The pioneers of Anglo-Saxon archaeology were C. Roach Smith and J.M. Kemble, beginning their studies in the 1840s (Lucy 2000). Even at this stage it was recognised that Anglo-Saxon material culture was similar to that of northern Germany. Inevitably, the following generations of scholars concentrated on establishing the basic typology of artefacts and linking the archaeology to what they knew of the historical events of the period. In the days before sophisticated theoretical models and without well-developed anthropological analogies, this approach was the only feasible way of interpreting the data. Key figures of the earlier scholarship were E.T. Leeds (1913, 1936), G. Baldwin Brown (1903-15) and N. Åberg (1926), whose works are still the basis for our current description of the period. Inevitably, their interpretations of Anglo-Saxon England were coloured by the cultural context of their own times. In an age of imperialism, and the acceptance of racial distinctions, the identity of modern English with Anglo-Saxons as an ethnic group is understandable. Seeing the Anglo-Saxons as an invading army moving in to take over and settle as pioneers a new country would also fit with the more recent activities of the English in their modern day migrations in the 'white empire'.

Later scholars developed this approach into the third quarter of the 20th century, to create what we might call the traditional and established interpretation of the period, e.g. S.C. Hawkes (1962), V. I. Evison (1965), J.N.L. Myres (1969, 1970, 1977). Material culture was seen to represent the existence of sharply defined ethnic groups, and the archaeological evidence could be related either in some detail or in general to the accepted scheme of historical events derived from documentary sources. Invasion and migration of large numbers of Anglo-Saxons brought with them a new culture that transformed the south east of what had been Roman Britain into Anglo-Saxon England.

By 1970, a revolution was beginning in archaeology, the so-called 'new archaeology' which emphasised trying to understand the past in its own terms, through systems analysis and the use of science. Instead of using archaeology to fill in the gaps of history, the goal of archaeological study was to understand the rules governing human behaviour and ways of all aspects of life in the past. Archaeologists had begun to examine the evidence of sites and landscapes rather than just artefacts or burials, and develop an understanding of ways of life as well as the broad sweep of historical events. This approach began in prehistoric archaeology and soon spread to the study of the Anglo-Saxons. These new directions were signalled in Wilson (1976). Hodges (1982) provided an early glimpse of the new perspectives on this period, with a full-blown application of the new archaeology arriving with Arnold's first edition of *An Archaeology of the Early Anglo-Saxon Kingdoms* in 1988. Arnold treated the period as essentially prehistoric (as did Esmonde Cleary in 1989), and, in keeping with current trends in prehistory, he rejected mass migration as a causal factor for change. Prehistorians had long been used to discounting migration in reaction against the excesses of diffusionist explanations for culture change. In place of an immigration of peoples, Arnold preferred to see only a Germanic elite coming over and somehow managing to assimilate the majority native population through their political or cultural superiority. At the same time, place-name studies were gaining maturity, and the works of Margaret Gelling (1978, 1984) brought this area of study into mainstream acceptance among archaeologists and historians. This helped to reassert the need to envisage migration by more than just a small social elite in order to explain the overwhelmingly English nature of these names.

Historical study of the Anglo-Saxons has a longer pedigree than for archaeology. It could be said that serious historical study of the early history of the Anglo-Saxons began with Bede in the 730s. Although Bede anticipated many of the methods used by modern historians, it is only in the last two hundred years that historians have advanced in method beyond what he achieved.

The earliest modern writer to look seriously at the documentary sources for the period was Sharon Turner, who published his *History of England from the earliest period to the Norman Conquest* between 1799 and 1805. Turner laid the foundations for Sir Francis Palgrave who, with his *History of the Anglo-Saxons* in 1831, was the major force in the study of Anglo-Saxon history during the early 19th century. It is striking how early the historians adopted a racial interpretation of the documentary evidence. Chief among Palgrave's successors were J. R. Green, E. A. Freeman and W. Stubbs, who from the 1870s, popularised the idea of mass replacement of native Britons by waves of incoming Anglo-Saxons (Higham 1992: 3), tied to a naïve, literal reading of the early sources. In an earlier, pre-imperial and pre-Darwinian generation, Kemble had shown a more nuanced interpretation of the period, allowing for a great deal of ethnic continuity from the native Britons.

Later generations of scholars provided greater detail and subtlety to the picture of the Germanic migrations to Britain. H.M. Chadwick's work (1905, 1907, 1912) on social systems and hierarchy placed the Anglo-Saxons in their Germanic context. His analysis could have provided a more nuanced interpretation of the social nature of migration and settlement. Myers in Collingwood & Myers (1936) provided a detailed synthesis of archaeological evidence with history to provide a narrative of mass Anglo-Saxon migration and takeover in Britain. The high point of traditional scholarship was reached in Sir Frank Stenton's magisterial survey of the whole Anglo-Saxon period (Stenton 1943), followed and amplified by such historians as Whitelock (1952) and Loyn (1962).

What the traditional scholarship lacked was a knowledge or understanding of the British side of the story. An awareness of the importance of looking at sources relating to the native British, rather than basing accounts only on Anglo-Saxon sources, began to seep into scholarship in the 1970s. In part, this was an attempt by historians and archaeologists to bring the subject of Arthur into mainstream study. It was also a reflection of recent work in the study of Celtic cultural history, e.g. Dillon & Chadwick 1967, Chadwick 1970. Among archaeologists, Leslie Alcock produced *Arthur's Britain* in 1971 as an attempt to bring some balance to the study of the 5th and 6th centuries. The major historical work was that of John Morris, whose work was summarised in *The Age of Arthur* (1975). Morris attempted to make accessible the wide range of insular and continental sources for the period, and based his interpretations of early medieval Britain on an unrivalled knowledge of these sources. Unfortunately, he was too willing to accept at face value many sources which needed a more careful investigation into their context and their reliability. Nevertheless, Morris brought a much needed fresh eye to the study of the period, and injected a host of new ideas into the debate about the transformation of Roman Britain into Anglo-Saxon England and Celtic Britain.

Morris's work produced the inevitable reaction that all radical rewritings of history face. It was David Dumville (1977) who attacked both Alcock and Morris, and began the close examination of the British historical sources. He did this with the explicit intention of demolishing the historicity of Arthur. While historians like Dumville were creating a vacuum in the 5th and 6th centuries, archaeologists like Reece (1980) were applying increasingly sophisticated analyses to the late Roman period and producing an early collapse for Roman Britain that extended the vacuum back into the 4th century.

Increasingly, the work of archaeologists and historians has come to be considered together, each feeding off the other. In spite of new evidence, and of new approaches – perhaps even because of both – there has been little consensus on the nature of events in the 5th and 6th centuries. The last 15 years has seen a frenzy of publication, and an exciting level of debate, with archaeological contributions from scholars like Esmonde Cleary (1989), Hills (1990, 2003), Welch (1990) and Faulkner (2000), as well as major historical studies from Bassett (1989), Yorke (1990), Kirby (1991) and Dark (1994, 2000). Some authors have sought to integrate historical and archaeological evidence within a strong narrative, e.g. Higham (1992, 1994, 1995, 1997). Some of the most interesting publications have tried to bring together not just historical and archaeological approaches but also the anthropological and sociological, e.g. Hines (1997), Frazer & Tyrrell (2000). The focus on the British has continued with writers beginning to treat the 5th century as a transition not from Roman Britain to Anglo-Saxon England, but to a post-Roman British society, (Snyder 1998) or event anti-Roman British society (Jones 1996), thus providing a necessary framework for the Anglo-Saxon migration and context (Snyder 1998). As well as looking at developments in Britain, scholars have also learned that Britain should be studied as part of the wider European context within the Roman Empire as a whole (Swift 2000).

New perspectives are being applied, new ways of looking at the data, even new techniques like archaeogenetics. These all help us to develop new models for the events of the 5th and 6th centuries. Ideas about what happened during these two centuries and explanations for these events are legion, with no consensus available and considerable disagreement between different models. Perhaps there never will be agreement, since the evidence for this period is too fragmentary and ambiguous. This is one of the fascinations of the period and every researcher can feel they have something new to add. What follows is my interpretation of the period, but it is not a comprehensive history of the two centuries. It is an exploration of Anglo-Saxon ethnic identity, and should be read with this in mind. Readers looking for a connected narrative history of the period should look at the Timeline and Appendices.

Migration and Conquest

If we are to understand what it means to be English, we must understand the origins of Englishness. The creation of this identification began well before the creation of a Kingdom of England. While it is straightforward to describe the events that led to the creation of a single English state, it is more difficult to describe the creation of an English nation; a people sharing certain values, outlook and cultural expression. What characterises the English people has changed greatly over time. What it means to be English in the 21st century under Elizabeth II is very different to what it meant in the 16th century under Elizabeth I. Nevertheless, a people identifying themselves as English have existed for around 1,600 years. This chapter will explore the origins of English identity at the beginnings of the medieval period. It should be read in conjunction with the Timeline and the Appendices, which provide the necessary chronological and other frameworks for understanding the narrative of events. The scheme of dates adopted for various events is explained in the Timeline.

The origins of the English lie in the immigration of Germanic speaking people to Britain from northern Europe in the fifth and sixth centuries AD. This is not to say that genetic origins of all people now living in England lie in those same settlers. The people of England have been the result of a constant series of migrations over many hundreds of years, adding to the native stock of the inhabitants of Roman Britain. However, England as a nation, as an idea, does have its origins in the movement of peoples from the Germanic areas of the continent. Over the last 30 years, there has been a bewildering variety of interpretations of the transition from Roman Britain to Anglo-Saxon England and Celtic Britain. The differences between them centre on the degree to which Roman civilisation and organisation survived into the post-imperial period, and the size and nature of the Germanic migrations to eastern Britain. Evidence for this migration comes from documentary sources of the time, traditions set down in writing over 300 years later, and from the archaeological remains of their material culture. The fragmentary nature of this evidence makes secure interpretation rather difficult. First hand, contemporary documentary sources are few, and those that do exist present problems of context and content. Recourse is therefore had to later secondary sources, with all the pitfalls that this entails. Archaeological evidence is subject to major problems of interpretation deriving from the subjective nature of analysis applied to evidence that cannot speak for itself. Place names have often been used as evidence for this period but secure interpretation of these depends largely on historical or archaeological evidence for its significance to be accurately assessed. Scholars working with particular types of evidence are seldom familiar with other kinds of evidence and often distrust or ignore what these have to offer. The inadequacy of the sources means that it is possible to attack both the documentary and archaeological evidence as unreliable and so cast doubt on the extent of the migration. However, as Woolf (2000: 99) has pointed out, to say that migration did not happen exactly as portrayed in the sources is not the same as saying the migrations did not happen at all. The personal backgrounds of scholars, the climate of the time in which they work, and the perspectives of other disciplines like anthropology or sociology also colour how we interpret the evidence (Hills 1990). Hills (1999: 180) has shown how approaches to the period have been coloured by the events of the modern era, including the rise and fall of empire, and two world wars with Germany. It is no surprise therefore that at present the reader can choose from any of at least eight interpretations. It is by no means certain that the latest in time are an improvement on earlier ones, merely that they have been developed in a different scholastic climate. The interpretations offer different views on the extent to which Roman culture and identity survived into the 5th century, but also on the size and nature of the Germanic migration into Britain after the island was withdrawn from the Roman Empire. As Sims-Williams (1983: 28) has pointed out: "the fact is the academic mind is so flexible that it can reconcile almost anything with almost anything else".

There are three basic views of the extent of Roman continuity:

- a transformation of Roman Britain into a Celtic Britain; involving a gradual decline of Roman civilisation (Frere 1967, Alcock 1971), the abandonment of Britain by Rome (Bassett 1989, Esmonde Cleary 1989), the collapse of Roman economy and politics in the 4th century (Reece 1980, Arnold 1984, Swift 2000, Faulkner 2000), or a British revolt against Rome (Jones 1996, Faulkner 2000);

- the maintenance of Roman ways either as Roman-Christian (Morris 1975), a version of Roman civilisation being called late antiquity (Dark 1994, 2000, Henig 2002), or as a hybrid Romano-Celtic culture (Snyder 1998);

- a division of Britain between a Romanised, late Antique east and a Celtic west (Higham 1992).

The view of Frere, and later Alcock, may be termed the traditional view and was that the structures of Roman Britain declined in the period 360-450, with the west of Britain reverting to a Celtic tribal identity and the east succumbing to large scale Germanic migration (Frere 1967, Alcock 1971). The classic case for Germanic migration within this model was put by Myers (1969). An early revision of this traditional view was the work of Morris; what might be called a minority view that Roman administrative structures largely survived at diocesan level until mid 6th century collapse, with an intense and long-lived struggle between native Britons and large numbers of incoming Anglo-Saxons (Morris 1975). Most people would now say that this was based on a largely uncritical acceptance of later documentary sources. A more recent partial revival of this view in a different guise is that Roman Britain did not collapse but was transformed into what can be called late antiquity (only becoming medieval after c.600), with more complex relationships than simple antagonism between the Britons and the newly arrived Anglo-Saxons (Dark 1994, Henig 2002). A modified version of survival is that post-Roman Britain was a unique kind of hybrid native/Roman society unlike anything seen elsewhere (Snyder 1998). The major revisionist view has been that instead of gradual decline or survival there was a complete collapse of Roman Britain. For some, this was due to the withdrawal of the army and Imperial administration in 410, with little left by c.430, and only small numbers of Germanic settlers arriving after this (Bassett 1989, Esmonde Cleary 1989). An alternative view is that the infrastructure of Roman Britain had effectively collapsed well before 400, leaving a prestige vacuum that would be filled by the native British adopting new elite Germanic fashions following a limited but high status Germanic settlement (Reece 1980, Arnold 1984, Swift 2000, also partly by Faulkner 2000). A more recent alternative is that the collapse of Roman Britain was due to a native revolt against Roman ways and values (Jones 1996, also partly by Faulkner 2000 but with a class war dimension). The more complex view is that elements of Roman civilisation remained into the 5th century, especially in the west (becoming Christian, employing Germanic soldiers, succumbing to a Germanic revolt and take over) while the east remained pagan and Celtic (able to defend itself, remaining independent but later adopting Christianity) (Higham 1992). The role of Germanic immigration in these models varies between acceptance of large scale migration (Frere, Alcock, Morris, Dark, Henig) and a much smaller scale immigration leading to a greater degree of acculturation to a minority Germanic military elite (Arnold, Cleary, Faulkner, Higham, Reece). This latter view has proved to be appealing to many archaeologists, who have been prone to interpret the presence of Germanic material culture as a simple case of local natives adopting new and exotic fashions (e.g. Pryor 2004).

Some trends in interpretation are apparent: an increasing acceptance that elements of Roman Britain survived into the 5th and even 6th centuries, and a downplaying of the size and role of the Germanic migrations (Hamerow 1997). Continuity between the Roman and medieval worlds now seems to be the preferred analytical framework. The extreme of this view is perhaps represented by Henig (2002) who could say "the 7th and 8th centuries can still be regarded as culturally late Roman". Henig's indicators of Roman identity are rather unspecific however, including the use of coins, speaking Latin and Christianity, which would make most of medieval England also Roman. The belief in cultural continuity is largely the result of the changing views of archaeologists (archaeologists like Arnold and Hodges were early exponents of a minimal view of the extent of Germanic migration, Hamerow 1997). Archaeology has become more confident in its ability to offer explanation independent of historical research and documentary frameworks. Whereas an emphasis on documentary sources of evidence for the period leads to an emphasis on changes at the level of the ruling elites and political structures, archaeological evidence yields different kinds of information that is more amenable to interpretation in terms of continuity. However, belief in continuity is due to more than this. Scholarly interpretation does not take place in a vacuum. In the days of empire, colonialism and military rivalry, it was natural to accept an interpretive model for the early middles ages that laid stress on conquest and models of population movement, with categorisation of the civilised and the barbarian. In more modern times, we are used to a world where the rights of minorities are protected, where colonialism and empire are regarded with regret or embarrassment, where conquest and military adventure are treated as illegal acts. In this kind of world, there is a reluctance to see invading hoards of Germans, an acceptance that even native Britons had rights, and that the gap between civilised and barbarian was more apparent than real.

It is easy to find examples of the trend in recent scholarship to downplay the extent of migration, e.g. Lucy 2000. It is now accepted that the interpretations of the post-Roman period in Britain have reflected the wider socio-political concerns of contemporary scholarship, chiefly attitudes towards Germany and towards Britain's place in Europe (Hamerow 1997, Ravn 2003). As has been well put by Richard Sermon, "archaeology, like history, is reinvented by each generation and is deeply affected by the political and social thinking of the time" (Sermon 2001: 37). Furthermore, advances in archaeological theory have been led in recent years by prehistorians. Over the past 30 years, explanations of cultural change in prehistory have been dominated by internal mechanisms in reaction against the now discredited models of earlier times which laid greater stress on the advance of civilisation through conquest and migration. Such models were partly the result of methodology for determining dates which relied on making stylistic links between cultural artefacts. These were later proved to be only partly valid and were largely replaced by the radio-carbon dating revolution (Renfrew 1974). Simplistic equations of cultural groupings with ethnic groups have rightly been questioned. However, this should not lead to a denial that material culture can play a role in signalling ethnic identities, and Hines (1996) has said that "the tendency in archaeology to dismiss ethnicity of cultural groups is unjustified". Changes in archaeological explanation were also the result of the rise of what was called the New Archaeology in the 1970s, which laid stress on understanding the internal dynamics of how societies worked, rather than relations between different societies. Prehistorians have adopted increasingly sophisticated theories focussing on economic, social or psychological motives for processes of change. As a result, migration became unfashionable in prehistoric studies (Chapman & Hamerow 1997: 3-4). Unfortunately, changes in academic thinking that result from the rejection of unfashionable models inevitably swing too far in the opposite direction. Other areas of archaeology have not been immune to this work, and medieval archaeology in particular has found it to be attractive in the absence of detailed or unequivocal historical evidence to provide its explanatory frameworks. Historians have hardly helped matters by the almost gleeful willingness of some to dismiss many of the documentary sources of evidence as untrustworthy or flawed. The main example of this tendency is Dumville (1977) who was unwilling to accept any source that could not be demonstrated to be unequivocally contemporary with the events it describes; what Ravn (2003: 89) calls self-destructing source-criticism. This tendency is not, however, new and goes back to the origins of modern study of the period with the attitude of John Kemble in 1849: "I am convinced that the received accounts of our migrations, our subsequent fortunes, and ultimate settlement, are devoid of historical truth in every detail." (Sims-Williams 1983: 1). Inevitably, this involves the rejection of most of the sources used by many to flesh out the narrative history of the 5th and 6th centuries. While historians like Dumville and Kemble have been quite right to argue that sources need to be used with a critical eye to their circumstances of production, their minimalist approach might well have thrown out the baby with the bath water. For example, Sims-Williams would go so far as to suggest (on what I take to be very tenuous 'evidence') that figures like Hengest or Oisc were purely mythical with no historical basis (Sims-Williams 1983). Archaeologists can be forgiven for assuming that the work of the minimalists like Dumville has reduced the migration period effectively to a prehistoric period, and treat it accordingly as pointed out by Yorke (1993). In my view this is wrong. Later sources can be used if 'health warnings' are properly given about their degrees of probable accuracy and an understanding of their context of production. We need to use all avenues of evidence with a full awareness of their reliability. To argue that what a document has to say about an event or figure cannot be corroborated or proven does not mean that it is wrong and can be ignored. As noted by Yorke (1993), to have reservations about historical sources does not mean that they have no historical value at all. It is not the same as proving it to be false by contradictory evidence. Dumville's 1977 article was written as a response to two particular works of history and archaeology, which accepted the historicity of the figure of Arthur at face value (Alcock 1971, Morris 1975). The existence of Arthur is an issue which tends to engender strong, emotive and polarised views. We need a more realistic and sober judgement of the reliability of evidence than either uncritical acceptance or hyper-critical dismissal. We should not embrace the counsel of despair as put forward by Sims Williams (1983: 40) who stated that "It is one thing to admit that there 'may be something in' the traditions reported by Bede and the *Chronicle*; it is quite another to imagine that we can divine what that something is.". We must take account of the possibility that the traditions recorded in later sources may have some relevance to what actually went on in the 5th and 6th centuries.

Although there are legitimate reasons to question the archaeological evidence, the most ardent expressions of the revisionist scholars may sound like a rejection of migration in any form, e.g. Carver 1998: 100:

> We still do not know exactly who they were or where they came from, or indeed whether they were incomers at all.

However, Carver himself happily belies his own quote to paint a picture of Germanic migration alongside native acculturation. Even the most dismissive find it hard to say that at least some migration did not take place, e.g. Lucy 2000: 179-180:

> This is not to say that there was no population movement in the fifth and sixth centuries. ... it does not mean dismissing the idea that people moved, merely the idea that in observing their movement you can account for all subsequent change.

What is debated is not whether there was a migration but the extent of that migration. The two main models of Germanic take-over of Britain involve either a minimal migration of elites with widespread acculturation of Britons to a Germanic identity, or a mass migration of Germanic settlers whose upper strata would eventually take over lowland Britain and mould a new insular Germanic identity for their people (Arnold 1997: 20-22). While archaeologists and historians have veered towards the more minimalist model, a fuller acceptance of migration has been the model followed by scholars of place-name studies (Gelling 1993). Moreover, as Ravn (2003: 89) has pointed out, the more revisionist interpretations have come from scholars who have little reading knowledge of German and tend to study the British evidenced in isolation from comparative material on the continent. Barnwell (1996) showed how an understanding of socio-economic and fiscal organisation in the period could be enhanced by placing the British evidence in its wider European context. Any explanation of the evidence must take into account the remarkably thorough transformation of Britain into Anglo-Saxon England (and into 'Celtic' Wales), as noted by Hines (1996). I think we can know a great deal, both of the broad outlines and some of the details of the creation of the Anglo-Saxons, and that this creation is intimately bound up with the act of migration of large numbers of Germanic speaking people from the continent to Britain in the 5th and 6th centuries. We cannot know the hearts and minds of the early settlers, but the fact of migration to a strange land, with natives of different speech and customs must have had an impact on the identity and attitudes of the migrants. The English were a new nation, in which the migrants' identity became that of all and which, over time, developed apart from their cousins on the continent.

It may be that future genetic studies will allow us to evaluate the extent of population movement independently of archaeological or historical evidence, and so also of the biases of archaeologists and historians (Hooke 1997). As pointed out by Wilson et al (2001), although the pendulum has swung away from migration to continuity, it is likely that cultural change has involved population movement in some cases while not in others. As yet unfortunately, genetic studies are in their infancy. Evison (2000) should be required reading for anyone who thinks that genetic analysis will provide a simple answer to questions of ethnicity. Genetic variation is complex, with different characteristics being shared by different populations. One feature can be shared by groups A and B, while another by groups A and C, and a third by groups B and C. Good genetic analysis will take a group of features and employ proper statistical analysis to discriminate between clusters of genetic variables. Genetic differences are simply too minor to stand out within the generally very mixed and similar genetic pool in north west Europe (Hills 2003: 67) without such detailed statistical analysis. Evison does point out that the very fact that the genetic pool is so mixed is a sign of frequent migration over many millennia and has little patience with current anti-migrationist fashions to be found in archaeology (Evison 2000: 289):

> Given the ideological form of criticism of migration in archaeology, it is ironic that the isolation inherent in extremely indigenist models would almost inevitably have led to genetic divergence (not to the genetic admixture which is apparent) and potentially, ultimately, to the development of separate races. Although it may be difficult to detect unambiguously migrants using skeletal or genetic evidence, it would be a mistake to relegate the movement of individuals and groups of people to a position of irrelevance as the fashionable indigenism seems to do. Such processes have always been and continue to be major social factors in Britain and elsewhere.

Other scientific techniques may also help us to analyse population movements. Looking at the relative concentrations of different isotopes of oxygen or strontium in human bone can help to show where a person spent their formative years and so could provide an indicator for first generation immigrants. This method has only just begun to be used however and it is too early say what results it will bring. A study of human remains from West Heslerton (Budd et al 2004) has enabled the identification of new migrants (perhaps one in six of the population) from Scandinavia. What is interesting about this is that the samples producing this result all came from women, and from women who were buried without grave goods. The rest of the population, including those identified as culturally Anglian originated in Britain. A majority of those sampled however came from areas to the west of the Pennines. This is not at all what we should expect and provides a necessary element of caution for all analyses based on purely artefactual evidence. Nevertheless, this is only one study - in an area marginal to the areas of supposed primary Germanic settlement in Yorkshire (which was in the southern Yorkshire Wolds). More analyses are needed from a wide variety of securely dated contexts.

It is genetic studies that will provide the greatest progress in helping us understand the broad patterns of possible migration. As Hills points out, a true genetic picture of a population should take in both the male and female ancestries of the group (Hills 2003: 67). While the male ancestry can be studied through the Y chromosome, the female ancestry is best approached through studies of mitochondrial DNA. A combination of both approaches has yet to be done for Britain with studies so far restricted to male or female lines of ancestry.

The few studies that have yet been undertaken have produced intriguing results. A study by Falsetti and Sokal (1993) yielded the existence of genetic boundaries in the British Isles. They suggested that variation in genetic data from the British Isles could only be explained by the "migration of different ethnic units". Sharp boundaries were identified separating the south west of England and Wales from the rest of England, and two boundaries were detected in East Anglia and Lincolnshire. Evison (2000) put forward the view that genetic boundaries could well be the result of geographical boundaries acting to separate population groups. This was discounted by Falsetti and Sokal in the case of the boundaries just described. Evison's idea that the two boundaries in eastern England reflected migration from different parts of the continent based on the likely natural landfall of travellers across the North Sea is an interesting suggestion, but one that may not take into account the naval abilities of seafarers of the time. Evison pointed out that the DNA of immigrant groups would be diluted by their reception into existing indigenous populations, and this is what we may be seeing in the evidence provided in a study of the Y chromosome in the British Isles (Capelli et al 2003). This showed "a continuing indigenous component in the English paternal genetic make-up" (Capelli et al 2003: 983) diluting the continental nature of the English genetic signature.

A more restricted study has been carried out on Y chromosome samples from a transect across central Britain from East Anglia to North Wales (Weale et al 2002). This found little genetic difference between the populations of the English towns but that the two north Welsh towns studied were significantly different from each other and from the English samples. They also found that there was no significant difference between their sample from Friesland and the English samples. A Norwegian sample was different to all the others however. As the authors state (Weale et al 2002: 1018):

> Our results indicate the presence of a strong genetic barrier between Central England and North Wales and a virtual absence of a barrier between Central England and Friesland.

Perhaps the most significant part of this study was that the authors attempted to model the size of migration from the continent to Britain; more precisely to model what proportion of the genetic pool in the English part of their transect came from continental sources. Depending on the assumptions made, the continental ancestry accounted for 50-65% at least of the English population. Much depends on the assumptions in their models and these figures should not be accepted at face value, only as indicative of a substantial migration event. One issue that this study could not solve was whether there was a large Danish Viking component in the English samples, which could account for the similarities with Friesland, since Danes and Frisians are genetically similar. The other disadvantage of the study was that it covered only a narrow transect across Britain and could say little about levels of migration to southern England.

The most comprehensive study yet undertaken in Britain seems to be the Capelli study (Capelli et al. 2003), which produced some fascinating results. Samples from Wales, Cornwall, Scotland and Ireland (with one anomalous exception) clustered separately from those from England. A degree of Norwegian Viking input could be seen in samples from the north west of Britain. The highest amount of similarity to German and Danish samples came from Yorkshire and East Anglia. Samples from Northumberland, the West Midlands and southern England were less continental in nature and much more like (although still separate from) the 'indigenous' samples. The study also found that Frisian samples were not significantly different to the German and Danish samples. The high continental input into the genetic make-up of Yorkshire and East Anglia could come therefore from either Anglo-Saxon or Viking populations. Just as there have been attempts to minimise the Anglo-Saxon migrations, there have also been attempts to minimise the extent of Viking settlement. It is interesting therefore to see how far the minimalist scholars are willing to accept Viking migration as a way to save their interpretation of minimal Anglo-Saxon migration!

The analysis of scientific data should go with openness to new ideas about the extent and nature of Germanic migration in this period. Dominant interpretations can be challenged and new thinking promoted. However, the power of fashionable models, dominant theories, can be very strong. Hills is strangely reluctant to accept genetic findings in their entirety, preferring to suggest that Weale et al.'s similarities between England and Friesland might have other explanations than simple migration of people from one to the other (Hills 2003: 70). She suggested that the English sample represents Viking migration or that Frisians and English both resulted from migration of Saxons southwards on both sides of the North Sea. Likewise, Evison (2000) quotes a genetic study showing a genetic similarity between part of Cumbria and Norway, that can be matched with the historical and place-name evidence to support the idea of Viking migration into the area. Yet, the authors of the study seemed unwilling to accept the obvious: "although consistent with other historical data, the genetic evidence of Scandinavian settlement is slight and open to alternative explanations" (Evison 2000: 282). To be fair, Evison also criticises simplistic migrationist models and the view that language and culture can be used as proxies for kinship.

It is clear that genetic studies still have some way to go in shedding light on population movements in this period. Nevertheless, the early results are encouraging. So far, studies have concentrated on identifying differences between Germanic genetic features and those of indigenous Britons. There needs to be a shift of focus towards identifying differences between populations within England. One key issue, identified by Capelli et al., is the low proportion of Germanic contribution to the genetic pool in the far south of England. The other key issue is the overlap between areas of Danish Viking and Anglian settlement in eastern England. The area of densest concentration of Danish place-names almost mirrors the area of densest concentration of the earliest Anglo-Saxon cemeteries in this part of Britain.

Actual kinship is only one aspect of ethnicity. Ethnic identities are not the same as racial groups, and it is the creation and manipulation of an Anglo-Saxon identity that is the interesting question this book seeks to explore. To analyse the evidence for the 5th and 6th centuries, we shall need to keep in mind the nature and construction of ethnicity as understood through sociology and anthropology. Only if we do this will we fully understand and interpret the evidence. It is only very recently that historians and archaeologists have begun to look at the work of sociologists and anthropologists to help shed light on the 5th and 6th centuries (Moreland 2000). The work of continental scholars has been in advance of those in Britain in this respect (Pohl 1997). In this chapter, I hope to show some ways in which this might be done to our advantage in understanding this period. As explained earlier, I adopt a Liberal interpretation of ethnicity based on individual choice which has much in common with social constructionist models as put forward by writers like Jenkins (1997). However, there are dangers in the social constructionist approach. In particular, it becomes too easy to assume that ethnic group identities have no basis in reality other than as a convenient fiction for individuals, and that they have no set boundaries. To say that a people is an imagined community (Davies 1994) is to mislead. A people may be a constructed community, but it is nevertheless very real (both for those who belong and for those who do not - witness the appalling story of the Balkans in the 1990s). The real ethnic group exists in time, and has an origin and a future. Members of the group may feel a direct connection with the same named group in past times and we must heed the caution of Smith (2000) who stresses the importance of historical continuities in the make up of ethnicity (a point accepted by Jenkins). However, the connection is direct from generation to generation through processes of procreation as well as socialisation.

Origins

The migration to England was of different groups at different times, in different circumstances and probably for different reasons. Bede, writing around 300 years after the earliest settlements, stated the traditional view of the Anglo-Saxons themselves that the migrants included Angles, Saxons and Jutes, as well as Frisians, Rugians, Danes and Bructeri (part of the Franks), and even non-Germanic Huns (Colgrave & Mynors 1969: 50, 476). Hines (1994) feels that Bede's list of peoples may have more to do with 8th century missionary activity on the continent than being an accurate memory of the 5th century migrations. However, that Bede may have been accurately reflecting genuine tradition is suggested by the evidence of burials at Fontenay in northern Gaul which betray the presence of people from the Black Sea area who could well have been Hunnish (Swift 2000: 86-88). No such burials have yet been found in Britain however. The Anglo-Saxons themselves felt that they were a Germanic people and as late as the 8th century the continental Saxons were expressing the view that they were of one kin with the Anglo-Saxons (Kylie 1924: 195).

Some modern place names still preserve the names of some of the tribal groups involved in the settlement (Cameron 1977: 72-73) and broadly confirm Bede's lists. However, interpreting place names as having ethnic labels can be hazardous, e.g. names containing *fyrs* (furze = gorse) have often been mistaken as indicating Frisian presence. The following list is generally accepted as the minimum number of place names based on tribal groups:

Alemanni	Almondbury? (Yorkshire);
Angles	Englefield (Berkshire), Englebourne (Devon), Engleton (Stafford);
Frisians	Freezingham, French Hay and Frenchhurst (Kent), two Frisbys (Leicester), Friesthorpe, two Friestons and two Firsbys (Lincoln), Freston and Friston (Suffolk);
Saxons	Saxton (Cambs.), Saxham (Suffolk), Saxondale (Nottingham), Saxton (Yorkshire);
Swabians	Swaffham (Cambs.), Swaffham (Norfolk), Swavesey (Cambs.).

The Byzantine historian Procopius mentioned Angles and Frisians as settled in Britain (Morris 1973: 281). On the other hand, Bremmer (1990) would minimise the Frisian contribution to Germanic settlement in Britain, pointing out that place-names like Frieston could have arisen through granting of lands to Frisian individuals long after the initial settlements (although this is less likely for other place-names). The settlers thus identified came mainly from the Baltic and North Sea Germanic speaking peoples. It was the Angles and Saxons, along with Jutes that provided the royal families for the later kingdoms and which thus became the dominant groups in the later mythology of settlement, and still dominate modern discussions of the period. However, it is as well to remember that various groups of settlers could have come from almost anywhere within the north-western Germanic area of the continent, and that we should not expect rigidly separated ethnic cohesion among the settlers in Britain. They did not settle as nations, but as groups of families and warriors, attracting fellow settlers as opportunity and ties of kinship arose. The archaeological evidence cannot be forced into a rigid three people model settling in carefully bounded regions of Britain, as many early historians and archaeologists tried to do.

The traditions about the settlement that were written down in the 8th century and later, related to the creation of the kingdoms of the Anglo-Saxons. These kingdoms emerged mostly in the 6th and 7th centuries, some years after the earliest settlements (Bassett 1989, Yorke 1990, Kirby 1991). The formation of these kingdoms has too often been projected back into the 5th century to provide ethnic identity for the archaeology of the earliest phases of the migration. As Myres (1970: 25) wisely noted, the divisions between Anglian and Saxon kingdoms "were far too precise and that they disguised by oversimplification the confused and chaotic conditions of the age of settlement". Each kingdom would have had its own origin legends, based on royal families of Anglian, Saxon or Jutish origins. However, few of these have been handed down in any detail in the historical sources. What was written down in later sources is a later transliteration and transformation of what must have been orally transmitted legends. Oral transmission is not the same as accurate written recording (Yorke 1993), and the realities of the past are often blurred and changed to fit later circumstances with myth and reality being mixed. For later generations of English, it was the legends that mattered. It is only modern historians who are concerned about the 'accuracy' of the legends.

The most detailed legends to have survived relate to the founding of Kent, the earliest of the kingdoms and the only one to have been founded at the same time as the original settlement. Kent was used by Bede to stand for the origins of the English as a whole. It may be that this was because the Kentish settlement was the earliest, but as a Christian writer, Bede may have given pride of place to Kent as the home of Anglo-Saxon Christianity. At any rate, the story of Kent came to stand as the primal origin myth of all the Anglo-Saxons. It is thus important to look at this story in some detail. The tale is preserved in later historical sources, both Anglo-Saxon and British, and can give us an insight into how each group saw the nature of the early migration.

The Kentish experience

The story of the Kentish settlement has been preserved in part by different sources, the chief of which are Bede's *Historia Ecclesiastica Gentis Anglorum* (Colgrave & Mynors 1969), the *Historia Brittonum* wrongly attributed to one Nennius (Morris 1980) and the *Anglo-Saxon Chronicle* (Bately 1986, Garmonsway 1954, Thorpe 1861). None of these accounts is contemporary with the events. As noted earlier, the sources themselves have not always been accepted as having any worthwhile information about the events of several centuries previously (e.g. Dumville 1977). However, it seems an exaggerated sense of caution to reject their testimony entirely. The incautious use of sources by scholars like Morris (1975) should not be balanced by an over-cautious unwillingness to accept any source that cannot be proven to be an eyewitness account of events. In practice, we must take the story they present as most likely a mix of genuine fact and legendary tale. Which part is fact and which only legend will always be a matter for debate. Yorke (1993) would have Hengest and Oisc being divine myths rather than historical persons, while I would accept that they were real.

Britain in the 4th century had been a diocese of the Roman Empire, divided into at least four (may be five) provinces, and into various '*civitates*' within each province. A revolt in 406 led to Britain coming under the rule of the usurper Constantinus III, who seized control of Gaul and Spain as part of his attempt to win control of the Empire during the confusion caused by a massive 'barbarian' invasion from across the Rhine. Constantine's position collapsed in civil war during 410, he himself being captured and executed in 411. In the confusion of 410, Britain threw off its allegiance to Constantinus but was unable to return to the Imperial fold. The Emperor's forces were fully occupied in Italy, and Britain was told to take up its own defence (although some scholars believe the reference to this event was actually to a town in southern Italy, e.g. Henig 2002). By the time Imperial rule had been restored to Gaul after 427, Britain had become independent, no longer part of the Roman Empire (Frere 1974: 408-409).

It may be that the former diocese was still united and ruled by a single person. If so, this may be Vortigern, mentioned in the sources as ruling from 425 (Morris 1980). He faced many threats to his rule, the Picts, the Irish and a rival named Ambrosius. He might also have feared that the Romans might return to reclaim Britain for the empire, especially in the context of the restoration of Imperial authority in Gaul by Aetius. Ambrosius may have been the major supporter of the restoration of Roman rule, an aristocrat wanting to reassert Britain's place as part of the Roman world and thereby secure his own position in Britain with Roman support (although this is pure supposition without any evidence to back it up). Perhaps we should see Vortigern as the British version of those Gaulish aristocrats who were establishing their native identities as an alternative to a Roman identity at around the same time (Geary 2002: 104-105). Matthews (2001) has noted that the attitudes towards Rome by some Britons seems to have been rather hostile, e.g. Gildas who described Rome as a foreign oppressor and occupier. The British church seems to have purposely ignored innovations in theology and religious practice made since independence as a conscious act of differentiation of Britain from the Empire (Harris 2003). Vortigern's solution to securing his position and the independence of Britain from Rome was the tried and tested Imperial method of engaging Germanic soldiers to fight for him. These were led by the brothers Hengest and Horsa, who were given lands and provisions in return for fighting off the Picts and others. They were settled at first in Thanet in Kent and recruits were brought over from the continent to join them. At least, that is the usual interpretation. The highly suspect version of Geoffrey of Monmouth would position Hengest in Lindsey first before moving to Kent. Sims-Williams has noted (1983: 21) that Bede himself does not actually say that Hengest landed, or was settled, in Kent. It is according to the *Historia Brittonum* (Morris 1980: 28) that Hengest gave his daughter in marriage to Vortigern and received in return the whole British Kingdom of Kent (the '*civitas*' of the *Cantii*). His son Octa and nephew Ebissa were summoned and settled near the wall in the north to defend Britain against the Picts and Irish. There is archaeological evidence for the employment of Germanic soldiers at Corbridge near Hadrian's

Wall in the 5th century (Snyder 1998: 170) which supports this historical tradition, although it cannot support identification of the soldiers with Octa and his men. Loveluck (2000) however would place the Anglian burials at Corbridge in the early/mid 6th century. The date of the first settlement by Hengest was placed by Bede between 449 and 456 (Colgrave & Mynors 1969: 48-50). Bede was basing his dates on the evidence of the 6th century writer Gildas and extrapolating from the one fixed chronological point in Gildas's work, the *De excidio Britanniae*. This was an appeal by the Britons to Aetius in 446. The *Anglo-Saxon Chronicle* followed Bede, but also put an appeal to the Angles for military help in 443 (Garmonsway 1954: 12-13). However, in the *Historia Brittonum* Hengest's arrival was placed in 428 (Morris 1980: 39). This earlier date is supported by the archaeological evidence for the earliest Germanic settlement (Higham 1992: 172-174, Hills 1978: 307, Myres 1989: 87, 108-109, Welch 1992: 102-103), which has been dated to the 420s or 430s (Jones 1996: 37). According to Hines (1990b), there are 15 sites that have produced certain or probable archaeological evidence of Germanic settlement before 450, the earliest occurring around Dorchester on Thames in the 420s. An early date for settlement is also supported by the pottery evidence. Myres (1977) in particular has noted the similarity between pottery found at a variety of sites in Britain with continental Germanic styles of the late 4th and early 5th centuries, e.g. the *Schalenurne* of Schleswig-Holstein. The evidence of the continental *Gallic Chronicle*, which noted the passing of Britain (i.e. the south coast?) under Saxon rule in 441/2 (Higham 1992: 155; Morris 1975: 38), presupposes a period of settlement some time before this, also supporting an early date for the first settlements. Sims-Williams (1983) has pointed out that Gildas may well have mistaken the historical context within which the appeal to Aetius was written (nearly a hundred years before he was writing) and so misplaced the sequence of events, thus misleading Bede and in turn generations of later historians.

The story as presented in the *Historia Brittonum* was that the Britons eventually became reluctant to pay for the increasing numbers of mercenaries and their families, who themselves were eager to share more directly in the riches of Britain. The result was that the Germanic settlers made a truce with the Picts and turned against the Britons. Fighting broke out led by Vortigern and his son, Vortimer, who besieged the mercenaries in Thanet while they sent for reinforcements from the continent. The later traditions of the *Anglo-Saxon Chronicle* recorded battles at Aylesford where Horsa was killed (455 by the *Anglo-Saxon Chronicle's* chronology or 434 by the chronology of the *Historia Brittonum*), further fighting at Crayford (457/438) and *Wippedesfleot* (465/444) and again in 473/452. These were perhaps based on the four battles of Vortimer recorded in the *Historia Brittonum* (Morris 1980: 31). After the death of Vortimer, both sides seem to have reached a stalemate. The two sides met in conference to talk about peace, but Hengest and his followers turned on their hosts killing most of the British leaders. Vortigern was then forced to cede Sussex and Essex as well as Kent to the control of Hengest. This might well be a later myth used to support Kentish claims to supremacy over its neighbours in the 7th and 8th centuries. Whatever the actual result of the revolt, the Anglo-Saxons were now firmly established as a permanent presence in Britain.

Hengest is the only name associated with the migration and conquest to have figured in later heroic verse tales (see below under *Myth and legend*). Hengest's reputation was as a Jutish leader associated with both Danes and Frisians, possibly an outsider to both. He was a man involved in bloody feuds and likely to have been forced to seek his fortune as an exile away from his native land. Hengest could thus be seen as the archetype of the Germanic immigrant to Britain; a lordless warrior, with loyalties only to himself, his family and followers, carving out for himself a position of power in a new and strange land.

According to the *Historia Brittonum*, after the death of Vortigern, leadership of the British resistance to the new settlers passed to Ambrosius Aurelianus who had some success at the beginning of a long war. After Hengest's death (488/467), his son Octa (grandson according to Bede) took over the leadership of the settlers in Kent. He, and probably other leaders like Ælle in Sussex, continued to fight against the Britons. By the end of the 5th century, these Britons might well have been led by Artorius (Arthur). Some historians deny that Arthur actually existed, while Henig's (2002) view is that Arthur was a by-name for Ambrosius Aurelianus. Many battles were fought, the last being at Badon Hill in which the Britons (under Arthur?) were victorious. The later *Welsh Annals* (Morris 1980) placed this in 516, but a reference by Gildas (Winterbottom 1978: 28) would place it c.495, as would Bede (using Gildas's chronology). In spite of Badon, the Britons could not expel the Anglo-Saxons, who stayed on and brought over reinforcements with their royal families from Germany. Their advance westwards may have been stopped but they were secure in their possession of parts of the east coast of Britain, and could continue to bring over fresh immigrants from the continent.

Germanic settlement

The nature of settlement

The reality of Germanic settlement in Britain is much more complex than the story presented above. Late Roman Britain was a world in full touch with the rest of the Empire and received immigrants from many of its provinces. It should come as no surprise then that Germanic peoples could be found in Britain while it was still part of the Empire. We know of Germanic military units serving in Britain, as they did elsewhere in the Empire. It seems that individual Germanic civilians were also to be found. Dark (2000) identifies a thin scatter of supporting arm and tutulus brooches from the 4th century as representing the presence of a few Germanic women in Britain at this time, albeit within a Roman social and settlement context. Swift (2000) has noted the increasing Germanic influence on Roman fashions and practices in the late Empire. We can no longer see an antithesis between civilised Roman citizens seeking to preserve the Empire against barbarian Germanic tribesmen. The late Empire was a symbiosis of Roman civilian and Germanic military seeking to coexist to mutual advantage. To be identified as Roman or German was not simply a matter of genetics. Society at that time must be seen as fluid with individuals able to switch identities and be both Roman and Germanic. Traditional Roman burial practices could exist alongside newer Germanic rites, used by both native Roman and Germanic newcomers, as in the Frankish *reihengräber* (Dark 2000: 23).

Evidence for Germanic migration to Britain has been identified in the form of pottery and metalworking, associated largely with burials. The main burial rite of the earliest Anglo-Saxons was cremation. This form of burial dominates the evidence north of the Thames (Higham 1992). Most Anglo-Saxon cremation burials come from just 10 large cemeteries (Myres 1969: 18, Higham 1992: 174): Caistor (Norfolk), South Elkington (Lincoln), Girton (Cambridge), Illington (Norfolk), Lackford (Suffolk), Loveden Hill (Lincoln), Newark (Nottingham), Sancton (East Riding), Spong Hill (Norfolk), Little Wilbraham (Cambridge). Such large cemeteries echo the large urnfields found on the continent. However, there are also a great many smaller cemeteries in Britain. The continental origins of the English cremations are demonstrated by the similarities between such continental cemeteries as Liebenau and their English counterparts like Apple Down in Sussex (Welch 1992: 66-68), especially the existence of four- and five-post 'houses of the dead'. To the south of the Thames and in Essex, it is the late Roman practice of inhumation that is dominant. Although some early cremations are found south of the Thames, they are the exception and do not form large cemeteries like those found farther north (Higham 1992: 170-72). These early inhumation burials with military fittings and quoit brooch style metalwork of late Roman inspiration may represent Germanic soldiers employed by the British authorities in the early 5th century. Archaeologists differ in their analysis of the quoit brooch style of metal belt fittings but the best explanation seems to be that the style was Romano-British in origin (Haselhoff 1974, Suzuki 2000). Hills (1978: 307) put forward the view that the fittings were Romano-British made but were worn by Germanic immigrants of some status (possibly military leaders), and might have been official issue to Germanic *foederati*. A recent technological study (Inker 2000) supports this view that the quoit brooch style was the product of Romano-British metalworking. It has been argued (Wood 1997) that within Britain the more southerly inhumations represent a more mixed Germanic origin with settlers from various parts of the continent, while the more northerly cremations were perhaps more homogeneous. This would support Higham who suggested that the southern burials represent Germanic soldiers from the Rhineland (Franks and Saxons) operating within a Roman style military system, while the more northerly cremation burials represent immigration of warrior communities from more northerly parts of Germany settling with their families (Higham 1992: 162-174). This echoes the remarks of Myres as long ago as 1936 who noted the differences between the evidence from East Anglia and from the south of the Thames which he interpreted as the difference between migration and conquest (Arnold 1997: 22). The differences between the areas to the north and south of the Thames have again been emphasised by Suzuki (2000), who noted that the early 5th century material culture of the south was markedly Roman and non-Germanic (and in the south east non-Celtic also), while Germanic cultural items occurred to the north. This could reflect the differences between soldiers serving under post-Roman authorities (*laeti*?) and Germanic settlers (*foederati*?). Similar differences in Roman material culture of the 4th century were identified by Hawkes and Dunning (1961). Belt fittings of types III to VII, made on the continent, were distributed in eastern Britain, associated by Hawkes and Dunning with the soldiers and officials brought over by Count Theodosius in 367. Fittings of types I and II were of native British manufacture and were distributed in the west and the midlands. These were interpreted by Hawkes and Dunning as part of the equipment of locally recruited military forces. Late Roman Britain was far from homogeneous and regional differences continued into the 5th century. Soldiers were perhaps much more likely to come from a variety of 'tribal' groups, while settlers were more likely to move as discrete groups from particular locations. It is noteworthy that the distribution of early 5th century burials with military fittings is in Kent, Surrey, Sussex, Hampshire, Dorchester, while women's brooches at this period are found mainly in Essex, Dorchester, East Anglia and Lincolnshire (Higham 1992, fig. 6.2). It was not until c.500 that women's brooches were present over the whole area from Hampshire through Dorchester up to Northamptonshire and Lincolnshire, and the East Riding (Higham 1992, fig. 6.3). Böhme has identified the settlement of family communities in East Anglia on the basis of finds of equal arm, supporting arm and early cruciform brooches (Carver 1989). This north-south split is echoed by the distribution of early runic inscriptions (Page 1999: 24). Artefacts bearing runic inscriptions that can be dated to before 650 are concentrated in eastern England and Kent with few finds south of the Thames. Could this be a reflection of a larger Germanic presence in these areas? Arnold's map of early Germanic burials (Arnold 1977: 214) shows the Anglian areas of Britain, with Kent, to have much heavier concentrations of burials. The existence of two separate areas in which settlement took place in different circumstances is also supported by the pottery evidence. Stamped wares like those of the Illington-Lackford workshop of the 6th century or granite tempered domestic pottery are limited to the northern, Anglian, area (Dark 2000). We must also take into account the findings of the genetic study by Capelli et al. (2003). There was a much lower Germanic component in the DNA of people in southern England than farther north, which they saw as one of their most surprising findings (Capelli et al. 2003: 982). Their findings may be accounted for by a difference in settlement between Saxon *laeti* and Anglian *foederati*. Anglian areas would be more open to a longer period of continued migration from across the North Sea than in the areas facing the English Channel and so a heavier Germanic settlement of these areas might be expected. Burials with Germanic artefacts increase over time in both density and geographical area. How much of this was due to increased immigration from the continent, natural increase in population of the early immigrants or to the cultural assimilation of the native Britons is difficult to determine (Campbell 1982: 35-36). The geographical distribution of early burials (5th century) is in the eastern part of lowland Britain, from the East Riding of Yorkshire, down through Lindsey and the areas bordering on the Fens (e.g. Northamptonshire) to East Anglia, along with Kent and the upper Thames (Oxfordshire). The western border of settlement by the mid 6th century ran along the East Riding, Lindsey, Kesteven, Leicester, Northampton, Oxford, Berkshire and Hampshire. There was only isolated Anglo-Saxon settlement outside this area.

The concentration of Germanic finds around the middle Thames, centred on Dorchester is one of the curiosities of the early 5th century. The area can hardly be thought of as strategically important for the defence of Britain. Deployment of Germanic mercenaries, some with their families perhaps, so far inland can only be for reasons of internal politics. What that reason was we cannot know, but we may have a glimpse of it in an obscure reference to a Battle at Wallop in Hampshire between Vitalinus and Ambrosius. We do not know who Vitalinus was, but Ambrosius was noted in later Welsh literature as an opponent of Vortigern. If the battle was fought as part of the political tensions between Vortigern and Ambrosius, then it may be that Hampshire was hostile territory for Vortigern, and a placement of Germanic soldiers loyal to the 'British government' would make strategic sense. Such soldiers would be placed under British control and loyal to the British administration. These would be ideal conditions for the creation of a mixed military grouping, with both Germanic and British components, as we see with the later kingdom of the *Gewisse*; an Anglo-Saxon kingdom with suspiciously British names among its early kings and centred on the middle Thames.

Further evidence that different parts of Britain had different experiences of Germanic settlement come from the distributions of imported goods. Kent was acting as the centre of distribution of a variety of goods imported from Gaul, central Europe and the Mediterranean, e.g. amethyst beads, gold coins, garnet, crystal balls and glass (Arnold 1997). Links between Kent and the continent seem to have been politically controlled and oriented to the major power centres of the old Roman world. Foreign imports elsewhere in Britain show a much more dispersed and less controlled distribution. They seem to show links across the North Sea on a widespread and decentralised basis, e.g. amber, crystal beads, ivory rings (of walrus as opposed to elephant ivory). The major exception to this is the distribution of type D bracteates which shows strong centralised links between Kent and Scandinavia, that is links between elites.

The densest areas of Germanic settlement were Lindsey, Kesteven, Leicester, Rutland, northern Northamptonshire, eastern Nottinghamshire, Norfolk and Suffolk, south Cambridgeshire, Kent, the upper Thames centred on Dorchester (Berkshire and Oxfordshire). Dark (2000) has noted that the evidence for different types of Germanic presence, together with survival of dominant Romano-British culture farther west seems to echo the geographical arrangement of Roman provinces. *Maxima Caesariensis* (centred on London) would cover the area of employment of Saxon mercenaries within a late Roman military system. The province of *Flavia Caesariensis* (centred on Lincoln) saw the immigration of Germanic settlers and their families. *Britannia Secunda* (based on York) was an area of British military strength, but also saw the employment of Anglian mercenaries and their families in the *civitas* of the *Parisii*. *Britannia Prima* (based on Cirencester) would have relied on native British military power and had no need for Germanic settlement. Carver (1989: 152) has identified East Anglia as the earliest area to be settled, based on the archaeological evidence. Todd (1992, 2001) adds the lower Thames, Kent and Lincolnshire, where early 5th century Germanic artefacts have been found at Romano-British settlements like Kirmington and Hibaldstow in Lindsey. Germanic cremation cemeteries began in Lindsey in the same period. Germanic evidence has also been found in other late Roman and post-Roman sites farther south like Portchester and Highdown (Todd 2001), although the latter site has also yielded evidence of 5th or 6th century Christian burials that should signify native British presence (Henig 2002). This picture of widespread early settlement conflicts with the documentary sources' emphasis on Kent alone. Examples of the earliest settlements are Mucking in Essex, Bishopstone in Sussex, and Caistor and West Stow in East Anglia (Welch 1992, Todd 2001). The first two of these may have been related to the strategic military needs of the post-Roman British authorities, but West Stow does not seem to have served any military function, being simply a community of settlers (Todd 1992).

Although some scholars are nowadays sceptical about the interpretation of the evidence as due to migration (e.g. Lucy 2000), I believe that the archaeological evidence largely backs up Bede's statement about the migration of various groups of peoples from northern Germany and southern Scandinavia, especially Angles, Saxons, Jutes and Frisians. Arnold (1997: 23) supports this view, although accepting that the correspondence between the archaeological evidence and Bede is not exact. Many people have noted the links in material culture between Kent and the Isle of Wight, and how these reflect later traditions of Jutish origin in both places. However, for Arnold (1997: 190), the similarities in material culture can only be sustained at the level of the minority elite on the island. This could be the result of intermarriage, as much as from common migratory origins. Hills (1999: 184) rightly points out that Bede may well have been providing an explanation for the observable divisions of his own time rather than providing an accurate portrait of 6th century events. We must beware of reading back into the 5th and early 6th centuries the political conditions of the 7th with its various kingdoms defined in monolithic ways as Saxon in the south or Anglian in the north. We should heed the words of Myres (1970: 31) that the evidence will reveal a "tumbled mass of early settlers whose local distribution was at first far more complex and varied than was afterwards apparent". However, the overall patterning is remarkably similar to what Bede tells us we should expect. Perhaps the identification of kingdoms in the 7th century was indeed a rough reflection of earlier realities.

Continental Germanic forebears

The first surviving references to *Angli* and *Frisii* are in Tacitus's *Germania*, written in 98 AD (Mattingley 1970). The Jutes also appear in Tacitus, as the *Eudoses*. The *Angli* and *Eudoses* are described together as part of a group of peoples bordering the western Baltic, worshipping a goddess Nerthus (equivalent of the later male Niorðr of the Vikings). The *Frisii* are located on the North Sea coast around the Ijsselmeer. *Saxones* first appeared later, in the work of Ptolemy of Alexandria c.150/75, centred on the River Elbe, and appear to have been either a renaming of an earlier group (perhaps the *Chauci*) or a merger of smaller peoples. The Germans themselves were first identified as a distinct people by Poseidonius of Apamea in c.100/75 BC (Todd 1975 & 1992). The term *Germani* was the name used by the Romans to distinguish this people from the other major group living in western Europe, the Celts. It is not a term that the Germans would have used to describe themselves, and most likely they would not have such a term other than their local 'tribal' name. Two of these 'tribes' had been identified by the Greek explorer Pytheas of Massilia - the *Gutones* (Goths?) and *Teutones* - in the late 4th century BC. The *Teutones* reappeared amongst the group of peoples who travelled south to attack southern Gaul in 109 -102 BC. It has been argued (Hedeager 1992) that Germanic society underwent a profound transformation around 175-200 AD and that earlier kin based tribal structures were replaced by warrior based groups in which warrior leaders competed for wealth with which to reward followers, with the result that ethnic identities were formed around particular royal families. Such units might adopt a particular ethnic label but could be composed of people from a variety of tribal backgrounds. This might well be true for the groups that invaded the Roman Empire in the 4th century, e.g. Goths and Vandals. Whether it holds true for all Germanic groups is more difficult to say. The Saxons for instance although appearing as a new group at around the right time, do not seem to have formed themselves into a unit based on a particular kingly family. In any case, the proposition that early Germanic society was based on unilineal kindreds such as royal families has been challenged (Murray 1983).

The chief artefacts that archaeologists have used to define ethnic identities are pots and brooches, with a few other items relating to different modes of dress. Recent studies of emblemic stylistic traits (e.g. Richards 1988, 1992) have shown how the use of such items at the time of their manufacture was closely linked to other kinds of identity as well, such as class, age or gender. Nevertheless, differences in form and decoration can still yield information about broad differences in ethnic categories. It has been noted that the Saxons on the continent had achieved a greater degree of ethnic marking in material culture than other groups farther to the north. Hines (1994) reported the work of Böhme in Germany showing the emergence between the lower Elbe and Weser rivers of distinctively Saxon items of dress by the later 4th century. These included the supporting and equal armed brooches, saucer brooches and associated styles of relief decoration. Cremation urns likewise became distinctively Saxon at the same time. Anglian cultural markers in dress came later, in the 5th century with particular styles of small-long brooch. Jutish identity remained only slightly marked in dress. The Jutes seem to have been happy to belong to a wider material culture province with a low sense of self-identity in dress fittings.

Links between the continent and Britain

Establishing links between Germanic areas of Britain and the continental homelands has been based largely on artefactual evidence. The evidence of settlements has not usually been part of the equation. It has been thought that settlements in Britain had little similarity with those on the continent, and that even house styles were completely unalike. Hamerow's ground-breaking study of settlement evidence from both sides of the North Sea has shown how far this was based on inadequate archaeology: too few sites excavated and too small an area of the settlements (Hamerow 2002). What is apparent is that settlement form on the continent was changing in the 5th century. Earlier settlements were characterised by enclosed farmsteads with long-houses in a regular layout. The newer styles of settlement comprised unenclosed farms with large numbers of *grubenhäuser* (sunken floored buildings) in a dispersed layout. This has been termed the Loxstedt type of settlement (Hamerow 2002: 94). With a greater knowledge of settlement archaeology we may at last be in a position to integrate the artefactual evidence with that from settlements. What is needed is more large scale excavations at settlements in areas of major Germanic immigration in Britain.

For now, most evidence of other difference still remains that of the artefacts. Analysis of pottery styles has revealed strong similarities between pots found in Britain and in the continental homelands of the settlers. Analysis of 5th and 6th century cremation urns in Britain has shown numerous links with the continent (Myres 1970, 1977, 1989). Although a great deal of the form and decoration of these pots can be found throughout the continental homelands of northern Europe and southern Scandinavia (e.g. horizontal linear and line & dot schemes of decoration), there are attributes that can be associated with more localised areas. Broadly speaking, Anglian and Jutish pottery on the continent tended to take the form of globular, wide mouthed bowls with incised decoration and lugs. Saxon pottery was more likely to consist of open carinated bowls with pedestal feet (Johnson 1980: 48-49).

Myres' identification of strong links between pots found in Britain and on the continent is invaluable for tracing the migration of settlers. In some cases, pots can be identified as having been made by the same potter or workshop (Myres 1977). Caistor in East Anglia is thus linked with Hammoor in Holstein and Sørup in Schleswig, while Bifrons in Kent is linked with Drengsted in Jutland, and sites in the upper Thames (Frilford, Long Wittenham and Sutton Courtenay) linked with Wehden in Saxony. Such linkages confirm Bede's identification of settlement by Angles, Saxons and Jutes. It is not only direct links which reveal this. There are many cases of strong resemblances between pottery from important cemeteries, e.g. from Sancton in the East Riding of Yorkshire and Borgstedt in Schleswig. In general, Anglian pottery can be traced back to Schleswig and Fyn, Saxon pottery to the northern parts of modern Lower Saxony. Pots from early 5th century Kent are similar to pots from the Ribe and Esbjerg areas of Jutland (Suzuki 2000). As we shall see later, other evidence confirms that Bede's division was overly neat and based on reading back the conditions of the 7th century rather than reflecting the reality of the 5th. It comes as no surprise therefore to see strong resemblances in pottery from sites in the 'Anglian' parts of Britain, like North Elmham, Loveden Hill, Kettering and Longthorpe, to pottery from Issendorf in Saxony, and that links can also be made between Markshall in East Anglia and Wehden in Saxony. It has been noted that groups of peoples were becoming mixed on the continent before the migration to Britain. The site at Issendorf in Saxony seems to have been a cultural melting pot and can be paralleled by British cemeteries like Spong Hill (Hills 1978: 317). The presence of Frisians in the settlement is revealed by links between Lackford, Eye and Cambridge St Johns in Britain with Rijnsburg and Wageningen in the Netherlands (notwithstanding the arguments of Bremmer, 1990, against such a connection being evidence of migration). Involvement by other Germanic peoples in the settlement of Britain might be revealed by other resemblances between the pottery of Swedish Gotland and sites in the east of Britain; at Kempston, Sancton and Sleaford. Some pottery seems to show links with parts of Norway in the early 6th century, particularly those pots with vertical and diagonal schemes of decoration combined with long bosses (e.g. at Linton Heath, Cambridgeshire, and Kempston in Bedfordshire, Myres 1977: 43). The archaeological picture is one of great variety in burial practice and material culture even over small areas. Cemeteries that are next to one another can show great dissimilarities (Moreland 2000).

Links with the continent can also be seen in metalwork. The Germanic animal art style began by the 3rd century (the earliest examples are from Thorsbjerg in Denmark). It developed through the Sösdala and then the Nydam style of c.400-475 into Style I (c.475-525) and Style II animal art. These were common styles that were shared by the Anglo-Saxons with Scandinavia and the Franks (Speake 1980). The place of Britain within a Scandinavian culture area has been noted by a number of scholars (e.g. Hedeager 1992, Hines 1992, Stevenson 1992). Style II art in Britain is found chiefly in Kent and at high status sites elsewhere, e.g. Sutton Hoo and Taplow (reflecting Kentish overlordship?). It has been suggested that the adoption of Style II ornament was linked with the desire of the newly emerging elite to identify themselves with their Germanic cousins in Gaul and Scandinavia (Lucy 2000: 21). Higham (1995) has suggested that Rædwald of East Anglia in the early 7th century was consciously asserting links with the homeland to bolster his traditionalist pagan conception of identity in the face of challenge from a newer, Christian and Frankish oriented identity. On the other hand, Hines (1984) has identified what he interpreted as clear signs of migration from southern Norway and Denmark into the Anglian areas of settlement in Britain, particularly East Anglia. These may continue earlier links between Anglian Holstein and Norway as revealed by some examples of pottery and small-long brooches. The links between Norway and Anglian settlers in Britain are marked by particular artefacts: sleeve clasps, equal armed brooches, phase 1 square-headed brooches, some types of scutiform pendants and C class bracteates. In particular, Hines sees the introduction of sleeve clasps as due to Norwegian presence in East Anglia and/or the Humber estuary from c.475. Other parts of Scandinavia were also linked with Britain, e.g. Denmark through early square-headed brooches and types of scutiform pendants. Hines's study of square-headed brooches (Hines 1997) has revealed that the earliest forms of brooch find their closest parallels with southern Scandinavia. Scandinavian art styles and bracteates link Kent and Jutland (Myres 1989), e.g. type D bracteates, as do early square-headed brooches (Suzuki 2000). As an additional link with Scandinavia, Ager (1985) would see the quoit brooch style of metalwork developing in Kent from origins in Jutland. However, this would not be supported by a technological analysis of the style (Inker 2000). It is as well to remember that metalworking links were not only with Scandinavia. For example, the earliest saucer brooches, belonging to East Anglia, Essex and Kent (Lucy 2000: 179), have links with the Saxon part of northern Germany, e.g. Perlberg (Myres 1989: 62). It has been suggested that the development of metalwork followed a simple scheme related to the mechanics of migration (Arnold 1984: 111). The earliest items to be deposited would be those brought over by the settlers from their homeland. These might be retained for some time before deposition as grave goods. Early attempts at manufacturing replacement would try to stick to the original template and the resulting artefacts would show little variation. Only later would indigenous production be able to break the mould and proceed to develop new and more varied forms. It is unclear how far this scheme holds true for all types of artefact and whether it can be given chronological precision. Nevertheless, it does demonstrate that the settlers would have an attachment to their continental identity that would take some time to develop along insular lines.

Anglian cultural material was restricted to the traditionally Anglian areas of Britain, but Saxon material was not restricted to the traditionally Saxon areas, e.g. the saucer brooches mentioned above. The early cemetery of Markshall was noticeably Saxon in its orientation with resemblances to Wehden, Gudendorf and Feddersen Wierde (Myres 1977), although it was sited near the Roman town of *Venta Icenorum* in East Anglia. Such Saxon presence in the Anglian areas was a feature of the 5th century and continued into the 6th, but declined markedly after about 550 (Hines 1994). The variety of cultural influences present in the Anglian areas of Britain is also seen in the distribution of annular brooches. These are very common to the north of the Thames but are not a continental Anglian style of brooch (Hills 1978: 316). Kent and the Isle of Wight share a different identity. Some would say that this indicates marriage of Kentish families into the Isle of Wight (Arnold 1997: 189), although there is no reason why the common Jutish background given in the later documentary sources could not lie behind the pattern.

It is clear that Anglo-Saxons were an intimate part of a northern Germanic cultural entity that spanned the North Sea. They used cultural markers from within this Germanic identity to reflect different types of Germanic identities within Britain.

Early English place-names

Place-names have long been regarded as an important source of information about early Germanic settlement. However, they need to be very carefully investigated if simplistic reasoning is not to produce spurious results. Gelling (1993) has pointed out that the evidence of place-names is for large scale immigration of modest farming families from the continent in precisely those areas with most abundant archaeological evidence for Germanic culture. It is now agreed (Cameron 1977, Gelling 1978, 1984, 1988) that the very earliest Germanic place-names are those that refer to topographical features, those that use the element -*hám* to denote settlement or township, and some of those that use the Roman term *vicus* in the English form *wic*. The topographical elements that were used in early names include -*burna* (stream), -*dún* (hill), -*eg* (island, dry area), -*feld* (open pasture), -*ford* (river crossing), -*wella* (spring), although these also could have a long life as an active name forming element. The term *vicus* also had a long life as a place-name element. Its earliest usage can be isolated in the form *wichám* or similar compounds. It is likely that the term denotes survival of a flourishing Romano-British settlement under Germanic political control, rather than a settlement of Germanic speakers (Gelling 1978). Of the 28 names in *wichám* listed by Gelling (1978), 75% occur in Kent, Sussex, Essex, Suffolk, and Lincolnshire in the south east of Britain, and in the upper Thames region in Berkshire and Oxfordshire. Early habitative names include -*ge* (district), -*burg* (fortified site) and especially -*hám* (estate). The distribution of sites in *hám* is concentrated in the east of Britain and coincides well with the areas of earliest Germanic burials. However, there are some areas where settlement is thought to have been equally early where names in -*hám* are rare, e.g. Warwickshire (Gelling 1978: 116).

Names that used to be seen as the earliest evidence for Germanic settlement include those ending in *-ingas* or *-ingahám*. It is now realised that these belong to a secondary phase of settlement, although still early and most likely within the 6th century. Using the examples given by Cameron (1977), we can see that the bulk of these names occur in core areas of early Germanic presence. Of the 174 names in *-ingas*, 72.5% are found in Kent, Sussex, Essex, Suffolk, Norfolk, Lincolnshire and the East Riding. Names in *-ingahám* are concentrated in the same areas.

Detailed studies may reveal something of the dynamics of settlement in a way that general studies may miss. As an example, I will look at the distribution of early English place-names in the British kingdom of Elmet, later to form the southern part of the old West Riding of Yorkshire. Documentary sources tell us that Elmet was annexed by Anglian Northumbria in 617. The area chosen for study is the wider Elmet from the River Wharfe southwards to the River Don as delineated by Taylor (1992). The earliest English place-names are not evenly distributed throughout this area. The pattern in paired wapentake units is shown in Table 2, listed in their geographical position from north to south.

Paired wapentakes	Total townships	Early English names	% of Early English names
Barkston-Skyrack	135	20	14.8
Agbrigg-Morley	111	8	7.2
Osgoldcross-Staincross	90	5	5.6
Upper & Lower Strafforth	135	9	6.7

Table 2: Early English township names in Elmet.

This gives the impression that the central part of Elmet was not favoured in the early Anglian take over but that the margins were, particularly the northernmost two wapentakes. If we plot the early names onto a map of Elmet, the pattern begins to make more sense. Figure 1 shows the distribution of place-names in *-hám, -dún, -burna, -eg, -hláw, -inga-* and *-wella*. Those in *-wic* are also added and conform to the same general pattern as the rest, suggesting that they might be broadly contemporary with the earliest names. In the case of *-ford* and *-feld*, the pattern is not so clear. Names in *-ford* do tend to occur in the same areas as early names but there is a scatter of them in the Humber Levels also, in which early names do not occur. Their occurrence in the Levels would be expected to have a long functional life given the importance of water crossing points in this area. Names in *-ford* from the levels are excluded from Figure 1 but *-ford* names elsewhere are included. Names in *-feld* show a wider general scatter with a group along the River Calder as well as the Humber levels. The Calder is a conspicuous gap in the distribution of early names. However, there are some *-feld* names that are found in the early name areas and the name Hatfield is known from early sources like Bede, although applied to a region rather than a particular township. It seems more likely that *-feld* was a generally longer-lived element in place-names as it has a general topographical application in all areas, and is therefore excluded from the map.

That some settlement of Anglian peoples took place in Elmet is likely, being the followers of new Anglian lords and their families, perhaps even Anglian soldiers brought in by British lords before 617. So far, archaeology has provided precious little evidence for such early Anglian settlement (Faull and Moorhouse 1981: 179-188). However, it is the township names that may reflect such actual settlement. These are not distributed randomly. Early English names in Morley and western Skyrack cluster around the River Aire, within and facing the Aire gap. This is the major east-west crossing point of the Pennines. There is a further cluster along the Roman road south of the River Wharfe leading to Tadcaster. The southward approach to Tadcaster is also covered by sites along the Roman road and by a cluster around the major crossing point of the Aire where it meets the River Calder, at Castleford. In the south, there is a line of townships covering the roads running northwards out of Doncaster and along the River Dearne where it reaches towards the River Don. There is also a small cluster around the meeting point of the two Roman roads running southwards and south-westwards from where the Don and River Rother meet, near Rotherham (an Anglian *-ham* name with a British river prefix). There are few townships with early Anglian names outside these clusters. The most obvious isolated name is Meltham, in the middle of the Pennines. Others are Wyke, Keresforth, East and West Ardsley. West Hardwick is also isolated but lies in the approaches to Castleford from the south while Braithwell and Todwick lie between the approaches to Rotherham and Doncaster.

The pattern is clearly non-random and shows a strategic regard to defending the approaches to York. The most obvious context for this would be after the take over of Elmet by Eadwine of Northumbria in 617. At this time, Mercia lay to the south of Elmet and was potentially hostile to Northumbria (it was certainly so later under Penda). The area to the west of the Pennines may still have been under the control of British Rheged. Its ruling family was important enough to provide a marriage partner for a later king of Northumbria a generation after 617. We can only speculate that the defences around the Aire gap were aimed at an independent British power, against Rheged, or even an enlarged Gwynedd.

There are two features of the minor, non-township, place-names that need further investigation and explanation. There is a concentration of early English minor names in the upper Calder Valley where it cuts through the Pennines. There are also Mercian dialect features in the area south of the Wharfe; not just in place-names but in the traditional English dialect of the area (Smith 1961-63 Part VII: 39-42). Particularly Mercian name elements are *-worð* and *-worðign*, *-wælla*, *-ród*, *-pihtel* and *-wang*. Other features are *alor* (alder) becoming owler (as Owlerton), 'o' for 'a' before nasals (e.g. Longwood) and *scép* (sheep) instead of Northumbrian *scíp* (e.g. Shepley). It has been noted that the core of Mercian forms is to be found in Agbrigg and Morley wapentakes. It is also in Morley where the upper Calder crossing of the Pennines lies. Indeed, the upper Calder gap is where Mercian forms in *-wælla* are to be found (Smith 1961-63 Part VII). It is difficult to believe that Anglian settlers from Mercia would have been brought into Elmet after its absorption into Northumbria. Mercia and Northumbria were long-standing enemies from the time of Penda and Eadwine. It is possible that this enmity did not occur before Penda and that Eadwine might have been able to introduce Mercians very early in his reign. However, given that their presence is revealed by minor names, not township names, it would seem perhaps more likely that the settlers were brought in by the British kings of Elmet to settle under established British lords. Mercians were not given townships as landowners; they were settled as followers within townships. The upper Calder gap leads into what is now southern Lancashire, below the Pennines. It does not face northwards against Rheged but southwards towards Chester. It may be that relations between the two British rulers of Elmet and what would later be Powys were less than cordial. This may explain the survival of Elmet during the reign of Eadwine's predecessor Æþelfrið who first created the kingdom of Northumbria. During his campaign against Powys, he would have had to pass through Elmet on his way to the Battle of Chester. Elmet may have been willing to accept Anglian overlordship as protection against its own enemies and Northumbria would gain a loyal ally guarding its south-western flank. King Ceredig of Elmet poisoned a member of the Deiran royal house at the behest of Æþelfrið. This act would thus be set in context, as would Eadwine of Deira's takeover of Elmet as soon as he came to power as King of Northumbria after his destruction of Æþelfrið. This is only a suggested hypothesis to explain Mercian linguistic features in Elmet. Against it may be cited the lack of archaeological evidence for Anglian settlement at this date. However, it should be noted that evidence for any settlement, Anglian or British, is equally lacking. The minor place-names of Morley wapentake themselves may contain evidence of early date in that they have the only examples in Elmet of heathen elements - Thunerton (Sowerby), Pike Law (Mytholmroyd), Killop Lawe, Miller Lowe (Todmorden) and Elm Lawe (Bradford). Four out of these five occur in the upper Calder gap. As ever though, it should be born in mind that the reliability of these names is compromised by being preserved only in late documents.

The bulk of the Aire gap lies in Craven, the other district name of British origin apart from Elmet within what was later to be Yorkshire. Indeed, it contains both the Aire and Ribble watershed and is the major east-west crossing point of the Pennines south of Stainmore. Within Craven itself, British township names are remarkably absent. It may be that there was less accommodation between the British and the new Anglian regime in this strategic Pennine crossing. It may also be that Craven was only part of a wider kingdom (Rheged) and that its landowners would have somewhere to flee to in the rest of the kingdom where they may have had other lands or relatives. There are 18 identifiably early English township names out of 121 recorded in the Domesday survey of 1086. This is a rather high figure, 14.9%, similar to the high figure for Barkston and Skyrack. It is not known when Craven became part of Northumbria, although shortly after 655 has been suggested (Wood 1996). The position of early names in Elmet facing the Aire gap against Craven would suggest that Craven was absorbed later than 617. The high proportion of early township names in the gap would seem to show that Craven's position was strategically crucial. Placing loyal Anglian lords in control of selected townships would be an obvious military strategy for the new Northumbrian kings. Thus, the settlement of Germanic peoples at different levels of society was subject to the realities of power and concerns of strategy. Such realities were long-lasting and the policies of the early Northumbrian kings would foreshadow the policy of the Norman William I in his settlement of loyal followers on strategically important estates some 450 years later (Kapelle1979: 143-145). It is in small-scale regional studies like this that the realities of Germanic settlement and conquest are likely to be revealed.

The British context of settlement

Germanic settlers were arriving in an island which was undoubtedly post-Roman; that is no longer part of the Roman Empire and no longer Romanised in its material culture (Esmonde Cleary 1999: 173). Employment of Germanic soldiers is not unexpected. Besides Kent, we see evidence of 5th century Germanic settlers in the Saxon Shore fort of Portchester (Snyder 1998: 173). What made Kent different was that it seems to have been handed over to the political control of the new settlers. At places like Portchester, the newcomers were most likely settling under British political authority. As already noted, there is a clear difference between the earliest Germanic burials in southern England and those of eastern England (Higham 1992: 169-175). The former appear to be of Germanic soldiers employed within the existing late Roman structures of the early 5th century, and so in a positive relationship to the Britons. Dark (2000) notes the Old English name of at least some the southern settlers, the *Gewisse*, can be interpreted as 'the reliable ones', a name that could have been adopted as a proud mark of service to British authority. The settlers in eastern Britain appear more like immigrations of whole communities, bringing over with them their own social structures and cultural practices, separated from but existing alongside the native inhabitants. Why there should be this difference has not as yet received the scholarly attention that it perhaps deserves. It may be, as already suggested by Dark (2000), that Roman provincial organisation survived in some way into the 5th century and determined the nature and extent of Germanic migration. If Germanic migrants were brought over to service the military needs of the British authorities, then it stands to reason that the distribution and nature of Germanic settlements should be related to the existing military dispositions of post-Roman Britain. It may be that it was not only the provincial organisation that survived but also the military organisation of the late Roman diocese. Perhaps it is the military structures whose traces are preserved in the *Notitia Dignitatum* that provide the context for Germanic employment in the 5th century.

The *Notitia Dignitatum* survives as an 11th century copy of a document of c.395, updated until the 420s, for the purposes of the headquarters of the western half of the Roman Empire (Jones 1964, Jones & Mattingly 1990). It listed all the civil and military officials and gave details of the quartering of army regiments in every diocese and province. The information for Britain relates to the period between 395 and 410. Although there is information missing from the British section, enough survives to give an overall picture of the military arrangements in the diocese at the end of Roman rule. By 410, Britain was divided into five civil provinces and three military commands. The *Dux Britanniarum* (Duke of the Britains) controlled the forces in the north, covering Hadrian's Wall, its hinterland, and the north-eastern and north-western coasts above the Humber and Mersey. The *Comes Litoris Saxonici* (Count of the Saxon Shore) had charge of the south and east coasts either side of the Thames from Brancaster to Portchester. The *Comes Britanniarum* (Count of the Britains) was in command of the mobile field army, whose headquarters remains unknown. Given the concentration of late Roman and early post-Roman finds at Dorchester on Thames, might this not have been the centre of operations for the *Comes*; allowing easy access to the south west, south Wales or the midlands? The distribution of continental military belt fittings of the 4th century, identified by Hawkes and Dunning (1961) was centred on Kent and Dorchester, perhaps the headquarters of the two Counts. In the 5th century, the successor of the *Comes* may have been employed to keep watch on internal opposition to the central British rule of Vortigern. The major omissions from the document are the known late Roman military sites of North Wales. It is striking that the earliest Anglian settlement in Britain lies between the areas of the *Dux Britanniarum* and the *Comes Litoris Saxonici*. The exception is the intrusion of Anglian settlement into East Anglia at the northern end of the Saxon Shore. We could envisage a situation where the command of the *Comes Litoris Saxonici* was diminished through shortages of manpower, the northern forts of the command being perhaps the least strategic if defence against the continent were needed. Hiring Anglian *foederati* would plug the defensive gap covering the North Sea. It would also be a sensible continuation of the 4th century military arrangements which included the formation of a local yeomanry. This is the interpretation of Hawkes and Dunning (1961), who saw belt fittings of type IIC as Anglian copies of Romano-British types, supporting the idea of Anglian settlers fitting into a Romano-British context of military employment. Germanic soldiers brought over to the south of Britain might have been placed within areas of existing military commands: the two *Comes*, and so the context of Germanic settlement in the south would have been very different. A placement of *laeti* would make more sense in the south where functioning late Roman military organisation might still have existed. It might even be that a Germanic warrior could find appointment as *Comes Litoris Saxonici*. After all, Germanic soldiers occupied the highest military commands within the Roman Empire itself. Was this the context for the settlement of Hengest in Kent at the heart of the Saxon Shore, and the basis for the later supremacy of Kentish kings over Sussex and Essex?

Positive relations with the native Britons, rather than racially motivated antagonism, are suggested by various pieces of evidence: the British origin of the names of various kingdoms (Kent, Lindsey, Deira, Bernicia), the presence of Celtic names in kingly genealogies, use of *wealh/walh* in personal names in the 7th century, e.g. Coenwalh, Æðilwalh (Faull 1975: 32), and occasional notices of historical relations between Anglo-Saxon and British kingdoms. The poorly recorded kingdom of Lindsey might well have been a good example of continuity with a British past (Yorke in Vince 1993). It was named after the Roman town of Lincoln (*Lindum*), in which some sort of civic authority still existed in the early 7th century. The arrival of Germanic settlers in the area as federate soldiers seems to have begun under Roman rule (Eagles in Bassett 1989: 208). The only genealogy that has been preserved for a king of Lindsey records the British name Cædbæd, who (assuming the genealogy to be true and accurate) would have lived sometime in the early-mid 6th century (Foot in Vince 1993). The political structure of the British, or even late Roman, period seems therefore to have been preserved particularly well in the some parts of the old Roman diocese. Some historians, e.g. Dark (2000), would accept that the Roman provincial authorities remained intact until the late 5th or early 6th century. The earliest stages of contact between the Britons and Germanic settlers would have been the employment of Germanic soldiers in defence of these provinces. The three capitals of London, Lincoln and York all have early Germanic sites in strategically defensive positions (Dark 2000), e.g. Mitcham, Croydon and Orpington guarding the approaches to London (Hines in Wood 1997). Likewise, the earliest Germanic cremations are sited near to contemporary British villages and towns, arguing for a defensive purpose to Germanic settlement.

Northumbria provides other examples of friendly relations between the Anglo-Saxons and Britons. King Oswiu of Bernicia had a British wife, Rhiainfellt of the kingdom of Rheged (Dumville in Bassett 1989: 220). Another British kingdom, Elmet, was still independent when Oswiu's father Æþelfrið had ruled all Northumbria. According to the *Historia Brittonum*, its annexation took place under Æþelfrið's successor and rival, Eadwine (Morris 1980). Bede described how Eadwine's nephew Hereric, the father of Hild of Whitby, had found refuge there as an exile, until his murder at the behest of Æþelfrið (Colgrave & Mynors 1969). British Elmet must therefore have been an ally/dependency of Anglo-Saxon Bernicia. Æþelfrið's rival, Eadwine of Deira, may himself have spent some time in exile in Gwynedd according to a reference in the medieval Welsh *Triads* (Bromwich 1978: 47-48). As with Lindsey, the names of Bernicia and Deira, the two kingdoms that formed the bulk of Northumbria, were of British origin - *Berneich* from *Bernacci (most likely referring to the mountain passes of the Pennines) and *Deur/Deivr* from *Deibhr (of unknown meaning) (Jackson 1953: 701-705 & 419-420, Jackson 1969: 80-81). Continuity in society and economy might be seen in the medieval estate structure of northern England. This had some strong similarities to that of north Wales, and it may well be that the pattern of estate organisation in both areas went back to Romano-British origins (Jones in Sawyer 1979). According to Loveluck (2000), there is good evidence of British continuity north of Hadrian's Wall at such sites as Huckhoe and Bamburgh. At Huckhoe early Romano-British round houses were replaced by rectangular houses in the 4th century, these continuing into the early 6th century with a purely British material culture. The Anglian takeover of Northumbria would therefore have involved the retention of the socio-economic and administrative practices of the former British ruling elite. It may also have seen continuity in settlement loci, either by replacement or acculturation of existing farms, e.g. at Milfield and Sprouston where Anglian farms directly overlie Roman period ones (Loveluck 2000). Adjustment by native Britons to new Anglo-Saxon practices may be seen in a number of burials in Northumbria, particularly in Bernicia (Higham 1993: 70). It was in the 7th century that Anglian conquest of the native Britons reached its peak in the north with Northumbrian annexation of Elmet and, in stages, Rheged. The conquest of both of these must have involved dispossession of the native aristocracy, but there is no reason to suppose that the social and economic structures that had supported them would also have been destroyed.

The two Anglian 'halves' of Northumbria - Bernicia and Deira - need not have come under Anglian rule in similar ways. Archaeological evidence for early Anglian populations is much commoner in Deira than in Bernicia (Cramp in Driscoll & Nieke 1988: 72-74). The eventual border between Deira and Bernicia may have been farther north than in later periods, with evidence for 6th century Anglian cemeteries and artefacts in what would later be County Durham that show links with the traditionally Deiran areas south of the Tees, e.g. Norton on Tees, Easington (Loveluck 2000). Anglian settlement in Deira may have begun with the employment of Anglo-Saxon soldiers by the British authorities at York, evidence for which may be seen in the cemeteries at Heworth and the Mount, just outside the city and guarding its northern and southern approaches. Later settlement of Germanic immigrants was centred on the old civitas of the Parisii, in the East Riding of Yorkshire around the Yorkshire Wolds. Medieval Welsh evidence (the *Annales Cambriae* and the *Triads*) points to York being in British hands up to 580 (Morris 1980: 45, Bromwich 1978: 488-491), with a relatively late take-over by Anglian rulers. This points to a long period of stable relations between the two peoples within what would become Deira. By contrast, it may well be that Bernicia was subject to an intrusive and small Anglian ruling elite, and that the bulk of the population remained British (Higham 1992: 185). The evidence from burials for social structure in Bernicia suggested a small Anglian elite was ruling a largely British population (Alcock 1981). Loveluck (2000) has pointed out that there is evidence for Anglian burials (or burials with Anglian artefacts) near, or in, former Roman forts in the 6th century, e.g. Benwell, Binchester, Corbridge, Piercebridge, which would presumably represent Anglian military presence. He also noted that the political centres of Bernicia were fortresses taken over by Anglian elites, i.e. Bamburgh and Dunbar. Even here though, these elites cannot have arrived in Britain as lone military units. Some followers must have come with them to found the farmsteads and hamlets than have been found in lowland Bernicia, e.g. in the Milfield basin and the Tweed valley like at Thirlings or New Bewick where sunken floored buildings and Anglian loom-weights occurred on a farmstead with no previous indication of British or Roman settlement (Loveluck 2000). The Welsh evidence of the *Historia Brittonum,* the *Triads* and the *Canu Taliesin* points to a long period of antagonism between British rulers and intrusive Anglian invaders in Bernicia (Morris 1980: 37-38, Pennar 1988, Williams 1968, Bromwich 1978: 516-520), which would thus conform to the 'official' model of migration and conquest (but note Higham 1993: 70-71 for a more complex view). Why this should be so for Bernicia but not perhaps for Deira may be accounted for by the survival in the north of military traditions inherited from the Roman army units placed at Hadrian's Wall. There is evidence for the continued use of the Hadrian's Wall forts in the 5th century, e.g. at Chesterholm, Housesteads and South Shields (Loveluck 2002). The traditional interpretation of this is that the army units of the Wall remained and became war-bands supported by local taxation in kind. As there is little evidence of continued civilian settlement associated with the forts, it is assumed that the military units became a new native British elite for both civilian and military alike, over much wider areas.

That outright opposition to all things British was not part of the mindset of all the Germanic invaders/migrants is suggested also by the early politics of Mercia. An alliance between heathen Anglian Mercia and Christian British Gwynedd seems to have been a long-standing feature of the early and mid 7th century (Higham 1995: 132-133). As late as 633, Cadwallon of Gwynedd had hopes of reversing the Anglo-Saxon conquest of Northumbria and restoring the area to British rule, but could only achieve this in alliance with Anglian Mercia.

The contrast between the official history of Anglo-Saxon origins and the reality is perhaps starkest in the case of Alfred the Great's own ancestral kingdom, Wessex. The story of the origins of Wessex, as told in the *Anglo-Saxon Chronicle* can tell us much about how the migration and conquest was seen by the later ruling elite of England. The origin of Wessex was attributed to Cerdic and his son Cynric, who came with five ships to *Cerdicesora* in an attack on the Britons (495). A major victory was eventually won over the British King Natanleod (508), and the Kingdom of the West Saxons was established some 24 years after their first appearance in Britain (519) following a further victory at *Cerdicesford*. Other battles followed, e.g. *Cerdicesleah* (527), and in 530 the Isle of Wight was added to Cerdic's rule. Cerdic was reputed to have died in 534, to be succeeded by his son Cynric. Cynric and the later West Saxon kings were portrayed as being in the forefront of the conquest of Britain from its native inhabitants. The early entries about Wessex in the Chronicle are dominated by notices of warfare against the Britons in the Thames Valley or the south-west.

Many scholars (e.g. Sims-Williams 1983) have noted that this account of West Saxon origins is inconsistent with both the archaeological evidence and with other historical material recorded in the 9th and 10th centuries, including the *Anglo-Saxon Chronicle* itself. The dating of events in the Chronicle seems to have been stretched to cover a longer and earlier time frame than was really the case (Yorke 1990: 131-132), in order to enhance the status of the royal family as pioneers of the conquest. Perhaps the most noteworthy feature of the West Saxon kingly genealogy is that it contains names that are purely British (Celtic), i.e. Cerdic himself, Ceawlin, Cædwalla in the 7th century and at least one name that may reflect 7th century intermarriage between Saxon and Briton, Coenwalh (Yorke 1990: 138-139; 1995: 49). Jackson (1953: 613-614) has pointed out that the name Cerdic must have been derived from the British *Caratícos through primitive Welsh *Car'dig by c.550. If the family had mixed Saxon and British origins, this would cast a completely different light on the nature of the dynasty and the origins of its power. The seat of the earliest bishop of the West Saxons was at Dorchester, an area of notably mixed British and Saxon archaeology. If this was the earliest seat of power of the dynasty, then the myth of their arrival and conquest as given in the *Anglo-Saxon Chronicle* must be a large scale re-adjustment of the facts. The early cemeteries of Wessex seem to contain mixed British and Saxon burial practices (Yorke 1995: 46) that could, as in Bernicia, indicate assimilation of Britons to an Anglo-Saxon cultural identity. Such assimilation seems to have occurred earliest in the eastern half of Wessex. There was a division between this area (Hampshire, Wiltshire, Berkshire) which was dominated by Anglo-Saxon material culture, and presumably settlement, and the west (Dorset, Somerset, Devon) in which native British culture was not assimilated until much later, and which may have had a lesser degree of Anglo-Saxon settlement (Yorke 1995: 69-72). This may be reflected in the fact that British Christian sites seem to have continued in use in this region and became part of the West Saxon ecclesiastical landscape (Yorke 1995: 177-179), e.g. Exeter, Wells, Wareham and Sherborne. While the laws of Ine in the 7th century discriminated against the Britons, it is nevertheless clear that the British contribution to Wessex was greater than a simple reading of the Chronicle would allow. It seems clear that the traditions of Wessex were reworked in the 9th century to fit the model of Anglo-Saxon immigration, conquest and settlement outlined by Bede for Kent. Alfred the Great and his circle wished to be seen as a continuing part of the English national myth (as given by Bede); the chosen people with a God-given right to rule over Britain.

The British contribution to Anglo-Saxon Britain

The incoming Anglo-Saxons did not arrive in an empty land, nor did they destroy all that they found. Some accounts of the migration period read as though the authors imagine that Britain was a blank slate, awaiting settlement by newcomers who were free to shape it according to their will on a basis of equal shares (Carver 1998: 104), perhaps showing the same cavalier disregard of the natives as shown by many of the settlers of the American west in the 19th century. The native Britons are conspicuous in such accounts by their absence. Incredibly, some scholars still talk of the possibility of genocide or population displacement (Ausenda 1997). Some seem to imagine Britain as some kind of frontier society, similar to the American west, with pioneers carving out civilisation from a wilderness inhabited by a few lowly natives (Arnold 1984: 140). This is surely wrong; the Germanic peoples migrated to an inhabited land with its own values, civilisation and social and political structures, with which the newcomers would have to reach some sort of accommodation. The land they came to was one carved out into landholdings, rents and taxations, fields and boundaries. In no way was it a virgin land. A great deal of native British society must have been incorporated into the new order of things during the 200 years of settlement and conquest. For example, a study of burials in Hampshire showed a great deal of continuity in physical type between Romano-British cemetery of Lankhills and later Anglo-Saxon rural cemeteries in the county (Arnold 1984: 129-130). There is evidence for the survival of town life of some sort into the 5th and 6th centuries (Campbell 1982: 39-41, Snyder 1998). The legionary headquarters at York was still in use at this time, and Canterbury was still the political centre of Kent under Æþelberht at the end of the 6th century. *Verulamium* (St Albans) was still inhabited in the 5th century and the cult of St Alban may well have continued from late Roman times. Bath might also have been still functioning as a spa. The best archaeological evidence for continuity of occupation into the post-Roman period comes from Wroxeter where timber buildings in Roman style were being built c.450 and continued in use until the mid 6th century, although many other towns have now also shown evidence for building and occupation during this period (Snyder 1998: 158-160), e.g. the famous Irish ogham inscription at Silchester, which has been recently dated to between 360 and 530 (www.silchester.rdg.ac.uk). However, the nature of this occupation in the post-Roman period is the subject of some debate. While the evidence for a 6th century (530/570) aisled house at Wroxeter has been interpreted as the residence of a bishop and therefore a specialised form of urban continuity, Matthews (2001) has emphasised that this house was not an isolated example and that the urban nature of the town may have been more 'normal' than we have hitherto suspected. Most scholars though would say that the functions of towns had changed and some archaeologists would see most towns of this period as being little more than rural settlements (Arnold 1984), decline having begun in the 4th century. The evidence of coinage would suggest that the market economy was in decline from c.350 (Arnold 1984: 91), which would have affected the economic functions of the towns. One of the main problems in interpreting the nature of urban occupation is the fragmentary state of archaeological excavation in towns, which tends to yield isolated keyhole views of structure or parts of structures, and makes it difficult to determine the presence of wooden buildings that were not earth-fast structures, as at Wroxeter. As Matthews (2001) has noted, the evidence from a town like Chester can be frustratingly tantalising, capable of suggesting but not proving post-Roman continuity. The three main urban centres in the east - London, Lincoln and York - all continued to become English capitals and cities.

Political continuity

The continuance of British political rulers can be demonstrated in the west of Britain where later documentary sources preserved their memory in the successor Welsh kingdoms. Where there were no kingdoms to keep alive British memory, notice of such authority has vanished. It is axiomatic in archaeology that absence of evidence is not evidence of absence, and this can be applied to the British political structures of the 5th and 6th centuries. Some writers seem to suppose that little or no centralised authority remained at diocesan, provincial or *civitas* level, almost painting a picture of descent into anarchy (e.g. Scull 1992, although contradicted later in the same article) allowing thrusting and aggressive Germanic newcomers to elbow aside native elites and seize power. Others write as though the growth of Anglo-Saxon kingdoms took place in an empty landscape creating totally from scratch political organisation out of this anarchy, e.g. Arnold (1997) talking about the emergence of kingdoms out of small competing units. This is not a picture to which I subscribe. I would prefer to see the continuance of British political structures at *civitas* level throughout the 5th and 6th centuries, and possibly at provincial or even diocesan level in the 5th. It has long been recognised that the later Anglo-Saxon kingdoms bear a general resemblance to the area of the Roman *civitates* and this must presuppose that the *civitates* maintained an identity for the Anglo-Saxons to take over and remould. Even Scull (1992) accepts "a pre-existing capacity for political integration in the social and economic configurations of the fifth and sixth centuries" in East Anglia, which for me can only mean the existence of British political organisation continuing on the basis of the *civitas* of the Iceni. While it is reasonable, as suggested by Newman (1992: 26), to adopt the rigorous methodology of prehistorians in gathering evidence, to treat the period as similar to prehistory because of the relative dearth of documentary sources should not lead archaeologists to suppose that political organisation was at the level of the Neolithic or Bronze Age. Scull himself notes that the *civitas* capital, *Venta Icenorum*, remained an important location until the 7th century. This must surely indicate some sort of political role for the town no matter what its changing economic or demographic importance. That some *civitas* in the east of Britain remained under British rule until the 6th century seems certain. Dark (2000) even identifies gaps in the distribution of Germanic burials to delineate where some of these *civitates* were located: London and the Chilterns, the Wash, the Weald, north Hampshire. However, the plotting of political control on the basis of burial distributions is a hazardous exercise (even when backed up by extremely partial archaeological evidence from towns and villas). It would seem sensible to suggest that most of the late Roman *civitates* continued under British rule until the late 6th century (Kent being the major exception) when control then passed into the hands of dynasties with varying degrees of connection to the Germanic migrants. Table 3 lists the possible late Roman *civitates* and their medieval kingdom successors, along with the dates when they fell under Anglo-Saxon political control. The exact boundaries and locations of the Roman provinces are my own guesswork, and should be 'taken with a pinch of salt'. The area under Anglo-Saxon control by 634 is shaded in grey. Further conquest of British areas would follow: Lothian in 638, the area of Maund next to Gwent c.650, eastern Powys c.655, Craven from Rheged c.658, the eastern part of Dumnonia in 658, all of Rheged in 682, and the Kyle area from Strathclyde in 750. Much later annexations would include Cornwall by 928 and the annexation of the Welsh principalities by Edward I in the 13th century.

It is not capable of proof, but we should accept it as a possibility that the Diocese of the Britains remained as a political unit into the early 6th century and that the provinces still had a part to play in political organisation. This is not a generally held view, although some writers do accept a role for provincial organisation into the 5th century (Dark 2000). The words of Geary (2002: 115) could stand for the view of many:

> In Britain, the Roman centralized government faded away, to be replaced by a plethora of small, mutually hostile kingdoms.

However, the small, mutually hostile kingdoms we do see in the historical record are visible only in the later part of the sixth century. The precious few records we have for a time earlier than this would make sense in a context of still existing wider political integration.

Although we do not know the precise boundaries of the provinces and the whereabouts of the province of *Valentia* are unknown, the four remaining provinces can be characterised as having different histories during and after the 5th century. As noted already, *Flavia Caesariensis* might well have allowed the influx of large numbers of non-Romanised Germanic settlers while *Maxima Caesariensis* was careful to employ Romanised Saxons within a late Roman military context. *Britannia Prima* relied on its own native forces and those of Irish immigrants and *Britannia Secunda* saw only small-scale adoption of Germanic soldiers (Dark 1994: 248-251). Might this also reflect Diocesan priorities with the more highly prized Germanic soldiers under Roman style military organisation guarding the south of Britain against possible Roman re-invasion in the 5th century?

Province	Civitas	Towns	Kingdom	Anglo-Saxon
Maxima Caesariensis	Cantiaci	Canterbury	Kent	430
	Regni	Chichester	Sussex	470
	Catuvellauni	London, St Albans	Essex	c.580?
	Trinovantes	Chelmsford, Colchester		c.570
	Belgae	Winchester	Gewisse	537
	Atrebates	Silchester		529
Britannia Prima	Durotriges A	Ilchester		614
	Durotriges B	Dorchester		614
	Dumnonii	Exeter	Devon	pt. 658
	Demetae	Carmarthen	Dyfed	
	Silures	Caerleon, Caerwent	Gwent	pt. c.650?
	Dobunni	Cirencester, Gloucester	Whych	582
Flavia Caesariensis	Iceni	Caistor	East Anglia	571
	Corieltauvi A	Water Newton	Middle Anglia	?
	Corieltauvi B	Leicester	Mercia	585
	Corieltauvi C	Lincoln	Lindsey	?
Valentia	Cornovii	Chester, Wroxeter	Powys	pt. c.655
	Deceangli	?	Gwynedd	
	Ordovices	Caernarfon		
	Carvetii	Carlisle	Rheged	655-682
Britannia Secunda	Parisii	Brough	Deira	c.430?
	Brigantes A	York, Aldbrough		580
	Brigantes B	?	Elmet	616
outside Britanniae	Votadini	Edinburgh	Lothian	638
			Bernicia	575
	Selgovae	?	to Rheged	682
	Novantae	?	Alclwyd	
	Damonii	Dumbarton		

Table 3: Roman civitas to medieval kingdom.

Manorial organisation

Greater continuity with the British past may be expected in rural life and in the extraction of key resources, e.g. the continuing 'industrial' organisation of various activities like salt production in Worcestershire and lead production in the Peak District. Many scholars have noticed that the organisation of local administration in support of the king in later medieval Wales has so much in common with that for Northumbria, western Mercia and southern Scotland that they must share a common origin in administrative arrangements of the early medieval period, the so-called multiple estate model (Jones 1975, 1979), perhaps better called the commote system. The origins and precise nature of the multiple estate are hotly debated and not everyone agrees that they began life as a Romano-British system of land organisation (e.g. Dark 1994: 148-150). However, the existence of similarities between later medieval England, Scotland and Wales do to my mind suggest a presumption in favour of Jones's model, and Hooke (1997) provides a sensible account of the model as it might be applied to the areas later under English control. The evidence of place-names suggests that early Germanic settlement in Britain was largely influenced by patterns of lordship (Hooke 1997: 72), and later estate centres often had British names, with a link between these centres and early churches, signified by names in *eccles* (Hooke 1997: 75-76). In the face of such evidence, we must surely reject the idea that there was a free-for-all egalitarian land grab of a landscape vacated by the British.

Under the commote model, a kingdom would have been divided into regional units, called hundreds (Welsh *cantref*, plural *cantrefau*), consisting of two commotes (Welsh *cwmwd*, plural *cwmydau*), each with a royal estate as its centre. The various townships of the commote would owe services to that centre. Most of the townships were grouped into estates (Welsh *maenor/maenol*, plural *maenorau/maenolau*), assigned either to officials and nobles, or farmed by bondmen directly for the king (Figure 1).

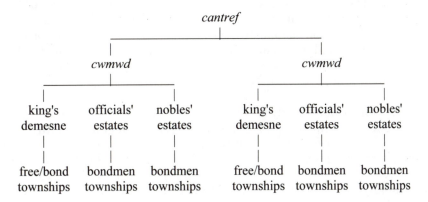

Figure 1: The organisation of *cantrefau*

The key features of the commote system were the rents and services owed to the king's townships from the whole commote, irrespective of who held the lordships of the estates, and the linking of townships together across more than one commote within the hundred - usually a means of linking arable with pasture, or winter grazing with summer grazing areas. The services owed included farming labour, carriage of goods and building work on the royal residence.

The easiest way for newly arrived Germanic landlords to take over British polities would be by allotting them existing *maenorau*. This is seen by Barnwell (1996) as the easiest way to explain the origin of the Anglo-Saxon unit of land assessment, the hide, in the assessment mechanisms of Roman Britain. The resident native bondmen would be kept on, which would lead easily to the later identification of the Welsh with slaves (Jones 1979: 28). The later evidence of charters can sometimes be used to reconstruct blocks of lands that might represent pre-existing British land units taken over by new Anglo-Saxon owners, e.g. the *Stoppingas* in Warwickshire (Hooke 1997). In Bernicia, later royal manors were often places with evidence of late Roman occupation, e.g. Yeavering, Milfield or Sprouston (Loveluck 2000). On the other hand, it is noteworthy that Romano-British estates names do not survive in Britain (Jackson 1953). Villa estates were often named after a person, using the ending -*acon* (Latin -*acum*), and names of this type have frequently survived in modern France (Jackson 1953: 233) but not in Britain, suggesting disruption of the pattern of landownership. Just perhaps, traces of these names did survive but have not been recognised. The 7th century tribute list known as the *Tribal Hidage*, contains names of peoples that have long puzzled scholars. Among the list of peoples are the *Noxgaga, Ohtgaga* and *Unecungaga*. The final -*a* is a sign of the genitive plural common to all the names in the list. A British -*acon* would have become -*ag* by the time of contact with the Anglo-Saxons through the process of lenition as described by Jackson (1953: 68). It must be a possibility that the puzzling names of the hidage represent British regions named from central villa estates.

It has been suggested that there are strong links between the location of early Anglo-Saxon minsters and previous British churches or monasteries, some founded on the sites of earlier villas (Dark 1994: 160-162; Morris 1989: 101). If so, this would signal the survival of British Christianity as an element of continuity underlying the supposed conversion of the Anglo-Saxons to Christianity by Irish and continental missionaries in the 7th century. The existence of place-names in *eccles* has long been accepted as showing the presence of British churches.

Goodier (1984) undertook a study of Anglo-Saxon burials which showed that the use of some burials as township or estate boundary markers arose in the 6th century. The association of burials with boundaries was far from general, most burials being in cemeteries near settlements or in communal cremation urnfields. Arnold particularly questions the statistical validity of such studies as that of Goodier (Arnold 1988: 37). However, within their limits such studies are useful. If some burials occurred on boundaries in the 6th century, this was not the case with the earliest burials of the 5th century. An association between burials and boundaries could have arisen either because a major redrawing of the administrative map occurred in the 6th century by the Anglo-Saxons, which saw the origins of many of the modern township boundaries (possible, but I think unlikely), or the earliest Anglo-Saxons did not have strong relationship with territorial divisions in the 5th century and only began signifying their connection with land units after such a relationship arose. In other words, the Anglo-Saxons only took over ownership of the land units in the 6th century and moved their places of burial to signal this. In the 5th century, they must have been settlers but not yet lords and masters. The corollary of this is that much of lowland Britain remained in British hands for some time after the initial settlement. If ethnic identity follows political mobilisation of that identity, then we should not expect the growth of separate ethnic consciousness until some time after the first settlements. However, we have to admit that it is also possible that a part of the British political elite remained under Germanic rule and began to adopt Germanic material culture and modes of behaviour (but only in the 6th century). This could help to explain the use of some burials in relation to land units which the same elite continued to control.

Britons remaining

The archaeological record does suggest that Britons remained within the areas of Germanic settlement and contributed towards aspects of the material culture of these areas. The evidence of burials shows a continuation of Roman burial rites alongside newer Germanic rites (Arnold 1997: 31), for example, the use of only one brooch rather than two, hobnail boots, crouched or beheaded inhumation and general lack of grave goods. British stone lined cist graves continue into the post-Roman period, e.g. at Castle Eden in Cumbria and elsewhere in what would later be northern England. Anglian artefacts begin to appear in these northern British graves only in the 6th and 7th centuries, probably marking trade or acculturation rather than settlement (Loveluck 2000). The coexistence of Britons and Germanic immigrants may well be reflected in the continued use of the Roman rite of inhumation in southern and eastern Britain. Whereas cremation cemeteries may have been largely Germanic, the inhumation cemeteries may have been mixed. Such may also have been the case in those cemeteries where cremation and inhumation are found together. It may be, as Dark (2000) suggests, that pagan Germans were coexisting alongside Christian and pagan Britons. However, we must always exercise caution in interpreting individual burials as British or Germanic. Crawford (1997) has pointed out that some of the anomalous burial practices that could be British can be exemplified by burial practices among the Germanic peoples themselves on the continent.

Among the artefacts of the time are forms which seem to signify continuity of, or links with, native Britons. This is clearly seen in the types of brooches found in heathen burials in the south-east of Britain (Lucy 2000), especially in the areas of 'Saxon' settlement (Dark 2000). Disc brooches of the mid 5th to mid 6th centuries are found concentrated in the region of the upper Thames. These are more likely based on British workmanship, having no continental parallels, although Hines (1994) claims for them a mainly Saxon origin. Scull (1992) notes the use of red enamel on Germanic metalwork of the 5th and 6th centuries as an example of the application of Romano-British craft skills in the service of new masters. Likewise, penannular brooches of the 6th century are of British not Germanic origin. The similar but distinct annular type of brooch, commonly found in the areas traditionally ascribed to Anglian settlement may also be of largely British origin. In particular, type G penannular brooches were of native manufacture under the control of the British elite in western Britain. Finds of these brooches in the east have been interpreted as evidence for high status trade between Britons and the Germanic settlers (Dark 1994) and as evidence for British women being married into Anglian elites (Loveluck 2000). As mentioned earlier, the origins of the more elaborate quoit brooch style of metalwork, including various disc, penannular and quoit brooches are now usually seen as Romano-British rather than Germanic in inspiration. The style originated in late 4th century metalworking styles, a prime example of continuity (Inker 2000). Hanging bowls, of the type found in the Sutton Hoo ship burial, have long been recognised as being of native Celtic design, although their distribution lies almost entirely in areas of Germanic settlement. However, since the dates for these bowls seem to be late 6th to 7th century, they are less of a candidate for British survival in the early phases of settlement and are more likely to be prestige imports signifying links between Anglo-Saxon and British elites during the period of kingdom formation. Harris (2003) has suggested that the Byzantine silver bowls found at Sutton Hoo could have been obtained from British rulers (as part of their diplomatic gifts from Constantinople) in western Britain as tribute or booty. An intriguing alternative might be that they came as diplomatic gifts closer to East Anglia, to the earlier British kings in the east of Britain. Humbler categories of artefact might also token continuing British presence in eastern Britain, e.g. grass tempered pottery or baked clay loom weights (Dark 2000: 86), although this would be questioned by some who dislike labelling items of material culture as ethnic markers (Moreland 2000). That archaeologists are now beginning to recognise British survival in the area that would become Anglo-Saxon England is reflected in the fact that settlements like Frilford and Chalton are now being put forward as settlements of Britons rather than Anglo-Saxons (Dark 2000). A site like Catholme in Staffordshire must indicate British survival (Welch 1992) since it spans the 5th to 9th centuries, either side of the incorporation of the area into Mercia. Härke (1997: 150) suggested that we could identify British enclaves within the areas of Germanic settlement, e.g. at the Queenford Farm Christian cemetery in the upper Thames Valley (Henig 2002) or in East Anglia represented by the practice of enamelling metal ornaments. Likewise, there are cemeteries which seem wholly British in form in areas of known early Germanic settlement, e.g. at Dorchester and Lewknor (Hinton 1900: 17-18).

It has often been claimed that evidence of Britons surviving in the Anglo-Saxon kingdoms can be found in the laws of 7th century kings. The laws of Ine of Wessex certainly refer to the existence of Welsh people within the kingdom. These however may be recently annexed populations in the west of the kingdom rather than survivals from the 5th or 6th centuries in the heartlands of Wessex. There is reference in the earlier laws of Æþelberht of Kent to a group of people called *læts*. This is found in chapter 26 of the laws:

> *Gif læt ofslæhð, þone selestan lxxx scll' forgelde; gif þane oþerne ofslæhð, lx scillingum forgelde; ðane þriddan xl scilling forgelde.*

> If he slays a *læt* of the best class, he shall pay 80 shillings; if he slays one of the second class, he shall pay 60 shillings; the third class, he shall pay 40 shillings. (Attenborough 1922)

The word *læt* is found nowhere else in English documents of the period, but is assumed to be the same as the Latin word *latus* used on the continent for a class intermediate between freemen and slaves. It is often presumed that this class represents either freed slaves or the remnants of indigenous, subject populations (Stenton 1971: 303), although this interpretation began only as a possibility, not a secure interpretation of the law (Attenborough 1922: 177). The basis for this presumption is less than clear, as is the wording of the chapter of the laws. Chapter 21 of the laws states that the *wergild*, the financial compensation for killing a freeman was 100 shillings. The *læt* as native Briton would be worth less than a free Anglo-Saxon, which would agree with the treatment of the Welsh in Ine's laws. Higham (1995) is happy to see the Kentish *læt* as representing the native Britons. On the other hand, is it possible that the word *læt* is the singular form derived from Latin *læti*, and the class referred to are the descendants of the Germanic mercenaries of the 5th century? If so, their lesser worth than the freeman (*ceorlas*) would reveal a sense of ranking or hierarchy among the Germanic settlers. This may be be worth further investigation.

Language

It is a major feature of Old English that there is very little contribution to it from the native Celtic British language. Very few words have been identified as having been borrowed into English from British. Serjeantson (1935) listed *assa* (ass), *bannoc* (small cake), *binn* (manger), *bratt* (cloak), *brocc* (badger), *carr* (rock), *dunn* (dark grey), *gafeluc* (small spear), *luh* (lake), *torr* (rock peak), to which Campbell (1959: 220) has added *becca* (fork), *mattuc* (mattock), *toroc* (bung), and to which *cumb* (valley) may also be added (Lass 1987, 1994). Not all these words would stand detailed scrutiny, but even if all are admitted this is not an impressive list. Wolff (1971) noted the existence of 280 Lombard words in Italian, 520 Frankish words in French, 90 Gothic words and 4,000 Arabic words in Spanish. Even more importantly, Jackson (1953) noted that the sound systems (pronunciation) of British and Germanic during the post-Roman period were very different. He pointed out that when British words were adopted into English as place-names, the Germanic sounds were substituted for the native sounds. We can see this in names like Charnwood in Leicestershire, which contains the British word that survives in Welsh as *carn* (= cairn). In other words, there was no influence by British on English pronunciation (Jackson 1953: 195). This is surprising given that areas of British speech may well have survived late into the period of Anglo-Saxon control, e.g. Chilterns, the Fens and the Suffolk Heathland, Yorkshire Moors, Pennines, Glendale, Durham, Dorset (Jackson 1953: 236-39). This must indicate a large element of population migration rather than acculturation. Surely, remnant British groups are only likely to have adopted an English pronunciation if it was the dominant speech of the area in which they lived. The continued existence of British populations is suggested by the extent of British influence on later English place-names, especially in the western parts of Britain. It has sometimes been claimed that the extent of this influence has been grossly underestimated by scholars trained to recognise Old English but not conversant with Old Welsh. This may be true. A recent study (Coates et al. 2000) into the problem has provided a better picture of the survival of Celtic place-names with a notable increase in numbers. However, the overall number of Celtic place-names is still only a very small proportion of the total stock of place-names.

That British peoples remained in the areas under English control and contributed to the genetic make-up of present day English men and women is suggested by the existence of counting systems in the folklore of various parts of England that can only come from a British original (Barry 1964). These systems were reputed to have been used for such purposes as counting sheep, knitting, in children's games and nursery rhymes. The north of England was the main area where these numerals were used, especially the pastoral upland areas of the Pennines and Lake District, but also taking in the Wolds of the East Riding and Lincolnshire. Such numerals also occurred in the south and east of England. These may be the result of migration of shepherds from the north rather than the independent survival of counting systems in these areas. That the numerals in the north were a survival from the British spoken in the area in the 6th and 7th centuries cannot be proven, and has been challenged by alternative views (Barry 1964: 82-87). However, survival is still the most likely explanation and a long period of spoken transmission within ritualised counting activities would account for the deviation of the numbers from their modern Welsh and Cornish analogues. A selection of the many recorded forms of numerals is given in Table 4. The numbers seem to have been chanted in pairs up to five and ten; so one & two, three & four, five, six & seven, eight & nine, ten. The numerals were the feminine forms, suitable for counting ewes, e.g. in Welsh *tair* instead of masculine *tri*. Each pair was made to rhyme (e.g. three with four and two with one) which has severely changed the form of some of the numerals. The numeral for seven seems to have been swapped round with six, and a new form created to rhyme with it for seven. The forms for six to nine have an added extra syllable to make them resemble three and four. This has obscured the British origin of the form for eight, upon which a new rhymed form of nine has been made. Nevertheless, the British origin of the numerals is still obvious.

Modern Welsh	Modern Cornish	Cumbria	Elmet	Lindsey	Suffolk	Sussex
un	ün	yan	eena	yan	ina	ein
dwy	dyw	tan	deena	tan	mina	tein
tair	týr	tethera	tethera	tethera	tethera	tuthera
pedair	peder	pethera	fethera	pethera	methera	futhera
pump	pymp	pimp	fips	pimp	pin	fim
chwech	whégh	sethera	saiyta	tethera	sithera	shavera
saith	seyth	lethera	ayta	lethera	lithera	lackera
wyth	éth	hovera	avera	hovera	cothera	ko
naw	naw	dovera	cavera	covera	hothra	debera
deg	dék	dik	dix	dik	dik	dik

Table 4: British derived numerals used in England (from Barry 1964).

The Frankish contribution
to Anglo-Saxon Britain

There are well attested, although sparse, links between the Anglo-Saxon migrants and power centres on the continent. To treat Britain as an island cut off from the continent is to falsify the early medieval reality. Likewise, to treat the Anglo-Saxons as a people of themselves is to ignore the relationships that undoubtedly placed them firmly within the Germanic world. Such evidence as does exist shows that the Kings of the Franks had a strong interest in Anglo-Saxon affairs and at times regarded themselves as exercising some sort of lordship or supremacy over various of the Anglo-Saxon kings (Wood 1992). Links between the Franks and political authorities in Britain are revealed in the Salian law code of 481/507, in which Frankish lords could plead in courts in Britain for the return of slaves (Wood 1997). There is however nothing in the laws to show whether the court was British or Germanic, although it is evident that slaves were still being taken 'across the sea' as late as the 630s when those doing the taking would have to be Anglo-Saxon (Haywood 1991). Frankish political influence in Britain had certainly begun by the reign of Theuderic I (511-34), who recruited insular Saxons to fight for him on the continent. According to Suzuki (2000), it is at this time, in the period 525-50, that Frankish luxury artefacts began to appear in burials in Kent. The Kentish elite was clearly reinforcing its position by forging economic, and presumably political links with the newly emergent Frankish kingdom. Frankish influence was particularly strong under Chilperic I (561-84), his son Chlothar II (584-629), and Dagobert I (623-39) - all kings of the northern part of the Frankish kingdom based on Soissons and Paris. This influence lasted well into the 7th century under the mayors of the palace Erchinoald and Ebroin. We cannot be sure whether the Anglo-Saxon kings themselves viewed their relationship with the Franks as one of subordination, or whether in fact they welcomed the protection of a stronger power and profited by Frankish influence. Esmonde Cleary (1993: 62) has put forward the idea that the Franks acted as a source of wealth, prestige and power for emerging Anglo-Saxon kings, very much in the pattern of the core-periphery models often used by prehistorians. The exact relationship between the Franks and their Germanic cousins in Britain is likely to be more complex than this model assumes.

Evidence for this relationship comes in the form of marriages between Anglo-Saxon kings and either minor members of the Frankish royal family or of the Frankish nobility. The strongest links are attested for Kent, the nearest of the Anglo-Saxon kingdoms to the Franks. Both King Æþelberht and his son Eadbald had Frankish wives, Berhta and Ymme respectively. Eadbald's son Eorcenberht called his son by the Frankish name Hloþhere (Chlothar), most likely after Chlothar II (584-629). It has been suggested that the Frankish name Sigeberht born by an East Anglian king shows that his father might also have had marriage links with the Franks (Wood 1992). Certainly Sigeberht sought refuge among the Franks when in exile between 628 and 631. Likewise, the name of Æþelberht of Kent's father, Eormenric, might well indicate that Frankish connections went back further than the time of Æþelberht himself. The evidence of these marriages suggests that the Anglo-Saxons were seen as lesser dependants by the Frankish kings, rather than equals (Wood 1992). It was not just the Kings of Kent who profited from Frankish alliances. East Anglian links with the Franks are revealed by the spectacular finds from the Sutton Hoo cemetery in Suffolk. The coins with the main burial, assumed to be that of King Rædwald, came from various Frankish mints (Carver 1998: 39) and could date to the period 613-22 (Wood 1994: 177). The sumptuous use of gold and garnet metalwork on many of the artefacts certainly reflects an aristocratic fashion associated with the Franks. It seems clear that the Franks were seeking to influence and control areas on the margins of the Frankish state. Whether it was a desire to control potential destabilising elements beyond the borders or genuine expansionism, the Frankish kings seem to have claimed political lordship over the Anglo-Saxons in Britain at this time, as noted by the Byzantine commentator Procopius for the period 548/53 (James 1988: 103). If Procopius can be accepted as a reliable source then the earliest Frankish claims in Britain might belong to Theudebert I, who ruled from 534 to 548 (Campbell 1971). Specific kings who claimed such lordship may have included Sigibert I (561-75), Chilperic I (561-84), and Theuderic II (596-613) and Theudebert II (596-612) (Wood 1994: 176).

Rare evidence of these links has been teased out of the continental evidence by Morris (1973: 286-291). It was Procopius who noted Frankish policy of allotting lands to Germanic settlers migrating from Britain. Indeed, there is evidence for Anglo-Saxon settlement behind Boulogne and Calais which may date to the early 6th century, while others may have been settled in what would later become Normandy (James 1988: 103). Saxon settlements are found in the Bessin (around Bayeux) and the mouth of the Loire, as well as Boulogne (Haywood 1991), although whether these came from Britain or from continental Saxony is impossible to tell. Myres (1977) noted that pottery from St Gilles in modern day Belgium was made in the same workshop as pottery from Desborough and Rothwell in Northamptonshire. He also noted that pots with vertical and diagonal schemes of decoration combined with stamps show parallels with pots in the Rhineland and southern Germany (Myres 1977: 43). This may be linked with later continental tradition of Anglo-Saxons returning from Britain to help the Franks subdue the Thuringians and being settled on lands by the Frankish kings.

The documentary sources are silent on links with the Franks in the 5th century, and there is no place-name evidence for Frankish settlement (a Frankley and two Franktons occur but in the west midlands, away from areas of early settlement and most likely refer to a personal name). However, the archaeological evidence can show that these links were in place in some form in the earliest phases of the migration. Evison (1965) has even argued that the early stages of settlement were organised under Frankish leadership. There are some burials in Britain that can best be interpreted as those of Frankish warriors, e.g. Alfriston, Abingdon and Petersfinger (Hills 1978: 315). As would be expected, there is archaeological evidence of Frankish links with Kent. Some artefact types are found in both Gaul and Kent, e.g. glass bowls (Knight 1999: 50). Indeed, one glass bowl from Darenth in Kent bears the names of two Gallo-Roman martyrs from the area around Soissons. Frankish artefacts in Britain can be interpreted as imports of luxury items through links between the Merovingian and Kentish elites (Loveluck 2000), but there is enough evidence to suggest that at least some Franks were themselves involved in the 5th century settlement of Britain (Todd 2001: 90). Hawkes and Dunning (1961) were willing to accept the few finds of continental style belt fittings of types IIIB and VB from the 5th century as indicating Frankish settlement in Britain.

The nature of Frankish relations with Anglo-Saxon kings was strengthened during the missionary phase of Christianity in the 7th century. Dagobert I would seem to have sponsored the missionary activities of Felix in East Anglia and Agilbert in Wessex, and English nuns were recruited to Frankish monasteries. Agilbert seems to have been close to the Frankish mayor of the palace Ebroin. It was King Coenwalh of Wessex who accepted Agilbert as his bishop, but who later fell out with him resulting in Agilbert's eventual return home to Paris. Bede reported that Coenwalh had grown tired of Agilbert's Frankish speech. This can only have been a coded way of saying that Coenwalh had tired of Frankish alliance, for he later tried to entice Agilbert to return. Although Agilbert refused, Coenwalh did accept his nephew the equally Frankish (and presumably Frankish speaking) Leuthere as his new bishop (670-676). It has further been suggested that Bishop Eorcenwald of London (675-693) might have had Frankish origins (Wood 1992). A much fuller exploration of the links between the Anglo-Saxon church and that of the Franks can be found in Campbell 1971. As Campbell says, the English Channel cannot be regarded as a strong cultural or even political boundary at this period. South-eastern Britain and north-eastern Gaul shared many similarities and were part of the same Germanic world.

An interesting picture emerges if we examine the chronology of Frankish relations with the Anglo-Saxons, and of Anglo-Saxon activity in Britain. (Table 5)

The events shown in Table 5 (over page) can be placed into four phases as follows.

Phase 1 (520s-550s): increasing Germanic settlement in Britain and the threat of their increased political power there threatened to destabilise the existing order on the continent and prompted the Franks to take a controlling interest in the Saxons and Britain through the Germanic rulers in Kent. The rulers of Kent gained from an alliance with the Austrasian Franks, their wealth and power, and submitted to Frankish interests.

Phase 2 (550s-60s): the dominance of Neustrian interests among the Franks led to unrest against Frankish control in Britain. Continental revolts against the Franks diverted attention away from adventures in Britain.

Phase 3 (570s-90s): Anglo-Saxon dynasties took advantage of division and civil war among the Franks to expand against the Britons. New kingdoms were established and British lands were taken over on a large scale.

Phase 4 (590s-630s): Frankish rulers attempted to restore their political interests in Britain, using the church and marriage ties. By seeking to control Britain, they could deprive the continental Saxons of overseas support and secure their eastern borders. Britain might also have been an arena for the playing out of political rivalries among the Frankish kings, especially that between Neustria and Austrasia/Burgundy.

The Germanic settlement and conquest of Britain did not take place in isolation from events elsewhere in Europe. It is unfortunate that many historians and archaeologists continue to treat Britain as though its island status made it somehow apart from the continent. It is clear that the Germanic settlers and their descendants were part of a wider world, in which the dominant power in the 6th century was the Franks.

Continent	Britain
	523? Cerdic began campaigning in the south
	527? Anglian settlers arrive in eastern Britain 529? Cerdic established a Kingdom in the south, the *Gewisse*
531 Theuderic I of Austrasia subdued the Saxons *531 Saxons from Britain under Heaðugeat fight for Theuderic in return for land*	
548/53 Angles were part of a Frankish embassy to the Eastern Empire	
	550s war between the Angles in Britain and the pro-Frankish Varni
555 Austrasia fell to the two western Frankish kings on the death of Theudebald 555/56 Saxon revolt against Chlothar I, put down by 561 558 Chlothar I reunited the Franks	
561 Franks split under four kings on the death of Chlothar I 561/75 Sigibert I & Chilperic I campaigned against the Saxons	560s the expansion of the *Gewisse* began but little other activity at this time
	571 Wuffa became King of the East Angles and Ceawlin of the *Gewisse*
	575 Ida established an Anglian Bernicia
	580? marriage of Æþelberht of Kent and Berhta 580 York fell under Anglian control 582 Battle of Bedcanford delivers the Chilterns to the Anglo-Saxons
	585 Mercia was established 587 major British defeat at the siege of Lindisfarne 588 Battle of Dyrham delivers the lower Severn to the Anglo-Saxons
	592 Æþelfrið became king in Bernicia 594 Æþelberht became king in Kent

Continent	Britain
	597 the mission of Augustine to Kent
	604 Æþelfrið united Northumbria under his rule
613 Franks reunited under Chlothar II	*614 Bishop Justus attended a synod at Paris*
623/29 Saxon revolt against Dagobert I	
	631 Sigibert returned to rule East Anglia from exile among the Franks *633 Eadwine's children given sanctuary by Dagobert I*
639 decline of Frankish power after the death of Dagobert I	

Table 5: Events in Gaul and Britain, 520s-630s.
Direct relations between Britain and the continent are shown in italics.

Myth and legend

The settlers in Britain were part of a wider family of Germanic speaking peoples. Their kinship with other speakers of Germanic dialects is revealed in the shared myths and legends which were written down in later manuscripts in both Britain and the continent. Myths were based on non-historical characters and cannot be localised in time or place, except for the unique story of Beowulf. Legends developed around known historical people and may reflect genuine history, but were most likely fictional embellishments of the original. Ardener (1989: 27-29) has shown how myths and legends can be transformed at different times and yet keep a common core of relationships and actions. He suggests that this constant core is likely to contain the historical reality. Most of the legendary tales found in later Anglo-Saxon manuscripts seem to belong to four broad cycles. There is a set of tales about figures widely known in Germanic literature (e.g. Sigemund). There is also a set of tales relating to the origins of the Anglo-Saxons themselves (e.g. Finn and Hengest, Freawine, Offa). The two other cycles relate to characters who date to the age of Germanic settlement in Britain. The first of these tells of characters based around the non-Germanic figure of Attila, the Hunnish king who dominated much of Europe in the 440s (Ætla, Guþhere, Hagena, Waldere). As the head of a multi-ethnic empire, Attila seems to have been a figure around whom myths and legends of heroes common to all the Germanic peoples could be based. The second cycle relates to the Baltic and North Sea in the early 6th century (Beowulf, Hroþgar, Hygelac, Ingeld, Ongenþeow, Þeodric). Other figures who appear in English sources are the Gothic ruler Eormanric and, the latest figure to appear in English literary sources, Ælfwine of the Lombards, active in the 560s. Thenceforth, from the middle of the 6th century, the age of migration to Britain gave way to the age of conquest and the carving out of kingdoms. Links with the continent became of lesser importance than the dynamics of conquest and relations between peoples in Britain itself. Arnold (1997) rightly points out that there are very few Anglo-Saxon migration myths and legends. The migration must have generated a whole set of indigenous legends but these have only survived in cursory form, if at all. It has been suggested (Howe 1989) that the experience of migration was reflected in later literature and in translations into English of relevant Biblical stories where the Christian originals have been altered to fit the Anglo-Saxon received myth of migration. Battles (2000) has provided a particularly good example of this, which will be explored in more detail later.

Common Germanic mythology

Some of the tales known among the Anglo-Saxons were shared in common with other Germanic peoples. As with all folk tales, they change in their details from one telling to another. There is no standard Germanic form for these tales, merely common elements which take different shape at different times and in different places.

Mœðhild (ON Magnhild) and Geat (ON Gauti)

Mæðhild foretold her own death by drowning in a river. This duly happened when a bridge she was on collapsed. Her husband Geat then played his magic harp and released her from the clutches of the water demon, restoring her to life. The story is preserved in the later English poem *Deor* and is also known from Norwegian and Icelandic ballads of the nineteenth century (Malone 1977).

Sigemund (ON Sigmund)

Referred to in Beowulf (Wrenn 1973: 47), Sigemund was the father of Sigeward (ON *Sigurðr*) and a chief actor in one of the most popular of Germanic mythological tales. The fullest account of Sigemund and his family is found in later, Old Norse, literature (Orchard 1997: 140-141, Hollander 1962, Auden & Taylor 1981). A famed warrior of many exploits, he was the only man who could pull out a magical sword which Oðinn had stuck into the trunk of tree. His father and brothers were killed by his sister's husband, *Siggeir* (OE Sigegar). His sister, *Signy*, lay with Sigemund to give birth to *Sinfiötli* (OE Fitela), who would help Sigemund avenge their deaths. *Signy* helped them kill *Siggeir* but chose to die with her husband. In old age, he married *Hiordis* and became father of *Sigurðr*. Shortly before *Sigurð*'s birth, he was killed in battle when Oðinn appeared and claimed him for Valhalla by breaking the magical sword. Norse legends had his son *Sigurðr* slay the dragon *Fafnir* and win a fabulous hoard of gold. In the English poem *Beowulf*, this deed was done by Sigemund himself.

Weland (ON Völund) and Beaduhild (ON Boðvild)

Weland was a famous smith who was taken captive by King Niðhad, placed in chains and hamstrung. One of his golden rings was given to Niðhad's daughter, Beaduhild, while his sword was taken by Niðhad himself. He managed to kill the King's two sons, making bowls and jewellery out of their skulls, eyes and teeth which he gave to Niðhad and his family. He then seduced Beaduhild, winning back his ring and escaped by making a coat of feathers and flying away. Weland's revenge was clearly a widespread and popular story. He appeared in later Norse literature as *Völund* (Orchard 1997: 179-180) as well as in English literature. He appears in the Old English poems *Deor*, *Waldere*, *Beowulf*, and his image was carved on the Frank's Casket, as well as being known by King Alfred (Wilson 1970: 11-14). His fame survived for a long time after the Norman Conquest.

Wudga and Hama (Go Vidigoia, MHG Witege, Heime)

Wudga (also Widia) was the son of Beaduhild by Weland. He and Hama were mentioned in the poems *Widsið* and *Waldere*, and were the subjects of various adventures, e.g. rescuing Þeodric from captivity by giants. According to the poem *Beowulf*, Hama was reputed to have stolen an important necklace from his enemy King Eormanric (Wrenn 1973: 46-47). Others tales existed but do not survive in Old English manuscript sources. Mention of them is made in later Middle English manuscripts. Stories of Wudga and Hama can be found in Middle High German literature and Wudga at least seems to have had a Gothic origin (Wilson 1970: 6-7). Hama may be a version of the Norse god *Heimdall* reduced to the status of a folk hero (see below under Religion).

Þeodric (MHG Dietrich, ON Þiðrik)

The story of the imprisonment of Þeodric by his uncle Eormanric is reflected in the poem *Waldere* (Zettersten 1979). Versions of the story also occur in later High German literature (Wilson 1977: 5-6). This Þeodric should not be confused with the Frankish Þeodric (see below). In continental Germanic legend, Þeodric was of Verona or Bern, ousted and exiled by Eormanric.

The ancestral English

Memories of figures directly connected with the Anglo-Saxons have been preserved, albeit sparsely. The key role played by the kingly families in creating and maintaining a sense of Germanic heritage is shown by the fact that the three main figures and stories that have been preserved relate to the ancestors of the Kings of Kent, Mercia and Wessex.

Finn and Hengest

These two characters are known from an episode in *Beowulf* and from a separate fragment of a larger tale (Wrenn 1973). Tolkien's reconstruction of the tale of Finn and Hengest (Tolkien 1982) places Hengest as a Jutish follower of Hnæf, a Danish prince ruling over part of Jutland. Other Jutes, who had been displaced by the Danish conquest, had found sanctuary among the Frisians. The Frisian ruler, Finn, had married Hnæf's sister, Hildeburh, and their son Friþuwulf was fostered with Hnæf. Friþuwulf was returning home, escorted by his uncle, accompanied by Hengest. It was inevitable that there would be friction between the Danes and their Jutish collaborators, and the Jutish exiles sheltered by Finn. Among these exiles was Garwulf, the heir to the Jutish kingship. The Jutish exiles mounted an attack on the Danes in the hall they had been given for their stay (most likely against Finn's wishes). During a five-day siege, both Hnæf and Friþuwulf were killed, leaving Hengest in command of the Danes. In their turn, the Jutish exiles and their Frisian allies had suffered great losses. A truce was arranged whereby Hengest and the Jutish Half-Danes were to stay over winter under Finn's lordship. In the spring, the Danes returned home, leaving Hengest and his Jutes in Frisia. When the Danes returned to extract vengeance for the death of Hnæf, Hengest was in a key position to betray Finn from the inside and pay his debt to the dead Danish king. Hengest thus played a key role in ensuring the destruction of Finn, but would have no choice but either to go back and live under the Danes or find a new career elsewhere. He followed the path of exile by collecting together a band of warriors and accepted an invitation to sail to Britain to enter the service of the British ruler Vortigern. In this way, he established himself and his men in Kent, beginning the long process of migration and conquest that would create England. We can only guess at how much historical truth lies behind the legends preserved in later literature. It would certainly be unsafe, although not impossible, to treat the literary tale as history.

Freawine (Da Frowinus)

The story of Freawine has been preserved in Danish legend (Davison & Fisher 1979/80). He was ruler of Schleswig under Wærmund of Angeln, who had married his son Offa to Freawine's daughter. He was killed by Eadgils, a renowned warrior King. His two sons Cet and Wig then challenged Eadgils to a duel. Wig broke the conditions of the duel by rushing in to help his brother who was being beaten and together they both killed Eadgils, revenging their father but earning shame in the process for fighting two against one. The story has not been preserved in any English literary source. However, the names Freawine and his son Wig have been preserved in a version of the West Saxon royal genealogy, as given in the *Anglo-Saxon Chronicle* (Garmonsway 1954: 66). This ought to mean some familiarity with the story, as well as a desire among the West Saxon kings to claim or acknowledge connections with the continental Germanic homeland.

Offa (Da Uffo), King of Angeln

Offa was reputed to be the ancestor of Offa of Mercia (757-96), ruling Angeln in Holstein. Extrapolating back from the historically known kings of Mercia who were his descendants, would give Offa of Angeln a reign in the latter half of the 4th century. Stories about Offa have been preserved in *Beowulf* and *Widsið* (Wrenn 1973, Wilson 1970). Danish legend also remembered Offa (Davidson & Fisher 1979 & 80). He was the son in old age of Wærmund, and although large in stature refused to speak and was considered an idiot. When Wærmund became senile and blind, the Saxons claimed the kingdom and Offa unexpectedly spoke up for his father. He challenged the Saxon king's son to a duel, defeating both him and a chosen champion to settle Angeln's southern boundary on the River Eider. His wife Þryð did not have such a good reputation, being remembered for cruelty, putting to death any men who openly looked upon her.

Other people remembered in continental sources were mentioned in the genealogical ancestries of the Anglo-Saxon royal families, and tales based on them may well have been known, e.g. Wihtlæg in the Mercian genealogy (the killer of Hamlet according to the Danish writer Saxo Grammaticus).

The migration period

The Germanic nature of the settlers in Britain is nowhere better demonstrated than in the preservation of stories about figures from the 'barbarian' world of late antiquity on the continent. There are two main sets of characters, those associated with the Hunnish onslaught on Rome, especially with Attila, and those found operating in and around the Baltic homelands of the Angles. There are many figures named in the literature, chiefly in *Widsið*. Most are just names, but to some we can determine their history or stories and so flesh out the details that lay behind their memories in Britain.

The Hunnish connection

Ætla (La Attila), King of the Huns

Ætla was the leader of the nomadic Huns who had come from central Asia and conquered much of Europe outside the Roman Empire. He ruled a multi-racial confederacy of tribes from 435 to 453 (Wolfram 1997). The Hunnic realm was made up of many peoples, including Germanic groups like the Goths and Gepids. Many legendary or mythical Germanic figures are associated with Ætla's court in literature, e.g escape from his court is the starting point for the poem *Waldere* (Zettersten 1979). At first he ruled with his elder brother Bleda, but he disposed of Bleda in 444/5 to gain sole rule of the Huns. He attacked the Balkans in 447 with great success and was then at the height of his power. His attack on Gaul in 451 was less successful, being defeated at the Battle of the Catalaunian Fields by the Gallic forces under Aetius. Both sides in this battle had Germanic soldiers. Ætla had Gepids, Goths, Heruli, Suebi and non-Germanic Sarmatians. Aetius also had Goths and Sarmatians, as well as Saxons, Bretons, Franks and Iranian Alans. Ætla moved into Italy in 452, taking Milan but his army was decimated by disease and the Empire refused to grant his demands. He died the following year. Although the Huns themselves were an Asian people, the realm of Ætla seems to have blended Hunnic and Gothic elements that made it at least partly Germanic (Wolfram 1997: 141-143). He was known in later Norse literature as a ruthless and cruel ruler (Orchard 1997), but to have attracted so many peoples he must also have been a generous lord and an able warrior.

Guþhere (MHG Gundohar, ON Gunnar), King of the Burgundians

Guþhere had founded Burgundian power by crossing the Rhine and setting up a kingdom at Worms inside Gaul c.411. He was killed in 436 in an attack by the Huns of Ætla on behalf of the Roman ruler of Gaul Aetius, his bodyguards dying to the last man around him. The remnants of the Burgundians found refuge in Gaul and eventually formed a new Kingdom based on Lyons (Todd 1992: 211). Guþhere is mentioned in *Widsið* but his main literary appearance is as a character in the *Niebelungenlied* in both German literature and its equivalents in Norse literature.

Heoden (ON Heðinn, MHG Hetel) and Hagena (ON Hogni, MHG Hagen)

These two characters were mentioned in *Widsið* and the dynasty of Heoden was also mentioned in *Deor*, which suggests some knowledge of his story among the audience for both poems. Both figures lived to the east of the Angles towards the estuary of the Vistula (Herbert 1993: 229). The basic version of the story is that Heoden was a close friend of Hagena but abducted or seduced his daughter Hild. They became enemies as a result. One resolution of the story is that they fought in single combat to the death. Hild then awakens them so that they return from the dead and fight each day to relive their quarrel. The story was retold with modifications in various works in both Old Norse and Middle High German (Herbert 1993), and also in the collection of Danish legends of Saxo Grammaticus (Davidson & Fisher 1979 & 80).

Waldere (La Waltharius, ON Valtari, MHG Walther), King of Aquitaine

The figure of Waldere was the subject of an Old English poem, now mostly lost and only preserved in two fragments of parchment (Zettersten 1979). Waldere was sent as a hostage to Ætla of the Huns. There he met Hildegyð of Burgundy and fled with her back to Aquitaine. On the way, they were attacked by Guðhere of Burgundy and Hagena, another former hostage of Ætla. Waldere survived but lost an arm, and returned to marry Hildegyð and become King. The story is preserved in German and Norse versions (Zettersten 1979: 3).

The Baltic

Beowulf

Beowulf was the subject of the only surviving complete heroic poem in Old English (Wrenn 1973). He was the mythical nephew of Hygelac of the Geats, a people lying between the Swedes and the Danes. Beowulf had taken part in the raid on Frisia in which Hygelac had been killed (c.521). He later succeeded Hygelac's son as the last king of the Geats. While king, he helped the exiled Eadgils regain the throne of the Swedes. His three legendary feats described in the poem were the killing of the monster Grendel who had terrorised the Danish Hroþgar's court at Heorot, the killing of Grendel's mother who was seeking vengeance for the death of her son, and the killing of the dragon that guarded a hoard of gold. The first two were performed in his youth. The last was an act of his old age, after a reign of 50 years. His death in the fight with the dragon brought to an end to the existence of the Geats as an independent people. There is no evidence that Beowulf was ever a real person. The Geats were probably taken under Swedish rule not long after the death of Hygelac.

Part of the significance of Beowulf must lie in the fact that there was an audience in England in the 8th century (the most likely time of composition) for stories set in southern Scandinavia. Newton (1992) has suggested that links between the Kings of East Anglia and Scandinavia, either real or assumed, lay behind this. In any case, it is striking that links between the Anglo-Saxons and a part of the Germanic homeland were still being recognised some 200 to 300 years after the migration.

Billing, King of the Werne

The Byzantine historian Procopius recorded an attack on the Werne by Angles from Britain in the 550s. Billing was possibly the subject of this attack since he was listed as King of the Werne in the poem *Widsið*.

Hroþgar (ON Hroarr) and Hroðwulf (ON Hrolfr), Kings of the Danes

Hroþgar's hall (Heorot) was based at Lejre in Jutland. Hroðwulf was his nephew, and had loyally helped his uncle repel an attack by Ingeld, Hroþgar's son-in-law. After Hroþgar's death, it was Hroþwulf who took over the kingdom by slaying Hroþgar's son Hreðric (c.525). Hroþgar's court was also the setting for the early adventures of Beowulf. The two kings were mentioned in *Widsið*, as well as in Danish legend (Davidson & Fisher 1979 & 80) and Old Norse literature (Wrenn 1973: 35).

Hygelac (Fr Chochilaicus), King of the Geats

The Geats lived in southern Sweden and were distant kin of the continental Goths. Hygelac was killed leading a raid on Frankish controlled Frisia in 521 (or between 511 and 525, see Wood in Ausenda 1995: 247). The Geats were soon afterwards absorbed into Sweden. His supposed nephew and later successor was Beowulf. Hygelac was mentioned in an eighth century English collection of stories about monsters as a man of huge size whose body was buried near the mouth of the Rhine (Wrenn 1973: 37-38).

Ingeld (Da Ingellus), King of the Heaðobards

Ingeld was married to Freawaru, the daughter of Hroþgar. The Danes had slain his father Froda, and Ingeld owed a duty of avenging him, even against his father-in-law. Thus, he was killed attacking Heorot (c.520). The story is referred to in *Beowulf* and in *Widsið* (Wrenn 1973: 41). His story was seemingly popular since Alcuin complained in a letter of 797 about monks listening to legendary stories, including those about 'Hinieldus'. Ingeld also figures in the Danish 'history' of Saxo Grammaticus (Davidson & Fisher 1979 & 80). His people, the Heaðobeardan cannot be located.

Ongenþeow (ON Angantyr), King of the Swedes

The centre of the Swedish Kingdom was Uppsala, north of the Geats. Ongenþeow had been at war with the Geats and was killed by them early in the reign of Hygelac. His son Onela (*Ali*) was married to Hroþgar's sister. He is mentioned in both *Beowulf* and in *Widsið* (Wrenn 1973: 40).

Other characters

Ælfwine (La Alboin), King of the Lombards

Ælfwine became King of the Lombards in Pannonia c.560 (Wolfram 1997: 284-291). After destroying the neighbouring Gepids, in 568 he invaded and took over northern Italy. He had captured and married Rosamund, the daughter of the Gepid King Kunimund, whom he had killed in 567. Rosamund poisoned him in revenge for her father in 572. He was mentioned in *Widsið*, but we do not know how much of his story was known by the audience.

Eormanric (Go Hermanaric), King of the Goths

Eormanric was ruler of the area north of the Black Sea, and built up an empire over several peoples around the Volga, Don and Urals as far as the Baltic (Wolfram 1988). He had two reputations. One for being warlike, cruel and treacherous, and the other for being a generous lord and mighty ruler. His empire was destroyed by the attacks of the Huns in 375, whereupon, he killed himself. There was a tradition that he had been attacked and wounded by two brothers, Ammius and Sarus. They had a sister, Sunhild, whom Eormanric had killed because of the treachery of her husband. He was mentioned in English legend in *Deor*, *Widsið* and *Beowulf*, as well as being found in Jordanes' history of the Goths (Mierow 1915), and occurs in Norse and German literature (Malone 1977, Hollander 1962). Eormanric was a figure around whom other heroes of legend were placed, much like Ætla or the later medieval Arthur.

Þeodric (Fr Theuderic), *King of the Franks*

Þeodric was a son of Clovis, and ruled at Rheims 511-34. According to Frankish legend, an evil counsellor, Sabene, advised him to kill one of his followers, Sigewald. His son Þeodberht helped Sigewald, the son of the executed man to escape. When he himself became King, Þeodberht recalled him and gave him back his father's estates. Þeodric was mentioned in both the Old English poems *Deor* and *Widsið* (Malone 1977: 9-13). It was Þeodric's kingdom that was attacked by Hygelac in 521. A runic passage carved in Sweden in the 9th century contains a legend that Þeodric was killed in an invasion of the Geatish homeland after Hygelac's raid. A Þeodric is also mentioned in the poem *Waldere*, but this is probably another figure of myth or legend, Þeodric the Goth, part of the circle of Eormanric (Wilson 1970: 5-6).

Conquest mythology

The Germanic peoples who settled in the Roman Empire had various origin tales that often incorporated genuine material in a mythical format. The materials in these tales would be selected and changed, often condensed with confused chronological horizons (Wolfram 1997: 32-34). Many of these tales have elements in common: a small people leaving their homeland, overcoming a geographical or military obstacle, the leadership of royal house receiving divine aid. The settlement in their new territory would often be accompanied by a change of religion or cult (e.g. Vanir to Æsir, or from pagan to Christian). As we shall see, the adoption of Christianity might mark the culmination of the process of migration and would have cemented the identification of the migrants with their new land through divine providence. A further element often found is the existence of a traditional enemy, whose opposition has to be overcome before the people's destiny can be fulfilled. The Germanic settlers in Britain were no exception to this model. The relation between origin myths and historical events is complicated. To be acceptable, the myths must have some basis in reality but are also likely to conform to certain patterns, as noted by Wolfram, and realised long ago by Kemble (Sims-Williams 1983: 4).

The origin myths of the Germanic settlers in Britain are based on the coming to power of various royal houses. They are not the origin myths of peoples, but of kingdoms. The creation of such myths was likely to be the result of a mix of court poets satisfying the dynastic ambitions of the ruling house and, as later written down, of clerical support for strong rulers who could guarantee the rights and privileges of the church (Yorke 2000). As Arnold (1997) has noted, there are remarkably few myths and legends concerning the migration and settlement of Germanic peoples in Britain. Arnold suggests that this may be because legends tend to be based on heroic failure and so would not be appropriate for successful migration and conquest. This is doubtful since myths do not have to be about failure. However, it may also be (again as noted by Arnold) that the migration and conquest was not one single act but a series of acts by various groups of people at various times. The only myths and legends to survive would be those of direct interest to the ruling elites of the new kingdoms that emerged after the later 6th century. Much of the history of the 5th and early 6th centuries would simply not be relevant. It may also be that the loss of so many documents from the archives of the early medieval period has resulted in only a few myths and legends surviving to modern times. Our sources for the legends that do survive are Bede and the *Anglo-Saxon Chronicle*, neither of them contemporary with the transfer of Germanic peoples to Britain.

The first of the tales to be related in these later sources is that of Kent. The narrative of the origins of Anglo-Saxon Kent is one of treachery and conquest. The reasoning behind the conquest was simply that Britain was a wealthy land, a prize worth fighting for. Historical 'facts' can be seen underlying the narrative, which may well reflect 5th century reality; the hiring of Anglo-Saxon mercenaries, the increase in numbers of the mercenaries, their demand for extra provisions and their desire for land they could call their own leading to revolt against their former paymasters. However, the story of the origins of Kent was not simply one of telling historical 'facts'. It was used to justify the conquest as a whole and its primacy in the historiography of the conquest enables us to treat it as the archetype for the whole Anglo-Saxon migration and conquest. The origins of Kent could be made to stand for the origins of the English as a whole because it was both the first of the Anglo-Saxon conquests and the earliest of the Christian kingdoms. Each of the later kingdoms must have had its own origin tales but the only early source for any of these is the *Anglo-Saxon Chronicle*, which gives an account only for the founding of Kent, Sussex and Wessex. Welsh sources give us additional information relating to Bernicia. For the rest, we have nothing other than a few names and vague indications of date. What the *Anglo-Saxon Chronicle* reveals is how the English elite of Alfred's day, and most likely his court circle, saw their own origins. The three stories presented in the *Anglo-Saxon Chronicle* share certain features; arrival, warfare against the native British and the creation of a kingdom. Some sharing of details is also apparent, e.g. the arrival in three ships. This could be simply a conventional mythical element. Yorke (1993: 25) has reminded us that there were shared Germanic foundation myths, and indeed shared mythic elements from a variety of sources that often were expected by the audiences for stories representing origin legends. On the other hand, it could be that three ships' companies was the size of the normal military unit for the period. After all, Columbus's expedition to America in 1492 was based on three ships and no one could argue that this was merely an invented myth (without disagreeing that the expedition has generated its own mythology since).

The outlines of the three myths as presented in the *Anglo-Saxon Chronicle* are as follows.

Kent

arrival   Hengest and Horsa landed at Thanet in 3 ships (449)
warfare   fought Vortigern (455), fought the Britons (457), fought
             the Welsh (465, 473)
kingdom succeeded to the kingdom (455), succession of Æsc (488)

Sussex

arrival   Ælle landed in 3 ships (477)
warfare   fought the Welsh (477, 485), fought the Britons (491)

Wessex

arrival   Cerdic landed in 5 ships (495), Port came with 2 ships (501), Stuf and Wihtgar came with 3 ships (514)

warfare   fought the Welsh (495, 508), fought the Britons (519, 527), took Wight (530)

kingdom   obtained the kingdom (519), succession of Cynric (534)

The process for all three was described in terms of conquest, linked to the establishment of kingly families. Being Anglo-Saxon was defined in terms of being non-British; i.e. allegiance to the kingly family, originating from outside Britain and being actively hostile to the native inhabitants of the island. There was no attempt to justify the migration or the conquest. Whether the events put down in the early entries in the Chronicle were accurately or truthfully presented is neither here nor there (the existence of figures such as Port is highly doubtful). The Chronicle reveals how the origins of England were seen in the 9th century as part of the ideology of Englishness. We have to turn to Bede to find a justification for the conquest of Britain by the Anglo-Saxons. Bede's *Ecclesiastical History of the English People* was part of the Anglo-Saxon intellectual heritage since the 8th century, and we may be sure that his reasons for the conquest were likewise part of the 'official ideology' of Englishness under Alfred. Bede presented a picture of native Britons wallowing in luxury and sin, having turned away from the righteous life ordained by the Christian faith. The Anglo-Saxons were thus God's punishment on a miscreant people (Colgrave & Mynors 1969: 46-49, 52-53).

> *Siquidem, ut breuiter dicam, accensus manibus paganorum ignis iustas de sceleribus populi Dei ultiones expetiit.*

> To put it briefly, the fire kindled by the hands of the heathen executed the just vengeance of God on the nation for its crimes.

> (Colgrave & Mynors 1969: 52-53)

The Anglo-Saxons were thus a chosen people, selected by God to punish the sinful Britons (Hills 2003: 26). The idea of being a chosen people has been a common characteristic of ethnic groups throughout history, and is not restricted to Christian societies (Smith in Hutchinson & Smith 1996: 190-194). It is no surprise that it should surface among the Anglo-Saxons, who conform to the emigrant colonist pattern of ethnicity put forward by Smith.

Justification of conquest went hand-in-hand with justification of title to rule. In the case of the new kingly families of Anglo-Saxon England this involved a mythology of descent. Two features of the descents of these families as recorded in later manuscripts stand out: the common descent from Woden for all but the East Saxon kingly family, and the mid-late 6th century as a chronological horizon (Carver 1998: 104) beyond which the genealogies become somewhat untrustworthy. The significance of this chronological horizon will become apparent later. The origin of royal families with Woden would provide the necessary divine sanction for the origins of the kingdoms themselves. Being chosen by the gods as a favoured royal line is clearly linked to the idea of being a chosen people.

Racial antagonism

Justification of the migration and conquest involved the denigration of the native Britons as an erring, therefore unworthy (and hence inferior), people. To some extent, this may have been simply a standard theme of Christian writers when dealing with invasions and conquests. It may also have been the common currency of Christian writers among the Britons themselves, e.g. Gildas (Winterbottom 1978). However, there can be no doubting Bede's dislike of, and contempt for, the British and his view of their church as heretical (Higham 1995: 14-18). There can also be no doubt that the native Britons (Welsh) were more widely treated, or thought of, as inferior. The laws of Ine of Wessex (688/94) laid down wergilds for the Welsh at a lower rate than for their English counterparts (Whitelock 1995: 367). The English word for a native Briton was *wealh* (itself the Germanic word for Romano-Celtic foreigner). By the 10th century, this word had come to have a secondary meaning of slave, and by the 11th century could be equated with the word *ungerad*, meaning rude, unskilled, foolish, ignorant (Faull 1975). Although this evidence of hostility towards the British comes from sources that are later than the migration, the idea of racial antagonism between the Anglo-Saxons and the Britons finds some support from the fact that there is little evidence of linguistic assimilation between Anglo-Saxon and Briton. As noted earlier, the number of British, as opposed to Vulgar Latin or Irish, words borrowed into English is pitifully few (Campbell 1977: 219-220; Lass 1987: 43). That people were aware of ethnic differences at this time is reflected in the legal prohibition against intermarriage between Roman and Goth in Italy. Once the barbarians groups settled within the Roman provinces they stopped being willing to accept new recruits from the native population and began to keep a certain legal and cultural difference between themselves and the Roman provincials (Geary 2002: 108). Awareness of difference need not involve hostility but the evidence of Gildas suggests that at least some Britons were extremely hostile to the Germanic newcomers, probably at the same time that other Britons were actively cooperating with them. The strength of Gildas's feelings can be in no doubt (Winterbottom 1978: 26 & 97): "*ferocissimi illi nefandi nominis Saxones deo hominibusque invisi*" ("the ferocious Saxons (name not to be spoken), hated by man and God"). As Higham (1994) has noted, the rhetoric of Gildas is full of animal metaphor, likening the Saxons to wolves and ferocious beasts. This may have been highly coloured rhetoric but rhetoric cannot work unless it strikes a cord in the listeners.

Some explanation for the depth of hostility between Britons and Germans can be attempted using Scheff's ideas for the psychological motivation of individuals (Scheff 1994). We have to account for two hostilities, of the Germanic settlers towards the Britons and of the Britons towards the settlers. Germanic attitudes to Rome and the Empire were a mix of hostility and an appreciation for wealth and career opportunities offered by Imperial service. The Empire was something they wanted to join and be part of, not to destroy. Waging war on the Empire was part of a strategy for having claims to service, payment or territory noticed. The settlers in Britain were not part of a cohesive people, under strong leadership. They were unlike the Goths or Vandals.

Moreover, they were heathens. We may surmise that the native Britons looked down upon these mercenary soldiers and their families for being outside the pale of civilisation. The Britons may also have felt a degree of defensiveness (in Scheff's term 'shame') about their having to rely on imported soldiers to maintain their new-found independence from the Empire itself. Early relations between the two peoples may well have been characterised by claims of superiority by the Britons and a feeling of inferiority among the Germans. Such would be a plausible setting for a psychology of low self-esteem being transmuted into feeling of hostility towards the Britons and of a reinforcement of Germanic identity. A negative feedback loop of shame would be built up (Scheff 1994) leading to anger being directed outwards between the two peoples. An independent Britain, no longer part of the Empire, feeling unsure of itself and its identity would reinforce solidarity through Christianity, a rediscovery of pre-Roman native identity (Geary 2002: 104-105) and feel resentful towards the 'barbarians' it saw itself relying on for its protection. Newly arrived Germanic settlers would feel excluded and discriminated against, angry about being excluded from the civilisation they wished to join and would overcome feelings of inferiority by holding onto their traditional religion and culture. Individuals would merge themselves into a group Germanic identity. Both sets of feelings would simply reinforce each other and lead to inevitable ethnic strife.

The myth of migration

The experience of migration seems to have left an echo in the later literature of the English (Howe 1989). This is seen particularly clearly in works that deal with episodes of Biblical history involving the migration of peoples. In his analysis of the poem *Genesis A*, Battles (2000) has shown how the description of the various migrations of the Jews has been described in terms which alter their original Biblical descriptions to fit a common pattern. This pattern would seem to reflect how the English saw their own migration history during the period when the poem was written (may be 8th century but certainly by the 10th century). Whether this consistent pattern of migration reflects the reality of events in the 5th and 6th centuries must be open to question. At the moment, we can neither prove nor disprove it. My own belief is that it should reflect reality for some parts of Britain at times during the immediate post-Roman period.

The picture presented in *Genesis A* is a simple one. The act of migration is portrayed in stages. There is the departure, the travel with household and family, the bringing of possessions and property, and the settling of fertile lands. The act of migration is provided with a motive: the search for more spacious territory. This would support the idea of overpopulation and rising sea levels putting pressure on resources as a factor in the Anglo-Saxon migration (Todd 1992). We can hardly use literary evidence on its own to support this idea. Nevertheless, the evidence of poems like *Genesis A* does allow us to identify how the English saw their own experience; how they articulated their own myth. A representative passage of the poem is lines 1730-1738:

Genesis (lines 1730-1738)
Gewat him þa mid cnosle ofer Caldea folc
feran mid feorme fæder Abrahames;
snotor mid gesibbum secean wolde
Cananea land. Hine cneowmægas,
metode gecorene mid siðedon
of þære eðeltyrf, Abraham & Loth.
Him þa cynegode on Carran,
æðelinga bearn, eard genamon,
weras mid wifum.

(Krapp 1931)

He took himself with his family through the people of Chaldea
journeying with his possessions the father of Abraham;
the wise man with his kin would seek
the land of Canaan. His kinsmen,
chosen by God travelled with him
from their native turf, Abraham and Lot.
Those nobles for themselves in the land of Harran,
sons of men, a homeland took,
men with their wives.

(Author's translation)

Within this passage, the key ideas are *gewat him þa mid cnosle, feran mid feorme, secean wolde land, of þære eðeltyrf, eard genamon, weras mid wifum* (they took themselves with their kin, journeying with their possessions, would seek land, from their native turf, took a homeland, men with their women). The settlement of Britain was thus seen not just as the Kentish myth would suggest, as the coming of soldiers, but as the true migration of families with women and children.

In Battles' view, the later English were not just revealing something of their myths, they were consciously aligning themselves with the Bible. A key element of this is the 'official' West Saxon myth of descent from one of the sons of Noah. The dispersal of the descendants of Noah was the founding act in the creation of the different peoples of the earth. One of these peoples was the English, a people coming into being through an act of migration. The last migration thus fulfilled the act of the first migration, recorded in the Bible. The Anglo-Saxon migrations were seen as a culmination of divine plan. In this sense, the later English could see themselves as a chosen people, and their rulers as the chosen leaders of this people. This cannot have been an original view of migration by the Angles, Saxons and others at the time but has considerable force as an after the fact justification, which could be a transformation of racial antagonism by some of the settlers at the time. Seeing the Britons as weaker, different or inferior, led to the view of being a divine scourge of the wicked Britons, which then became transformed into being the divinely ordained descendants of Noah, fulfilling God's plan for his people. Likewise, the divinely descended heathen kings could be transformed into Christians without losing their status as ordained rulers. In these ways, the views of the 5th or 6th centuries were transmitted in new guises into the 9th and 10th centuries.

Ethnic labels

Names and tribal groups

The use of names as ethnic labels is an important part of creating and maintaining ethnic identities. However, such names are themselves artificial constructs applied differently by members of the group and by outsiders; often with a carelessness that leaves the modern historian gasping in frustration. Names of peoples in the early medieval period were transient, changing in their usage according to context (Hines 1995, Pohl 1997). They might denote a particular people, or be applied to a geographical region. The same people may appear under a variety of names at the same time, depending on who is describing them or there might be various names used for different levels of social integration; the local, regional or general. We must also be aware that the names used by modern writers are often rationalisations masking these complexities.

For the period of the migration and conquest it is highly anachronistic to use the term Anglo-Saxons as though it were a contemporary term. The earliest usage of the term dates from the late 8th century on the continent, and 9th century in Britain (Pohl 1997). If used for this period, it must be accepted that it is a modern term being used as a convenient shorthand to describe the various Germanic peoples involved in the settlement of Britain at this time. We do not know how the settlers described themselves in the 5th century. We only know how others described them at this time. It is important to note that contemporaries seem to have thought of the Germanic settlers as one people, even though they may have been of mixed origins, e.g. Gildas who terms them all Saxons (York 2000). Saxons was the terms used most often by the British, Irish and Franks (following Roman Gaulish usage?). As well as Gildas, the *Life of Germanus* and the *Gallic Chronicle* all use the term Saxons. *Angles* was the term preferred by Bede and the Papacy, itself following Imperial Byzantine usage. The Angles could thus be contrasted with the Saxons still living on the continent (York 2000). Bede is our only informant that the Anglo-Saxons were also identified by the Britons as Germans, i.e. *Garmani* from the vulgar Latin form of *Germani* (Jackson 1953: 281). Bede actually used both the terms *Angli* and *Saxones*, sometimes explicitly as equivalents for each other (*Angli vel/sive Saxones*, i.e. Angles or Saxons). He did however tend to distinguish between them according to context. *Saxones* appear in his *Historia Ecclesiastica Gentis Anglorum* in military contexts, while *Angli* tend to appear in religious contexts (Pohl 1997: 19). It has often been stated that the influence of the Papacy using the term *Angli* for the Germanic peoples of Britain might have been the dominant influence for the use of the word in Christian circles (Wormald 1983).

The earliest historical evidence for the terminology referring to the Germanic settlers is largely continental. Pope Gregory consistently referred to them in his letters as the Angles, e.g. a letter to Candidus in 595 (Colgrave & Mynors 1969). He also referred to King Æþelberht of Kent as King of the Angles in a letter to him (Colgrave & Mynors 1969: 110) and he explicitly called the new Christian church the new church of the English *(nova Anglorum ecclesia)* in a letter to Archbishop Augustine (Colgrave & Mynors 1969: 104). By the 7th century, terminology was becoming more mixed. Papal letters to Eadwine of Northumbria addressed him as King of the English (Colgrave & Mynors 1969: 166 & 194), but a letter of Pope Vitalian to King Oswiu of Northumbria referred to him as King of the Saxons (Kirby 1991: 13). The fact that their Germanic cousins living in the old homeland were also known as Saxons could have led to confusion. The report of the Papal legation of 786 spoke of the land occupied by the Anglo-Saxons as English Saxony but the people as Angles.

The earliest native references begin in the later 7th century. The record of the Council of Hatfield in 679 referred to the language of the people as Saxon. The laws of Ine of the West Saxons use the term English as a racial opposite to Welsh, although the laws only survive in a copy made by King Ælfred in the 9th century (Whitelock 1955: 367). The Life of Wilfrið in c.710 used the term 'Saxon' in opposition to Pict when referring to Anglian Northumbria, and also described Wilfrið himself as Bishop of the Saxons. However, a *Life of Ceolfrið* (c.716), while referring to the island of 'Britain' as a collective geographical name, used 'English' for the name of the people and at one point also used the term 'England'. Felix's *Life of Guðlac* (730/49) referred to King Æþelred of Mercia as King of the English but later used the terms 'English' and 'Saxon' as synonyms. The West Saxon Wynfrið, better known as Boniface, the apostle of Germany, in letters of 736 and 738 used 'English' when referring to the church of the Anglo-Saxons and the Anglo-Saxon people as a whole. When writing to Æþelbald of Mercia in 746/47, he addressed him as 'King of the English'. However, he also identified his fellow missionary the Anglian Willibrord as a Saxon. Other 8th century writers also expressed a preference for the term 'English', e.g. Cuþberht in 754, Alhwine (Alcuin) in 787/96 and 797 in letters to Offa of Mercia and Osberht of Northumbria. A letter of King Cenwulf of Mercia in 798 to the Pope likewise referred to the English nation but to the Saxon land. The 'English people' were referred to in the decree of the synod of Clofesho in 803.

The fundamental document of the 8th century which provided a 'national' history for the Anglo-Saxons was the *Historia Ecclesiastica Gentis Anglorum* of Bede, written in 731. The very title of the work established the English as the people whose history he related, while also describing the Germanic settlers of Britain as being a mixture of Angles, Saxons, Jutes, Frisians and others. While he also referred at times to several peoples of the English *(gentes* or *populi Anglorum,* Fanning 1991), he also referred to Pope Gregory as having made 'our nation' *(nostram gentem)* into a church, echoing the words of Gregory in his letter to Augustine. For Bede, the English were the Germanic settlers of Britain who belonged to the Christian church owing allegiance to Rome. Others as we have seen seem to have been less sure how to describe their ethnic status.

An ecclesiastical origin for the use of the term *Angli* is doubted by Higham (1995: 250-254). He has suggested that the fact that Pope Gregory addressed King Æþelberht as *rex Anglorum* means that the term was accepted and recognised by the English themselves as entirely appropriate to them. He argues, it must therefore have been a currently used term during the 6th century before the Papal mission. Why this should be he feels may have been due to racial antagonism. If the terms *Saxones* and *Germani* were used by the Britons, then it may have been a choice by the Germanic settlers themselves not to use terms used by their enemies.

It is possible that a preference for English as opposed to Saxon may have been due to the connotations of each. The Saxons were soldiers in the employ Rome or Britain, *foederati*, and were the 'foreign barbarians'. This may have been somehow alien to the Germanic self-image, providing instead an image that was part of a Romano-British context. Settlers coming over as a community self-describing themselves and settling as *laeti*, with their customs and identities intact, were less dependent on their Romano-British context and could maintain a fully Germanic self-image as *Angli*. On the other hand, most scholars today would more likely agree with Hills (2003: 14-15) "It is no accident that the English call themselves by the name sanctified by the Church as that of a people chosen by God, whereas their enemies use the name originally applied to piratical raiders."

For reference when reading original documents, the various forms and grammatical cases of the ethnic terms used in Latin are as follows:

	nominative	accusative	genitive	dative	ablative
singular	*Saxo*	*Saxonem*	*Saxonis*	*Saxoni*	*Saxone*
plural	*Saxones*	*Saxones*	*Saxonum*	*Saxonibus*	*Saxonibus*
singular	*Anglus*	*Anglum*	*Angli*	*Anglo*	*Anglo*
plural	*Angli*	*Anglos*	*Anglorum*	*Anglis*	*Anglis*
singular	*Germanus*	*Germanum*	*Germanis*	*Germani*	*Germane*
plural	*Germani*	*Germanos*	*Germanorum*	*Germanis*	*Germanis*

In later Old English, the commonest ethnic terms used would be *Engle* for the Angles or English generally, *Seaxe* or *Seaxan* for the Saxons, and *Iote* (also *Eote* and *Iete/Yte* by regular sound changes in different dialects) for the Jutes. The genitive plurals would be *Engla*, *Seaxna* and *Iota*, the dative plurals would be *Englum*, *Seaxum* and *Iotum*. The descendants of the Britons (the Welsh and Cornish), along with the Irish (and their descendants the Gaelic Scots), still use instead the ancient terminology to describe the English, i.e. Saxons rather than Angles. To the Welsh the English people are the *Saeson* (Cornish *Sawson*), the English language is *Saesneg* (Cornish *Sawsnek*). For the Irish, the English are the *Sasanach* (Scots Gaelic *Sasunnach*).

On the other hand, the modern Welsh for England is *Lloegr*. It has been suggested that this means the 'land near the border' (Hamp 1982). Is it possible however that the word is related to modern Welsh *llogi,* meaning 'to hire'? In Old Welsh, the word *Lloegyr* is used to denote the land, and *Lloegrwys* the people, e.g. in the *Canu Taliesin* (Williams 1968: 3). Could it be that *Lloegrwys* had the original meaning of 'the hired ones', i.e. the mercenaries? Only those who have detailed knowledge of early British phonological changes could say (and I am not one of those).

Language

Germanic background

One of the most fundamental effects of the Germanic settlement of Britain was to change the language spoken by the inhabitants in most of the island from the native Celtic dialects to the Germanic language of English (e.g. Hines 1994). This is often put forward as one of the most powerful arguments in favour of substantial Germanic migration to Britain (Hooke 1997: 68). Although Hines (1990a) has questioned the supposition that language is a more reliable ethnic marker than material culture, he has accepted that in post-Roman Britain large numbers of migrants were needed to bring about the complete change in language of the south and east of the island. In the view of Charles-Edwards (2003), language was the primary ethnic marker in this period signalling the opposition between British and English.

We need to think carefully about how language contact and change could occur in the 5th or 6th centuries. Either a British population adopted English as their speech from a small group of elite overlords, or that speech was brought over to Britain by a large Germanic speaking population. The adoption of Germanic speech by a British population should have left discernible effects on the resulting Germanic dialect – either in vocabulary, or more likely in phonology (the sounds of speech) or grammar (e.g. word order, use of set phrases). Modern Welsh or Irish speakers of English cannot be mistaken for English speakers of English in that their forms of English are heavily influenced by the rhythms and grammar of Welsh and Irish. No such British influences have ever been detected in Old English. This would seem to show that any adoption of Germanic speech must have been by contact with a Germanic population that was large enough to swamp the British by providing an identifiable speech community; a community with its own recognisably right ways of speaking. A rural community of British speakers can only be influenced in its speech by contact with outsiders. These outsiders can be identified. There would be resident outsiders: clergy and estate officials (some of whom though may also be native to the village). There would also be visiting outsiders such as merchants, or outsiders that the villagers might themselves be visiting, such as in towns. Soldiers passing through or living nearby would be another source of contact; as would service in the army by selected villagers. These contacts are the dynamics of language contact and change. In 5th and early 6th century Britain, the clergy would have been British. It is likely that any merchants, as well as any urban populations that still existed would also be British. Of course, all three groups might speak Latin as much as British but would most likely be bilingual rather than monoglot Latin. The speech of the estate officials would depend on that of the landlords they represented but they must also have been able to speak with the villagers. For most of this period, the bulk of landlords in most areas may have been British and their officials likewise. In selected areas of Britain, there might have been Germanic lords and some Germanic officials. The army would have been the main transmitters of Germanic speech in direct contact with the villagers. It seems unlikely that armies passing through an area could be a transmitter of language change. Only a resident army with its families and followers amounting to a large influx of people could have overcome the reinforcement of British speech through the church, trade and towns, or the work of the local estate managers. We really do need to accept that a large number of migrants is needed to carry the Germanic language to Britain. British acculturation to Germanic would be more likely when the balance of speech contacts had changed as a result of political control passing into Anglo-Saxon hands in the 7th and 8th centuries. In these circumstances, the church and local officials, merchants and towns would be more likely to be dominated by English speakers, so long as that political control was based on large scale demographic support.

Date	Place	Inscription	Meaning
c.200	Nøvling (Denmark)	biðawarijaz talʒiðai	Biðawarijaz has carved
c.300	Torsbjærg (Denmark)	owlþuþewaz ni wajemariz	property of Ull's servant, of no ill fame
300/400	Pietroassa (Romania)	ʒutani o wihailaʒ	Goths' property, inviolate and holy
c.400	Einang (Norway)	.. ..ðaʒaz þaz runo faihiðo	(I Go)ðagastiz carved these runes
c.400	Gallehus (Denmark)	ek hlewaʒastiz holtijaz horna tawiðo	I Hlewagastiz of Holt made the horn
c.400	Stenmagle (Denmark)	haʒiradaz tawide	Hagiradaz made
c.500	Sjaelland (Denmark)	hariuha haitika fara uisa ʒibu auja	I am called Hariuha, the travel-wise, I give a chance
c.500/50	Lindholm (Sweden)	ek erilaz sa wilaʒaz hateka	I Erilaz, am called the cunning one

Table 6: Examples of early Germanic inscriptions.

English is a Germanic language that shares a common origin with such modern languages as Danish, Swedish, Dutch, Frisian and German. The earliest extensive evidence of Germanic languages is preserved in manuscripts of the 6th century onwards, or in earlier runic inscriptions. These now go back as far as 50/100 AD but are found mostly after c.200 AD. The area in which Germanic speech seems to have developed was southern Scandinavia, the southern shores of the Baltic and northern Germany. Germanic characteristics may have arisen in the local Indo-European dialects at around 500 BC (Mallory 1989). The Germanic homeland has been associated with the Jastorf archaeological culture centred on northern Germany and Jutland (Mallory 1989: 86-87). As already noted, scholars are now wary of associating particular archaeological cultures with communities of language speakers and it is likely that the earliest Germanic speakers occurred over a wider area than this. Early Germanic underwent several hundred years of development before emerging in the earliest runic inscriptions, yet these early inscriptions preserve a stage of Germanic before the development of the different languages recognised in later manuscripts (Page 1987). These early inscriptions can be hard to interpret. Some examples are given in Table 6. The various changes that produced the later literary languages began at different times in different places, e.g. Old High German changes beginning in the 7th century, Old Norse appearing in runes in the 8th century.

We do not have enough evidence to reconstruct in full the Germanic language of the 5th century as it was spoken in the English ancestral homelands. Instead, we have to make comparisons between the earliest manuscript English and the earliest manuscript forms of its continental cousins.

All Germanic languages share certain features that mark them out as a distinct group within the overall Indo-European family of languages (the family that includes among others Latin, Slavonic, Greek, Persian and Hindi). The most important of these are:

- Grimm's Law, or the first sound shift, whereby the pronunciation of various consonantal sounds was changed;
- Verner's Law, further changes to some of the consonants;
- stressed pronunciation on the first syllable of most words;
- treatment of the vowels 'o' and 'á';
- a set of parallel 'weak' endings for adjectives in addition to the normal 'strong' forms;
- a 'weak' past tense of verbs using endings based of the consonant 'd';
- a past tense for 'strong' verbs developed out of an original perfect tense.

Details of these features are given in Appendix 1. For now, it is enough to note that the language of the first English settlers was made up of the dialects of Germanic spoken along the shores of the North Sea and Baltic. It would be false to imagine that there was an English language before the migration to Britain. The settlers would have spoken various dialects of a common Germanic speech. These dialects were similar to the other dialects of continental Germanic spoken farther south and in Scandinavia. At the end of the 6th century, the Latin speaking Christian missionaries brought Frankish interpreters with them to Kent in order to speak with the Germanic settlers there (Webster & Backhouse 1991: 17). Frankish and English were evidently similar enough for mutual understanding. Given the absence of abundant inscriptions or documents, we cannot be sure at what date the innovations that marked English as different to its Germanic cousins began. Changes in the runic alphabet that reflect changes in the pronunciation in English can be seen from the early 6th century. When those changes became enough to demarcate English as a separate language from its cousins is impossible to say, but certainly not before completion of specifically English sound changes, such as the treatment of the sounds 'a', 'ai', 'au', 'á', 'æ', by the 8th century century. It is in that century that Willibald's life of Boniface referred to the Frisians as naming the Zuider Zee Aelmere "in their tongue", and to "the borders of those who are called in the native language Ostor- and Westeraeche" as though the continental languages were then separate from English (Whitelock: 717).

The similarity between English and its Germanic cousins can be seen by comparing the early versions of the first three lines of the Lord's prayer in each major language (Lass 1987: 39). It should be born in mind that the examples given vary in date and are mostly much later than the age of migration. They also use different spelling conventions to represent similar sounds. In the list below, the closest relative of Old English is Old Saxon, and the last in the list, Gothic, is the most distant.

Old English   *Fæder ure, þu þe eart in heofonum, si þin nama gehalgod, to becume þin rice, geweorðe þin willa on eorþan swa swa on heofonum*

Old Saxon   *Fader usa, thu bist an them himila rikea, geuuihid si thin namo, cuma thin riki, uuertha thin uuilleo, so sama an ertho, so an them himilo rikea*

Old High German   *Fater unser, thu in himilon bist, geuuihit si namo thin, quaeme richi thin, uuerdhe uuilleo thin, sama so in himile endi in erdhu*

Old Norse   *Faþer varr, sa þu ert i hifne, helgesk nafn þitt, til kome þitt rike, verþe þinn vile, sua a iorþ sem a hifne*

Gothic   *Atta unsar, þu in himinam, weihnai namo · þein, qimai þiudinassus þeins, waírþai wilja þeins, swe in himina jah ana aírþai*

The Germanic speech of Britain shared many features with the other dialects of western Germanic, which were not shared by dialects farther to the north or east. For example, nasal consonants were lost in certain combinations: 'mf', 'ns', 'nþ'. As a result, English is clearly closer to a language like Old Saxon than it is to Norse: English *fíf, us, óðer* (five, us, other), Old Saxon *fíf, us, oðar*, Old Norse *fimm, oss, annar*. In some circumstances, consonants were doubled in West Germanic, e.g. Old English *sellan* (sell = to give), Old Saxon *sellian*, Old Icelandic *selja*. A final '-ð' became '-d', e.g. Old English *gód* (good), Old Saxon *gód*, Old Icelandic *góðr*.

Even at the present day after 1,500 years of separate linguistic development, English as spoken is still recognisably a Germanic language. Its nearest relation is Frisian, now largely confined to Friesland in the northern Netherlands. Compare the opening to the Lord's Prayer in the modern versions of the two languages:

English   Our Father who art in heaven, hallowed be thy name, thy kingdom come, thy will be done, on earth as it is in heaven.

Frisian   *Us Heit yn 'e himel, lit jo namme hillige wurde, lit jo keninkryk komme, lit jo wil dien wurde op ierde likegoed as yn 'e himel.*

(Our father in the heaven, let your name holy be, let your kingdom come, let your will done be on earth like-good as in the heaven)

(from website:
http://www.georgetown.edu/cball/oe/pater_noster_germanic.html)

The runic alphabet

The early Anglo-Saxon settlers of Britain brought with them the runic alphabet as a means of writing down their language (Page 1999). This is preserved as inscriptions on articles such as brooches, weapon mounts, pots and bracteates (medallions). The total number of inscriptions surviving is very small and is an even smaller proportion of the total that must once have existed (Derolez 1990: 400-401). The letter forms found in the earliest inscriptions, of the 5th and 6th centuries, are the same as those used throughout the Germanic speaking areas on the continent. Particular early letter forms have more in common with runes from Scandinavia than from elsewhere in the Germanic area. The runes found at Vadstena and Grumpan in Gotland are particularly close to those found in England (Elliott 1989).

ᚠ	ᚢ	Þ	F	R	ᚲ	X	P
f	u	th	a	r	k	g	w

N	ᚿ	I	ᛢ	ᛣ	ᛤ	Y	ᛥ
h	n	i	j	é	p	z	s

↑	ᛒ	M	ᛗ	ᛚ	◇	ᛞ	ᛟ
t	b	e	m	l	ng	d	o

The only identifiably Anglo-Saxon variant in the early forms of letters is in ᚠ for the continental ᛥ ('s'). Among the other letters, the northern single-barred form N was used in preference to the more southerly double-barred ᚼ (which was the more usual form in later Anglo-Saxon runes). This is not surprising given the northern affinities of many of the Germanic settlers in Britain, e.g. the location of Angles in Schleswig and the origin of the Jutes in Jutland. Hines (1991) regards the northern N as a sign of Anglian affinity, as is the use of word dividers in the earliest inscriptions. Links with the Frisians can be seen in the Chessel Down sword inscription of the early-mid 6th century. This has a letter form unique to Anglo-Saxon and Frisian runes, ᚠ ('o'), the letter ᛟ being used to represent 'oi' (the 'o' mutated by a following syllable containing 'i'). Hines (1991) sees the ᚠ rune as an innovation of the 6th century, and another new rune, ᚠ used to differentiate 'a' from 'æ', as a Frisian innovation of the 7th century, adopted by the Anglo-Saxons from their cousins. Derolez on the other hand would see the new letters as having originated in the early 5th century on the continent before the Germanic settlement of Britain (Derolez 1990: 420). The new rune Y may also be an early form added to represent the 'æo' derived from Germanic 'au' (Derolez 1990).

Early runes are found on a variety of artefacts. Inscriptions are often carelessly applied, the act of inscribing being more important than leaving a visual form to be read (Page 1999: 113-114). Examples of early English inscriptions are given in Table 7 (Elliott 1989, Page 1999). Hines (1990b) lists all the known early runic inscriptions from Britain, and another useful listing of early runic inscriptions in Britain can be found at: www.ub.rug.nl/eldoc/dis/arts/j.h.looijenga/c8.pdf.

Century	Artefact	Inscription	Reading	Meaning
425/75	Caistor bone	ᚱᚨᛋᚺᚨᚾ	raihan	the roe deer's
400/600	Loveden Hill urn	ᚺᛋ ᚦᚠ ᛒᚠᚺ ᛁᛁᚦ ᛚᛅ ᚠ ᛁᛁ ᚺᚻᚠ	si þæ bædiiþ ic wiihlæ or siþæbæd þiuw hlaw	He orders it, I divine or Siþæbæd, the maid/servant, her grave
475/525	Chessel Down sword	ᚠᛚᚠ ᛬ ᛣᛟᚱᛁ	æco soiri	increase in sorrow
520/70	Watchfield fitting	ᚺᚠᚱᛁᛒᚠ ᛁ᛬ᚹᛚ ᚺᚠ	hariboki wusa	to Hariboc from Wusa
500/600	Ash-Gilton pommel	ᛗᚻᚺᛁᚷᛁᚺᛗᚱ	em sigimer	I am Sigimer
c.650	Harford Farm brooch	ᛚᛅᚺᚠ᛬ᚷᛁᛒᛟ ᛏᚠᚺᛁᚷᛁᛚᚠ	Luda giboetæ sigilæ	Luda mended the brooch

Table 7: Examples of early English inscriptions.

As noted by Hines (1991), the earliest inscriptions, of the 5th century, are all from East Anglia. This is one of the areas where Germanic settlement seems to have been earliest and densest. It is only in the 6th century that runes are found more widely. Up to c.625, runes were used mostly on high status artefacts; although not in prominently displayed positions (indeed, often hidden). After this date, the use of runes became more widespread and obvious, partly in emulation of the usage of the new Latin alphabet brought over by the Christian monks and priests (Hines 1991).

Personal Names

The Anglo-Saxon settlers shared the types of personal names they used with the rest of the Germanic peoples. Names in use among the English were of two main types: those formed from one word (the earliest type), and those from two (usually more aristocratic and/or later in date). Most Old English names have only survived in modern English use as surnames.

One-word names were either a noun, e.g. fugol (fowl = bird), adjective, e.g. hwita (white = fair) or a meaningless syllable, e.g. Lulla. Such names could be masculine or feminine. Names ending in -a would change this to -e for the feminine. Examples of one-word names (with a modern equivalent) are: Æsca (Ash), Alda (Old), Bassa (Bass), Cola (Cole), Dodda (Dodd), Ecga (Edge), Fisc (Fish), Goda (Good), Hudda (Hudd), Ifa (Ives?), Lilla (Lill), Manna (Man), Nunna (Nunn), Odda (Odd), Pymma (Pym), Rudda (Rud), Sweta (Sweet), Tata

(Tate), Þeoda (Theed), Ucca (Huck), Wada (Wade), Ycca (Hick?). Some names of this type acquired an extra syllable; e.g. Dudel, Duduc, Dudig, Tilne, Lullede. A common ending for names of this type by the 11th century was -ing, e.g. Bruning (Browning), Duning (Downing), Golding (Golding), Hearding (Harding), Leofing (Levinge), Manning (Manning), Sweting (Sweeting).

Two-word names were compounds of nouns or adjectives, e.g. Ælf (= elf) with gar (= spear) to give Ælfgar (Algar or Elgar). Any one word could be combined in principle with any other word, e.g. Ead with -gar, -mund, -red, -ward, -wulf etc. The words used for the second element were either solely masculine or solely feminine. Examples of male names are: Ælfstan (Allston), Æþelgeat (Aylett), Brihtmær (Brightmore), Cyneward (Kenward), Eadwulf (Edolls), Ealdnoð (Alnatt), Godric (Goodrich), Leofwine (Lewin), Ordwig (Ordway), Oswald, Sægar (Seager), Sigered (Sired), Wulfsige (Wolsey), Wigmund (Wyman). Examples of women's names are Ælflæd (Alflatt), Æþelgyfu (Ayliffe), Brihtwyn (Brightween), Cwenhild (Quenell), Eadgyð (Edith), Ealdþryð (Audrey), Mildburh (Milborrow), Sæfaru (Seavers).

English	Frankish	Gothic	Norse
Forewords			
Ald, Ælf, **Æþel**, Blæc, Cæd, Ceol, Coen, Cuð, Cweld, Cwen, Cwic, **Cyne**, **Ead**, **Ean**, Ecg, **Eormen**, Eorp, **Friðu**, **Here**, **Os**, Ræd, **Rice**, Sæ, Seax, **Sige**, **Þeod**	Bert, Bil, **Chari**, Child, Chilp, Chlod/th, Chrod, Dag, Gund, Ing, Mer, **Sigi**, **Theud**	**Ath**, **Athal**, **Airmn**, **Ans**, **Friþu**, Hild, **Kuni**, Ges, Gunþ, Hild, Himin, Huni, Liuf, **Reiki**, Sidu, **Sigi**, Swinþ, **Þiud**, Þuris, Wal, Wald, Wiþ, Wulþ	**Ead**, **Ean**, Frea, Heard, Heoro, **Here**, Hreð, Hroð, Hyge, Oht, Wealh
Afterwords - men			
bæd, **bald**, **berht**, **frið**, **gils**, helm, man, **red**, **ric**, **wald**, walh, **ward**, wine, wiu, **wulf**	**bad**, **bald**, **bert**, car, har, mer, **oald**, ram, **ric**, vech	**bad**, **frid**, gild, gis, **gisl**, mers, munds, **red/rid**, **reiks**, **wulfs**	**bald**, cyn, gar, **gils**, here, lac, mod, mund, **red**, ric, þeow, **ward**, **wulf**
Afterwords - women			
burh	berga, feld, hild, swintha	bairga, linda, merca, nanda, swinþa	þeow, waru

Table 8: Elements of personal names during the migration period.

A variety of words were used throughout the Germanic speaking area for forming names, many of which were common to several of the dialects. On the other hand, each dialect would also have its own preferred choices of words not found elsewhere. Some of the commonest elements found from the 5th to early 6th centuries are listed below (Table 8). These are names chiefly occurring among the royal families of the period; the best attested names in the sources of the time and in legend. Frankish names are taken from Wood (1994) and Gothic names from Wolfram (1988). Sources for Norse names of this period are scarce and rather than rely on the dubious historicity of Saxo Grammaticus, I have taken the Norse names that appear in *Beowulf* (Wrenn 1973), in their English spellings. Elements that are shared between the Anglo-Saxons and other groups are shown in bold. Of course, the names shown are not the only ones that would have been in use at the time and they ignore the one-element names. Nevertheless, they show something of the wide range of elements in use, and how much the English names formed part of an overall Germanic stock of names (in spite of some elements, e.g. *Cæd*, which is likely to be British in origin rather than Germanic).

The creation of English

The speech of the Germanic migrants to Britain was part of a relatively homogeneous north west Germanic language area. People living towards the western part of this area had begun to innovate in their speech by the time of the migration (Hines 1994: 55) and although the Anglo-Saxons were part of this innovating area, there was in no sense an English language at this time. In the period of migration and settlement, there must have been a great variety of dialects and mixing of linguistic forms from various parts of the north west Germanic area. Hines (1994: 56) notes the existence of northerly features within the predominantly western orientation of later Old English which could reflect this mixing of dialects. For example, Old English resembled Old Norse in dropping the consonant *h* between vowels, as in *séon* (to see) (Old Saxon *sehan*, Old Norse *sjá*). The combination *hs* became *x* in both Old English and Old Norse, e.g. OE *siex*, ON *sex*, OS *sehs*. These northern Germanic features are particularly notable within Anglian dialects of English, e.g. *we aron* (we are), Old Saxon *wi sind*, Old Norse *ver erum*. Nevertheless, these Scandinavian features are marginal in extent and do not affect the overall West Germanic nature of Old English (Hines 1990a). Language does not operate in isolation. People speak within social and political contexts and language is subject to forces which act above the conscious individual choice of the speaker. The growth of kingdoms from the late 6th century might well have involved a degree of standardisation of linguistic forms based around the preferred dialect of the new ruling families. Hines (1990a) has suggested that deliberate linguistic convergence was adopted in the Anglian areas to stress a common ethnic identity, merging forms from various parts of the Germanic homelands to create a language distinct from that of the continent. It may be that the growth of English as separate language was a consequence of political unification and must date from after the late 6th century. Hines (1990a) however would see the normalisation process as having taken place by c.600, presumably as a result of emulation among the newly created royal houses of the Anglo-Saxons. This would be a linguistic equivalent of the creation of a common material culture at the same time. We can question whether changes in language and material culture would move quite so closely in tandem. It is unfortunate that there is little evidence for the speech of the Germanic settlers in Britain until after the development of Christian literacy in the 7th century. The earliest occurrences in the fragmentary runic record in Britain show new letterforms reflecting distinctive English changes in pronunciation which can help to date the development of English. The letter ᚠ (a) is found in the admittedly Frisian 6th century gold solidus inscribed ᚻᛚᚱᛏᚠ ᛗᚠ ᚻᚾ. The letter ᚠ (o) is found firstly in the Undley bracteate, perhaps made in the early 5th century in southern Scandinavian (the Anglo-Saxon homeland). If correct, this is highly significant and shows English to have been developing distinctive features while its speakers were still on the continent. More certain is the letter's occurrence on the Chessel Down sword mount of the early 6th century. This suggests that English had arisen by the mid 6th century. This early form of English would have a great many dialectal varieties. With the rise of the Anglo-Saxon kingdoms, linguistic standards would be adopted to iron out the differences in dialect, although building on changes in pronunciation probably already begun while on the continent. It may be that this is the significance of Aþelberht's laws being written in English not Latin (as in Francia). He may have seen the use of the new Christian literacy allied with the royal prerogative of declaring law as part of a strategy to create and maintain a Germanic identity at the same time as claiming to be the heir to Roman Britain (Wormald 1999: 101). The Anglian and Saxon areas of England adopted different standards for their speech, which must reflect some desire to be differentiated from each other. How far this reflects a different mode of origin for the Saxon kingdoms in the 5th and 6th centuries must remain for the moment an open but fascinating question.

Model of language replacement

British communities must have remained even in the areas of heaviest Germanic settlement. In areas conquered in the 7th century, Britons must have been in the majority. We lack the detailed knowledge to construct a map of where languages were spoken locally in this period and so can only model by guesswork the process of language replacement by which British was replaced by Germanic as the spoken language of the native-born people of south eastern Britain. We need to be cautious about the processes of language change in the days before state education and mass media. Such change must have been geographically varied and possibly much slower than we think. Some writers now accept that replacement of British speech by Germanic dialects was likely to have been a complex and extended phenomenon (Hills 2003: 55). Assimilation and loss of language by the British would be a result of low social as well as political status (Härke 1997).

What would be the fastest realistic model of replacement in originally British speaking communities? We need to assume that the first generation born after Anglo-Saxon rule grew up monolingual British. Their parents would be monolingual British, as would their neighbours and friends. Their contacts with Germanic speakers would be minimal, and at most they might pick up an understanding of some Germanic words or phrases. We might assume that their children would grow up in a world of greater Germanic contact and be bilingual; speaking British at home and English to many of their neighbours or to officials of the new landlords and kings. Let us then assume that their children grow up monolingual English, no longer needing to speak British to their parents and family and content to speak the language most useful within their social relations outside the home. Let us further assume that marriage took place at around 25 years of age and that few people would live beyond 60. We can call this a three generation model of replacement. (Such a model ignores the likely realities of language contact and should be regarded only as an intellectual exercise.)

We can follow the implications of a three-generation model by applying it to the first of the Germanic kingdoms on British soil, Kent. To estimate the earliest possible loss of British speech, we will assume an early time-scale for Germanic control, i.e. political takeover of Kent in 434. The results are presented in Table 9.

Stage of life	1st generation	2nd generation	3rd generation
birth	434	460	486
marriage	459	485	511
death	494	520	546

Table 9: Stages of loss of British speech in Kent.

We can see that the last monoglot British speakers would die out around 500, and that British speech would stop altogether around 530 with only a few aged bilingual speakers surviving after 520. Similar figures are presented in Table 10 for the Wessex heartland, Bernicia and Elmet (see Appendix 2 for an explanation of the 530 and 575 dates for Wessex and Bernicia).

Stage of life	Wessex	Bernicia	Elmet
birth	530-556-582	575-601-627	616-642-668
marriage	555-581-607	600-626-652	641-667-693
death	590-616-642	635-661-687	676-702-728
British dies out	c. 620	c. 670	c. 710

Table 10: British survival in other parts of England.

The last bilingual British speakers would reach 60 years of age c.85 years after Germanic takeover. If we allowed for a later age at marriage and a handful of people living to 75 then the extinction of British could have happened c.105 years after takeover. It must be emphasised that a three-generation model is the most rapid model of language replacement. It is highly likely that most communities took longer than this. In the case of Cornish, whose decline can be measured, it took 600 years from the first loss of Cornish speech in the modern County of Cornwall for the language to disappear as English advanced westwards towards the last Cornish stronghold in Penwith (Gardner 2002). If British replacement was at all slower than the three-generation model, as the likely context of language contact and change would suggest, then it is perfectly feasible to see British speech lasting well into the 8th century in parts of Anglo-Saxon Britain. It may be these communities which lie behind the Walton place-names which occur all over the country, as Gelling (1993) has pointed out. Late survival of British is demonstrated in various sources. Gelling (1978: 100) notes that for Lichfield in Staffordshire to derive from the British *Letocetum* it would have to pass through Primitive Welsh *Luitged* some time after 675. The latest parts of Britain to be annexed from the British lay in eastern Powys (around the Wrekin), Maund, Craven, Rheged, and Devon. These were incorporated into the new Anglo-Saxon kingdoms in the mid to late 7th century, and it is likely that British speech would have continued up to the end of the 8th century. It is even conceivable that pockets of British speech might have survived into the 9th century in these areas, although we have no evidence to support this other than place-names using the racial term *Bretta*, which might have been coined by Vikings. One peculiarity of areas like Devon, Craven and eastern Powys (Shropshire) is that their place-names are overwhelmingly English, with a very low survival of British names (Gelling 1993). Devon can be contrasted with Cornwall, taken over only 200 years later, where the stock of names is mostly British. Gelling suggests that these areas may have a stock of names that is largely administrative in nature rather than deriving from popular speech. Upon annexation, their landlords and churches became English but there was no large-scale immigration of Anglo-Saxon farmers, leaving the natives in place and British speech to survive longer than elsewhere, hidden behind an administrative geography. Gelling may well be right but the reasons are likely to be more complex than this. The difference between the English annexation of these areas and other regions farther east is that they were taken under English rule by Anglo-Saxon kings in charge of the administrative apparatus of an existing kingdom. They were also brought under the rule of Christian kings, who could therefore take over the apparatus of a landowning church from the British with little disruption. We should also not forget that both Devon and Shropshire (and Craven) were border areas, facing British opposition from neighbouring kingdoms. They would need securing with a thoroughly loyal Anglo-Saxon landowning class, and presumably a class of warriors at lower level to provide a kind of 'gentry' that might have been more thoroughly Anglo-Saxon than back in the east. British villages would find themselves in contact with English speaking clergy, most likely English speaking estate officials, English speaking merchants and by this period English speech in such towns as preserved urban functions. Their situation would thus be different to their cousins in the east of Britain, in the 5th and 6th centuries, whose speech might leave more of an impact on place-names.

Literary evidence for the survival of British speech is rare. It is sometimes said that the *Life of Guðlac* by Felix has evidence of language survival in the Fens in the 8th century. Guðlac was subject to visions in which he was attacked by what he interpreted as demons speaking British. The vision occurred at a time (704/09) of Welsh attacks on Mercia and Colgrave (1956) saw the British speech of the demons as part of an attempt to demonise the Welsh enemy, and so could not be taken as evidence for British speech around Guðlac's Fenland retreat. More secure evidence for British speech in areas under English rule comes from the *Life of Wilfrið* by Stephanus. Around 670, Wilfrið brought back to life the son of a woman in Tidover, near Harrogate. He claimed the boy for a monastic life when he was seven years old but the mother objected and ran away with her son. They were eventually found by Wilfrið's reeve "hidden among others of the British race" (Colgrave 1927). It has been suggested that the place they were found was Walton Head, not that far from Tidover (Faull & Stinson 1986), and showing by its name the late survival of British speakers (Jones 1979: 33). Both places were part of a multiple estate that might have a British origin (Jones 1979). The boy was taken for the monastic life and given a new name, the impeccably English Eodwald, thus hiding his original ethnicity.

Jackson has provided the most detailed examination of the geography of British survival in place-names in southern Britain (Jackson 1953: 220-241). He identified 4 zones with different linguistic characteristics. Zone one coincides with the area of primary Germanic settlement and the heaviest concentration of early Anglo-Saxon material culture. It extends from the Yorkshire Wolds southwards, covering eastern England through the east midlands to the middle Thames and on to include the North and South Downs. British place-names in this zone are very rare and are confined mainly to major features of the landscape. Zone two extends from the north east of England through Yorkshire and the Peak District into the west midlands and Cotswolds southwards to the Wessex Downs. British names are commoner in this area and extend to smaller landscape features. Zone three consists of discrete areas: to the east of the Pennines, to the west of the Severn and the south west of England from the two River Avons (Hampshire and Somerset) as far as the Tamar. In this area, British names are much commoner and survive for small local landscape features. It is only in zone three that we must modify the statement that there is no British influence on English pronunciation. There are a few place-names in this zone in which the British stress pattern has been preserved in modern place-names (Jackson 1953: 226), e.g. Clovélly in Devon ('é' indicating the main bearer of stress). That zones one and two were settled by Germanic groups much earlier than zone three is shown by the fact that names in these zones preserve the ancient Celtic word order of adjective coming before the noun it modifies, while zone three has the more modern order of noun before its modifying adjective. Zone four consists of Cornwall, Wales and the south west corner of Herefordshire. British names dominate this zone with little sign of English influence. The characteristics of the first three zones are summarised in Table 11.

Survival of British settlement names, as opposed to landscape features, in areas of Anglo-Saxon rule is very rare. Some English place-names incorporate Latin words and must have been in use in Roman Britain, e.g. *campus* (plain), *castra* (fort, walled town), *ecclesia* (church), *fons* (spring), *portus* (harbour), *strata* (road), *vicus* (village, township) (Gelling 1978). It is interesting that the distribution of many of these, e.g. *campus, fons, portus*, is concentrated in the southern part of Britain in a way that does not relate to Jackson's zones (Gelling 1978: 85). Indeed, they seem to be restricted largely to the areas of Britain under Saxon rather than Anglian control or settlement. It is yet another line of evidence that suggests that Saxon settlement was different in kind to that of the Angles, and may have taken place within a functioning late Roman administrative structure.

Features	British names Zone 1	British names Zone 2	British names Zone 3
towns	yes	yes	yes
villages	very rare	rare	yes
rivers	few	some	common
streams	none	none	yes
hills	few	some	common
woods	few	some	common
language	early compounds e.g. *Noviomagos* = new field	early compounds e.g. Malvern = bald hill	late compounds e.g. Cardew = black fort

Table 11: Zones of British place-names.

The British words that survive in English place-names tend to be those that denote topographical features. Many still survive in Welsh, Cornish and have related forms in Gaelic names (Table 12).

Some place-names seem to indicate the existence of British speakers well into the period of English rule. These are those that refer directly to the Britons themselves; compounds of *Bretta-*, *Cumbra-* and *Wealla-* (respectively the Britons', the Cumbrians', the Welsh). It has been suggested that names in *Bretta-* could be Scandinavian in origin as well as English and so do not have the same significance as the others, perhaps denoting Britons arriving in England with the Vikings (Cameron 1977: 43). However, survival of British speech into the 9th century is perhaps just as likely, as noted above. Names in *Cumbra-* are found throughout Jackson's zones 2 and 3, and occasionally in zone 1, but are hardly plentiful. Much commoner are names in *Wealla-*. Unfortunately, these can be confused with names deriving from *wall* (wall), *wald* (wood) and *walle* (well or spring). If compounded with late place-name elements like -*tun* or -*cot*, they could also refer to the use of *wealla* to means slaves' settlement (Gelling 1978). However, it does seem that a large number of names like Walton (from *Weallatun*) refer to survival of British speaking populations into the 8th century. The element *tun* is the commonest term for a township applied after the period of settlement and belongs largely to the 8th and 9th centuries, denoting newly nucleated townships (Hooke 1997).

Welsh	Cornish	Gaelic	meaning
cadair	cadar	cathair	seat, stronghold
cam	cam	cam	crooked, bent
cefn	keyn	(droim)	ridge
cil	kyl	cuil	recess, corner
coed	cos	(coille)	wood
craig	*crak	creag	rock
crug	cruk	cruach	mound
crwm	crom	crom	crooked, bent
cwm	*comm	(gleann)	valley
du	du	dubh	black
dwr/dwfr	dowr	dobhar	water
egwlys	eglos	eaglais	church
glyn	*glynn	gleann	deep valley
pen	pen	ceann	head, top, end
pwll	pol	poll	pool, pit
rhos	*ros	(riasg)	moor

Table 12: Some surviving Celtic elements in modern place-names.

Gelling (1978) rightly pointed out that Jackson's map was produced on the basis of surveys which would now be considered inadequate. His zones can only be provisional until detailed studies have been made of the whole of England to a similar standard of detail by scholars sensitive to the possibilities of British survival. Nevertheless, the broad outlines are likely to remain unchallenged, while greater detail may elaborate the picture. Gelling (1978: 90) also noted that where detailed studies of place names have been undertaken, they often reveal clusters of British names within a region, suggestive of population survival at a local scale. Studies of how British place-names in these areas were adopted into English can reveal evidence for late retention of British speech. Names may preserve changes in the pronunciation of British that occurred after the mid 7th century, as already mentioned, e.g. Lichfield in Staffordshire (Gelling 1978: 100-101).

One area that we know was not taken under English rule until the 7th century was the kingdom of Elmet (map p. 268), annexed by Northumbria in 617. Taking Elmet as the area between the Rivers Wharfe and Don (Taylor 1992), an examination of township names shows there is little patterning in the survival of British names. There are three *castra* names, all on major river crossings along the Roman road north to south from York. Other names are scattered randomly throughout the area, from the low-lying Humberhead Levels to the upland Pennines. The only concentration of names is a small group of British names, or names showing British survival, between the River Calder and the upper River Dearne (Walton, Chevet, Crigglestone and West Bretton). This area is at the geographical centre of Elmet, well away from any of its borders. There is no concentration near any of the three *castra* sites. The pattern seems best explained by chance random survival of British speech during the Anglicisation of the area during the 7th and 8th centuries, perhaps in pockets where British landowners remained under the new regime. If so, then the British landowners may have been more tolerated in the middle of Elmet, away from its potentially sensitive borders. This would be supported by the evidence of the early English place-names in Elmet presented earlier.

Religion

The importance of religion for ethnicity is that it offers a set of rituals and a way of structuring opinions and views for the group to observe and take part in. Religion is a way of sharing an identity that may be 'above' ethnicity but its political context ensures that ethnicity and religion mutually support one another. Religions differ widely in their practices and organisation, with the result that ethnic marking by religion is not uniform (Enloe 1996). Religions with elaborate hierarchy and well-defined ritual practices provide the rich tapestry of symbolism and behaviour which can more easily be mobilised in the service of signalling ethnic difference than those with little structure and varied, less structured beliefs. We shall see that little differences in practice can assume great significance within highly structured religions if the political context demands the marking of ethnic boundaries. In the context of early medieval Britain, we might expect that native British Christians would use their religious beliefs as an important signifier of identity whereas the heathen Germanic peoples might lay less stress on their religious beliefs and use other means to emphasise their difference. Once the Germanic peoples in Britain adopted Christianity, we should not be surprised to see minor differences in practice become emphasised in order to maintain the differences between Anglo-Saxon and Briton at a time of intense political competition between the two.

Heathen Germanic settlers were migrating to a Britain that was nominally Christian. Although some writers maintain that Christianity was an important part of a Roman cultural identity (e.g. Loveluck 2002), the dominant position of Christianity was a recent phenomenon. It was only after 391 that the Imperial government made Christianity the sole religion of the Empire by officially closing the pagan temples and making pagan worship unlawful. This decision seems not to have been implemented fully in Britain, and paganism continued as the preferred religion of some of the elite in the diocese (Dark 1994: 20 & 34, Henig 2002). It may be that Christianity only became dominant in Britain in association with the events that led to the usurpation of Constantinus III, who might have been a representative of a militant and aggressive Christianity (Dark 1994). The first Germanic settlers would thus arrive in a land where late Roman paganism was flourishing within living memory, and might still have been the preferred private belief of some among the native British elite. By the mid 5th century, most practising pagans will have died and any opposition to the new Christian order would have to be kept alive by their children and grandchildren.

It is in this context that we must see any alliances and contacts between the native elite and Germanic families. The Germanic migrants remained heathen with no signs of conversion by the native Britons. Acculturation of Britons to a Germanic identity would thus involve a conversion of religion for any Christian. It might also involve a re-emergence of latent paganism, in which adoption of Germanic identity would allow opposition to be expressed to the dominant Christianity by certain disaffected elite families. Germanic political control of British *civitates* or provinces would not be welcomed by most Britons so long as the Germans remained heathen (Dark 2000). On the other hand, Britons who were less attached to the new Christianity might welcome association with Germanic settlers and even be prepared to adopt a Germanic identity. Thus, it is in religion that we may have a positive factor in favour of acculturation for some Britons. Perhaps an anti-Christian stance might lie behind the curious concentration of Germanic artefacts around the area of Dorchester on Thames, in an area that has produced evidence for late Roman paganism (Dark 1994: 11). It is precisely this area that seems to be the core of the *Gewisse*, later known as the West Saxons - ruled by a royal family with a collection of notably Celtic names in its early pedigree.

Evidence for Anglo-Saxon heathenism

When trying to understand the religion of the Germanic peoples in the 5th and 6th centuries, too much reliance is often placed on the literary sources for Norse mythology, committed to parchment in the 12th century at the earliest. The mythology of the later Norse documents cannot be applied uncritically to all earlier Germanic peoples, as should be evident from the evidence of Tacitus for different beliefs among the Germanic peoples of the 1st century. Branston (1957: 186-187) however would allow that there is much in common between English and Norse mythology. This is certainly true for the gods worshipped by the Germanic settlers in Britain. However, the evidence for Germanic paganism in Britain is slight. Archaeological evidence is rare and seldom incontestably pagan (Dark 2000: 82). It is the documentary and place-name evidence which gives us our best picture of Germanic religious belief and practice, albeit partial and distorted. However, the documentary evidence is also not without its problems, being both Christian in origin and late (Hines 1997).

Place-names are a major strand of evidence for Germanic heathen belief in Britain. However, we are faced with the difficulty that many of the place names, especially those of townships, might well originate in later times when the memory of heathenism was stronger than its practice. Unless we know that a name was coined during the early phases of migration, we cannot be certain that religious practice took place. We can though suggest that names that are compounded with words meaning temple or shrine can reasonably be supposed to indicate that religious practices did take place there. The lists of place-names given below have been compiled from Branston (1957: 41-43), Gelling (1978: 158-161), Hines (1997: 385), and Wilson (1992: 7-21). Names no longer in use but surviving in historical documents are in italics, and a question mark indicates a name that does not certainly contain the element indicated.

Ealh (also *alh*)

This was the term usually used to translate temple:

Alkham (Kent)

Hearg (also *hearh*)

This term seems to have indicated a tribal shrine, often located on a hill top (probably as a convenient communal meeting place):

Harrow-on-the-Hill (Middlesex), Harrough (Suffolk), Harrow Hill? (Northampton), Harrow Hill? (Sussex), Harrow Hill? (Warwick), Harrow Hill? (Worcester), Harrow Hill Field? (Warwick), Harrowden (Bedford), Harrowden (Northampton), Harrowdown? (Essex), *Haregedon* (Sussex), *Harowedownehulle*? (Oxford), Peper Harrow (Surrey), Mount Harry? (Sussex), *Besingahearh* (Surrey), *Cheseharegh* (Sussex).

Wíg (also *wíh, wéog, wéoh*)

These were probably wayside shrines in personal ownership rather than tribal:

Wye (Kent), Weedon (Buckingham), Weedon Beck (Northampton), Weedon Lois (Northampton), Waden Hill? (Wiltshire), Weeford (Stafford), Wyfordby? (Leicester), Wyham (Lindsey), Weyhill?? (Hampshire), Weoland? (Wiltshire), Wheely Down (Hampshire), Whiligh? (Sussex), Willey (Surrey), Willey? (Warwick), Weoley? (Worcester), Wysall? (Nottingham), Wyville (Kesteven), *Cusanweoh* (Surrey), Patchway (Sussex).

In addition to these, as suggested by John Dodgson, it may be that names in 'wing' also preserve this element (Hines 1997: 387), e.g. Wing (Buck.) or Wingham (Kent).

The names of various gods are also preserved in place-names. It is difficult to say whether the attribution of a name shows that the god was worshipped at that place or whether he/she was a figure of myth to which strange landscape features could be attributed, especially man-made features like barrows or dykes, e.g. Wansdyke. Nevertheless, the names do show which gods were part of the intellectual universe of the population.

Ós (plural possessive *ésa*)

This means simply a god and was used in its possessive plural form to mean the place of the gods. None of the following place-names are certainly derived from the word:

Eisey? (Wiltshire), Easole? (Kent), Easewrithe? (Sussex)

Wóden

Woden was the equivalent of the Norse *Óðinn*; the ruling god of wisdom and battle. He was referred to in later English sources as the ancestor of kings, in one of the charms of the late 10th century (the *Nine Herbs Charm*, Branston 1957) and in the *Maxims* copied in the Exeter Book of Old English poetry (as the creator of idols and ruler of all creation). He may be the god (*os*) referred to in the Rune Poem as the origin of all speech (*os byð ordfruma ælcre spræce*, Dobbie

1942: 28). If so, this is an early form of his link with eloquence that is seen in Norse mythology. Equated with the Roman god Mercury, he was also mentioned in *Salamon and Saturn* as the creator of writing, a clear evocation of the Norse myth of his creation of runes (Owen 1981: 11). Associated with Woden is the spear, and spear shaped amulets have been found on women's bodies in burials (Owen 1981: 15-18). Names including Wóden are:

Woodnesborough (Kent), Wednesbury (Stafford), *Wodnesbeorg* (Wiltshire), *Wodnesdene* (Wiltshire), Wansdyke (Somerset), Wansdyke (Wiltshire), *Wedynsfeld*? (Essex), *Wodnesfeld* (Essex), Wednesfield (Stafford), *Woddesgeat* (Wiltshire), Wensley (Derby), *Wodneslawe* (Bedford), Wormshill?? (Kent).

Woden's by-name of *Grim* is also found in place-names:

Grimsdyke/ditch 18 instances in 11 shires (Berkshire, Cambridge, Cheshire x4, Essex, Hertford, Middlessx, Nottingham, Oxford x2, Surrey x2, Wiltshire x3, Yorkshire), Grimsbury (Berkshire, Oxford), Grimes Graves (Norfolk), Grim's Hill (Gloucester), Grimspound (Devon), *Grimeswrosne* (Hereford, Warwick).

Þunor (also Þunur, Þuner)

Still surviving as the modern English word thunder, he was the equivalent of Norse *Þórr*; the protector of the gods against the giants (the personified forces of nature) and so popular with crop growing farmers. His characteristic weapon was the hammer, amulets of which have been found in graves in Kent (Owen 1981: 25). It may be noteworthy that most of his place-names are in the Saxon areas of Britain. However, the swastika symbol usually associated with Þunor is found widely on burial urns within the area of Anglian Britain (Owen 1981, Wilson 1992). This same symbol can also be found in the Lindisfarne Gospels, on the carpet page of St John's Gospel; not a place we would expect a reference to Þunor! Þunor is mentioned in an entry in the *Anglo-Saxon Chronicle* under 640, where two sons of King Eormenred of Kent are said to have been martyred by him (*wurðan gemartirode of Ðunore*). Þunor is found in place-names as follows:

Thundersbarrow? (Sussex), Thunderfield (Surrey), *Thunresfeld* (Wiltshire), Thunderhill? (Surrey), *Thunreslau* (Essex), *Thunoreshlæw* (Kent), Thunderley (Essex), Thundersley (Essex), *Thunreslea* (Hampshire x2), Thursley (Surrey), *Thunorslege* (Sussex), Thurstable?? (Essex), Thundridge?? (Hertford), *Thureslege*?? (Rutland).

Tíw (also Tíg)

As the English equivalent of Norse *Tyr*, he was the god of courage and war; perhaps more important in earlier times. The runic letter ↑, representing the god's name, is often found inscribed on weapons of the period, invoking his protection. This practice was described in the 13th century Norse *Sigrdrifumal* (Owen 1981: 28). Tiw was possibly a god of importance to indivdiduals like warriors but not to communities. Only a few places contain the name of Tíw:

Tysoe (Warwick), *Tislea* (Hampshire), Tuesley? (Surrey), *Tyesmere* (Worcester), Tiffield?? (Northampton).

Fríg (also Fréo)

The only goddess possibly mentioned in place-names, she was the equivalent of Norse *Frigg*, the wife of *Óðinn*. There is also the possibility that her name has been confused with that of the Norse *Freyr*, the goddess of fertility. Places that may include her name are:

Frobury? (Hampshire), Friden? (Derby), Freefolk? (Hampshire), Froyle? (Hampshire), Fryup? (North Riding), Frethern? (Gloucester).

The names of the gods are also preserved in later literary sources. Indeed, we still use them in the days of the week, an inheritance we share with our continental cousins, as Table 13 shows.

Modern English	Old English	German	Old Icelandic
Monday	Monandæg	Montag	Mánadagr
Tuesday	Tiwesdæg	Dienstag	Tysdagr
Wednesday	Wodnesdæg	Mittwoch	Óðinsdagr
Thursday	Þunresdæg	Donnerstag	Þórsdagr
Friday	Frigedæg	Freitag	Frjádagr
Saturday	Sæternesdæg	Samstag	Laugardagr
Sunday	Sunnandæg	Sonntag	Sunnudagr

Table 13: Names for days of the week.

Branston has shown (1957) that other figures from the world of the gods might also be mentioned in later literature. The legend of Norse *Heimdall* retrieving the Brosingamene necklace of *Freyja* was referred to in Beowulf (ll 1197-1200 as *Hama*). The legend of Norse *Baldr* might also have been known among the early Anglo-Saxons and could have influenced the depiction of Christ's crucifixion in the *Dream of the Rood*; notably the description of Christ as wounded with darts, and the weeping of all creation on his behalf (Branston 1957: 168-169). Even where no legends survive, the names themselves might still occur as ordinary names: Norse *Freyr* as *frea* meaning lord, Norse *Baldr* as *bealdor* also meaning lord, Norse *Ullr* as *wuldor* meaning splendour. *Freyr* was also known under the by-name *Ingvi-Freyr* and might be represented by the figure of Ing in the *Rune Poem* (Owen 1981: 30). His association with the boar might lie behind the use of boars as decorative motifs on archaeological finds of the time (Owen 1981). One of the less well-known gods was *Seaxnet*, preserved as the ancestor of the kings of the East Saxons. He does not occur in Norse myth, but was named in an 8th century Old Saxon oath, alongside Woden and Thunor (Wilson 1992: 38).

Literary sources provide some evidence of links with continental Germanic religious practices and beliefs. Bede made some incidental reference to religious practice when he noted that priests were forbidden to bear arms or ride stallions (Colgrave & Mynors 1969: 185). This might relate to the information given by Tacitus some 700 years earlier who noted that arms were forbidden among the Angli during the worship of *Nerthus* (Mattingley & Handford 1970: 135). Tacitus also reported that priests would dress as women among at least one of the Germanic tribes (Mattingley & Handford 1970: 137). Could this denial of male sexuality be a link with the ban on riding stallions? Pope Gregory also referred to heathen practices when he mentioned the sacrifice of oxen as part of religious rituals. This might receive archaeological confirmation from the find of over 1,000 ox skulls at Harrow Hill in Sussex (Owen 1981: 45).

It must be said that the archaeological evidence for religious practice - as opposed to burial ritual - is very weak. There is only one clear case of a temple having been excavated, that at Yeavering royal palace by Brian Hope-Taylor. This was a rectangular building with opposed entrances in the middle of the long sides. The building was 11 metres (36 feet) long and 5½ metres (18 feet) wide. It was aligned north-south and inside its southern end was a line of three free-standing posts (most likely idols representing gods). A pit inside and next to one of the doors contained animal bones, including fragments of ox skulls, the probable remains of sacrifices. No other convincing case has yet been made for the excavation of a temple of this period, although various structures have been found associated with cemeteries which might best be regarded as shrines or memorial structures. Bede described a temple with idols within an enclosure at Goodmanham but this has not been found archaeologically. Unfortunately, archaeological evidence for temples elsewhere in the Germanic world is equally rare. Our only comparative example might be at Hofstaðir in Iceland (Orchard 1997), where a building containing animal bones and charcoal in a pit was interpreted as the temple attached to the farmstead described in a 13th century saga. The saga described the temple as having a door in its side wall and images of the gods in one part of the building. It also had a choir like construction and an altar, for which there was no archaeological evidence. There are certainly similarities with the temple at Yeavering but we should like to have a wider selection of excavated sites to be absolutely certain that Yeavering belonged firmly within a Germanic tradition.

The combination of the above, varied evidence means that there can be little doubt that Germanic religion was practised in Britain and must have been brought to these shores by Germanic settlers. It would have strongly differentiated them from the Christian British. The religious beliefs and practices of the settlers should also have been noticeably different to those of the Britons who had kept to their pagan heritage. Although parallels can be drawn between Celtic and Germanic religion, the specific details of the two were quite different. Names of the British gods can be found in place-names of the Roman period surviving at the present day, e.g. Carlisle (from *Luguvalium* containing the name of the Celtic god Lugos, Jackson 1953: 39). However, there are no certain traces of the British gods in the English language or in the evidence for heathen religion among the Germanic settlers. The exception to this may be the reference by Bede to the festival of *Modranect* (mothers' night) on the 25th December (Owen 1981). The idea of a group of mothers (in Latin *matres* or *matrones*), earth mothers and guardians of the land's fertility, is found among the Celts (MacCana 1983: 43-48) and might have been a British heathen festival. However, the idea of mother goddesses was also familiar to the Germanic peoples (Davidson 1993: 47-48), so we cannot be sure this is a Celtic religious survival among the Anglo-Saxons (Owen 1981: 34-37).

The beginnings of Christianity

The adoption of Christianity marked a break with traditional links between the Germans in Britain and their continental past, and emphasised instead strong links with the Christian rulers of the Franks and with Rome. Although the conversion may have been an act of faith for some, for others it was as a political act by the newly emerging Anglo-Saxon kings as part of a way of enhancing their power and prestige. This is not to deny that faith may have played a part but religion was deeply embedded in the society and politics of the time. Religious change cannot be considered apart from material considerations. The advantage of conversion was that it strengthened the role of the king and acted as a way of binding together the newly emergent kingdoms. On the one hand, it brought the Anglo-Saxon kingdoms into a closer relationship with the Franks and with Rome, but on the other it must have entailed a rejection of old alliances and connections with cousins across the North Sea among the as yet heathen Frisians and Saxons. Attempts to heal this breach would take place in Christian missions to the continent of the 7th and 8th centuries.

The importance of Christianity for the Germanic peoples of Britain as a means of asserting a new identity cannot be underestimated. At a time of political disunity and conflict, it was the adherence to Roman Christianity and the authority of Canterbury that would eventually provide a unifying framework whereby the Germanic inhabitants could think of themselves as one people. However, this could not happen until the bulk of the Germanic settlers had been converted. Christianity in the early 7th century was a divisive force that had little part to play in forging ethnic identity. The advent of Christianity among the Germanic kingdoms took place in a piecemeal fashion, intimately connected with the fortunes and ambitions of the various kings. The first conversion, of Æþelberht of Kent after 597 has been placed in a plausible and wider political context by Higham (1997). This was largely shaped by the events of Frankish dynastic politics and the desire of the Kentish kings to achieve greater political standing by exploiting their Frankish connections. The later conversions of Essex and East Anglia took place against a backdrop of Kentish supremacy in southern Britain. Essex relapsed into heathenism after Æþelberht's death in 616. Rædwald's conversion to Christianity in East Anglia was dubious, and the kingdom had to wait until after 631 for Christianity to be securely established. Even Kent relapsed between 616 and 624. The conversion of Edwin of Northumbria in 627 was part of a strategy to achieve political dominance in southern Britain. The Germanic peoples of Britain must have remained largely heathen in belief and sentiment until well into the 7th century. It was not until the episcopate of Archbishop Theodore of Canterbury in 669-690 that the Anglo-Saxons could be said to be fully and finally Christian.

A useful starting point for understanding the mechanism of conversion is the work of Higham (1997) who applies insights from anthropology and sociology to the Christianisation of the Anglo-Saxon kingdoms. He points out that we should resist setting up too great an opposition between heathenism and Christianity, as though they were two opposing world systems. Germanic folk had long been in touch with and aware of Christianity through their contacts with the Roman Empire. Furthermore, our knowledge of Germanic heathenism in the 5th and 6th century is very limited and gained through the filter of later Christian writers. Conversion to Christianity may not have been seen in the same way by the Angle or Saxon as by the Christian missionary. Heathen religions are often of low intensity and their beliefs not always structured according to fixed rules of dogma. They are thus capable of change and receptive to new influences. Being baptised would not necessarily be recognised as involving a rejection of the familiar, traditional rituals and beliefs. It is also important to realise that religion is not a separate aspect of life that can be divorced from other aspects of society. Religions in the medieval world operated within a political context. When the main impetus for conversion came from the newly emergent Anglo-Saxon kings, then a political motive for the adoption of Christianity must be considered. In Higham's view, Christianity was the religion of the ruling elite and it took a long while before the mass of the population could be considered as practising Christians (Higham 1997).

Christianity was useful to kings in various ways and there were specific advantages of the moment for particular conversions by the kings. The earliest of the Germanic kings in Britain to accept Christianity was Æþelberht of Kent. Higham (1997) has put forward the idea that Kent was a militarily weak kingdom, reliant on Frankish connections to gain access to the wealth that enabled it to dominate its neighbours. This connection was maintained partly by marriage. That of Æþelberht and Berhta brought with it a Christian bishop, Liudhard, to the Kentish court c.575/81. Liudhard's role may have been to cater for the needs of the Christian Berhta but he might also have been the political agent of King Chilperic of Neustria. After Chilperic's death in 584, he was succeeded by his son Chlothar II. Liudhard remained in Kent until his death, possibly c.595. Meanwhile, the union of Austrasia and Burgundy under Childebert II in 593 had tilted the balance of power among the Franks decisively away from Chlothar. The mission of Augustine to Kent then makes sense as part of a diplomatic realignment of Kentish politics. Augustine was the envoy of Pope Gregory in Rome, an ally of the dominant Austrasian/Burgundian axis in Gaul. Æþelberht gain more powerful allies from his acceptance of Augustine. He also gained a powerful tool in his strategy of dominance within Britain. Augustine's meeting with Christian British clergy in 602/04 should be seen as an attempt to bring British kings within the orbit of Kentish domination. If so, Christianity was being seen by Æþelberht as a non-ethnic set of beliefs and practices that could cross the Germanic-British divide. In other words, Christianity in the 6th and early 7th centuries cannot be seen as an ethnic trait among the Anglo-Saxons. This is not to deny that it may have had ethnic significance to the British rulers in the west of the island after generations of defence against the heathen Germanic newcomers. In practice, the isolation of the British church from Papal reforms of the last 200 years meant that Roman and British Christianity were dissimilar enough to act as ethnic signifiers to later generations, once the Anglo-Saxons had decided to follow the Roman path to Christian unity in the later 7th century.

There seems to have been negligible British influence on the Christianity of the Anglo-Saxons. The Celtic influence that there was on the church came in the 7th century from contacts with Ireland. One hint that there might have been more influence, at popular level, than appears in the documentary sources comes from studies of place-names (e.g. Gelling 1978). One of the few Romano-British terms to survive in place-names in England appears in modern English as Eccles. This comes from the Latin *ecclesia*, which is the source of the modern Welsh *eglwys*, Cornish *eglos*, and means a church. Names in Eccles are not common but do occur in all areas of England, and lowland Scotland. Eccles on its own occurs in all Jackson's zones 1, 2 and 3; in Kent, Norfolk, Derbyshire and Lancashire as well as Scotland. It is also found compounded with Old English *-halh* (e.g. Ecclesall) in Staffordshire, Warwickshire and the West Riding, with *-ton* in Cheshire and Lancashire, with *-hyll* in Lancashire and the West Riding, and *-feld* in Cumberland and the West Riding (all in zones 2 and 3). This must mean that British churches were a surviving part of the landscape and of people's lives at the time the names were coined. Henig has noted the existence of British churches in Lincoln, Canterbury and St Albans, which were recognised as such by the Anglo-Saxons (Henig 2002). A rare reference to British churches and priests occurs in the *Life of Wilfrið* by Stephanus (Colgrave 1927). Among the lands given to the church at Ripon under Wilfrið were properties in the area of Craven, from which British clergy had recently fled in the face of English conquest. It must be that some clergy remained in other parts of Britain during the 6th and 7th century conquests of British territory. Bede recorded that in the 7th century, Bishop Wine of Wessex consecrated Chad to be Bishop of Mercia with the help of two British Bishops, who might as well have been from within Wessex as from neighbouring Welsh kingdoms (Colgrave & Mynors 1969: 316-317).

A major advance in the adoption of Christianity by the Anglo-Saxons came with the conversion of Eadwine of Northumbria in 627. Higham (1997) has constructed a plausible scenario which explains the conversion in largely political terms. Æþelberht's successor as dominant king (*Brytenwalda* or *Bretwalda*) was the heathen Rædwald of East Anglia. Rædwald was the protector of Eadwine but died c.625. Eadwine was ruling a powerful kingdom, well able to exercise dominance of other kings to the south. It was natural therefore that he should seek alliance with the successor of Æþelberht in Kent, Eadbald, a king with still strong Frankish connections, and Eadwine's obvious rival for dominance. Neutralising potential rivalry by alliance would be a shrewd move but entailed the arrival of Bishop Paulinus and Christianity at the court of Northumbria. It might well have been the case that Eadwine was personally receptive to Christianity but his kingdom was probably less open to persuasion. Other advantages to Eadwine were the potential for Frankish alliance, the possibility of neutralising support for the Christian sons of his predecessor Æþelfrið and possibly making his rule more attractive to any British Christians among his subjects or allies, e.g. in the recently annexed Elmet. Other attractions of Christianity noted by Higham were the use of literate priests as an early bureaucracy, and the associations of the Roman church with authority, Imperial power and hierarchy; all of which emphasise the political importance of the Church to rulers like Eadwine. As with Kent, we cannot see the adoption of Christianity in Northumbria under Eadwine simply in ethnic terms. In so far as kings thought at all in ethnic terms, religion cannot have been seen as an ethnic unifier when one considers that Eadwine was eventually overthrown by a combined invasion of the British Christian Cadwallon of Gwynedd and the Germanic heathen Penda of Mercia. The 7th century was an age of *realpolitik*, in which religion was merely one of many factors to be manipulated in the search for greater security, influence and power. Higham sees Eadwine's use of Christianity as a 'dynastic weapon' and a 'force for state creation' (Higham 1997: 188). The link between religion and politics would lead in time to the identification of religion with an Anglo-Saxon identity, but this had to await the full conversion of all the Anglo-Saxon kingdoms later in the century.

Ethnicity in action

Mechanisms of settlement and conquest

The inadequate nature of the sources for the period unfortunately means that there is no scholarly consensus on the nature or scale of the Germanic migration to Britain. Most people now accept that the population of Britain would have been mixed with incomers from across the North Sea living alongside the native Britons (Henig 2000). This simple statement however begs many questions about the nature of the mixing. We can only surmise at the context within which social groups moved from the continent to Britain and the effect that this had on how ideas of identity were acted out in daily life. The two main, rival views are that the settlement was carried out either by a small military elite or involved large scale movement of population from all sectors of society (Hamerow 1997: 34-35). It is possible that the movement of 'peoples' in late Roman Europe in general was more usually a movement of armies. Amory (1997) notes that the barbarian peoples had much in common with the late Roman army regiments and we do not know how far they included families, slaves and camp followers. I agree with Hamerow (1997) that we need to address regional variation in the size and nature of the migration. We need to take into account the fact that the settlement of Britain was not a single act undertaken at one point in time but the result of many different choices by individuals and families over the course of perhaps 150 years in different parts of Britain within different political circumstances, as has been recognised by others (Scull 1992: 8; 1993: 70). Glasswell (2002: 16) also accepts that the reality of the Anglo-Saxon migrations was probably more complex than entailed in a simple invasion hypothesis and that the processes involved would have varied between different areas. It may be that the elite and the large scale views are both right for different parts of Britain. Scholars have now put forward a view that foederate settlements of a military nature under aristocratic warrior leadership might have been the norm in the south of Britain, with non-military settlement by whole communities of all social groups in the midlands and north (Scull 1992, Dark 2000). While this may well be true, we must avoid a simplistic split between military and civilian for the bulk of settlement. It is still possible that early settlements in the northern areas of Germanic immigration in Britain were also military in nature, albeit of a different nature to that of the south. The siting of early cemeteries near access routes to important towns like *Venta Icenorum* (Caistor) or *Eburacum* (York) would suggest military roles for the very earliest settlers throughout Britain.

Migration

Few archaeologists visualise precise explanations rather than general factors for the transference of artefact types and styles that underlie their distribution patterns. Prevailing views are exemplified by Todd (1992) who put forward rising population, rising sea level reducing the land area available and the presence of opportunities for wealth in Britain as causes of the Anglo-Saxon migration. That rising sea levels reducing the area available for settlement in northern Germany were a factor in kick-starting the migration can be demonstrated (Lamb 1995: 163-164). Welch (1992) suggested overpopulation and soil exhaustion as prime motives for the abandonment of continental settlements in the early 5th century. In the case of Hines (1984), trade, a limited amount of settlement, exogamy and travelling craftsmen are all invoked to explain the spread of Scandinavian artefacts and styles southwards on the continent, with a more prominent role for migration between Scandinavia and Britain. In particular, he interpreted the distribution of sleeve clasps indicating styles of women's dress as being due to the presence of few but highly influential Norwegian migrants. Härke (Wood 1997) put forward the view that migration was triggered by Roman economic collapse depriving peoples outside the Empire of their trading links with the Empire.

We will only begin to make sense of what happened if we treat the process of migration in a more sophisticated manner than has hitherto been the case among historians and archaeologists. Simply putting forward overpopulation as a prime mover of migration will no longer serve, as with Hines (1984) when discussing Norwegian migration to Britain in the 5th century. The potential reasons for undertaking migration have been ably summarised by Anthony (1997). For migration to proceed, four conditions must be met:

- negative social or economic conditions at home;
- attractive social or economic conditions elsewhere;
- information flow about the conditions in the area to which people are moving;
- an available means of transport.

People will seek to move if it is in their self-interest to do so. For most people, in normal times, that interest will take the form of opportunities for social or economic advancement. For economic pressure to be the main reason, there has to be a greater disparity of wealth between the two areas than can be overcome by simple trade or raiding. Potential settlers would need information about where to settle. Early visitors or settlers could report back to the homeland the advantages of the new settlements and attract kin or other settlers to join them. There will thus be nodal points around which new settlements will cluster. The attraction of settling near to pre-existing settlements would continue long after the initial conditions leading to settlement might have changed. It may be that these clusters formed the centres from which later kings could base their conquest of the Romano-British *civitates*. The distribution of early Germanic graves indeed shows clusters at regional level (Arnold 1997: 214), which could be the centres of origin for the later Kings of Kent, Essex, East Anglia, Mercia, Lindsey and Deira. Other kingdoms seem to have had much weaker centres, e.g. Sussex, Wessex and the *Hwicce*. The social identity of the migrants would be maintained by ties of kinship among themselves, and with relations back in the homeland. New social ties to other kin groups in the same region of settlement would add an extra dimension of identity to this. This would be especially the case with the type of migration identified by Tilley as a chain migration (Anthony 1997: 26-27), where settlement proceeds by people coming over to join their kin. It is possible that some of the Germanic migrants were what Tilley calls career migrants (Anthony 1997: 27), in which case settlement would take place according to the dictates of a host organisation hiring specialist labour for its own needs. This is the type of migration that the tales of Hengest conform to. Chain migration would be less well attested historically, being less connected with the kind of political contexts likely to be recorded in documentary sources. However, the archaeological evidence for early settlement in East Anglia and the midlands might well reveal this kind of migration, as might the enigmatic statement in the 12th century chronicle of Henry of Huntingdon referring to settlement by various disparate groups under numerous kings around 527 (possibly 515, Scull 1992). It is likely that these were kinship groups, moving into areas already settled by previous (and perhaps related) generations of migrants. This is supported by Crawford (1997: 69) who has interpreted the archaeological evidence as reflecting settlement by families, keeping their social structures intact. Ethnic identity would exist at perhaps two levels in a chain migration to Britain. There would be an overall Germanic identity and a smaller scale kin-group identity. For career migrants, there may be less kin based relationships and a more direct connection with an identity based on profession, or on political relations with the host organisation. An overall Germanic nature might be fused with other influences, and this might be a suitable context for the development of the Germanic input into the decorative motifs of the undoubtedly Romano-British Quoit brooch style of ornamentation (Ager 1985).

If the earliest Germanic settlers were initially brought over to Britain as soldiers then we might expect an ethnic identity to arise which would fit the pattern seen later in a number of mercenary groups (Enloe in Hutchinson & Smith 1996: 282-285). These groups were often seen as marginal, often in border areas or not integrated into their host society. But, they would be greatly respected for their military prowess. One thinks today of the Gurkhas in the British army. One major difference between the Germanic groups and these later ethnic mercenaries is that they would be serving under their own leaders, not under Roman or British officers. At least we can presume this to be the case in Kent and the Anglian regions of Britain. The situation might have been different for the Saxons in southern Britain. A military based ethnic identity would fit very well with both Enloe and the evidence of weapon burials.

The burial of weapons as signifying Germanic identity has been investigated by Härke (1992). It is clear that the weapons - arrows, swords, spears, shields, axes and *seaxes* (knives) - were often buried with people who could not have been functioning warriors, e.g. children under 12. It seems clear that the act of depositing weapons as grave goods was meant to signify a particular image, the warrior, associated with a particular segment of the population and that the skeletal evidence suggests that this segment was genetically distinct from the rest of the population. Härke's interpretation of skeletal differences has not gone unchallenged, and geneticists are particularly sceptical about the use of skeletal traits as an ethnic marker. Characteristics like height are heavily influenced by environmental factors such as diet and differences in height could reflect class differences rather than ethnic differences (Evison 2000). However, this need not invalidate the identification of weapon burials with incoming Germanic groups, although this must be a presumption rather than a proven fact. What is interesting is that a warrior ideology was clearly serving some purpose of group identification. It is reasonable to suggest that an incoming Germanic population might be identified with a warrior ideology, acted out at the graveside rather than on the battlefield. Hines (1995) has noted that weapons are commoner in Britain than they are in the Germanic homelands and has suggested that elite competition for power and status during the upheaval of migration might be responsible for this. Emphasis on a Germanic military identity by migrants of marginal social position in an alien society is just as likely.

Emergence of local identities has been revealed in the study by Fisher (1988), who looked at burial practices in East and Middle Anglia. Fisher found that burial practices showed significant variation between cemeteries of different areas and that the greatest difference occurred between those of East Anglia and those of Middle Anglia. This emphasises that the geography of settlement in this period was localised. At some point the Roman diocese of Britain ceased to be a single unit, and cultural fragmentation increased along with political division. In a sense it is wrong to talk of Britain or the Anglo-Saxons as though they were a single unit by the 6th century. The sphere of action of most people would have been their township or hundred, with only the upper strata of society acting over larger regional areas. Loyalty, kinship and social action at this level would occur within well-defined cores of what would later become the historical kingdoms of the Anglo-Saxons.

Arnold used polygons centred on the locations of rich burials to delimit the early political territories of the mid 6th century in southern Britain. His territories are largely in agreement with the picture derived from documentary sources. Marking of identity in these burials would then be related to signifying of elite status and competition between different emerging royal families, rather than any sense of ethnic identity as Saxons, Angles or Jutes. The major exception is the area that would later be Wessex, which is revealed as split between several centres of wealth (Arnold 1988: 186).

Suzuki's detailed examination of the Quoit brooch style of belt-fittings and brooches (Suzuki 2000) provides a possible scenario for Germanic settlement within 5th century Kent. The style would have begun with adaptation of Romano-British belt-fittings for use by Germanic soldiers in the service of post-Roman authorities. Suzuki sees these belt-fittings as the product of a 'sub-Roman' elite using native British templates to make an explicit statement about an independent British identity (Suzuki 2000: 84). The soldiers employed by the

British would include Hengest and his forces in Kent. Their revolt against the British would naturally lead to a greater desire to signal an independent Germanic identity by fusing the artistic style of the belt-fittings with a more appropriate cultural idiom, the display brooch, drawing on technology and form from Scandinavian models of the soldiers' homeland. The brooches in the Quoit-brooch style are indeed concentrated in Kent, whereas the earlier belt-fittings were manufactured farther to the west and have a wider distribution. Nevertheless, the revolt was limited, with the Quoit-style brooches signalling a desire to operate still with the 'sub-Roman' framework. The Jutish material culture (pottery and cruciform brooches) of these early settlers was low status, reflecting the social origins of the settlers. It would seem natural that their elite should adopt Romano-British models to signal their status within a political framework that must have remained Romano-British. The employment of career migrants as *laeti* would fit this situation. It was only later that Kent adopted a more explicitly anti-British, pro-Germanic stance. It was towards the end of the 5th century, possibly in the 490s according to Suzuki, that a secondary migration brought Germanic immigrants of higher status using bracteates and square-headed brooches. These new immigrants continued the connection between Kent and their original homeland. The styles of bracteates used in Kent were most like those used in central Jutland. It was this second migration (a chain migration?), in Suzuki's view, that brought the ruling royal family of Kent, the Oiscingas, to Britain. This new elite had a high status from the beginning and would feel more comfortable about signalling its position using its own, Germanic high status markers. A major question that Suzuki felt unable to answer was the relationship between the earlier settlers and the later 'reinforcements' from Jutland. Artefacts decorated in Germanic Style I used by the 6th century elite show no influence from the earlier Quoit-brooch style of metalwork. Was this part of a conscious rejection of Romano-British connections? Or was it simply the acceptance by the existing settlers of the higher status of the newcomers and assimilation to their identity? Whatever, the reason the change in material culture ought to signal some underlying change of importance in the political/social orientation of Kent.

Mechanisms of settlement

Relations between Anglo-Saxons and Britons had to be acted out on a daily basis and in the context of civilian and military life. The origins of Anglo-Saxon Britain are fundamentally acts of conquest and acts of migration. The acting out of these must have formed an important psychological reference point for later generations and helped forge attitudes on either side of the Germanic-British divide. Contact between Roman provincials and Germanic settlers was nothing new. Such settlers had been accepted into Gaul since the 3rd century, known as *laeti* (Hills 1978: 300). These were settled as farming families on vacant lands and furnished soldiers for the army, to serve in Roman army units under Roman officers. The political control of such settlers was also in the hands of Roman officials, *praefecti laetorum*. The distinction between these settlers and the indigenous inhabitants - the Roman citizens - was rigidly maintained. A 4th century law forbade intermarriage between the two. It would be perfectly natural for this to be adopted as a model of how to regulate relations between them by the British authorities in at least some areas of Britain.

Another category of Germanic settler was that of *foederati* - tribal groups under the control of their own leaders, serving as soldiers in their own native formations. As coherent units under their own political leaders, they are more likely to have kept their own customs and Germanic laws and culture (Hills 1978). *Foederati* were bound by treaty to the empire whereby a native king and his people became subject to the emperor. They could be bound by that treaty to provide soldiers to fight for Rome. This could easily become a contract of employment between Romano-British authorities and a Germanic leader with military followers. This may have been the model for the employment of Hengest in Kent. In return for this treaty, the soldiers could receive payments or gifts on a regular basis. A government that was having to make cuts in spending would be tempted to reduce or default on these payments. Such a reduction was the cause of a revolt in 365 by the Alemanni (Heather 1997: 70). The tradition of Hengest's revolt in Kent conforms to this pattern.

So, although the details of Anglo-Saxon settlement in Britain remain unclear, it may have involved both *laeti* and *foederati*. In practice, there may have been little difference between *foederati* and *laeti* in the 5th century. The key differences was more likely between the employment of soldiers in return for supplies and the settling of farming communities with a military obligation in return for land. The employment of Germanic units as soldiers by the Roman authorities was given the name of *hospitalitas*. Two models have been put forward for how this operated in practice (James 1989). The traditional view was that the estates of existing Roman landowners were divided with a portion being given to support the new Germanic soldiers in their midst. The leading Germans would then become landowners alongside the existing aristocratic families and be able to settle their followers on their lands. A more recent interpretation is that what was given to the Germanic leaders was the right to collect and appropriate the tax revenues of the Roman estates. This would have given the newcomers a stake in maintaining the existing social and political set-up. There is explicit reference to the giving of lands to the followers of Hengest, along with supplies and payments. These references are not contemporary with the events depicted and are capable of interpretation in a variety of ways. It unlikely that all the Germanic settlements in Britain proceeded according to the same plan. While leaders of the settlers may have been given tax revenues (the right to a portion of agricultural produce or the assignment of whole estates), the settlers themselves will have needed lands to live on for themselves and their families. It is likely that different patterns were followed in different parts of Britain.

Anglo-Saxon kingdoms were erected largely on the basis of the Romano-British *civitates* (Yorke 2000). The Germanic peoples did not settle and conquer a blank landscape but accommodated themselves to existing institutions and borders. Regional identities remained but were 'rebadged'. For example, the *Iceni* and *Trinovantes* still remained as separate people with their local loyalties, but learnt instead to think of themselves as East Angles and East Saxons. At the level of sub-divisions of the kingdoms, the long-lived nature of Welsh *cantref* boundaries from the 6th to 16th centuries, and the possibility that some *cantrefau* were incorporated and renamed to survive as English units of administration, e.g. names of peoples in -*sæte* (as in Dorset), might indicate that the administrations of the *civitates* were taken over substantially intact by the new Anglo-Saxon rulers (Dark 1994). It may be that Germanic warrior groups were made up of what the Lombards and Burgundians termed *farae* (Barnwell 1996). Each *fara* would be a group of warriors and their families under the leadership of one particular warrior who would be responsible for ensuring that the other warriors were ready to serve the king, and for making sure that they were given the supplies or rents that were their due. Barnwell (1996) has suggested that such groups might have existed among the Germanic settlers in Britain. The leader of the group may be referred to by the term *ceorl* in the Kentish laws of the 7th century, and the dependant warriors by the term *hlafæta*, the 'consumer of the bread' (the lord being the *hlaford/hlafward*, the 'guardian of the bread'). The land that the group was given to support it would have been an existing Roman-British estate, possibly rated in units called a *centuria*. The remnants of some such allotment may be preserved in the evidence of place-names in *wic-* from Latin *vicus*, which Balkwill (1993) proposes as examples of Germanic settlement at still functioning centres of Roman administration. The *centuria* was a notional 125 acres in size, curiously similar to the notional 120 acres of the Anglo-Saxon hide. Both the *centuria* and the hide were units of assessment as well as units describing amounts of land. This may yet be another strand of evidence supporting the British origin of the Anglo-Saxon estate and fiscal structure. The estates would pay their taxation to the regional centre, the king's manor at the heart of the multiple estate (the British *cantref* or shire), and in turn be consumed or passed on to the king himself at the level of the kingdom or province (the Roman *civitas* or kingdom).

The disruption caused by conquest would therefore be minimised for the bulk of the population who would have found much continued as it always had under their new ruler. The obligations to landlords and kings, and the functioning of administration and justice might well have remained familiar, so easing relations between the new lords and their British subjects in those areas without substantial Germanic settlers.

Population

Population decline?

A key variable is missing from our knowledge of the period. We do not know the level of population, and its increase or decrease over time. Not surprisingly, given the lack of evidence, there has been some debate among archaeologists and historians about the size of the migration to Britain and the size of the receiving British population (Jones 1996). We suspect very strongly that the late Roman population was higher than that of England in 1086, as measured in the Domesday Book. Estimates vary but most would probably accept a figure of around 4 or 5 million people, with a lower limit of 3 million and an upper limit of 6 million (Jones 1996, Fowler in Hooke 1997); all of which figures entail a decline over 700 years to the Domesday level of 1¾ to 2 million people. Whatever happened between 400 and 1066 must have had a drastic and catastrophic effect on population levels (Hooke 1997). The reliability of these estimates is open to question and Ausenda (1997) has argued that comparative studies with non-western societies at the present day can be used to suggest an upper level of 2 million for the population of Britain during the migration period. Esmonde Cleary in 1989 took a middle position with a Roman peak of around 3 million. Most people argue that the peak of population was reached c.300 with decline setting in the 4th century. However, a great deal of work remains to establish the extent and chronology of this decline. Arnold (1984) has suggested that the decline began early in the 4th century, with towns being the first affected and later the rural areas. He accepts that many Roman period settlements in the south east of Britain were abandoned and the pattern of dispersed farmsteads of the early Anglo-Saxon period really does indicate a "shrinkage in the size of the population" (Arnold 1984: 79). Wolfram (1997) noted that the decline was a general phenomenon in the Imperial west, and the existence of population decline (with a retreat in the extent of farming) in Britain has long been assumed (Hoskins 1955). The low taxation revenues of the west of the Roman Empire in comparison to the east may be a reflection of this (although tax avoidance by the wealthy must be a possible alternative). Higham (1992: 77-80) would see a long-term population decline under the impact of worsening climate in the 5th and 6th centuries. Unfortunately, we have conflicting or ambiguous evidence for when or how that decline occurred. Archaeological evidence was presented by Hodges (1983) for population decline in late Roman and early post-Roman times in Italy. Faulkner (2000: 144-148) suggested that land was being abandoned during the 4th century in Britain, and that the pottery industry was running down during this period. Both phenomena could be the result of declining population. Esmonde Cleary suggested that there was no evidence for regeneration of woodland at the expense of agriculture until the 6th century (1989: 174). He noted that the climate was becoming cooler and wetter at the time, but stressed that the effects of this would be felt mostly on marginal farming lands. Although he accepts that the population must have declined between the 4th century and 1086, he has cast considerable doubt on whether decline was a factor in the transition from Roman Britain to early medieval England (Esmonde Cleary 1995). There is pollen evidence for the regrowth of woodland on marginal land in the north, possibly centred on the 6th century (Loveluck 2002). Hinton however, (Hinton 1990: 10-11) pointed out that there is evidence for lands going out of cultivation after the Roman period on land which is not usually thought of as marginal, e.g. on the Hampshire Downs and in north Nottinghamshire. Sites on heavy soils seem to have been abandoned in preference for farming easier, lighter soils. Continuity between fields and boundaries from the Roman period into medieval and modern times can be demonstrated in many places (Esmonde Cleary 1995), and this has been presented as evidence for continuity of cultivation, and so of no decline in levels of population. However, simple continuity of cultivation need not have a direct link with the size of population. Continuity in the extent, intensity and methods of cultivation needs to be demonstrated. Even then, continuity could still conceal population increase or decrease in urban and non-agricultural sectors. Population decline will not affect all areas of cultivation; it will be selective in operation. A study in Cornwall suggested that there was dislocation and retraction of settlement in that county by the 6th century (Rose & Preston 1995). An intensive study by

Newman (1992) in one area of Suffolk suggested that 5th century settlement was at a much lower density than that of the Roman period and that there might have been a decline in population from c. 350/75, coupled with a retreat of settlement from some types of soil and a change in location of settlement in other areas. Even Esmonde Cleary (1995: 22) accepted that there is evidence for intensive Roman farming not surviving into the post-Roman period in various areas, e.g. the Thames Valley. Some archaeologists would accept a period of catastrophic population decline in the post-Roman period, although this is not a generally agreed position (Jones 1996: 229). As Hills (1990) elegantly put it: "The difference between Roman and Saxon in most areas is so striking that it must reflect a real fall in population, but this has been exaggerated by the nature of the evidence. We have not yet worked out how to allow for this distortion." It is possible that climatic conditions, and the increase in warfare, might have had a downward effect on population levels during the 5th century. There is evidence for a sharp worsening of climate at c.400 (Jones 1996: 189-198). However, although there is some archaeological evidence for land going out of production in the uplands, there is no general evidence of decreasing productivity of farming during this period. There is evidence of specific changes in the distribution of settlement and type of farming, e.g. retreat to higher terraces of the Thames Valley, and abandonment of areas prone to flooding. It may be that population decline was more a feature of the 6th century than the 5th. Scull (1992) undertook a detailed study of East Anglia (whose implications were supported by Newman's more intensive local study, Newman 1992) which showed that although the general distribution of Anglo-Saxon sites was remarkably similar to that of earlier Romano-British period, it differed in two important ways. The density of Anglo-Saxon sites was much lower, which might indicate that population levels had declined, although Scull rightly pointed out that this cannot be automatically assumed. He also noted that the precise location of Anglo-Saxon settlement was different to that of their Romano-British forebears. Such dislocation of settlement awaits proper explanation. Powlesland, based on his work at West Heslerton in Yorkshire, called this dislocation the 'early Saxon shuffle', proposing that it was a widespread phenomenon that probably began in the late Roman period and may be related to a relaxing of social controls over settlement location (Powlesland 1997). However, the problems in dating late Roman material (assumptions of 4th century dating rather than continuity into the 5th) make it difficult at present to say whether the new settlements grew up alongside British sites or replaced them. There is general agreement that most Romano-British villas were abandoned, although archaeological interpretation of villa abandonment can be challenged in some cases. Most villas did not last into the second half of the 5th century. At Whitley Grange in Shropshire the last firing of the baths has been dated to 470 ±50 (Matthews 2001). This might be due to general population decline undercutting the economic base which allowed such villas to be maintained, although writers like Dark (1994) would rather see this as part of a revolution ousting an elite too closely identified with a discredited Roman pagan ideology.

The difficulties in assessing population levels from archaeological evidence have made some scholars reluctant to make the attempt. As pointed out by Arnold (194: 133), using the evidence of archaeologically recorded cemeteries, the population of Roman Britain would be just 2000 people! What then would be the point of trying to assess population levels in the 5th and 6th centuries? For Hines (1994), comparisons between British and Germanic levels of population in this period "are very obscure" and therefore "somewhat pointlessly disputed". However, I think the evidence (numbers and sizes of settlements) does suggest that we must accept population decline in Britain as part of the dynamic of the period. What has yet to be explored are the implications this has for relations between the Britons and incoming Germanic settlers. If populations were falling then it must affect the dynamics of these relations. If there were a lower level of population, generalised throughout Britain, then there would have been plenty of empty land for settlement with a minimum of disruption to the existing population. There are two principle effects of falling British populations. The structures which supported the British elites and governments would become progressively short of resources, not just people but also agricultural produce and rents/taxes. The existence of a chronic manpower shortage was a generally accepted feature of late Roman Britain (Arnold 1984). British authorities would find it harder to mobilise military forces, or engage in large scale building works. The employment of Germanic mercenaries would fit quite naturally into such a situation. The other effect would be to free up land for settlement. Falling populations should lead to marginal lands falling out of cultivation, villages shrinking and farmsteads being abandoned. Space would exist for new settlers to come in without unduly straining the social and economic relations and position of the native Britons. Germanic settlers would have had a demographic edge in areas where they clustered. We need to realise that they could replenish their population by immigration from their homelands on the continent. A demographic pendulum might begin to swing to the disadvantage of the native inhabitants.

The size of the migration

The size of the initial employment of Germanic soldiers by the British might have been quite small. Jones (1996) accepts the figures given in the historical sources for an initial force of 3 ships followed by 16 more for the men under Hengest's command with a total of 60 men to each ship; in all 1,140 men. A larger force of 2,400 men would have served under Octa in the north. These figures are used to put forward a view of minimal Anglo-Saxon settlement. It may be unwise to accept the traditional figures handed down in the myths of the migration and settlement (Sims Williams 1983). A small number of Germanic mercenaries would not have been an adequate substitute for the late Roman army in Britain, which as been estimated at c.30,000 men at the end of the 4th century (Jones 1996: 214). This was divided into three commands the northern frontier under the *Dux Britanniarum*, the south east coast under the *Comes Litoris Saxonici* and the central mobile field army under the *Comes Britanniarum*. The employment of the Germanic troops suggests that they were meant to replace or augment the northern frontier and south-east coastal commands. The nature of their rebellion, initially successful but later put down until a chance occurred to advance once more and force a stalemate suggests that the Germanic units were not so small that they could be easily defeated and yet not large enough to overwhelm British opposition. It is unlikely that they were a small force augmenting largely intact frontier defences. Many of the Imperial troops would have been taken to the continent by Constantinus III, presumably never to return. It is more probable that they were of some size and that the numbers given in the sources represent a lower limit to the numbers employed, brought up to greater strength by additional recruitment from the continent.

In any event, the figures for the military force employed by the Britons need have little bearing on the size of the Anglo-Saxon migration. This depended on a long period of contact across the North Sea allowing families to migrate to a new life. Although, we do not know how long was the period of time in which migration took place, Hamerow (1997) has pointed out that it was likely to have been at least 100 years (150 to 200 years might be nearer the mark). We might assume migration of families once the control of Kent was assured, lasting perhaps until the victory at Badon slowed down the opportunities for taking new lands, say a period of 60 years. Further migration would occur during the 6th century. After the political conquest of sout-east Britain, we might then see an increased rate of migration as new opportunities arose for settlement and land ownership. Wood (1997) felt that migration might well have continued until the mid 7th century. The size of the migration seems to have been substantial. Bede noted that the homelands of the Angles lay deserted by the early 8th century, supported by the historical and archaeological disappearance of the Angles from the continent (Todd 1992). Hamerow's recent study suggests that this was a real phenomenon (Hamerow 2003). On the other hand, natural increase in the resident Anglo-Saxon population would provide many of the new landowners and settlers for the newly conquered British territories. Newman's study of the Sandlings area of Suffolk (Newman 1992) showed an increase in settlement density from the late 5th century which might reflect the combined effects of migration and natural increase in population.

In an impressive review of the evidence for the period in 1978, Hills stated that the nature of the archaeological evidence could

> be explained only in terms of substantial immigration of people who came in sufficient force to retain their religion and way of life - not to become absorbed into the existing society but to absorb the remains of that society into their own.

(Hills 1978: 313)

While she has made the case for considerable migration Hills (1990), she has also accepted that the British contribution to the new society must have been considerable. She made the important point that it is the relationships between the Germanic settlers and the Britons which should be a key area of study.

If the number of settlers was small and eastern Britain became Germanic by assimilation of the native British majority, why did this not happen in the rest of Britain? It is always dangerous to argue from the absence of evidence, yet, those who argue that eastern Britain became Germanic by assimilation or for reasons of fashion need to explain why this did not happen in the west of the island. Up to 570, it is reasonable to assume that the British were still politically dominant in most of south-eastern Britain and so the Britons could not have assimilated to non-existant Germanic political superiors. Possibly the dominance of Germanic identity in the archaeology of the east before this date is more apparent than real - an artefact of the invisibility of the native population. Such invisibility, was explained by Alcock (1971) as due to declining population and the lack of burial traditions involving grave goods. We might add, the lack of coinage and mass-produced pottery, perhaps with an increasing taste for material cultural expression in forms that would have low archaeological visibility (Dark 2000). Another possibility is that, as suggested by Hedeager (1992), the British elites feeling secure in their position as rulers felt no need to bolster their personal political identities through artefact display. He noted that groups not under stress were more likely to devote their wealth to the gods, reinforcing their divine relationship and political position by serving the interests of the community. Might it be that the British elites were signalling their status and power through endowment and offerings to British churches and monasteries? The main era of foundation for most early Welsh churches and monasteries seems to have been the 5th century at the latest (Davies 1982). There is no reason to treat what would become Wales as any different to the rest of Britain at this time. Churches in eastern Britain would be effectively despoiled and their wealth recycled by the Anglo-Saxons in the 7th century. Harris (2003) has made the suggestion that the Byzantine silver goods found in the burial at Sutton Hoo could have originated as gifts to British rulers before finding their way as tribute or trade into Germanic hands. Is it possible that we can catch a glimpse here of the very act of despoilation and recycling that must have occurred on a much wider scale? The evidence of imported goods shows that Britain was divided into two economic zones (Harris 2003). The west had access to eastern Byzantine goods through diplomatic relations with the Roman Empire, yielding finds of pottery in the south and west of Britain. The east had access to Germanic goods through trade as part of the Frankish economic networks based on the Rhine. We could therefore suppose that we have a sharply defined British west and a Germanic ruled east during the late 5th and early 6th centuries. On the other hand, Byzantine pottery has been found in London and St Albans and the antique Byzantine silver from Sutton Hoo could have arrived in Britain as diplomatic gifts to British rulers in the east in previous generations. At the same time, the Franks may have been supplying goods to the Germanic elite in Kent who would then pass this on to appropriate communities in the rest of Britain. Nearby British rulers might have bypassed the opportunities for such trade with Rhineland networks in favour of the higher prestige of Imperial contacts with distant Constantinople. In other words, the Britons were there and ruling in the east, but the evidence no longer exists (having been in perishable artefacts, and recycled or melted down for later Germanic use). The Germanic settlers are highly visible but they may not have been the politically dominant element of the population until the rise of the kings in the later 6th century.

Migration to Britain needed an adequate naval technology as an available means of transport (Anthony 1997). One question that is impossible to answer is how many ships a year crossed the North Sea to bring new settlers to Britain? Boats of this period can be exemplified by those found at Nydam in Jutland (dated 310/20) and Sutton Hoo (c.625). The largest of the Nydam ships was 76 feet (23.5 m) long and would have had 28 oars (Rieck 1997), the smaller ship was 61 feet long (19 m) and would have had 22 oars (Haywood 1991). The Sutton Hoo ship (early 7th century) at 89 feet (27m) most likely had 40 oars (Brøgger & Shetelig 1951, Evans 1986). The contemporary ship from Gredstedbro in Jutland was up to 75 feet (23 m) long. This gives us an average of 20-40 oars for a ship at this period. A notice of Herul raids on Gaul reported 400 men from 7 ships, between 55 and 60 men to a ship (Haywood 1991). This might suggest that each oar had two men, so an average of crew of 60 would be a reasonable assumption. By the 7th century it is clear that large and exceptional ships could carry a crew of around 120 (Haywood 1991: 74). At a very conservative estimate, one ship every year holding 60 soldiers, with another ship for their wives and families, would bring just 14,000 people over 120 years between 430 and 560. It would take only 10 ships a year to bring over 140,000 people in that time. The capacity to bring sizeable numbers of people from the continent clearly existed, as did the capability to maintain regular contact between Britain and the Germanic homelands. Ships carrying sails could expect to travel 120 miles in a day with a fair wind (Haywood 1991). The distance from the Elbe to East Anglia is c.300 miles, a sailing time of three days with perhaps two landfalls along the way. Britain may be an island but we cannot analyse the Germanic settlements as though they involved the same degree of isolation of difficulty as the early European settlements in North America.

Political structures

Kingship

Kingship has a key role to play in creating national identity in the medieval period (James 1989). Todd (2001) makes the point that communal identity (ethnicity) is likely to have arisen in the migration period only once groups had a recognised territory with stable settlement; achieved usually through integration into kingdoms. Unfortunately, the term *king* was used to cover a variety of different types of leadership. The usual Latin term *rex* was most likely used to translate more than one Germanic term. The Goths used *þiudans* for the permanent civil leadership of the community (judicial and religious in function), and *reiks* for the temporary war leadership of the whole people. Bede noted that a similar system of local tribal leadership and a wider war leadership seems also to have been in existence among the continental Saxons (Colgrave & Mynors 1969: 481-482). There were thus two aspects to the leadership of communities in the early medieval period, generalship in war and judicial arbitration of disputes (Woolf 2000). The experience of migration and employment as soldiers by the later Roman or post-Roman power structures will inevitably have increased the importance of military kingship. The case of the Franks exemplifies this very clearly (James 1989).

It is generally thought that early Anglo-Saxon leaders were 'kinglets', leading small-scale polities based on family connections or the lordship of retainers (Arnold 1988: 112-113). There is a tradition preserved in the chronicle of Henry of Huntingdon in the 12th century of a phase of settlement in East Anglia and Mercia by small bands of settlers under a variety of 'kings' in 527 (Greenway 1996). How these kings described themselves we have no way of knowing. Nor do we know how their following was made up: of extended family lineages, of people from one area of settlement on the continent or of a collection of individuals and families brought together from a variety of backgrounds and places. Ausenda (1995) has shown how the scale of social units in pre-industrial societies can be very small with the basic unit of the lineage being perhaps 20-50 households in size, maybe 100-300 individuals. It is also not necessarily the case that a lineage and a residential unit would be the same. More than one lineage could be found within an area of settlement. We still have a long way to go before we can fully understand the social realities that underlie the identity of the groups preserved in later settlement and region names in *-ingas*, which can be based on named individuals (Cameron 1977). However, it is clear that such groups would have operated over a very localised scale and were not the basis for the later Anglo-Saxon kingdoms.

The earliest settlements of Germanic people must have occurred under native British political authority. In such a situation, there would have been no political arena for most of the Germanic kings to act within and therefore little access to patronage. Their role in defining ethnic identity could only be activated once they had replaced the British rulers and taken over the political leadership of their area. The royal families of the later Anglo-Saxon kingdoms had various origins. Unravelling these is no easy task since much of their early history is preserved in much later documents and in genealogies, both of which were capable of being manipulated to serve later political purposes. Genealogies have a poor reputation among modern historians because of their inconsistencies and capacity for being manipulated to mirror current political realities rather than historical truths. The surviving genealogies of the Anglo-Saxon kingly families go back to a historical horizon of c.550-575 before which they cannot be accepted as reliable without external verification (Arnold 1988: 119-120). This date may be significant as the time when these families began to take over political leadership and establish themselves as more than leaders of local kindred groups or war bands.

It may be that although many of the later Anglo-Saxon royal families claimed descent from continental kings, the authority wielded by these families in the Germanic homelands was rather limited. A series of remarkably wealthy archaeological sites has been uncovered in southern Scandinavia which are larger than normal villages (although without a planned, dense urban-style layout), near to the coast and with evidence for craft production and trade yielding large quantities of gold, silver, weapons and items like bracteates and other religious symbols. The most well-known of these sites are Gudme on Fyn, and Lejre in Jutland. Such sites can only be centres of power for early kings and were at their peak between 400 and 600 (Hamerow 2002: 163-165). Similar sites have not been found in Anglian or Saxon areas. Neither have they been found in Britain, suggesting that the leaders of the Germanic settlers were not in a position to monopolise access to trade and contacts with sources of wealth. It is not until the 7th century that the Germanic areas of Britain produce evidence for centres of trade and craft production, and hence monopolisation of wealth as the basis of political power. The existence of sites like Ipswich or *Hamwic* parallels sites like Hedeby on the continent at the same period. There are no such parallels for sites like Gudme or Lejre. The preservation of political power in British hands and a delayed acquisition of power by Germanic elites until after c.570 would fit such a lack of evidence for Germanic power centres until the 7th century.

We need to ask how far the Anglo-Saxon kingdoms that were set up towards the end of the 6th century resembled the Germanic kingdoms set up on Roman soil on the continent in the 5th and 6th centuries. Wolfram (1997) has described the continental kingdoms as late Roman, not Germanic, institutions exercising vice-Imperial authority of military and judicial nature, supported by Imperial tax revenues, and established by treaty with the Emperor. They were moreover literate, bureaucratic and Christian states (albeit heretic Arian Christian). The kingdoms that were established (beginning with the Burgundians in 413 at Worms and the Visigoths in Toulouse in 418) were set up over *civitates* and groups of *civitates*. They did not take over existing provincial or diocesan structures outside Italy. The kings maintained their rule through Imperial style officials: *comites* in the household or at *civitas* level, *duces* as military officials in charge of groups of *civitates* and border districts. The one new institution adopted in the Germanic states was retainership. However, even this had late

Roman precedent. Emperors had been trying to legislate against Roman citizens building up bodies of retainers, thus showing that the practice must have been common before the Germanic takeover. It may be that the model of an Imperial derived kingdom can be applied to Britain only in the case of Kent, the one kingdom established in the 5th century by treaty. The settlement of Germanic foederates in Kent might well have been a conscious, smaller scale, imitation of the settlement of Visigothic foederates in Toulouse not long before. The picture we have of the 6th century Anglo-Saxon kingdoms is not one of literate, bureaucratic, Christian states. In any case, their creation would seem to result more from conquest than treaty. However, we may be misled by the poverty of our documentary sources and the possibility of a more legalistic and ordered transition from British to Anglo-Saxon rule cannot be ruled out. The Anglo-Saxon kingdoms in the south east of Britain inherited their organisation from the Roman period (Hines 1995). That some sort of Roman administrative tradition continued after 410 is increasingly apparent. The genealogy of the Kings of the East Angles may contain a hint of this when they place Caser (Caesar) among the king's ancestors. This must at the very least signal a desire to acknowledge Roman Imperial symbols as legitimation of their rule. In spite of the archaeological tendency to see the Anglo-Saxons as colonists of an empty land, reduced to a primitive and localised level of organisation with the collapse of the Roman imperial superstructure (Scull 1993), the Anglo-Saxon (and British) kingdoms were not established in a political vacuum. To quote Dumville (1995: 183):

> There could be much in the sixth- and seventh-century political history
> of Britain explicable in terms of an imperial tradition of rulership.

It is certain that kings had an important role in shaping the identities of the Germanic parts of Britain (Yorke 2000). Allegiance to the king would replace any other form of group membership and ethnic identity would become based on the royal house. It is Amory's view (Amory 1997) that the barbarian peoples of the 5th and 6th centuries can be seen as military groups exercising political roles. The role of kings as war leaders would provide a mechanism for integrating political control and action in ways that strengthened group solidarity, no matter what the racial (genetic) origin of the soldiers serving the king. A key factor in transforming them into ethnic groups was played by service to their kings. Military success, official Roman status and office, and divine sanction (whether the sanctity of descent from the Germanic heathen gods or of Christian kingship) would all attract followers into adopting identity with the ruler's ethnic identification. The arrival of the original military group would become the founding migration myth of the people and elements of native and Germanic tradition would become fused (Amory 1997: 34-35). Elements of this certainly occurred in the case of the Anglo-Saxons in Britain, and the role of kings must be considered crucial in the fusing of ethnic identities. That kings would maintain their Germanic identity as the basis for this fusion must though reflect a sizeable Germanic following for these kings.

Social structures

Hierarchy

The social structure of the incoming Germanic settlers, and even of the native Britons, is poorly understood due to lack of documentary evidence from the period. Some commentators like Esmonde Cleary (1995) would see the change from Roman to early medieval Britain as due to the withdrawal of the Roman army, bureaucracy, Imperial landholdings and the collapse of towns. This would have removed the need to produce agricultural surpluses and reduced society to a non-hierarchical low-level and local subsistence economy. However, this would seem to ignore the position of any native aristocracy and the continued need to support military forces. Increasing evidence for continuity in town life would also contradict such a model. British society is largely invisible. On the other hand, the *visible* Germanic society being transplanted into Britain was not noticeably hierarchical or differentiated. Attention has been paid to the role of gender and age in early insular Germanic society (Härke 1997). It seems that the act of migration had little discernible effect on gender roles and does not seem to have loosened the social norms unlike other historical migrations. It is likely that hierarchy was maintained and that we have to face a recurrent problem in archaeology. How far is lack of evidence, evidence of absence?

The continental societies from which the migrants were drawn were highly varied in their social organisation, from those with a low level of centralised power, e.g. Saxons, to those that seem to have been highly stratified with centralised power structures, e.g. Franks or Danes (Wood 1997). The Germanic societies that settled inside the Roman Empire on the continent were highly stratified (Wolfram 1997). Even in non-military contexts, the Germanic peoples of the continent were a hierarchical society, not at all egalitarian peasant farmers (Higham 1992: 165). The king stood at the apex with a circle of officials - his *comites* and *duces* - and a layer of highborn nobles. These would have their retainers of various types living in their households and free tenants living on the land, and the bottom of the social pyramid would be formed of the unfree bondmen and slaves. What marked people as free and of higher status was service in the army. Documentary sources tell us that low born Roman citizens were joining the armies to escape their position and enhance their status; a practice prohibited by Theodoric in Italy where Romans were willing to become Goths in return for higher status. It is in this context that we may see the significance of the rite of weapon burial in eastern Britain as a symbol of Germanic identity.

The archaeological evidence has usually been taken to show a low degree of social differentiation in early Germanic burials in Britain. There are some possible indications that high status could be signified in these earlier Germanic burials. Scull (1992) put forward the idea that occasional graves which contain high status items of metalwork like equal-armed brooches, as at Spong Hill and Westgarth Gardens in East Anglia, could be remains of members of the 5th century elite. The use of the late Roman practice of inhumation in cemeteries where the Germanic practice of cremation had been the prevailing rite might also have been part of signalling elite status.

In the case of 6th century Britain, a general analysis of the evidence from burials reveals an increase in the marking of social status. Obviously wealthy burials begin to appear in the mid and second half of the 6th century. Until then, we cannot say that the Germanic settlers were egalitarian, merely that differences of status were signified in other ways. As Charles-Edwards (2003) has noted, there cannot have been an absence of power relations, and he would see instead more fluidity and uncertainty of such relations in the earlier 6th century. In an agricultural and complex society like early medieval Europe, there will have been inequalities in access to political power, land and wealth. The use of burial to signal such inequalities must mark a meaningful shift in behaviour. An interesting feature of these wealthy burials is that they were commoner in the later 6th century than in the 7th, but that the early 7th century saw a few spectacularly rich burials, e.g. Taplow in Buckinghamshire, Broomfield in Essex, Prittlewell in Essex, and of course Sutton Hoo in Suffolk. While female rich burials occured in the 6th century, they are rare after this. The evidence suggests that Germanic elites were gaining access to wealth and power in unprecedented ways from the mid 6th century, and that this wealth and power was becoming concentrated into fewer hands during the 7th century. What is significant is the absence of elite burials before the mid 6th century. The Germanic elites were either excluded from opportunities to exercise power or were refusing to signal their status at death. The former of these alternatives would be a natural consequence of settlements taking place within political contexts that were still British. The archaeological evidence supports the historical evidence for the growth in power of Anglo-Saxon kings after c.570. As well as increasing social stratification among burials (and a possible decline in status of ordinary freemen), a settlement hierarchy emerged in the late 6th and 7th centuries with new well defined high status sites, e.g. royal residences and ecclesiastical sites (Härke 1997). Particular buildings can be identified as significantly larger than the average household dwelling, e.g. Cowdery's Down in Hampshire. It has long been noted that early Germanic buildings in Britain were smaller and simpler than those on the continent: aisled long houses with byres on the continent but open halls without byres in Britain. Hamerow (2002: 46-51) has shown how the Germanic halls in Britain can have parallels on the content but also suggested that Germanic households in Britain in the 5th and 6th centuries did not have access to the social capital necessary for building large and more complex long houses. In other words, the heads of families could not draw upon networks of retainers and tenants to build their houses. Before the growth of the Anglo-Saxon kingdoms, the Germanic households were simply not in positions of power.

Assimilation

Elite Germanic burials of this period could be interpreted as reflecting a patrilineal kinship structure - that is reckoning membership of the group according by descent from the father (Scull 1993). This would run counter however to the prevailing bilateral (reckoning descent from both mother and father) interpretation of early Germanic kinship (Lancaster 1958, Murray 1983). This is not to say that bilateral systems cannot exhibit bias towards patrilineal descent, pretty much like the picture derived from documentary sources for the newly developed Anglo-Saxon royal families. The bilateral interpretation of Germanic kinship structure has been challenged (Ausenda 1995), and a more complex picture involving both agnatic (links by birth) and cognatic (links by marriage) elements is more likely to have been the true situation. Evidence from Roman Iron Age burials in Denmark has been interpreted as showing both bilateral and patrilineal kinship in different regions of southern Scandinavia (Ravn 2003: 26-27).

Early Germanic society in Britain must have been affected by the act and nature of migration. Much depends on the type of migration. A small military elite will of necessity have a different set of social relations among themselves and with native Britons than a large population of mainly civilian settler families. Scull (1992) proposed that the 'refugees' who formed the bulk of settlers north of the Thames would be likely to bring with them their social structures and hierarchies intact across the North Sea. Whether this was the case needs to be demonstrated rather than assumed, but is an interesting working hypothesis. Newman (1992) has noted that the pattern of British settlement in one area of Suffolk was dispersed farmsteads and that although there was a great degree of dislocation between this pattern and that of the early Anglo-Saxon period, the 5th and 6th century was still characterised by dispersed farmsteads. This would suggest that the social structure of the new settlers was not that different from the native Britons, and that they were able to slot into the existing social frameworks rather than set up isolated villages among a sea of natives. On the other hand, the undeniably early Germanic hamlet of West Stow also occurs in Suffolk so not all farmsteads were dispersed.

It seems that the fundamental unit of society was not the family but the household made up of a kinship unit and its dependants, with differences in status within the household rather than between households (Härke 1997: 140). Such a household might have on average a man and wife, 4 children, perhaps a parent and brother, and up to 4 servants. However, the true picture will be one of considerable variation and it is likely that household structure will vary between different parts of eastern Britain. While the servants in such households might well be British, not all Britons can have been subsumed within Germanic households. Arnold (1984: 130) has suggested that, at least in the Saxon area south of the Thames, the Germanic settlers were mostly men marrying native British women who were acculturating themselves to their husbands' ethnic identity. We must envisage a variety of social structures and household arrangements linking the British and Germanic agnatic kindred (kin by marriage – the in-laws); a situation that bilateral kinship is ideally placed to accommodate. Arnold (1984: 134-136) has highlighted the fact that there was a shortage of women in the burials of later Roman Britain. If this is a true state of affairs then marriage with local British women may not have been a general option and bringing over wives from the continent may have been commoner than Arnold supposed.

An interesting study by Anthony of the Luo in southern Sudan provides insight into processes of elite takeover. Social integration between different ethnic groups resulted in the adoption of the Luo language by the local population (Anthony 1997: 29). The process of assimilation consisted of five elements: the insertion of the elite into positions of political power, access to wealth allowing the widespread giving of gifts to cement vertical social relations, a monopoly of military power, a monopoly of trade and the willingness to intermarry with local native families and thereby receive natives into the kinship structure of the elite. In spite of Anthony's assertion that these elements do not seem to have been present and therefore were not used by early medieval Germanic settlers, it would seem that there is a case for accepting that the emergent Anglo-Saxon kings did indeed use the Luo type strategy in the creation of political units after the 570s, e.g. the control of trade evidenced by the burials at Sutton Hoo. The integration of the native Britons into an English identity might well belong to this phase of the Anglo-Saxon conquest. Härke (1997: 152) has suggested indeed that this is the case and that the integration took place largely in the 7th century.

If Scull (1993) is right and Germanic settlers were organised in patrilineal clans, this would make integration difficult as social units would be more bounded and fixed. However, the preferred model of bilateral kinship groups as the norm for Germanic society at this period (Lancaster 1958, Murray 1983) would accommodate integration better. In areas where family were less important and Germanic migration was more individually based, e.g. in Saxon areas where settlement seems to have been by soldiers within the Romano-British political and social system, a bilateral system would easily enable the complex mix of British and Germanic features that has often been noted in the early history of the West Saxons. In Anglian areas, if settlement was by patrilineal kin groups this could have helped them to maintain their separate identities for some time.

Material culture

Native British culture

If native Britons were still holding power in eastern Britain throughout most of the 5th and 6th centuries, we are faced with the considerable difficulty that they are largely invisible. A major problem in the archaeology of the 5th and 6th centuries is the identification of the native Britons. Archaeological evidence for them after the ending of Roman rule is hard to find. The minting of coins, the large scale production of domestic pottery and the use of stone for building had all come to an end, making sites of this period hard to identify. Esmonde Cleary (1989, 1993) has forcefully put forward the idea that many elements of Roman 'civilisation' were in decline from the fourth century and that the Germanic settlers migrated to a land without an existing Roman framework. This would be disputed by others, e.g. Dark 1994, 2000, who would rather see a Roman Britain transforming itself using different cultural norms. The extreme nature of Esmonde Cleary's position is evident when he put forward the scenario of the material culture of Roman Britain reducing itself not to pre-Roman Iron Age levels but effectively disappearing altogether. The Germanic settlers could thus walk into a vacuum, bring their own culture with them and be left to create from primitive beginnings a new civilisation (Esmonde Cleary 1989). This is not a convincing picture. Examples of the total disappearance of a culture and its socio-political structures would be hard to think of, and is unlikely to have happened in reality. We are instead faced with different forms of cultural expression in the 5th and 6th centuries by the native Britons; forms which are, sadly, less archaeologically visible than those of the Romans.

The minting of coins seems to have been linked very closely to payments of wages to the army (Arnold 1984: 89). There is a lack of Roman coins in Britain minted after 402. Further, the failure of the bid for the throne by Constantinus III, and the independence of Britain from the Empire after 410, ensured that Imperial coinage supplies would cease. Imported Mediterranean pottery is one of the rare items of artefactual evidence for native life at this time (Alcock 1992). However, these are found mostly in the west of Britain, e.g. Tintagel, South Cadbury or Dinas Powys (Henig 2002). A newspaper report *(The Independent*, 6 August 2001) of the newly discovered 6th century site near Bantham in Devon mentioned the finding of remains of pots from North Africa, Palestine and Anatolia, all in the Byzantine Empire, along with evidence of feasting, showing links between the British elites of *Dumnonia* with the remaining power centre of the late Roman Empire. The major evidence for British survival though comes from burials. The prevailing burial rite of the late Roman period was inhumation, especially with the body crouched on its side. Post-Roman cemeteries of east-west oriented inhumations without grave goods are now being recognised (Esmonde Cleary 1989: 184-185), e.g. Cannington, which have been interpreted as the burials of the native British. In other cases, late Roman cemeteries may well have continued as burial places for the native British into the 6th century, e.g. Colchester and Kelvedon (Campbell 1982: 41, Hamerow 1997: 37). The Germanic peoples on the continent largely favoured cremation (although inhumation was not unknown, Welch 1992: 56). Not all cremations need be of Germanic peoples, since the rite was used on occasion in late 4th century Roman burials, e.g. Lankhills (Lucy 2000: 144). However, it must be accepted that the use of cremation by whole communities rather than individuals does have ethnic meaning (Arnold 1984: 128). In spite of increasing recognition of British inhumations, the 5th century British population in the eastern half of the island is still largely archaeologically invisible. However, there is some evidence that new Germanic settlements in the early 5th century were made on poorer farming lands, e.g. West Stow, Mucking. It may well be that these were placed in the gaps between where the British settlements may have been on the better soils (Esmonde Cleary 1989: 196-197). Mixing of ethnic groups in cemeteries ought to be expected since, as has already been noted, there is some documentary evidence for the survival of British speaking populations in Anglo-Saxon ruled areas. This raises the possibility of native Christian burial rituals being used alongside Germanic heathen rites. There are some cemeteries with both British and Germanic burial practices, e.g. Wasperton. Interpreting these is not easy. A site like Wasperton may show either that a Germanic family displaced a native British one in the 5th century, or that a native British family adopted Germanic material culture (Esmonde Cleary 1989: 201). Another mixed cemetery is Spong Hill, where a British community may have been inhuming its dead within an otherwise Germanic cremation cemetery (Esmonde Cleary 1989: 203). Later Roman skeletons tend to represent slightly built bodies, and contrast strongly with later burials of tall strongly built men accompanied by weapons that may be the remains of Germanic migrants (Welch

1992: 60, Jones 1996: 31). Studies in Hampshire have shown that the average height for late Roman men was 5 feet 7 inches, but 5 feet 9 inches for 7th century men (Arnold 1984). By contrast the average height for women remained at around 5 feet 2 inches. Although not everyone accepts the interpretation of the weapon burials, the case for them being the remains of Germanic migrants has been made and restated very persuasively by Härke (1992). However, at least one such 5th century burial at Itchen Abbas in Hampshire is outside the area of primary settlement in Britain and thus seems indeed to be more likely a native Briton than a Germanic settler (Lucy 2000: 150).

There was a distinct western British material culture during this period (Arnold 1971). This is reflected in artefacts like penannular brooches, pins, hanging bowls and pottery. This latter is not the commercial pottery of the Roman period, which had already begun to disappear in the 4th century (Esmonde Cleary 1989). There were wheel-made calcite gritted wares but more usually hand-made types like the Richborough pottery of c.425/50, the Welsh Marches thick, gritty wares of the 5th century, and various wares in the Cotswolds and Cornwall. Perhaps the most spectacular evidence from the west of Britain is the imported wares (Alcock 1971: 201-209 & 1992). Class A red slip dishes & bowls from the eastern Mediterranean and Africa (Phocaean and African Red Slip Wares) date to c.460-600. Class Bi pinkish amphorae with close set grooves on the upper body dating to c.475-576, Class Bii buff amphorae with irregular ridges and fluting dating between c.375-675, and Class Biv red, micaceous amphorae with wide shallow fluting dating to c.400-550 all originated from the eastern Mediterranean and Black Sea. The Byzantine historian Procopius mentioned that Justinian sent subsidies to Britain (Wood 1997). Procopius describes the people in receipt of these as barbarians, implying that he means the Germanic settlers but it is more likely that they were the Britons in light of the distributions of the Mediterranean pottery. The presence of these wares in Britain seems to reflect direct diplomatic contacts between Britain and the Roman Empire at Constantinople between c.475 and c.550 (Harris 2003). This was part of the Empire's attempt to re-establish its influence in the lost areas of the Empire in the west and this attempt was not limited to Britain. Other imported pottery in western Britain is the Class D blue-black mortaria, bowls and goblets from south and west Gaul, and Class E hard, thin-walled and rough-surfaced kitchen ware also from Gaul. However, both D and E wares date to the 7th and 8th centuries. The earlier A and B wares are concentrated on the south western peninsular of Britain, unlike the later E ware, with its focus on Dal Riata in modern Scotland (Charles-Edwards 2003). Imported Byzantine wares are rare in eastern Britain, although sherds have been found in both London and St Albans (Harris 2003). Finds of Byzantine coins of the period are increasingly being made, with evidence that they have been used as pendants within Britain rather than as commercial coinage.

One intriguing class of artefact is the hanging bowls, which were largely of native Celtic craftsmanship but are mostly found in Anglo-Saxon burials. This may signify the existence of local British craftsmen under Anglo-Saxon control or they might have been acquired through tribute, as plunder or through trade (Alcock 1971). While the quoit brooch style of metalwork is unique to Britain and can be accepted as Romano-British in origin, it is likely that the wearers of items in this style were incoming Germans. As Inker (2000) points out, this is a situation somewhat similar to that of the hanging bowls; native artefacts found in what would be accepted by most as Germanic contexts.

Possible continuity or contact between Britons and Germans can also be seen in building styles and landholding patterns. Arnold (1988: 34) makes the point that the building styles of the period show evidence of both Roman and Germanic influences (also Hinton 1990). There are some archaeologists who would accept that the house types of the Anglo-Saxons are essentially Germanic in form and structure (Hamerow 1997: 39), while others would stress their Romano-British origins (Dixon 1982). The few Anglo-Saxon halls that have been excavated do indeed look very different to the aisled long houses with byres that have been found on the continent. The wooden halls at Mucking look as though they may have been built using Romano-British norms and techniques (Dixon 1993), and 5th and 6th century house styles had a long history within Roman Britain. There are similarities between 5th to 9th century houses at Catholme in Staffordshire and Romano-British houses at Dunstan's Clump in Nottinghamshire (Welch 1992: 39). Some of the differences between houses in Britain and the continent could be due to differences in climate (Arnold 1984: 70). Welch (1992: 36-42) would attribute the differences between houses in Britain and the continent, chiefly the lack of an integral byre for stalling cattle, to the milder British climate making winter stalling of cattle unnecessary, and a greater emphasis on sheep rearing than keeping cattle. Arnold (1984) points out that it may be difficult to assign buildings to either native or Anglo-Saxon ownership/use, and that the influence of local geology or economic factors may be more important than ethnicity in determining building type. It is worth noting that recent excavations on the continent have found more evidence for open halls without byres, so that Germanic halls in Britain may be less strange than they have hitherto appeared (Hamerow 2002). The same templates of size and organisation of space can be seen in both British and continental houses. The aisled long house itself was declining in importance on the continent during the 5th century and open halls were becoming much commoner in the very centuries which saw Germanic settlement in Britain (Hamerow 2002: 50). British influence on Anglo-Saxon halls may be more apparent than real.

The commonest type of brooch in Anglian areas is the annular brooch, being used from the late 5th to the 7th century. This is a ring and pin rather than a safety pin type. Most people would accept a native British origin for these brooches, although Hines (1984) has cast doubt on this. Penannular brooches, with a gap in the ring, are undoubtedly of native British origin, going back to the Iron Age. Similar in style were the quoit brooches consisting of flat metal ring, a pin and a notch on one side of the ring. These were also probably of Romano-British origin but for use by Germanic soldiers. The same origin accounts for the disc brooches, of safety pin type, from c.450-c.550 in the upper Thames valley.

It is now recognised that town life continued after the end of Roman rule and would have formed an important element of British influence. Not only Wroxeter, but also other walled towns like York and Gloucester have produced evidence for 5th century occupation (Hinton 1990: 6-7). Even smaller, market towns have evidence for continuity, e.g. Heybridge in Essex with intrusive features like *grubenhäuser* (houses with a basement or ground floor dug into the ground) and Germanic pottery in the latest levels of a Romano-British site (Hines 1990a). At Exeter, Dorchester and St Albans, there is evidence for large-scale processing of agricultural produce. Were these rents in kind, or supplies to be redistributed to the armies of the 5th century? Hinton regards the lack of processing evidence in the 6th century as due to the collapse of coercive centralised authority. However, we might also regard the evidence as suggesting that payments for soldiers were no longer needed. Early employment of Germanic mercenaries or British units might have relied on payment of supplies. In this context, it would make sense for British authorities to welcome the arrival of Germanic families who could feed and support their menfolk without the necessity of being provided for by the British landowners. By the 6th century, it might be that soldiers were more directly supplying themselves.

The New Germanic culture

One of the most obvious types of artefact that has been identified as Germanic in style and origin is the pottery found in eastern Britain. Variation in pottery style can carry meaning for various types and levels of social differentiation. Some features of pottery form and decoration may be linked with ethnic identity, but others seem to be representative of other kinds of group identity (Richards 1988). Incised vertical lines may well be an Anglian feature, but incised arches seem to have some social meaning within the group that is not now obvious, being associated in burials with miniature iron blades and shears belonging to children or young adults. Separate elements of decoration had clear associations with gender and age. Applied raised bosses seem to have been associated with adult males, while incised hanging arches were more linked with women and children (Richards 1995).

There are some attributes of pottery which seem to have been an indicator of particular ethnic identities. These were identified by Myres (1977, 1989). Anglian features included high shouldered forms in the late 5th century, upright rims, what Myres called the vertical and diagonal style of decoration, and linear and corrugated decoration which was horizontal on the neck and vertical on the shoulder. Jutish pottery was distinguished by linear chevrons and raised collars, and tall pedestal jars with elongated bosses. Saxon styles favoured sub-biconical forms, large decorated bosses, *stehende bogen* (upright arches, also a Frisian characteristic), and chevron decoration. Frisian pots were marked by long bosses, pedestal bases and foot-stands.

After settlement, the form and decoration of pottery began to develop distinctly insular attributes, distinguishing insular Germanic pottery from that on the continent (Myres 1977). The earliest Germanic pottery in Britain has incised linear decoration, or is faceted and carinated. Peculiarly insular developments included the use of stamps, line and dot decoration in enclosed zones and pendant triangles. However, some features remained in common between Britain and the continent until quite a late date, e.g. *stehende bogen* schemes and *buckelurnen* (urns with elaborate bosses).

The other major Germanic artefact was the metal brooch. These have often been used as an ethnic indicator, although the reality of their use is somewhat more complex than a simple equation of a type of brooch with a particular people. Lucy (2000) provides an admirable summary of the state of knowledge of these brooches, upon which the following paragraphs are based.

Cruciform brooches were of the 'safety pin' type consisting of a head-plate ornamented with three lobes and an animal headed terminal at the 'pin end' of the brooch. Some types of cruciform brooch were common to both Britain and the continent; chiefly the less ornamented and simpler types. The earliest types of cruciform brooch might well have been made on the continent in the early fifth century and were worn for some considerable time before being deposited with burials. The latest examples belonged to the early 7th century. Their main distribution is in Kent and can be considered as part of Jutish material culture, before being adopted more widely in Anglian areas in the later 6th century. Another artefact whose distribution is centred on Kent is the bracteate (Lucy 2000). These medallions based originally on the design of Roman gold coins seem to have originated around 450 in southern Scandinavia and spread shortly afterwards to other parts of the continent and Britain (Hines 1984).

Anglian square-headed brooches have a rectangular head plate and a lozenge or diamond shaped foot. Hines's studies of these brooches have shown that they resulted from southern Scandinavian influence in the early 6th century. The type is dated to between c.500 and c.570, with three phases: 500-20, 510-25/50, and 525-70 (Hines 1997). The Jutish version of these brooches tends to be earlier, smaller and has different forms of decoration. They are found in Kent and the Isle of Wight, belonging to the period 450-500 (Suzuki 2000). The earliest examples might have been brought over from Jutland in the 480s. Hines regards these brooches as cultural indicators of the Germanic elite.

Small-long brooches are simpler and plainer alternatives to the two elaborate types outlined above. They were a peculiarly insular type of brooch, only found in Britain, especially in the Anglian areas of the midlands, and beginning in the 5th century.

Other types of long, safety pin style Germanic brooch are found in Britain, regarded as imports made on the continent and not leading to any insular production. They would be brought over as the personal possessions of settlers, whose descendants were happy to use other types of brooch manufactured in Britain. Equal-armed brooches originated in Saxony in the late 5th century. A group of equal-armed brooches with trapezoidal head-plates from early 6th century East Anglia might have been the result of contacts with Norway. Northern Germany was the source for a variety of rare types, including supporting-arm brooches and tutulus brooches (from early 5th century contexts). Radiate and bird brooches were associated with the Franks.

As well as the elongated safety-pin type of brooch, there were also round safety pin brooches. Saucer brooches have been regarded as one of the classic markers of Saxon as opposed to Anglian identity, but have a marked concentration in the upper Thames valley rather than south of the Thames. They are circular in plan with an upraised rim, and belong to the 5th and 6th centuries, either having applied decoration or being solid cast. Although continental in origin they developed in Britain as an insular type of brooch. Button brooches are smaller types of brooch with simpler decoration and date to between c.450-c.600. They are also most likely to have been a Saxon product, although Arnold (1984: 105) seems to suggest that they have a British origin. Plated and composite disc brooches with inset garnets on the other hand were Kentish, belonging to the mid 6th century and lasting well into the 7th century, even as late as c.720. A minor type of brooch is the swastika brooch. This is a disc with part cut away to reveal a swastika design of Germanic origin.

To summarise, the various types of brooches have associations with different aspects of Germanic ethnic identity (Lucy 2000: 133-137). Square-headed, cruciform and short-long brooches were Anglian and Kentish, although square-headed and short-long brooches are also found in small quantities in Saxon areas. Good markers of Anglian identity were also swastika brooches, along with other items of female attire like girdle hangers (also Kentish) and sleeve clasps. Saucer brooches were centred on the upper Thames valley and Cotswolds but did spread into both Saxon and Anglian areas. Disc brooches have a similar distribution. It is the button brooches that are limited to Saxon areas (and Kent). It would seem that Anglian identity was more clearly marked than Saxon or Jutish in the 5th and 6th centuries. This should alert us to the possibility of different contexts and mechanisms for Germanic settlement in different parts of Britain.

The evidence from burials indicates strong regional differences in Germanic women's fashions (Welch 1992: 62-64). Saxon preference was for a long tubular outer dress fastened at each shoulder by a brooch, and for a third brooch over the chest to be used to fasten a scarf or cloak. Strings of beads would hang between the two shoulder brooches. Anglian women would have a long sleeved undergarment which was fastened at the sleeves by metal wrist claps. Silver bracelets and key like ornaments called girdle hangers would be worn from a belt at the waist. Jutish fashions were very different and shared many features with the continental Franks. A long sleeved jacket was worn above a long skirt. The jacket was fastened by two round brooches above the breast and two square-headed brooches at the waist. A woven head band might also be worn. On the other hand, Fisher (1988) found that some types of dress fastener did not show any significant association with geographical areas, while others did so but not in any consistent way. Small-scale local variations in use were more evident than larger scale regional patterns. These local indicators included annular and swastika brooches and pins, the easiest to produce and perhaps the easiest to use to assert individual identity. Other types of fastener (cruciform, square-headed, penannular and applied brooches) reflected an overall Anglian identity, and were not being used to discriminate between more local identities. The use of distinctive styles of dress and their associated fasteners to signal regional identity seems to have died out in the late 6th century. At a time when newly emergent kings were seeking to establish their power, the material culture of personal appearance was coming to stress an overall Anglo-Saxon identity rather than an identity based on differences between the recently created kingdoms (Lucy 2000: 25).

The development of styles of decoration on metalwork (brooches, strap ends etc.) clearly shows the origins of Anglo-Saxon design to lie in continental Germanic art styles; albeit that these in turn owe a great deal to late Roman prototypes. The eastern side of Britain belonged to a Scandinavian culture province embracing either side of the North Sea (Stevenson 1992). Haselhoff (1974) has shown that Scandinavia was a key area for the development of the Nydam style of ornament from c.400 to c.475, which in turn developed into Salin's Style I animal ornament (c.475 to c.525). It is phases C and D of Style I that were developed in the North Sea region and served to unite the culture of the Anglo-Saxons of Britain with their homeland on the continent. The Jutish connections of Kent as noted by Bede are reinforced by the archaeology, although Jutish culture was not simply transferred wholesale. Kent was not a copy of Jutland and archaeology reveals differences in the use of material culture between the two areas (Lucy 2000: 179). However, Kent soon reoriented its identity towards that of neighbouring Gaul just across the Channel (Hines 1994). For instance, there are some brooches that can be identified as having strong Jutish links, e.g. at Bifrons, Finglesham, Gilton and Richborough in Kent, but also occurring elsewhere in the Germanic areas of Europe, e.g. the Rhineland and the Alps. A Frankish overlay was thus imposed over a Jutish base.

One key element of material culture that seems to signify something very different to traditional Roman ideas of identity and status is that of weaponry. Roman citizens were civilians by law, forbidden to own or use weapons. It is therefore significant that a high proportion of the Germanic burials in Britain have weapons as grave goods. Similar weapon burials have been found also in Gaul, where they are widely accepted as representing Germanic warriors (Hills 1978). However, burials with weapons are much commoner in Britain than among the Germans on the continent: 18% of burials in Britain but only 4% on the continent (Jones 1996: 29). This amounts to 47% of adult male burials and must represent a warrior class born out of the circumstances of migration. This supports the traditional evidence for the employment of Germanic soldiers by British authorities as a key event in defining an insular Germanic identity. However, not all weapons were buried with adult males (e.g. 8% were found with boys under 12) and the weapons themselves seem to have been largely symbolic in function. One key feature of the skeletons buried with weapons is that they were on average 2-5 cm taller than bodies buried without weapons in the same cemetery. Skeletal evidence also suggests that weapon burials in at least two cemeteries were associated with particular family groups. The evidence of other grave goods supports the idea that the weapon burial represented the wealthier sections of society. Whether they symbolised Germanic soldiers and their families among civilian Britons or a fighting over-class among Germanic immigrants is not as yet possible to say. Härke (1990, 1997) and Jones (1996: 31) strongly suggest that ethnic differentiation is the only likely explanation, although the ethnic significance of the skeletal traits associated with weapon burials has not gone unchallenged (Hills 2003: 59-62). If this is the case, then we have a powerful indication that the proportion of Germanic incomers to native Britons could have been very high. No doubt the newcomers attracted or acquired British dependants who accommodated themselves to the culture of their new masters by being buried in the same cemeteries, presumably with similar rites. Some of the shorter skeletons buried with weapons have been claimed as those of acculturating Britons (Härke 1992). Differences in stature though could come from different upbringings and access to nutrition, and so have a class as well as ethnic significance.

Summary

Transformation through opposition

Partition and transformation

We are accustomed to speaking of Roman Britain as though it were a unit. True, it was a single diocese of the Empire but its five provinces had very different characteristics and histories. The complex variety of these characteristics can perhaps be simplified into a twofold distinction between a highly Romanised south and east, and a more traditionally British north and west. The distribution of villas and of late-occupied hill forts are largely exclusive, although there is a zone of overlap between them (Dark 1994: 40-41). The characteristics of the Roman way of life, as reflected by the distribution of towns and villas, were concentrated in an area to the south and east of the rivers Trent, Avon, Severn and Parret (Jones & Mattingly 1990: 151). That this reflects some long established pattern is suggested by the fact that this is the same area that was moving towards urbanisation and minting coins in the late Iron Age (Jones & Mattingly 1990: 46). Native elites in Gaul were re-emphasising their Gaulish identity at the expense of their Roman identity as early as the 4th century (Geary 2002: 104-105), and it may be that the south east of Britain was likewise more British in sentiment while at the same time holding onto the material wealth and ways of life they had become accustomed to. By the early 7th century, this duality between British and Roman cultures had been replaced by a pagan Germanic south and east and a Christian Romano-British north and west. Whereas the Roman diocese served to integrate the different parts of Britain, the new order was divisive and the old diocese would not be brought under a single authority again until the late 13th century.

The reality of partition of Britain between a Germanic and a Celtic sphere is revealed by the archaeology. Although archaeological artefacts cannot reveal the genetic make-up of their users, there is no doubt that the west and north of Britain rejected assimilation into a Germanic identity, while the south and east became dominated by Germanic culture. It is unlikely that this division was the result simply of personal taste in fashion. Gildas referred to a partition of Britain, complaining that some Christian sites could no longer be visited since they were in areas ruled by "the barbarians" (Winterbottom 1978: 19). There must have been some substantial movement of population to enable Germanic culture to achieve superiority in lowland Britain, and to enable a heathen rule to block Christian pilgrimage. If it were merely a matter of the British majority acculturating themselves to a powerful but small Germanic warrior minority, we need to ask why this acculturation was accepted only in part of the island, and resisted elsewhere. The advance of English culture and English speech did not continue to take over the whole of former Roman Britain (Hooke 1995: 3-4). Some scholars have suggested that some of the later royal houses of the Anglo-Saxons had British origins (e.g. Arnold 1997). The same question needs also to be asked of them; why did they feel the need to change their ethnic affiliation, unlike their cousins farther west? The answer must surely lie in the relative numbers of settlers, rather than just social superiority. A minority elite is just as likely to assimilate itself to the majority population it rules (cf. the Normans in Normandy, England and Sicily), and yet this did not happen in south eastern Britain. The reality of an Irish origin to the royal houses and presumably aristocracy of Dyfed and Brycheiniog during this same period of Germanic migration is widely accepted (Dark 1994: 79-83). Yet, it is noteworthy that this Irish element, although dominant and socially superior, acculturated themselves to the native British. The Irish were no less strange to the Britons than the Germans in terms of language and culture. If Irish and British were both Celtic languages, it must be doubtful whether they were in any way mutually intelligible at this period. The Irish were also traditional enemies of the Britons, having raided the shores of the diocese for many years. We must then explain why eastern Britain became England while Dyfed did not become Irish in its culture and language, although Dark (2000) suggested that Irish was a living language in Britain at this time. As noted above, I believe the explanation for this lies in the massive movement of population from the continent to Britain altering the demographic balance against the native inhabitants in the east. Evidence for such a massive migration of Irish (as opposed to the movement of elites) into Dyfed is lacking.

In accounting for why British identity disappeared in the east of Britain, we must acknowledge that British political power remained in the area for some time. Most of the Anglo-Saxon kingdoms were not established until the later 6th century, leaving someone else – the Britons – to be still governing the old *civitates* and perhaps even the old provinces. Post-Roman Britain was not an empty land without government for over 150 years. Even after the establishment of Germanic kingdoms, some pockets of native rule might have remained. One curiosity about the foundation of churches under Anglo-Saxon rule is revealed in the maps plotted by Arnold (1988:140). These reveal a gap in the location of churches founded in the 7th century in the region north of London. This area also coincides with a gap in the distribution of heathen Anglo-Saxon burials and has been suggested as an area of late British control that did not pass under Germanic rule until later than surrounding areas (Dark 1994: 86-89). The region is approximately that of the old *civitates* of the Catuvellauni and Trinovantes. Could it be that churches here were still in existence from the time of the first introduction of Christianity in the 4th century, protected by British rule? There is no hint of this in the surviving documentary sources for the conversion of the Anglo-Saxons, but since these focus on the conversion of royal families, this is perhaps not surprising. Harris (2003) has pointed out that the few finds of Byzantine pottery in eastern Britain, which might be evidence for Byzantine diplomatic contacts with British rulers, come from London and St Albans, both within this possible British enclave. On the other hand, the grave of St. Alban is mentioned by Gildas as being among the places unavailable for Christian pilgrims after the partition of Britain, which would not be the case if the area were still under British rule when Gildas was writing.

The partition of Britain did not happen overnight. Germanic migration was a process taking many decades. The process also involved a transformation not only of the Romanised south-east but also of the Germanic settlers themselves. Just as their relations with the native Britons changed over time, so did their organisation and self-identification. A variety of pagan Germanic families and social units would become a handful of Anglo-Saxon kingdoms. The only constant features to remain were their Germanic cultural identity and the resulting resistance to becoming British. The defining act of their identity would become that of migration. As the British speaking populations in the south and east became absorbed into the new Anglo-Saxon identity in the 7th and 8th centuries, a cultural unity based on Christianity would arise to weld together the new societies, and into which migration as a chosen people could be fitted as an essential part of the national myth.

The transformation of Roman Britain into Anglo-Saxon England and British Wales can be broken down into various processes:

- the 5th and 6th centuries saw the settlement in Britain of various people from the Germanic areas of the continent, in different circumstances and numbers in different parts of the former Roman diocese;
- these migrants maintained a self-identification as Germans, keeping up links with their homelands and the wider north-western Germanic world;
- the settlers gradually created an insular Germanic culture adapting their own continental customs and culture, alongside those of the Romano-Britons;
- some native Britons adopted this insular Germanic identity and shared in its creation;
- from c.570 various Germanic and Britto-Germanic families took over existing power structures and began to create kingdoms which were self-consciously Anglo-Saxon in identity, and which sought to expand and control eastern Britain.

These processes can be allotted to two phases: migration followed by conquest. This is similar to the view of Hines (1996) who also sees a phase of migration followed by a phase of expansion through conquest leading to assimilation of native Britons in the west of the conquered areas.

Phase 1: migration

It must be emphasised that there was no single migration episode common to all the Anglo-Saxons. To speak of 'the Anglo-Saxon migrations' or of the Germanic settlements in Britain as a single episode or phenomenon would be wrong. It is however all too common in discussions of the period. In part, this stems from a projection of English unity back into the early phases of Germanic presence in Britain. It also stems from an assumption of unity in the later Roman diocese of Britain. Neither is a tenable assumption. We should recognise that late Roman Britain was varied in its political and military arrangements, and in its culture. We should also accept that the settlement of Germanic immigrants in Britain was undertaken by different groups, under different leaders, for different reasons and within different British contexts. One early settlement was in Kent, where the Germanic settlers and their elite chose to signal their identity in different ways to other Germanic settlers in other parts of Britain. Styles of brooch were one way of signalling this difference, another was the differences in the styles and metallic composition of the high status bracteates. The initial employment of Germanic soldiers by British authorities was most likely a federate agreement. Other, later settlements were probably of *laeti* and *foederati* by separate provincial authorities. A revolt by some of these soldiers was followed by increasing numbers of Germanic settlers being placed in areas still under British political control in the east of the island. Some settlements of *foederati* would have been under strong royal or aristocratic leadership, maintaining contact with homelands across the North Sea.

Germanic identity was being more forcefully expressed in Britain than it was on the continent (Crawford 1997: 69). This would fit the circumstances of migration with the need to assert identity in a period of uncertainty and political/social change. It may also be one reason for the greater visibility of Germanic material culture relative to that of the native Britons. The difference between the two may be depositional and that non-material aspects of culture like language may have been more important to the Britons as ethnic signifiers (Hines 2003). As suggested earlier, display of wealth and position might have taken the form of endowments to the church rather than ostentatious personal display. Nevertheless, there does seem to be much more deliberate marking of identity among the migrant Germanic settlers than among other neighbouring groups of the same time.

The act of migration itself did not create an Anglo-Saxon identity although it would be used later a reference point for that identity. The Germanic migrations to Britain were not isolated. They were part of a wider move by Germanic settlers into various parts of the Roman Empire. Saxon migration was not limited to Britain but was a phenomenon taking place either side of the Channel. Migrants had been moving into the Empire from the 4th century onwards, directing themselves primarily towards northern Gaul. Germanic brooch styles evolved together on either side of the Imperial frontier in Gaul up to the early 5th century, at which time migration changed its direction towards Britain (Hills 1978). It is worth reminding ourselves that Saxons settlers have been identified in the Calvados area around Bayeux, the Loire estuary and near Boulogne and Calais. The Saxon leader Adovacrius (Eadwacer) was fighting in the Loire Valley in 464. Much later, Saxons were found fighting in support of the Frankish invasion of Armorica in 578 (Haywood 1991). Unfortunately, we cannot know whether links between the Saxons in Britain and Gaul were maintained but it is likely.

Germanic settlers in Britain were not cutting themselves off from their homelands. Contact across the North Sea was maintained (Hills 1978: 317, Scull 1993: 70). Britain was not isolated but part of interrelated maritime zones centred on the North and Irish Seas, in which Germanic contact between Britain and the continent was intense (Hills 1999). We can see this in, among other ways, the importing of luxury goods (Arnold 1997) and in the shared myths and legends of the period. Germanic myths current among the Anglo-Saxons included figures from the continent up to the 560s. As late as the 550s, there is record of a war between the Angles in Britain and neighbours from their old homeland, the Werne, in the 6th century. Mechanisms of settlement across the North Sea need to be balanced by mechanisms of continued communication. In time, it would be inevitable that the Germanic settlers in Britain would develop a separate identity, differing from that of their cousins on the continent. Styles of decoration in pottery for instance involve much greater use of stamped ornament and panel designs in Britain during the 6th century (Myres 1977). The new insular-based Germanic identity might be based around a core ethnicity of Angle or Saxon but could adopt its signifiers of identity from a variety of cultural markers from throughout the area of the Germanic homeland. It is Hines's view (Hines 1995) that a new Anglo-Saxon identity was created very quickly, soon after migration out of various elements of Germanic material culture, or to be more accurate, Anglian, Saxon and Jutish identities. Others might prefer to see this happening over a longer time-span.

Germanic identity in Britain in its earliest stages was probably twofold. A Saxon identity would have been shared across the Channel with Gaul, while an Anglian identity would have been spread across the North Sea. The Jutes were moving from one to the other identity during this period. Hines (1994) has reiterated his belief in an Anglian orientation towards Scandinavian cultural norms to signal their ethnicity in a way which excluded Saxons farther south. Anglian areas of Britain were not only more mixed culturally than Saxon areas, they were also more intensively marked by material culture (Hines 1995). There is strong evidence of two-way links archaeologically across the North Sea (Wood 1997), especially of 'Anglo-Saxon' evidence in the Rhineland and of close parallels in pottery styles between Britain and Frisia. The maintenance of networks of relationships across the North Sea in this period for East Anglia has already been noted (Scull 1992). The links with the continent were not only one-way. Reverse migration back from Britain undoubtedly took place. The Germanic settlers were still fully part of a northern European world and the leading power in that world was the Franks. Settlement of Angles from Britain was sponsored by the Franks in 531 to help in the subjugation of Thuringia. Angles were also present as slaves in Frankish Gaul. A letter of Pope Gregory in 595 makes it clear that he expected to be able to buy Anglian slaves in the slave markets of Gaul as part of the preparation for the Christian mission to Kent (Colgrave 1968: 145). Some 20 years earlier, between 575 and 579, Gregory had come across Anglian slaves being sold at market in Rome (Colgrave 1968, Colgrave & Mynors 1969). We would dearly like to know how they came to be there. Were they captured in war, were they part of tribute, were they gained though trade?

The nature of Frankish influence in Britain during the 6th century remains something of a mystery. The Franks themselves based their power in Gaul partly on Roman institutions, beginning as foederate governors of *Belgica Secunda* (Barnwell 1992: 93-94). There is however no evidence for the survival of prefectural or diocesan power in Gaul. If the Frankish kings were claiming prefectural power then they would naturally seek to resurrect prefectural supervision of the British diocese. That the Franks had interests in Britain is certain (Campbell et al 1982: 37-38). However, it would seem that Frankish links with Kent were more likely to be based on Germanic personal overlordship than revived Roman institutions.

Thus far, discussion of the transition from Roman Britain to Anglo-Saxon England has proceeded along very simplistic lines with an assumption that the numbers of migrating Saxons were related solely to the number of soldiers employed by the Britons in the early 5th century. It must surely be the case that the number of settlers depended rather on both natural increase and immigration over a period of perhaps 150 years or more. The migration was a prolonged series of acts, not a single action (Hamerow 1997: 41). Using the pottery evidence, Myres (1977) saw settlement beginning in the early 5th century, increasing greatly after c.450 and then continuing into the 6th century but declining by the end of that century. Arnold (1997: 26) has suggested that there is evidence from the dating of sleeve claps that migration was largely over by 525/50 (although this would relate only to migration from one part of the Germanic world). Fieldwork in East Anglia has revealed an intensification of new Germanic settlement in the late 5th and 6th centuries (Carver 1989: 144). As a result, the Germanic element of the population of south east Britain could be continually stocked up by immigration from the continental homeland. It is unlikely that Britons in the same part of Britain could replenish themselves to the same degree by migration from the north west of the island. Bede painted a picture of a depopulated homeland on the continent due to the extent of the migration to Britain, a picture largely supported by the archaeology for certain areas (Hamerow 1997: 33). North Sea coastal settlements like Feddersen Wierde, Wijster, Flögeln-Eekhöltjen and Vorbasse were abandoned by c.450 (Welch 1992), although it cannot be assumed that the population moved to Britain rather than elsewhere on the continent (Johnson 1980: 45-47, Welch 1992: 34). In some areas, increased excavation has revealed a picture of shifting settlement and a change in the patterns of settlement. There was a general trend at continental farmsteads around the North Sea for them to become less enclosed, more loosely structured, with shorter long houses and fewer granaries (Hamerow 2003: 88-89). Increasing population pressure leading to agricultural crisis is often cited as the main cause for these changes. In some areas, the traditional picture of depopulation is still the best interpretation of the evidence, as in Schleswig-Holstein, the original Anglian homeland (Hamerow 2003: 108-114). The evidence comes not only from settlements but also of place-names and pollen cores. One response to any agricultural crisis might well have been migration to Britain of surplus population. Todd (1992) noted that the pottery of the continental site of Feddersen Wierde is noticeably similar to that of the early 5th century site of Mucking in Essex, where Germanic settlers seem to have been placed by, or under, late Roman style officials.

Phase 1 then was a period of post-Roman British independence involving the employment of Germanic mercenaries from various parts of the continent; areas bordering the North Sea and in southern Scandinavia. The Germanic settlers were still part of a functioning North Sea Germanic cultural area. Links between Britain and the continent continued into the 6th century, tending to be with Saxony and Frisia rather than the Anglian or Jutish homelands (the latter areas being those depopulated according to Bede). Given the lack of extensive Germanic political power in Britain and the continued links with the continent, we cannot really speak of Anglo-Saxon history in this phase. Until the rise of kingdoms stressing that identity, it is perhaps better and more accurate to speak of Germanic peoples within a post-Roman or Late Antique Britain (Dark 2000: 25).

It is likely that the political unity of Britain as a Roman diocese was broken during this period and that the economic and political strength of the succeeding British authorities was undermined. Some writers would see post-Roman Britain as highly localised and fragmented in the 5th century immediately after withdrawal from the Roman Empire, with small units later combining into the larger kingdoms of the 6th century (e.g. Loveluck 2000). I would argue that this is too catastrophic a picture and that some sort of post-Roman unity was maintained for much or all of the 5th century – the true 'dark age' of British history. The key question for the 5th and early 6th centuries is not the extent of Germanic migration to Britain but the nature of British unity and power, and its later fragmentation and decline. Secure evidence for fragmentation of Britain only comes from the 6th century, after the putative reign of Artorius/Arthur.

Phase 2: conquest

It is this period which saw the creation of an Anglo-Saxon identity. This was achieved by the takeover of much of Britain from existing British authorities. This allowed the linking of political power with Germanic ethnicity and thereby mobilising a sense of being Anglo-Saxon. An insular Germanic identity in Britain was emerging in the years after 500 (Moreland 2000). We should realise that this needed to be focussed on structures of political power to become the Anglo-Saxon identity we see in the 7th century (as understood by Hines, 1996, when he wrote of the creation of a normative Anglo-Saxon identity hostile to pluralist culture and linked to royal power). This would also have involved the creation of insular linguistic norms, creating an English variant of north west Germanic speech. The Germanic kingdoms that took over lowland Britain were independent of the continental homeland, but some were possibly reliant on Frankish support and maintained links across the Channel.

The establishment of Germanic kingship in Britain has been identified on archaeological grounds as belonging to the late 6th century (Carver 1989: 158), which would support the documentary evidence for the founding of new dynasties from the 570s onwards. The documentary evidence may be illusory, simply reflecting a limit of oral memory that could not go back further than the later 6th century. However, the archaeological evidence and the documentary record of military conquests in the later 6th century would suggest that this period really did see the emergence of something new. Is it significant that Bede could not supply evidence of the original homelands of the Anglo-Saxon royal families, even of his own Bernician royal family. His statement of the original homelands of the Germanic settlers in Britain is remarkably unspecific, in contrast to the origin tales of the Goths and Lombards as related in Jordanes and Paul (Mierow 1915, Pohl 1997). This suggests strongly that the new kings in Britain were not of ancient stock, except perhaps for Mercia - the traditional enemy of Northumbria and so unlikely to be given an origin story by Bede that would elevate them above their neighbours. Most of the new kingdoms were a recent phenomenon that did not look back to their continental roots but forged new Britain-based Anglian or Saxon identities.

The key period for the expansion of Anglo-Saxon political control over Britain seems to have begun c.570. At about this time, the documentary evidence reveals the establishment of several new dynasties and the beginnings of major conquests from the Britons. This period also saw the emergence of wealthy elites using Germanic material culture to signal their wealth (Carver 1998: 104). With the establishment of political control came greater access to resources and a chance to accumulate wealth that was denied before this time. The establishment of new ruling families involved the reorientation of material culture to express hierarchical status rather more than ethnic identity. Hines (1984) dated this change in material culture to around 560, a period that saw the end of shared elements of material culture between Anglian Britain and Scandinavia - A to C type sleeve clasps, square-headed and relief brooches, A, C and D type bracteates and cruciform brooches - and the end of a shared style 1 ornament. Arnold (1997: 24-26) suggested that the development of sleeve clasps and square-headed brooches would suggest that migration or colonisation of Germanic settlers was coming to an end at around 550. Social bonds based on loyalty to the king seem to have overridden bonds based on kinship. The new political units, although based on elements of ethnicity, themselves were capable of mobilising an identity for their people based on that of their lords. An Anglian kingdom became Anglian through its ruling house as much as because it had an Anglian population. The kingdoms of Anglo-Saxon England therefore provide examples of a process Smith has identified in what he calls his imperfect ancient and medieval ethnic states (Smith 1986: 90). The process involves an aristocratic *ethnie* using the powers of the state to create a political unity, whereby they impose and filter down their ethnic identity to dependent populations. Ethnicity would have provided the social cohesion necessary for the elite to govern effectively (Hines 1995). On the other hand, it is noteworthy in Smith's model that pockets of alternative identities often remain, a situation lacking in the Anglo-Saxon kingdoms. An elite needs more than simply prestige to assimilate its subject populations. It is hard to see how an elite without a substantial base of ethnically similar followers could mobilise ethnic feeling or identity on its behalf.

The archaeological evidence for the break with the continent at 550-575 is paralleled by the breaking of contact with the continent in literature at around the same time; the latest common Germanic figure included in the cultural stock being Ælfwine (Alboin) of the Lombards (568-72). This represents a cultural break rather than any break in physical contact. It symbolises a feeling that the Anglo-Saxons were no longer part of a common Germanic heritage but henceforth could find their own indigenous heroes. As Hines put it (Hines 1995: 83), "... at least the conditions for the emergence of a common English identity then existed". This same period coincides with the disappearance of regional differences in Germanic identities in Britain, as expressed in artefacts, and the emergence of a general Anglo-Saxon style of material culture (Hines 1994: 54). However, it must not be thought that a single Anglo-Saxon culture was uniform. Some regional differences in material culture, e.g. brooches and manuscript illumination, were maintained well into the 7th century (Hines 1995), albeit within a general Anglo-Saxon cultural sphere.

The trigger for indigenous 'independence' might have been the growing Frankish control over the continental cousins of the Anglo-Saxons. Continental Saxon resistance to Frankish overlordship was being subdued in the 550s and 560s. Saxon desire for freedom could henceforth be satisfied in Britain under independent kings. On the other hand, the power of Kent was being enhanced by acceptance of Frankish sponsorship, allowing access to the wealth of the Frankish state. Perhaps the establishment of Anglo-Saxon kings was a way of resisting Kentish power as part of the attempt to resist Frankish power over the Saxons.

The Frankish state was prone to rivalry between different kings, each using links with peoples outside the borders of the state to strengthen his own position. The Franks also sought a position of superiority over other Germanic peoples in western Europe generally. It is into this pattern of Frankish politics that we should fit Procopius's story of the war between the Angles and Varni in the 550s. The Varni themselves were remembered by the Anglo-Saxons in the poem *Widsið* as the Werne or Wærne under their king Billing. The war began over a broken promise of marriage in which the Werne sought alliance with the Franks rather than the British based Angles. An Anglian attack on the Werne would therefore signal hostility to such Frankish links. Frankish attempts to bring northern Germany into its orbit were bound to involve relations of hostility or alliance with Germanic peoples settled in Britain, as long as these were maintaining contacts with their ancestral homelands. A key period in establishing Frankish supremacy over the continental Saxons seems to have been the 560s, with the campaign of Chilperic I and Sigibert I against the Saxons (James 1988: 105). Would this have given the Franks a vested interest in newly emergent Germanic kingdoms in Britain in the 570s? Frankish attempts to influence and control the Anglo-Saxon kingdoms could be either a cause or a result of the emergence of the historical dynasties in Britain. Either way, Frankish policy would have been to try to prevent Anglo-Saxon interference in continental Saxony. The Franks could have actively promoted the position and power of the Kentish kings as a way of doing this. The rise of new kingdoms might have been an independent development forcing a Frankish response. One intriguing possibility is that the new kingdoms were founded by elite families fleeing Frankish power in Old Saxony and Angeln. Unfortunately, the meagre state of the historical sources does not enable us to investigate this any further.

Halsall (1992) pointed out that the same period that saw the rise of Anglo-Saxon kingdoms also saw profound social changes in Merovingian Gaul. Material culture and burial practices changed radically at c.600, dated more precisely to the period of royal minorities and instability between 575 and 612. The previously dependant nobility became much more hereditary in nature and more securely entrenched in its rights, able to cream off part of the taxation surplus that would otherwise have gone to the king. The rise of Anglo-Saxon nobility in Britain to kingly status might be part of the same process. Their military expansion could proceed unchecked.

One key question yet to be tackled is why did British resistance to Anglo-Saxon advance collapse in the period 570-634? One answer to this might be that the Mediterranean trade networks that the British elites had relied upon since the ending of Roman rule came to an end at this time. The invasion of Italy by the Lombards in 568 broke Imperial Roman rule over Italy, so recently reconstructed by Justinian. This ushered in a period of crisis for the Roman Empire (not just in Italy) which effectively ended its attempt to re-establish its domination of the Mediterranean. One result of this seems to have been the collapse of Mediterranean long distance trade along the sea routes to Britain, as reflected in imported pottery Classes A and B (Hodges 1989: 31-34, Alcock 1992). The time of this collapse is usually put as either late 6th century or c. 600 (Hodges 1983, 1989, Hinton 1990, Higham 1992). The evidence of the imported wares suggests a replacement of eastern Mediterranean links (A and B wares) by trade with southern Gaul (D and E wares) in the 6th century (Alcock 1992). Some of the pottery classes were long lived but E ware is usually dated late 6th to late 7th century, while A ware is usually dated to c.475-550, which seems to place the change in trade to 550/75. The lessening of links with the Mediterranean after c.550 has also been accepted by Dark (1994) as a crucial feature of the history of Britain. For Dark, Justinian's failure to recreate the Roman Empire in the west led to the 7th century replacement of late Antiquity by early medieval forms of culture, settlement and organisation throughout much of Europe.

At about the same time, Anglo-Saxon trade with the Frankish state, and through them with the Mediterranean, was becoming more firmly established. The emporia of Kent (e.g. Sarre) and of East Anglia (Ipswich) were becoming linked with continental sites like Quentovic and Dorestad. The wealth that could be mobilised by the Anglo-Saxon kings is amply demonstrated by the treasures of Sutton Hoo (Carver 1998). Any dynasty like the Oiscingas in Kent or the Wuffingas in East Anglia that could control access to trade with the Franks and Scandinavia might well have had a key advantage in establishing their power and challenging the Britons for political control of the south east of Britain. Seeking independence from Frankish control would be balanced against the desire for the wealth that Frankish contacts could bring.

Carver suggested that a North Sea Germanic identity was being consciously maintained in opposition to a post-Roman Christian British identity that looked back to the days of the Empire (Carver 1998: 103). The late 6th and early 7th centuries would then become a time of conflict between two world orders, leading to aggressive assertions of paganism such as the Sutton Hoo cemetery. The dominant power acting as the core area for heathen Germanic culture was Denmark (Hedeager 1992). This was probably the most powerful Germanic state maintaining itself in opposition to the other core area, the Franks of Merovingian Gaul. The Franks acted as the heirs of Roman Christianity, although transformed through Germanic ethnicity. It was the Franks that were the core, to which Britain was the periphery in Esmonde Cleary's analysis of this period (Esmonde Cleary 1993). Britain, in particular the Anglian settled area of eastern Britain, was caught up as a border area between the two conflicting cores. The dominance of the Scandinavian connection was being maintained during the migration and settlement, but with Frankish influence growing through the 6th century, finally to triumph in the 7th. The influence of the two core areas would form a backdrop to the rivalries between the Anglo-Saxon kingdoms in Britain. As noted by Hines (1992), the Kings of East Anglia evidently chose to emphasise their Scandinavian links, most likely in opposition to the growing Frankish influence of Kent which was setting itself up as the most powerful of the new Germanic kingdoms in Britain.

To place ourselves into the mindset of the people of the time and imagine a clash between different world orders is tempting and the case is persuasive. Unfortunately, we have no way of verifying such a suggestion in the absence of the documentary voice of the heathen opposition to Christianity. It seems more likely that the newly emerging ruling families were confirming their status by reference to familiar ideologies that their subject people would support, and by establishing links with outside sources of patronage that could deliver moveable wealth. The identity expressed at sites like Sutton Hoo is just as likely to be status identity as an ethnic identity (not that the two are mutually incompatible). The flow of patronage across the North Sea and Channel would be part of the elite's strategy of enhancing its own position, channelling trade through itself, and there need be no contradiction between receiving Frankish gold coins and maintaining traditional links with Scandinavia. Rather than be squeezed between two world views, the new elite could be more interested in establishing its own independent identity; a British based Germanic Anglo-Saxon world conscious of its North Sea origins (this might explain the adoption of sleeve clasps from Norway without the adoption of other aspects of Norwegian culture, Hines 1992), but also using the power of Merovingian Gaul to its own advantage.

Creating and manipulating ethnicity

Ethnicity is primarily a matter of symbolising the difference of one's own group from that of others. The characteristics chosen to achieve this are the primary and secondary markers of ethnicity which have been discussed above. The evidence from this period is that, in general, the primary markers were particular to each set of settlers and may have marked Anglian identity off from Saxon as much as Germanic from British. The only common marker shared by the Germanic settlers was the act of migration.

As far as kinship was concerned, we may surmise that in the Anglian parts of Britain, chain migrants were organised in kindreds; small groups of settlers tightly bound by family ties. In the Saxon and Jutish areas, it may be that career migrants were more heterogeneous and less tied to family units, being part instead of professionally defined warbands. The origins of the different groups to cross the North Sea will have varied. If it was the case that southern Britain was settled by career migrant soldiers and the areas to the north by chain migrant families then no single origin event or even homeland could act to define the settlers as a whole. Their experience of migration would have been different, and their reception by the Britons would also have varied; not just the emotional reception but also the practical logistics of settlement. The only experience in common would have been the act of crossing the North Sea to start a new life. These differences may lie behind the adoption of different ethnic names between north and south, i.e. Saxons or Angles. Unfortunately, we do not know what the peoples of the 5th or 6th century called themselves when referring to the whole of Britain but we can be sure that the Britons were conscious of a unity among them by the use of the term Saxons as a blanket term for all Germanic settlers and their descendants, the English of today.

It is the secondary markers that assume a larger role in the symbolising and creation of an Anglo-Saxon identity. In the case of language we can assume a great deal of dialectal variety, although the evidence is largely lacking. It is likely that any attempt at establishing linguistic norms or standards could not be undertaken until the establishment of royal courts and centres of political power and status. However, the various dialects were probably not that different to one another and the language of the Germanic peoples at this time was probably commonly understood, and certainly provided a strong contrast to that of the Britons. A stronger common tie might have been religion. Again, this would provide a strong contrast with the native Britons, whether pagan or Christian. The acting out of daily life would take place on a local or regional scale. However, a common framework of military action against the Britons in phase 2 would provide a degree of common action, as would a military role within British society in phase 1. The existence of a militarist ethos may be reflected in the weapon burials of the period. Political action and structures would provide an arena for ethnic identity in phase 2. They would be crucial for the creation of specific named identities that could override the local and regionally based identities to create a wider ethnic consciousness. In material culture, what we see at first is only local or regional culture, partly British and partly Germanic. Only later, beginning in phase 2, would material expression be adopted on an island wide Anglo-Saxon basis. It would seem that language and religion were the major island-wide markers of Anglo-Saxon identity in phase 1, joined by material culture in phase 2 and later. Political structures integrating the different kingdoms remained weakly developed and the Anglo-Saxons would struggle to find unity through politics in the course of the 7th century. The major markers of identity were thus secondary, rather than primary. As such they were in theory capable of being abandoned. That they were maintained and even adopted by the native inhabitants must be related to the balance of advantage between the two populations. As a mix of immigration and ethnic fusion, Anglo-Saxon ethnicity was fundamentally a creation within the island of Britain.

Ethnicity through opposition

The use of a Liberal model of ethnicity allows us to ask some of the key questions which lie at the heart of the changes of the 5th and 6th centuries:

a. what incentive would there have been for a Germanic settler to adopt native British culture?

b. what incentive would there have been for a Briton to adopt the incoming Germanic culture?

Asking the questions of course is easier than providing answers to them. My intuition is that culture switching would only be undertaken where it was in the interest of the individual to do this. What advantages would there be for the individual in post-Roman Britain? Individuals would seek different things depending of their status, capabilities and character. Wealth, position or power would be acceptable forms of self-gratification. A plot of land or lordship over several lands, with attendant income in rents and services would set someone and their family up for life. Grants of gold and silver, or gifts of treasure, would be expected in return for service in the post-salaried economy of post-Roman Britain. None of these things in themselves would necessarily involve a change in ethnic marking. Switching ethnicity involves joining the social and political structures of the other culture, becoming part of networks in which the newcomer is made to feel welcome and can achieve fulfilment. The receiving culture must be prepared to open itself to outsiders. Barriers between the two cultures must be permeable, at least in one direction. A further consideration would be the relative isolation of the individual. Someone who was living apart, or estranged from, his native social networks would be less likely to feel he was leaving something behind by switching ethnicities. Also, the relative status of groups would effect switching of certain traits like language, where low social status ascribed to one language can be a powerful motivating factor in adopting the speech of the perceived higher status group. If, as Higham believes (1995), the Britons were a subject population, unfree, under an Anglo-Saxon ruling elite, then switching speech to English could be part of attempts to better their status; to caste off the burden of being unfree. Such may have been the case for British 'gentry' in areas in where a British upper class was not wholly dispossessed, but is less likely for the mass of unfree Britons, where adopting English speech would have no effect on their status. On the other hand, the same reasons would hold for immigrant Germans coming into an eastern Britain under British government, and we might expect immigrants to have abundant incentive to adopt British speech.

It would seem then that there was incentive for Germanic settlers to adopt a British identity in the 5th century. They were arriving into a political and social world which offered them great rewards. This world was undoubtedly of higher status, unless there had been an unimaginable and catastrophic collapse in civilisation after the Roman withdrawal (in spite of assertions by historians and archaeologists I regard this as unlikely). What prevented the settlers from merging into their host society? Perhaps some did merge, especially in the south of Britain, but strong evidence for this is lacking. The strongest difference in cultures at this time was religion. The attitude of Christianity was markedly hostile to paganism, especially after the legislation of the 390s making

Christianity the sole religion of the Empire. Was this the impermeable barrier that prevented acceptance of the pagan Germanic soldiers into British society? If religion was the barrier, why were the settlers not willing to abandon their paganism and become Christian, as many Germanic people did on the continent? Evidence of marking of Germanic identity was weakest in the Saxon areas of Britain, within which were possible pockets of late Romano-British paganism. This may be a reflection of a merging of Germanic soldiers with pagan Britons, where cultural barriers would be weakest.

Perhaps there was a difference of perspective. For Higham (1995), the difference was conditioned by deep-seated racial antagonism. However, this is simply to say that Britons and Germans were opposed because they happened to be Britons and Germans. We need a more sophisticated understanding of the ideology underlying the differences between them. If the difference between the two groups was seen by the Britons as a difference between Christian and pagan, the view from the Germanic side of the barrier might have had more to do with the difference between soldier and civilian. The relations between the two might have been characterised by a mutual contempt; of the warrior for the effete civilian, of the civilised Christian for the uncouth pagan soldier. Each would feel superior to the other, and so each would feel that to cross the barrier and join the other would be to step down in status. This might be avoided if such a step involved the acquisition of enough power and wealth to maintain status.

So far this discussion has proceeded along lines similar to that of Jenkins (1997), who sees ethnicity as a social transaction. Key issues in such a view are the categorisation of the other and of the self; in other words name and status. Such a categorisation in the post-Roman period would be achieved through action: judicial, financial or military. The acting out of judicial or financial roles would take place within the political structures of the day. Those who had political power would be in a superior position by virtue of controlling these aspects of daily life. In phase 1, we should envisage the Britons as dominant politically. In phase 2, this would change with the political levers of power being taken over by the Germanic settlers. We would thus have a switch between British superior opposed to Germanic inferior (Phase 1) to Germanic superior opposed to British inferior (phase 2).

My question a) above would be key in phase 1, while question b) would be key in phase 2. While an answer for the first question has been explored above, we still need an answer for the second question. As noted by Geary (2002: 106-107), many of the poorer and marginal sectors of Roman society on the continent were willing to join 'barbarian' bands as a way of escaping their condition within the Roman social system. Becoming 'barbarian' or a 'Goth' or a 'Hun' was a matter of choice for some Roman citizens; a choice willingly exercised. We have no literary sources to tell us whether this happened in Britain, but it must be a possibility. However, it is clear that on the continent this option was pursued only by a few, and did not affect the position of the majority of those tied to the land, or making a living in the cities. Assimilation of most Britons living in the south and east to a Germanic identity would not occur until the states in which they lived had become thoroughly Germanic in political leadership; a leadership backed by a sizeable demographic advantage in favour of Germanic identity. It may be even then that the assimilation of Britons into a Germanic identity could not proceed until the adoption of Christianity by the new Anglo-Saxon rulers. This in itself would be a powerful motivating factor for the Germanic rulers to adopt the new religion once they had achieved superior status over the Britons. But to make sure that becoming Christian was on Germanic terms, the new religion was adopted in a form that allowed the new rulers to link themselves directly with Rome, and position themselves as the true heirs of Roman Britain. Thus would they maintain their difference and superiority from the Britons they had displaced.

The Anglo-Saxon triangle

We can summarise the above by saying that there were three elements of Anglo-Saxon identity. This identity as it arose in the 7th century, out of 5th and 6th century roots, was Germanic in its ethnic affiliation, Roman in its operational context and conditioned by its opposition to things British (Green 1995 has explored a similar notion of threefold identity for *Germania*). The Germanic aspect of its identity was conditioned by the act of migration and militarism, and signalled by language and religion. Its Roman context arose in its take-over of administrative structures and polities, and its adoption of a new religion. An essential aspect of identity is being defined by reference to another, stating what you are not is as important as stating what you are. For the Anglo-Saxons, the others were the Britons. The relationship between them came in time to be marked by conflict, by political and religious opposition. This is not to say that there could not be cooperation at times between them (as in the alliance between Penda of Mercia and Cadwallon of Gwynedd in the 7th century) or that the infrastructure of the British economy would not be taken over and used to advantage. This triangular identity developed over the course of 200 years. On their way to becoming Anglo-Saxon the Germanic settlers in Britain had passed through various stages. The process of becoming Anglo-Saxon would develop at different rates in different areas. According to Woolf (2000), Anglian identity was more coherent, self-confident and established early on, while Saxon identity was established later. In the 5th century, Anglian identity was Germanic and pagan as opposed to Romano-British Christian. Saxon identity might have been more accommodating to Roman input. The 6th century saw tensions between a new Frankish neo-Roman and a traditional North Sea Germanic orientation, with a more aggressive anti-British stance, especially in the Saxon areas. This led to the general adoption of a Roman Christian identity in the 7th century as opposed to a heathen or British Christian characterisation. The 7th century also saw the final creation of a common insular Anglo-Saxon identity, Germanic but independent and different from their cousins on the continent.

How the Anglo-Saxon identity would develop further would be a matter for the following centuries and would depend on the political fortunes of various kingdoms. Nevertheless, the beginnings had been made and the first steps taken along the road towards an English nation.

Conclusion

The 5th and 6th centuries in Britain, as on the continent, were a time of fundamental change in the signalling of group identities. A Roman identity, which had begun to break down already in the 4th century, was replaced by a greater allegiance to a variety of regional identities based on complex relationships between native Romanised elites and newly arrived, largely Germanic warrior groups. Britain was not immune to continental currents but achieved an independence from Roman control (willingly or not) earlier than most. We can only surmise what the political arrangements in Britain were. A breakdown of central authority with power devolving to *civitas*-based elites is possible but it seems equally possible that later historical traditions give us a pale and distorted reflection of the continued existence of some kind of central British authority or *imperium*. The political dynamics of this period might well have involved oppositions based on, or exploiting, conflicting identities: 'Celt' or Roman, Christian or pagan. In common with other parts of the Roman Empire, the native elites took the step of employing Germanic soldiers to defend strategic parts of the former diocese. The initial employment seems to have been followed by others at later dates, organised perhaps on a more regional basis and taking different forms in different parts of Britain. In the south, Germanic soldiers probably fitted into a strongly post-Roman and British identity, while farther north, Germanic settlers seem to have come over and formed a greater density of civilian settlement transforming the demographic balance at least locally in their favour. In the far north of the former diocese, a Germanic warrior elite was most likely operating alongside native British warrior groups for control of the area. It was not until the mid-6th century that we can see a patchwork of independent British kingdoms and no existing trace of strong central British control. This provided the basis for Germanic take over of British areas on a piecemeal basis in the last quarter of the century, and the creation in their stead of a series of Anglo-Saxon kingdoms. Once royal families had been established, either of genuinely Germanic origin, of native stock accommodating themselves to a new identity, or of mixed origin (which may have been the case among the *Gewisse*), the conquest of more territory from the Britons quickly followed. After Cadwallaun of Gwynedd's attempt to eradicate Anglo-Saxon Northumbria failed in 634, there was no way back for the Britons and within another generation the basic geographical outlines of what would later form the Kingdom of England had been largely settled.

The 200 hundred years since the withdrawal of Britain from the Roman Empire were thus times of uncertainty and change. Geographical and social mobility may well have been greater at this time than before or since. Individuals would have had opportunities to change their station in life and advance themselves, either through migration or through taking advantage of military opportunities. If advancement entailed the adoption of new identities then so be it. Opportunities to change identity though may have been limited to relatively small sections of the population. Kings might find their ability to manipulate identity constrained by the need to carry their followers with them. Where those followers were themselves of mixed origin then manipulating identity might be more possible. Individual soldiers would perhaps have greater room to establish their identities by being able to sell their services wherever needed. The same might be true of groups of soldiers. On the other hand, groups of settlers would bring their social networks with them when moving to new areas. The framework of relationships binding the individual to the group would be stronger where settlers came over as a community. For native populations, we have to imagine what would be pressures forcing either a reinforcing of existing identities or a move towards the identity of incoming groups? We might also ask how far the different identities of the time were conflicting or complementary? Was the line between Christian and pagan belief for most of the population as sharp as monastic or clerical writers would have us believe? Were Germanic peoples and native Britons implacable racial foes?

Unfortunately, we are not in a position to investigate the full range of ethnic markers that could have constituted ethnic identity at this time. Among the primary constituents of ethnicity is kinship. It may well be that Germanic employment in the south of Britain involved the incoming settlers in bilateral kinship networks which were relatively open to British participation. Such networks could allow the assimilation of Germanic soldiers to a native British society or work the other way to assimilate Britons to the Germanic military elite. The direction of ethnic flow would surely depend on the balance of advantage to be assessed by the individual. The wider context of relations between southern Britain and areas providing access to wealth and prestige, and hence the power and position of the southern elites would be key. It may be that the position of Kent as a bridge between the insular world of Britain and a wealthier continent dominated by the Franks would encourage the southern aristocracy to lean towards a Germanic expression of its identity. In Anglian areas, it seems more likely that Germanic settlers arrive as groups, maintaining their social networks and perhaps allowing a greater role for patrilineal kinship as the dominant binding for relationships. Division between native Briton and Germanic incomer may have been more reinforced. Conquest and expulsion might have played a greater role than absorption and assimilation in the creation of Germanic political and social control in these areas.

It is clear that origin myths were an important part of the self-identification of the Anglo-Saxon kings and thence of their kingdoms. There could be no origin myth common to all Anglo-Saxons since Germanic migration to Britain was not a single act, neither did it take place at a single point in time. Of all the possible origin myths, it is only the Kentish myth that belongs to the earliest phases of settlement. Possibly because of this, or because of Kent's primary position in the conversion of the Anglo-Saxons to Christianity, the Kentish myth could be used emblematically to act as a reference point for all the later Germanic settlements. It was Bede's skill to combine this myth with the strictures of Gildas to provide a rationale for the coming of the Anglo-Saxons to Britain which placed them in a direct relationship to the Christian god, and thus a divinely sanctioned origin for their identity as a people. The use of such an idea of their origins in later centuries would allow a homogeneous Anglo-Saxon identity in contrast to that of the Britons; a contrast based on difference and superiority. Whether we can project this notion of the divinely sanctioned and superior Germans arriving to wrest Britain from the wicked and inferior Britons backwards into the 5th and 6th centuries is extremely doubtful.

Many peoples have, or claim to have, undergone a particularly intense and formative experience that helps to define them as a nation. In the case of the later Anglo-Saxons, it seems that this experience may well have been the act of migration. Whether this act, or in reality a series of acts, would have been such a formative influence at the time is open to question. We should not imagine the migrants as akin to the 17th century English travelling to a continent like North America to tame a new land in the face of tremendous hardships and overcoming hostile natives. The Anglo-Saxons were not the Pilgrim Fathers! The land of Britain was not empty but was filled with existing estates, farms, property rights and boundaries. The migrants in Anglian areas would have to fit themselves into existing structures, even if modifying these structures by their acts of settlement. Rather than struggling to carve out a new society, they may instead have felt the need coming into an existing British society and polity to create a comfort zone of reinforced Germanic identity. This may have been less important for migration of military elites in Saxon areas, and in areas without accompanying civilian settlers, as perhaps to the north of the former Roman border, in Bernicia.

While it is clear that what is signified by an ethnic name can change over time, nevertheless, ethnic names have considerable significance. Without a name there can scarcely be an ethnic identity. We only know what the Britons called the Germans and what the descendants of the settlers called themselves. We do not know the settlers' own names. It may be that Bede's names of peoples that were thought to have taken part in the migration is a reflection of oral traditions and so give some indication of how the migrants saw themselves. If so, then it is perhaps significant that there was no one name but a variety of identities for the migrants. This reinforces the notion that the migration was a series of acts without overall coordination by a Germanic king, unlike most of the migrations on the continent. It perhaps also fits in with the idea that migration took place within a context of British political control. Incoming Germanic identities were small scale and local. Larger political identities would have been those of the controlling British polities. It can be no surprise that when some of these units passed under Germanic control they kept their original British names; most notably Kent, the earliest of all to fall under Germanic rule.

Whether there was an ethnic attachment to the land among the Germanic communities is extremely hard to establish. Rather than divine providence, it is more likely that the Germanic settlers looked upon their title to the land as based on the legal frameworks of the post-Roman British state or states. The survival of place-names attributed to the gods, like Woden or Thunor, and the presence of places linked to early dynastic founders in the later mythology of the founding of kingdoms suggests that there may have been a more emotive attachment to the land, in someway bound up with dynastic or cultural identity. However, the fluidity of the borders of kingdoms and the unsettled nature of the names of most of the kingdoms until the mid-7th century would argue that ethnic identification with specific geographical areas was likely to have been the result of overt creation and manipulation rather than deep-seated identification.

Secondary, behavioural markers of ethnicity were more subject to day-to-day manipulation and negotiation by creating identity through continued repetition within aspects of daily life. Perhaps, the single most important of these markers, certainly to modern scholars, is language. There is no doubt that the English language of today derives largely in its basic grammar and vocabulary from the English language of the Anglo-Saxons, and that this language is an alien intrusion into the cultural make-up of Britain. It is also striking that the early English language shows remarkably little influence of the native Celtic dialects of Britain. Any explanation of the transformation of areas of Roman Britain into Anglo-Saxon England must account for this alien presence and its linguistic domination of southern and eastern Britain. Thus far, there has been very little exploration of the nature of language change and the mechanisms whereby one language is displaced by another in pre-modern contexts. We should take it as a reasonable working hypothesis that such complete language change cannot proceed without a considerable influx of people speaking the new language. Social dominance and fashion by themselves cannot be satisfactory explanations in the days before mass communication media and state schooling.

An important aspect of identity was the religious beliefs and rituals of the people. The utility of this as a group identifier may have varied from religion to religion. For Christians with their exclusive nature of divine revelation (as compared with the remarkable tolerance of pagan beliefs), the attitudes towards other faiths could be characterised by hostility. The Gothic rulers on the continent certainly used doctrinal differences within Christianity (Arian as opposed to Catholic) to maintain difference between their own elites and the native inhabitants of the Roman provinces. Within post-Roman Britain, we have little knowledge of the religious patchwork of the former diocese. We have Christian writings that show Christian communities and the presence of Pelagian ideas, but we have little idea of how strong Christianity was, nor how far pockets of pagan belief had survived. It is possible that there was a three-way religious triangle of British Christian, British pagan and Germanic heathen. Such a situation would allow the British pagan the option of acculturation to either of the other two. The possible importance of this for the British elites and Germanic soldiers of the upper Thames area have been noted. The presence of possibly religious iconography in Germanic metalwork of the period may signal a conscious desire to use religion as an ethnic badge in reaction to the attitudes of the Roman Christians, and might lead us to accept a more important role for heathen beliefs in the self-identification of the Germanic peoples. The fact that it was a mission from Rome itself that began the conversion of the southern Anglo-Saxon elite to Christianity, rather than missionary efforts by the British must surely be a significant reflection of religious hostility forged during the previous 150 years of Germanic presence in Britain.

Whether we can identify the actions, the conscious or unconscious aspects of personal behaviour, that reflected identities in this period is doubtful. This is not to say we cannot identify differences in such aspects of behaviour as costume through the archaeological evidence, but that we cannot identify the characteristics which would come under the heading of 'this is the way we do this', whether this be forms of greeting, methods of eating or styles of cutting the hair. It seems likely that Germanic settlers were distinguished from Britons by more than just their differences of language and dress but we have no way of knowing what these were in the absence of relevant documentary sources.

We are equally at a loss to describe the social and political structures of the earliest migrants to Britain. Attempts have been made to infer the broad outlines of social structure, but even here there is disagreement as to whether society was bilateral or patrilineal. What is clear is that the Germanic migrants did not as a rule form a clear social stratum or class distinct from the native British. In Anglian areas, they came across as families and communities, fitting into the local area as farmers and workers as well as soldiers. They did not arrive as a conquering upper class lording it over subservient natives. Only in the far north, in Bernicia, above the Wall that marked the old border of Roman Britain, was this a likely situation. In the south, the migrants who came to accept the designation of Saxon did probably form a military and aristocratic elite. Yet, the suggestions from the genealogy of the Gewissan royal house are that it was an open elite, ready to intermarry with the Britons and able to accommodate a mixed ethnic identity. Connections seem to have been maintained with kin on the continent for some time and we should envisage social networks as not purely insular, but extending across the North Sea. While we know that the Germanic settlers and native inhabitants were organised into kingdoms under Anglo-Saxon ruling houses from the latter part of the 6th century, we should be wary about projecting this backwards into earlier decades. The only early kingship we know of is the kingship of Kent, and if the sources are to be trusted, this was the result of the grant of a pre-existing polity to an incoming Germanic chieftain. It was the Roman-British grant that made the kingdom, not lordship over a Germanic following. It seems inherently likely that the political context of early Germanic settlement was British, that is either a centralised post-Roman diocesan power, or more local *civitas* or even provincial political units. The use of Germanic political power to create and define an Anglo-Saxon identity belongs much more the 7th century than earlier. Whatever, the earlier situation, the nature of political power by the last quarter of the 6th century seems to have been decentralised and fragmented. A single, Britain-wide authority and unity was no more than a memory or an aspiration than a political reality. The Germanic conquest and establishment of Anglo-Saxon power took place as a series of kingdoms or rival royal houses, not as a single state. While we can speak of a Frankish, Burgundian or Gothic kingdom, we cannot speak of an Anglo-Saxon kingdom. Politics may have been a mechanism for the enhancement of a few royal or aristocratic families, it could not serve to distinguish an ethnic identity for the Anglo-Saxons as a whole.

Where we can make statements about differences between ethnic groups is in material culture, but we must be aware that the ethnic significance of artefacts is not necessarily tied to genetic affiliation between people. Such affiliation cannot be assumed in all cases and must be demonstrated. We must await scientific studies to supply the quality and quantity of data that will help us to resolve the genetic and migrational histories of the population in general. There was no single set of cultural markers that served to identify a unified Anglo-Saxon identity. Rather, there was a varied set of artefacts and design elements from different parts of the northern Germanic world, that would be used and combined in Britain in new ways. It would not be until there was a Germanic elite mobilising identity for political control in the new Anglo-Saxon kingdoms that there would emerge a common material culture for the new Anglo-Saxon ethnicity. The elements of Germanic style that were used in Britain came from a wide area of the North Sea coasts facing Britain. There is little reason to doubt that Bede was essentially right in portraying the migrants as a disparate group of peoples with a variety of previous ethnic identities. It would be wrong to talk of the settlers as Anglo-Saxons until the takeover of political control by royal houses identifying themselves as Angles or Saxons from the late 6th century. It is clear that the material culture of the earliest Germanic presence in Britain was both fragmented and eclectic (e.g. Hines 1996). What the artefacts of the period show us is a patchwork of Germanic cultural features. This was a culture created out of thousands of individual choices as acts of manipulation and negotiation of identities. Individuals had the opportunity to create a new life for themselves in post-Roman Britain. They also had the chance to reinforce identities as well as establish new ones. These identities, and their manipulation, though had to take into account accepted realities of kinship and traditional norms of cultural expression.

What then can we say of the adoption of Germanic identity in Britain after 410? It is important to realise that we see this identity from the outside. It comes to us through the markers used by the people living at the time, markers whose uses may not have been exclusively ethnic. Status and role would also have a part to play in creating a social identity. Nevertheless, we can see how certain markers did serve to identify people within a continental Germanic world, in distinction to the world of the native British. The most important of the markers were language, religion and material culture, especially artefacts designed for display. These are all markers that function in a context of social communication. They serve to identify to others and create shared social networks where the individual can feel they belong to a welcoming and supportive group. They suggest that individuals found security and satisfaction through identifying with a familiar and comforting group identity; that the act of migration involved communities, not just individuals. Individual choice may have been possible for those willing to strike out on their own, or for those who had a 'career path' within a particular role that allowed escape from traditional ties of kinship, such as soldiers. The fact that these markers of ethnicity survived shows that they must have been handed down from one generation to the next. If the original settlers chose to maintain their identities in a new land, then their descendants likewise chose to continue this rather than begin adopting features from the native cultural templates. Second, third and later generations showed little desire to dilute their Germanic identities, rather they were creating a new insular Germanic identity while keeping connections with the continent. These continental connections should not be underestimated and it is a matter of regret than modern British historians and archaeologists have only recently begun to look at the wider continental background to Anglo-Saxon identity.

Who were the bearers of Germanic culture? This is perhaps a more interesting way of stating the traditional question - how many Anglo-Saxons migrated to Britain? This has at times dominated discussion and been argued with little understanding of the complexities and assumptions underlying the question. This is now beginning to change as scholars understand better the sociology and anthropology of social groups and identity. We are also beginning to realise how important it is to look at the regional and even local variety of experience in the post-Roman period. While it is likely that there was considerable population migration from the continent in eastern Britain, it is less certain that migration was similar in scale or type in southern areas. Towards the north and west, the degree of migration would drop away and acculturation through conquest would be more important in transmitting Anglo-Saxon identity. Areas conquered in the 7th century, the more westerly parts of what is now England, would have received a new Anglo-Saxon elite but less likely any large influx of settlers. Anglo-Saxon identity would emerge from living within a kingdom whose kings maintained an Anglian or Saxon origin for themselves. How long native Britons would have maintained an identity tied to their own ethnic markers like language or religion is one of the more fascinating aspects of the period yet to be explored in any detail. Anglo-Saxons in the 7th and 8th centuries were likely to a genetic mix of the descendants of incomers and natives; both Germanic and British. On the other hand, during the immediate post-Roman period, it seems likely that bearers of Germanic culture were indeed of Germanic origin. There were few power structures controlled by the Germanic elite (apart from in Kent), and there would be little incentive for the majority of native Britons to acculturate to an identity offering little advantage.

How then did people become Anglo-Saxon? The simplest answer is that people were Anglo-Saxon because they were subjects of an Anglo-Saxon king. This will serve as an answer from c.570 onwards when there were such kings. The language of the ruler, his culture and that of his officials and landowners would assert themselves as the means of marking an Anglo-Saxon identity. They could only do this through monopolising the channels of communication between people: the churches, assemblies/courts, the administration of estates and service in the army. Slowly but surely local people would come into contact with others for whom English was the main means of speech and find it advantageous to adopt the same. However, this process could only be slow in days before mass communication media and without compulsory and widespread education. If the ruling elite had had to deal with large numbers of Britons in their churches, as their officials or in the army then the balance of advantage would have lain with their adopting British speech instead. Behind the establishment of the Anglo-Saxon kingdoms, there lay a long history of migration and settlement by Germanic peoples in Britain; up to 150 years or more by the early 7th century. Long enough for five or six generations to establish themselves and maintain their identities. Long enough also for repeated acts of migration to build up a Germanic population in Britain that did not have to rely only on the natural cycle of birth and death to determine its population size. During this period before the establishment of Anglo-Saxon kings, political power, officials and landowners must have remained British. It would be wrong to speak of south-east Britain as Anglo-Saxon at this time. Incentives to change identity should have led to the eventual merging of Germanic identities into those of their native hosts, with selected Germanic features like personal names or styles of decoration held as remnants being used to denote status rather than ethnicity. That Britain did not end up as an insular equivalent of France or Spain has always been explained by the collapse of Roman administration and society, somehow creating a blank environment in which Germanic settlers could impose themselves and have the natives blindly follow. This will not do. Administration did not collapse, landowners and rulers were still there. More importantly perhaps the church was still there; all vehicles capable of transmitting British culture to the incomers. The vital factor was political conquest from the later 6th century, based on a secure population base in the east of England that had kept its cultural identities and allowed the new aristocracy to keep in touch with its Germanic origins on the continent. This provided access to manpower and wealth without the need to gain both by submission to British social networks.

One of the most difficult questions to answer in history is 'why' since we seldom have access to explicit statements by those involved. This is especially so for this period. If the Germanic settlers were maintaining links with their homelands and persevering with an ethnic identity that must have 'stuck out like a sore thumb' within Britain, we should like to know why this was so. In the continental provinces of the Roman Empire, newly arrived 'barbarians' had to find an accommodation with a notion of belonging to the state through citizenship. If the Roman provinces were becoming more and more inward looking, more parochial and less imperial in their outlook, they nevertheless retained the idea of being citizens with rights in the body politic based on law rather than ethnic descent. It was only in Britain that the local population succeeded in reviving a pre-Roman identity based on ethnicity. A rediscovery of 'Celtic' Britishness must have subtly changed the notion of what it meant to be British. The fact that Britain was the only province to officially leave the Empire made a rejection of Roman identity and legal norms perhaps more likely. Germanic groups would then have entered a world more comfortable with the idea of ethnically based identities in which being German involved being unable to be British, because to be British demanded being 'Celtic'. The citizen can look down upon the 'barbarian' but accepts that the 'barbarian' could change his ways and eventually become a citizen. A distinction between groups based on ethnic identifiers is perhaps less open to receiving new citizens. The mutual hostility between Briton and German can be overstated but some such opposition of different identities must be involved in the relations between the two. It may be that this opposition was thought of as not so much racial as religious; the opposition of Christian and heathen. While some of the soldiers employed by the Britons in the early 5th century may well have been happy to function within a post-Roman context (especially in the far south), in the long run, even these areas became Anglo-Saxon. If the *Gewisse* were indeed partly British in origin, eventually they would become just as Anglo-Saxon as any other of the kingdoms in eastern Britain. Something must have shifted the balance of advantage away from being British, but only for them, not for their neighbours to the west.

We are so used to treating the early medieval period as a unit that we forget how long it was. There is an absurd habit in Britain today of treating the whole length of time from 410 to 1066 as one Anglo-Saxon period. I will not fall into that trap. The period covered in this book is roughly from the first employment of Germanic soldiers by the British authorities in perhaps 428 to the failure of the last British attempt to defeat and destroy an emerging Anglo-Saxon kingdom, Cadwallon of Gwynedd's attack on Northumbria in 634. This in itself covers 206 years, the same length of time as now separates us from Nelson's victory at the Battle of the Nile, just a year before the coup that brought General Bonaparte to power in revolutionary France in 1799. The world of 634 was a very different place from the world of 410. I have suggested that the 570s were the key turning point of the period in Britain, when the Anglo-Saxon kings began to take over political rule of southern and eastern Britain. Why was this? It seems sensible to look at what was happening on the continent at this time. The collapse of Roman power in the central Mediterranean and the ruin of Justinian's dream of recreating the Roman Empire in the west may well be the key. At the same time there was Frankish pressure on the Saxons throughout the 550s to 570s that could have created the conditions for ambitious energies to be expended in safer areas away from Frankish domination. The lure of Roman wealth and trade receded to a memory and was replaced by the reality of Germanic Frankish power as the dominant force within western Europe. A more sensible beginning to the Anglo-Saxon period may well be c.570, with the 160 years before this assigned to a post-Roman British classification. At least this would present a more honest assessment of wherein political power lay during the first few generations of Germanic settlement in Britain.

No study of the past can answer every question that arises. Even if they answer some of the questions they set out to, they inevitably yield new questions that demand further study. Here are just a few that are only just beginning to be asked:

- what were the benefits for individuals in the choice of ethnic identities in the early-mid 5th century?;
- what was the nature of political power in Britain after the Roman withdrawal?;
- why are the British elites in the east of Britain so hard to see archaeologically?;
- what were the economic structures that upheld landowning elites and military forces?;
- was there a decline in levels of population and if so, how severe was this?;
- how long was central authority in Britain maintained after 410, did this collapse in the early-mid 6th century (assuming such power really did persist until then)?

The period in question is one in which the meaning behind ethnicity can be analysed and shown for what it really is: a social construct but based on an underlying reality or core. The core identities lie within the elites of the day and form a complex of political, military, religious and landowning hierarchies. They may be based around any convenient shorthand that can be used to symbolise a set of values that can bind the group together. This could be a notion of being Roman, a citizen and heir to a legal and classical tradition. It could be based on being Christian, an exclusive religion governing social relations among its members and providing a sense of being specially favoured by the divine. It might be based on being German, through membership of kinship networks and a society with hierarchies and a military role at its core. It might also be based on being British, harking back to an earlier time and an identity through opposition to things Roman or German. Although the core identities are very real, individual membership of the group may be open to negotiation. At some point, large numbers of Britons will have become Anglo-Saxon, some possibly even at the highest of social levels. When we are told by Bede that the earliest poet of the English language (in the later 7th century) was a man named Cædmon, were are introduced to someone given a wholly British name by his parents, what the Welsh would come to know as Cadfan. That his parents might themselves have been British is a possibility we have to admit. This may give us a glimpse of the change from one identity to another within one particular family at this time, a change that must have been experienced by many others.

It seems a truism to say that ethnic identities will form in reaction and opposition to those of others. One consequence of this would be that ethnic signification should be more intense at time of conflict and competition for resources or power. The explosion of elaborated metalwork in this period must give the impression that the archaeology of the time can be summed up in the study of its brooches. This is not so, brooches are only one aspect of the culture of the time, even though the study of brooches has dominated many studies of the period. However, the use of decoration and metalwork does seem to reflect a heightened concern with marking identity at this time. The circumstances of migration involving communities from different parts of the Germanic world could well lead to this, as would the cultural oppositions between Germanic and British or Roman, and between heathen and Christian. What we see over time however is a reduction in the variety and intensity of ethnic marking as the Anglo-Saxon kings established themselves and successfully won power from the native Britons. The core identities changed and the varied Germanic identities merged into something new, an Anglo-Saxon identity, at once continental in its origins but insular in its precise forms. The marking of ethnicity is not set in stone, it changes and yet has continuity with the past. The English of today are not the Anglo-Saxons of Bede, and yet it is in the events of these far off days that we can trace the beginnings of a new ethnicity, one formed by both group enterprise and by individuals in the period that has often been aptly named the age of migrations.

What is left from this period? What did it contribute to the English identity of today? The most obvious legacy is the speech of the people. English has changed greatly over the last 1,500 years but it is still a recognisably Germanic language, whose roots lie in the period of migration. A less obvious legacy, because less visible to the naked eye, is a genetic component in the people. The extent of this component will become clearer as archaeo-genetic studies become commoner and more sophisticated. The geo-political legacy is a Britain that is divided, with a core that is England and what is sometimes referred to, rather dismissively, as the Celtic fringe. The fact that today we have Scottish and Welsh identities (not forgetting Cornish) alongside an English identity within the one island is due to the events of the post-Roman period. A major legacy of this early period for future generations is perhaps a feeling of divine providence, that the Anglo-Saxons had a divine right to be in Britain and had a superior right over the heads of the native inhabitants to rule the whole of the island. Ruling over the whole of Britain we have a royal family that can trace its origin back to the *Gewisse* of the 6th century, and even, albeit through admittedly treacherous genealogies, to the continental Angles of the 4th century. Whether we can lay the discontinuity with the Roman past, in both settlement location and form, at the door of the Germanic settlers is debatable. However, it would be interesting to consider whether Britain without the Germanic migrations would have developed a Romance speaking core with continuity of bishops, *civitates* and cities. This did not happen of course and instead we had Anglo-Saxons kings, a church that had to be reintroduced and towns re-founded. We would dearly love to know the social and economic details of the Germanic settlements and how they fitted into or disrupted existing British patterns of settlement, social hierarchy and landholding. Finally, if the English are, and have been, an intensely individualistic people, parochial in focus, tolerant of diversity and proud of their freedom to act as they see fit, may these have been features of settlers trying to establish themselves in a new life in a new land? We may never know. What is clear though is that without the events of the two hundred years after 410, there would be no English people.

Appendix 1

Rulers Outside Britain

The Germanic settlement of Britain and the politics of post-Roman rule in the island took place in the context of wider political events on the continent. The two most important states that effected events in Britain were the Roman Empire and the Kingdom of the Franks. The Roman Empire was normally divided into an eastern and western half until the late 5th century. Each half often had a common royal family but passed its own laws independently from the other after 438. The break up of the western Empire began after 410 when Rome was sacked by the Goths and for a time lost control of Gaul and Spain. Vandals, Alans and Swabians were made foederati in Spain, Burgundians in Gaul and Goths in Aquitaine by 418. Africa was wholly lost to the Vandals as an independent state in 442. Roman power was restored in Gaul and Spain, although the foederates remained. It was the assassination of Emperor Valentinian in 455 that led to the final destruction of Roman power in the west. Most of the Western Emperors had been weak and relied on their Commander-in-Chief (*Magister Militum*), often of Germanic origin, for their power. The main Commanders were Stilicho 395-408, Constantius 411-421, Aetius 430-432 & 433-454, Ricimer 456-472, Orestes 472-476 and Odovacer 476-493. Only Constantius III and Majorian were active and effective Emperors in this period. From 456, the Empire was dominated by the attempts of the Commanders Ricimer and then Orestes to find pliable Emperors or sanction from the East to enable them to remain in power. From 461, northern Gaul was under Roman rule in the person of Aegidius but no longer recognising the sovereignty of Rome. From 466, the Goths under Euric threw off any loyalty to Rome and began a conquest of Aquitaine and Spain, being recognised as fully independent in 475. Another Germanic General, Odovacer ended the pretence of Western Imperial power and took control of Italy in his own right, saving an official but nominal allegiance to the Emperor in the East. From 476, there was once again only one Emperor. It would be left to Iustinianus to try to make this a reality by reconquering Italy and much of Spain. The presence of eastern Mediterranean artefacts in Britain at this time needs to be seen as part of the Empire's attempt to revive its power throughout the old lands of the West. Western rulers still paid nominal (and Popes a real) allegiance to the Emperors at Constantinople. However, the attempt to revive the old Empire would fail. Latin remained the official language of the Empire until the reign of Heraclius, who accepted the logic of the final loss of power in the west by adopting Greek as the official language of an Empire which was now Byzantine rather than Roman. A list of Emperors is given in Table 14. (next page)

189

WEST	EAST
Honorius 395-423 + Constantius III 421	Arcadius 395-408
	Theodosius II 408-450
Iohannes 423-425	
Valentinianus III 425-455	
	Marcianus 450-457
Petronius 455	
Avitus 455-456	
Maiorianus 457-461	Leo I 457-474
Libius Severus 461-65	
Anthemius 467-472	
Olybrius 472	
Glycerius 473-474	
Iulius Nepos 474-480	Zeno 474-491
Romulus 475-476	
Anastasius 491-518	
Iustinus I 518-527	
Iustinianus 527-565	
Iustinus II 565-578	
Tiberius II 578-582	
Mauricius 582-602	
Phocas 602-610	
Heraclius 610-641	

Table 14: The Roman Emperors 395-641

The Frankish kingdom began life in c.470 as a foederate establishment in the Roman province of *Belgica Secunda*, based on Reims. It was the second king, Chlodovech (usually referred to as Clovis), who expanded Frankish power. He ended the rule of the last Roman authority in Gaul, Syagrius of Soissons (the son and successor of Aegidius), in 486, annexed the Germanic tribe of the Alemanni in 496, and took Aquitaine from the Goths in 507. A further burst of annexations followed a generation later with Thuringia, Burgundy, Provence and Bavaria being added between 531 and 539. The weakness of the kingdom was its division between the sons of the king. The rivalry between the kings meant that a united Frankish state was seldom achieved after the death of Chlodovech I in 511.

Chlothar I 558-61, Chlothar II 613-29 and Dagobert I 632-38 were the only kings to rule over an undivided Frankish state during this period. With the edict of 614, Chlothar gave up appointment to the office of count to the local aristocracy. The rise in power of the counts would fatally weaken the kings in the 7th century. The same edict formalised the earlier *ad hoc* division of the kingdom into three parts: Austrasia, Neustria and Burgundy. After the death of Dagobert I, power would lie with the chief officials of each of the kingdoms, the Mayors of the Palace.

The Franks struggled to gain control over the Saxons during the 6th century. They were able to achieve recognition of overlordship but never managed to integrate Saxony into the kingdom in the same way as its other provinces. Saxony seems to have been first subdued by Theuderic I c. 530. The major phase of campaigning against the Saxons was from 555 to 575.

The political struggles between the different branches of the family are bewildering and hard to follow. The divisions of Gaul between the different Merovingian kings were not neat and tidy. The lands of each king tended to centre around a core area but could form a patchwork with that of his rivals until the consolidation of Austrasia, Burgundy and Neustria. Austrasia would be the basis of what would later become Germany, while Neustria was the core around which France would be built. The Frankish kings are detailed in Table 15.

Childeric 460			
Chlodovech I 481			
Paris	*Orleans*	*Soissons*	*Rheims*
Childebert I 511-58	Chlodomer 511-24	Chlothar I 511-61	Theuderic I 511-33
			Theudebert I 533-47
			Theudebald 547-55

NEUSTRIA Paris & Soissons	*BURGUNDY* Orleans	*AUSTRASIA* Rheims
Charibert I 561-67	Guntram 561-92	Sigibert I 561-75
& Chilperic I 561-84		Childebert II 575-96
Chlothar II 584-629		
	Theuderic II 596-613	Theudebert II 596-612
	Sigibert II 613	
Dagobert I 629-638	Charibert I 629-32	Dagobert I 629-38

Table 15: Kings of the Franks 460-639

Appendix 2

The Early Kingdoms of the Anglo-Saxons

Most Anglo-Saxon kingdoms were created between c.570 and c.650. It is those that were established before the end of the 6th century which would be the longest lasting and show the greatest degree of independent existence. In the early genealogies and chronicles, the founder of the royal house and the person described as the first king were often different. This may reflect the fact that the founder was the person first bringing the family to Britain but within a British political context, and only later did the family take over political power to establish the historically documented kingdoms. The early forms of the names of the kingdoms are given below, as are some of the key sources for dates or people. These are supplied in brackets using abbreviations.

Abbreviations

ASC	*Anglo-Saxon Chronicle*
HB	*Historia Brittonum*
HE	*Historia Ecclesiastica Gentis Anglorum*
HH	Henry of Huntingdon
LG	Life of Guðlac
RW	Roger of Wendover
TH	*Tribal Hidage*

Bernicia

name
: From British *Bernacci, meaning the people of the mountain passes (the northern Pennines)

early forms Bernicia (HE); Berneich, Birneich (HB)

royal house Founded by Oesa, said to be the first to come to Britain (Dumville 1973). Oesa might have been remembered more widely. The Ravenna Cosmographer gave the leader of a group of Saxons settling in Britain as 'Ansehis'. This might well have become Oesa by regular linguistic change between the 5th and 8th centuries (but see Kent below).

first king Ida (HE)

heartland Bamburgh

date
: The beginning of Ida's reign was given the date 547 by Bede. This was worked out on the basis of a king list, reckoning backwards from the documented date of death for King Æþelfrið in 616. However, the king list can be reconciled with other historical events only if we assume that it represents three separate lineages after Ida (see note below). On that basis, Ida would have begun to reign in 575. Assuming 25/30 years for a generation, that would put his grandfather Oesa's activity at around 515/25.

kings
: Ida 575-87, Glappa 587-588, Æþelric 588-592, Þeodric 588-595, Adda 588-596, Æþelfrið 592-616, Friþuwald 595-601, Hussa 596-603, under Deira 616-633, Eanfrið 633-634

Deira

name
: Of unknown meaning (Jackson 1953), derived from British *Deibhr.

early forms Deira, Dera (HE, land), Deiri, Deri (HE, people); Deur (HB)

royal house Founded by Soemil? (HB).

first king Ælle (HE, but not described as the first king)

heartland Yorkshire Wolds, centred on Driffield

date
: Ælle began to reign in 560 according to the Anglo-Saxon Chronicle. However, his reign had been wrongly worked out according to the reign lengths for the Deiran kings as given in the Chronicle. His successor Æþelric reigned 5 years and was expelled in 604, placing Ælle's 30-year reign as 569-599. The genealogies would make Soemil his ancestor in the fifth generation, placing Soemil around 419/444.

kings
: Ælle 571-599, Æþelric 599-604, under Bernicia 604-616, Eadwine 616-633, Osric 633-634

East Anglia

name   The East Angles

early forms East Engle (TH); Angli Orientales (HE); Easteranglii (HB)

royal house Known as Wuffingas (HE) after Wuffa 571 (RW).

first king Wehha (HB)

heartland   South east Suffolk?

date   Roger of Wendover in the 13th century dated the beginning of Wuffa's reign to 571. The source of Roger's information is unknown and we cannot know how accurate this is. Wuffa's father Wehha would have been active around 541/46.

kings   Wuffa 571-578, Tytla 578-c.599, Rædwald c.599-c.625, Eorpwald c.625-c.627, Riceberht c.627-c.631, Sigeberht c.631-c.638

Essex

name   The East Saxons

early forms East Sexe (TH); Saxones Orientales (HE); Estsexum (HB)

first king Eorcenwine (HH) in 527 (RW), whose name is given as Æscwine in the genealogies of the royal house, or Slædde (WM). Yorke (1985) has suggested that the names have a Kentish appearance and might point to Kentish origins for the kingdom.

heartland   Near Southend?

date   Although Eorcenwine is said by Roger of Wendover to have begun to reign in 527, this would give him an implausibly long reign. He was succeeded by Slædde, in turn succeeded by Sæberht who died in 616. Roger gives a date of 587 for Eorcenwine's death and a perhaps more realistic estimate of the length of Eorcenwine's reign would have it begin around 570.

kings   Eorcenwine c.570-587, Sledda 587-597, Sæberht 597-c.616, Seaxred c.616-623, Sæward c.616-623, Seaxbald c.616-623, Sigeberht I 623-c.650

Kent

name — From the Roman *civitas* of Cantium, the people being the Cantii or Cantiaci, meaning the land on the edge or the corner.

early forms Cantware (TH); Cantia, Cantuarii (HE); Chent, Cantia (HB)

royal house Known as Oiscingas (HE)

first king Hengest (HE) 434

heartland Canterbury and east Kent

date — Bede famously dated Hengest's arrival in Kent between 449 and 455. The Anglo-Saxon Chronicle stated that Hengest took over the kingdom 6 years after his arrival. The *Historia Brittonum* put Hengest's arrival in 428. Most people accept that for once Bede seems to have made a mistake in his reckoning. The date of 428 may well be near the mark. The first securely dated King of Kent is Æþelberht, who died in 616 and perhaps was born in 560, four generations after Hengest. This would put Hengest beginning his career at around 460/480. The genealogies in this case are highly suspect. The naming of the dynasty after Oisc may be significant. Suzuki (2000) and Yorke (1993) would identify Oisc as the same person as the Ravenna Cosmographer's 'Ansehis', alternatively thought to be Oesa in the Bernician genealogy. Oisc was three generations above Æþelberht and could have been born around 470. This would accord better with the Anglo-Saxon Chronicle's date of 488 for the beginning of his reign. It may be that Hengest was not really connected with the later Oiscingas but was added to the genealogy because of his known position as the first King of the area.

kings — Hengest 434?-467?, Octa 467?-488/491?, Oisc 488/491-?, (the succession of kings as recorded in the genealogists is obviously defective with names missing from the early 6th century), Eormenric, Æþelberht I 594-616, Eadbald 616-640

Mercia

name — The people of the march, the border province.

early forms Myrce (TH); Mercii (HE); Mercii (HB)

royal house Known as Iclingas (LG) after Icel.

first king Crioda 585 (HH)

heartland The middle Trent valley

date — Crioda was given a date of 585 as the beginning of his reign by the 12th century historian Henry of Huntingdon. We do not know where Henry got his information for this, and there is no way of checking whether Henry's date is accurate. Crioda's great grandfather Icel would have been active around 495/510.

kings — Crioda 585-593, Pybba 593-606, Cearl 606-626, Penda 626-655

Sussex

name · The South Saxons

early forms Suþsexe (TH); Saxones Meridiani or Saxones Australes (HE); Sutsaxum (HB)

first king Ælle (ASC)

heartland Between the Ouse and the Cuckmere.

date Ælle was said to have come to Britain in 477 according to the Anglo-Saxon Chronicle, perhaps taking power in Sussex after successfully taking the town of Pevensey in 491. However, we do not know how these dates were derived and we cannot reckon back from later kings, who are largely undocumented. Ælle 's arrival seems to be 11 years before the death of Hengest. If tied to a revised chronology for Hengest, then an earlier dating for this arrival would be 456.

kings Ælle 456-493? (later kings are unknown) ·

Wessex

name The West Saxons, earlier the *Gewisse*, possibly meaning 'the reliable ones', relating perhaps to loyal Saxon service to the British.

early forms West Sexe (TH); Saxones Occidentales, Saxones Occidui or Geuissae (HE)

royal house Founded by Cerdic (ASC).

first king Cerdic (ASC)

heartland Upper Thames valley, around Dorchester on Thames.

date The dates given in the Anglo-Saxon Chronicle of 495 for Cerdic's arrival do not tally with a reckoning back using the lengths of reigns given for him and his successors. Such a reckoning would give a date of 523 or 532 (see the Timeline). His taking of the Kingdom could be dated 6 years or 24 years after this, depending on how we interpret the Chronicle. Cerdic, his successor Cynric, and his successor Ceawlin all have non-Germanic names.

kings Cerdic 529?-545?, Cynric 545?-571?, Ceawlin 571?-589, Ceol 589-594, Ceolwulf 594-611, Cynegils 611-642.

Wight

name   From Latin and British Vectis/Vecta, possibly referring to the island's position at the fork of two estuaries.

early forms Wihtgara (TH); Vecta (HE land), Victuarii (HE people); Gueith (HB)

first king Unknown but reputed to be settled by Stuf and Wihtgar (ASC).

date   The arrival of Stuf and Wihtgar was dated to 514 in the Anglo-Saxon Chronicle. If this was dated 19 years after the supposed arrival of Cerdic, this would make the real date of their presence in Wight as 542 or 551.

kings   Largely unknown, the last king of the island was Arwald (died 686).

Note: The Kings of Bernicia

The dates of the early kings of Bernicia have been hopelessly garbled in the early sources. The earliest historical date for Northumbrian history is 616. This is the year in which Eadwine replaced Æþelfrið as King, in the Battle of the River Idle. According to Bede, Eadwine was baptised a Christian on the 12th April 627 in his 11th year as King, and died on the 12th October 633 after a reign of 17 years. This would put his accession, and the death of Æþelfrið, between 13th April and 11th October 616. The succession of Kings of Bernica is preserved in genealogies and king-lists as Ida 12 years, Glappa 1 year, Adda 8 years, Æþelric 4 years, Ðeodric 7 years, Friþuwald 6 years, Hussa 8 years and Æþelfrið 24 years. By counting back from 616 for Æþelfrið's death a date of 547 emerges for the accession of Ida, and this is indeed the date that Bede gave for the founding of Bernicia. However, it is difficult to accept such a simple counting back. The *Historia Brittonum* stated that the introduction of Christianity to Kent occurred in the time of Friþuwald. His reign by count-back would have been 579-85, which would have ended 12 years before Augustine's mission arrived in Kent. Furthermore, Adda, Æþelric and Ðeodric were stated to have been brothers and it is possible that they might have shared the rule of Bernicia between them. Joint rule by brothers is well attested in the southern Anglo-Saxon Kingdoms. A partition of Bernicia could have led to the three brothers' sons succeeding them in turn and if we assume this to be the case then we can construct a possible series of dates as follows.

Æþelfrið was the son of Æþelric and we will assume that he succeeded his father over a portion of Bernicia. A reign of 24 years counting back from 616 would give 592 for his accession and 588 for the accession of Æþelric. If the Kingdom was divided between Æþelric and his brothers then we can place their accession to the same year. Adda would then rule from 588 to 596, and Ðeodric from 588 to 595. What of Friþuwald and Hussa? We need to make a further assumption, that the king-list was prepared by giving Ida, then his successor, then Ida's sons in order of age, then their sons in order of accession. Æþelfrið however outlived the others by a large margin and was the immediate predecessor of Eadwine, and so he was taken out of sequence and placed before his successor. Friþuwald would then become the successor of Þeodric, ruling 595-602, and Hussa of Adda, ruling 596-603. According to this scheme of dates, Friþuwald would indeed be reigning during the Christian mission to Kent. The death of Hussa in 603 would make sense of the Battle of Degsastan that same year. A strike by Aedan of Dalriata across intervening Strathclyde into Bernicia makes more sense when it is realised that the invasion was accompanied by Hussa's son, Hering. Hering did not merely guide the invasion force but was the occasion of the war. He was seeking to succeed his father, a succession prevented by Æþelfrið's reuniting of Bernicia under one ruler. The revised scheme of dates might also support the Welsh tradition that the death of Gwrgi and Peredur of York was at the hands of 'Eda'. The Welsh Annals give a date of 580 for their death, within the revised reign of Ida (Eda?) of 575-87.

The establishment of the kingdoms

It is useful to tabulate (Table 16) some of the above information to make clearer the chronological relationships between the different kingdoms and the process of Germanic take-over of Britain.

Decade	Arrival	Established (traditional date)	Established (revised date)
580s		Mercia 585	Mercia 585
570s		Essex 570	Bernicia 575 East Anglia 571 Essex 570
560s		Deira 560	Deira 569
550s			
540s	East Anglia 541/6	Bernicia 547 East Anglia 541	Wight 548
530s			
520s	Wessex 523		Wessex 529
510s	Bernicia 515/25	Wessex 519 Wight 514	
500s			
490s	Mercia 495/510	Sussex 491	
480s			(Kent – Oisc 488)
470s			
460s			
450s		Kent 455	Sussex 456
440s			
430s			Kent 434
420s	Kent 428		
410s	Deira 419/44		

Table 16: The chronology of the establishment of the kingdoms.

The ancestry of the kingly houses

Genealogies of the early Anglo-Saxon kings are found in several manuscripts. Some of these have been discussed by Dumville (1976). Genealogies are also found in the *Anglo-Saxon Chronicle*, and made their way into Welsh sources like the *Historia Brittonum*. Other, later manuscripts also contain genealogies and king lists. Dumville has shown that the Anglo-Saxon genealogies go back in origin to the 8th century, extended and preserved in later copies, somewhat removed from the era of the original settlements. We cannot be sure how far the genealogies as preserved in later manuscripts reflect the realities of the 5th and 6th centuries rather than the political considerations of the 8th and 9th centuries. Although we tend today to look on early royal family trees with a great deal of suspicion, Ó Corráin (1998) has pointed out that the early Irish genealogies could be remarkably accurate, if flexible in accommodating the reality of kinship to political needs by amending genealogical links where necessary.

The genealogies listed here are from the following sources:

- Bæda: the *Historia Ecclesiastica Gentis Anglorum* of Bede, written in 731;

- Vesp. Bvi: British Library Cotton Vespasian B vi, compiled 805/14 in Mercia, derived from the Northumbrian genealogies of 765/74;

- Hist. Britt.: a version of the above genealogy from 787/96 used in the compilation of the *Historia Brittonum* in 829;

- BL Add. 23211: British Library Add. 23211, compiled 871/99 (Essex);

- A-S Chron.: in the *Anglo-Saxon* Chronicle, compiled from earlier materials in c.892;

- CCCC 183: Cambridge Corpus Christi College 183, compiled 934/37 possibly in Glastonbury, a copy of the Northumbrian genealogical collection, with added West Saxon material.

Bernicia

Vesp. Bvi	*Hist. Britt.*	*A-S Chron.*
Uoden	Woden	Woden
Beldæg	Beldeg	Bældæg
		Brand
Beornic	Beornec	Benoc
Wegbrand	Gechbrond	
Ingibrand		
Alusa	Aluson	Aloc
Angengeot	Inguec	Angenwit
Eðilberht	Aedibrith	Ingui
Oesa	Ossa	Esa
Eoppa	Eobba	Eoppa
Ida	Ida	Ida

Deira

Vesp. Bvi	*Hist. Britt.*	*A-S Chron.*
Uoden	Woden	Woden
Uedæg	Beldeyg	Wægdæg
	Brond	
Siggar	Siggar	Sigegar
Suebdæg		Swebdæg
Siggeot		Sigegeat
Saebald	Sebald	Sæbald
Saefugul	Zegulf	Sæfugl
Soemel	Soemil	
Uestorualcna	Sguerthing	Westerfalca
Uilgils	Giulglis	Wilgisl
Uuscfrea	Usfrean	Uxfrea
Yffi	Iffi	Yffe
Aelle	Ulli	Ælle

East Anglia

Vesp. Bvi	*Hist. Britt.*
Uoden	Woden
Caser	Casser
Tyttman	Titinon
Trygil	Trigil
Hroðmund	Rodmunt
Hryp	Rippan
Wilhelm	Guillem-
Wehha	-Guechan
Wuffa	Guffan
Tyttla	Tydil
Eni	Ecni

Essex

BL Add. 23211	*Henry of Huntingdon*
Seaxnet	Saxnat
Gesecg	Andesc
Antsecg	Gesac
Swæppa	Spoewe
Sigefugl	Sigewulf
Bedca	Biedcan
Offa	Offa
Æscwine	Erchenwine
Sledd	Sledd

203

Kent

Vesp. Bvi	*Hist. Britt.*	*Bæda*
Uoden	Woden	Uoden
Uegdæg	Guectha	Uecta
Uihtgils	Guitta	Uitta
Uitta	Guictglis	Uictgisl
Hengest	Hengest	Hengist
Ocga	Octha	Oisc (Oeric)
Oese	Ossa	Octa
Iurmenric	Eormoric	Irminric
Eðilberht	Ealdbert	Aedilberct

Mercia

Sussex

no genealogy known

Wessex

CCCC 183	*A-S Chron.*
Woden	Woden
Bældæg	Bældæg
Brand	Brand
	Friþugar
	Freawine
	Wig
Giwis	Gewis
	Esla
Aluca	Elesa
Cerdic	Cerdic

Wight

no genealogy known

Summary family tree

The genealogies of the different royal houses are gathered together in one diagram (Figure 2). The versions of the genealogies given in British Library Cotton Vespasian B vi are used in the diagram, along with that given by Henry of Huntingdon for Essex, and that of the Anglo-Saxon Chronicle for the West Saxons. The ancestry of the 8th century King Aldfrið of Lindsey has been included for the sake of completeness.

Bernicia	Wessex	Deira	Kent	Mercia	Lindsey	E. Anglia	Essex
			Woden				Saxnot
Bældæg		Wegdæg		Weðolgeot	Winta	Caser	Andesc
Beornic	Brand	Sigegar	Wihtgils	Wihtlæg	Cretta	Tyttman	Gesac
Wegbrand	Friþugar	Swefdæg	Witta	Wermund	Cweldgils	Trygil	Spoewe
Ingibrand	Freawine	Sigeggeot	Hengest	Offa	Cædbæd	Hroðmund	Sigewulf
Alusa	Wig	Sæbald	Ocga	Angengeot	Bubba	Hryp	Biedcan
Angengeot	Gewis	Sæfugol	Oesa	Eamer	Beda	Wilhelm	Offa
Æþelberht	Esla	Soemel	Eormenric	Icel	Biscop	Wehha	Eorcenwine
Oesa	Elesa	Wwalcna	Æþelberht	Cnebba	Eanferð	Wuffa	Slædde
Eoppa	Cerdic	Wilgils		Cynewald	Eatta	Tytla	
Ida		Uscfrea		Crioda	Aldfrið	Ene	
		Yffe					
		Ælle					

Figure 2: Anglo-Saxon kingly genealogies

Appendix 3

The Tribal Hidage

The Tribal Hidage is a tribute list, preserved in three versions (Dumville 1989). The earliest is version A, MS British Library Harley 3271, a copy made in c.1025. Version B is a copy made by Henry Spelman in 1626 of a now lost original Anglo-Saxon manuscript. Version C is preserved in 6 different manuscripts of the 13th and 14th centuries.

The date of the original version is much disputed. Dumville (1989) would attribute it to King Wulfhere of Mercia, c.670. Hart (1977) would rather see it as a Mercian document of King Offa (757-96). Higham (1995) has produced the most radical suggestion that it was produced c.625/26 for King Eadwine of Northumbria. It seems to me that Higham's idea has a great deal of merit.

The list is in two halves, with the names of 'peoples' given in the genitive, e.g. *East Sexena* = of the East Saxons. The Old English genitive plural ended in -a, -na or -ena, while the nominative forms would end in -e. Each kingdom or province is given a number of hides; a unit of assessment for the purposes of taxation. This bears some broad relation to size and status but could be manipulated for political reasons. For instance, the high value for the West Saxons might well be a punitive rate, while the low value for Elmet might be a reduction to ensure loyalty from a recently annexed province. Not all the provinces listed need be Anglo-Saxon. It has been plausibly suggested that units in *-sæte* were provinces under existing or recent British rule. We might also admit the possibility that the obscure *Noxgaga, Ohtgaga, Unecungaga* and *Hendrica* might also be British.

The lists are given below as they are in BL Harley 3271 (with variations of the names as given in version B in brackets). Major differences between this and the other versions are that the *Hendrica* are given 3,000 hides in the B version, and the *Hwinca* are given 6,000 hides in the C version. Most of the units listed can be identified to some extent. In some cases, they are identical in name to known kingdoms, in other cases their names are preserved in later place-names. Provinces that cannot be located with any certainty include the *Hendrica* and *Unecungaga*. These are placed between the *Cilternsæte* and the *Arosæte* (assumed to be in Warwickshire but this would make little geo-political sense) and so they have been assumed to be somewhere to the north of the Thames. The large provinces of the *Noxgaga* and *Ohtgaga* are placed after the Isle of Wight. They have been placed in later-day Surrey and Berkshire, but could really be anywhere. Somewhere next to the *Gewisse*, e.g. Dorset and Somerset, is just as likely. The *Westerne* are usually assumed to be the people later referred to as the *Magonsæte* around the area of Maund in Herefordshire and Shropshire, although Higham would prefer to see them as a reference to Gwynedd.

Kingdom/province	Location	Hides	Notes
Myrcnalandes	Mercia	30,000	Anglo-Saxon kingdom
Wocensætna	Wrekin	7,000	British Eastern Powys?
Westerna	'The Westerners'	7,000	
Pecsætna	Peak	1,200	Former British province?
Elmedsætna	Elmet	600	Former British kingdom
Lindesfarona	Lindsey		
mid Hæþfeldland	with Hatfield	7,000	Former British province
Suþ Gyrwa	Fens	600	Middle Anglian district
Norþ Gyrwa	Fens	600	Middle Anglian district
East Wixna	R. Ouse (Camb.)	300	Middle Anglian district
West Wixna	R. Ouse (Camb.)	600	Middle Anglian district
Spalda	Spalding (Holl.)	600	Middle Anglian district
Wigesta	Wiggenhall (Norf.)	900	Middle Anglian district
Herefinna	(Hunts. & Northants.)	1,200	Middle Anglian district
Sweordora	Whittlesey Mere (Hunts.)	300	Middle Anglian district
Gifla (Eyfla)	R. Ivel (Beds.)	300	Middle Anglian district
Hicca (Wicca)	Hitchin (Herts.)	300	Middle Anglian district
Wihtgara	Isle of Wight	600	Anglo-Saxon kingdom
Noxgaga	?	5,000	
Ohtgaga	?	2,000	
Hwinca (Hwynca)	Whych (*Hwicce*)	7,000	Anglo-Saxon kingdom
Cilternsætna	Chiltern	4,000	
Hendrica	?	3,500	
Unecungaga	?	1,200	
Arosætna (Aroseatna)	R. Arrow? (Warw.)	600	
Færpinga (Fearfinga)	Charlbury? (Oxf.)	300	Middle Anglian district
Bilmiga (Belmiga)	Belmesthorpe (Rut.)	600	Middle Anglian district
Widerigga (Witherigga)	Wittering (Peterb.)	600	Middle Anglian district
East Willa	R. Cam (Camb.)	600	Middle Anglian district
West Willa	R. Cam (Camb.)	600	Middle Anglian district
East Engla	East Angles	30,000	Anglo-Saxon kingdom
East Sexena	East Saxons	7,000	Anglo-Saxon kingdom
Cantwarena	Kent	15,000	Anglo-Saxon kingdom
Suþ Sexena	South Saxons	7,000	Anglo-Saxon kingdom
West Sexena	West Saxons	100,000	Anglo-Saxon kingdom

Appendix 4

Key Features of
the Germanic Languages

The Germanic languages developed out of Indo-European dialects spoken in northern Europe during the pre-Roman Iron Age. The Indo-European languages are widely spread across Europe and Asia. The only major indigenous European languages that are not Indo-European are Basque, Hungarian, Finnish, Estonian, and Lapp. There are various groups of modern day languages within Indo-European:

Germanic	e.g. German, English, Danish
Celtic	e.g. Irish, Scots Gaelic, Breton, Welsh, Cornish
Romance	e.g. French, Italian, Spanish, Romanian
Illyrian	Albanian
Baltic	Latvian, Lithuanian
Slavic	e.g. Russian, Polish, Bulgarian
Indic	e.g. Hindi, Punjabi, Bengali
Iranian	e.g. Persian, Kurdish, Pashto
Armenian	Armenian
Greek	Greek

Various features marked out those languages which became Germanic from the other Indo-European dialects. The stage of development before the various dialects became differentiated into the different Germanic languages is known as Proto-Germanic. The most important of the Germanic language characteristics are detailed below.

Germanic languages are traditionally placed into groups depending on how closely related they are. These groupings have some validity but do not tell the whole story of influences, borrowings and relationships between the different languages. Nevertheless, they are a simple way of providing an overall categorisation and listing of the languages. Most branches of the Germanic language family survive to the present day. The exception is the Eastern branch, which is now extinct. Its major known representative in history was Gothic. This is thought to have survived in pockets in the Crimea as late as the 16th century.

In the examples below, the various Germanic and other languages are referred by the following abbreviations: Go - Gothic, Gr - Greek, La - Latin, OE - Old English, OHG - Old High German, ON - Old Norse, PG - Primitive Germanic. All Primitive Germanic Forms are hypothetical reconstructions.

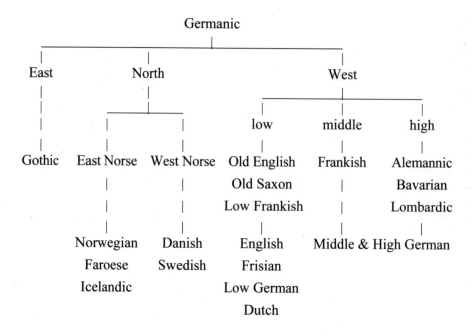

Figure 3: The Germanic language family.

Phonology

Treatment of vowels

Most Germanic vowels were pronounced as they had been in Indo-European but there were a few exceptions. Their pronunciation was then sometimes further changed in particular languages. Examples are:

Indo-European *o/oi/ou* became Germanic *a/ai/au*

- e.g. La *quod* = Go *hwa*, ON *hvat*, OE *hwæt*, OHG *hwaz* (what)
- e.g. Gr *oide* = Go *wait*, ON *veit*, OE *wát*, OHG *weiz* (he knows)
- e.g. La *rufus* (from **roufus*) = Go *rauþs*, ON *rauðr*, OE *read*, OHG *rót* (red)

Indo-European *á* became Germanic *ó*

- e.g. La *frater* = Go *bróþar*, ON *bróðir*, OE *bróþor*, OHG *bruoder* (brother)

Indo-European *é* changed to a variety of sounds in different Germanic languages

- e.g. La *édimus* = Go *étum*, ON *átum*, OE *ǽton*, OHG *ázum* (we ate)

Indo-European *ei* became Germanic *í*

- e.g. Gr *steigo* = Go *steiga* (pronounced *stíga*), ON *stíg*, OE *stígu*, OHG *stígu* (I go up)

Grimm's Law

Consonants underwent a greater degree of change from Indo-European to Germanic. The changes are referred to as the First Sound Shift, or Grimm's Law. This affected particular consonants as follows (with further changes later in Old High German):

- *p > f*   La *pisces* = Go *fisks*, ON *fiskr*, OE *fisc*, OHG *fisk* (fish)
- *t > þ*   La *tres* = Go *þreis*, ON *þrír*, OE *þrie*, OHG *drí* (three)
- *k > h*   La *canis* = Go *hunds*, ON *hundr*, OE *hund*, OHG *hunt* (hound)
- *b > p*   La *lubricus* = Go *sliupan*, ON *sleppa*, OE *slupan*, OHG *slioffan* (slippery/to slip)
- *d > t*   La *edere* = Go *itan*, ON *eta*, OE *etan*, OHG *ezzan* (to eat)
- *g > k*   La *ego* = Go *ik*, ON *ek*, OE *ic*, OHG *ih* (I)
- *bh > b* La *frater* = Go *bróþar*, ON *bróðir*, OE *bróþor*, OHG *bruoder* (brother)
  or *> ƀ* La *libido* = Go *liufs*, ON *ljúfr*, OE *léof*, OHG *liob* (dear)
- *dh > d* Gr *thugater* = Go *dauhtar*, ON *dottir*, OE *dohtor*, OHG *tohter (daughter)*
  or *> ð* Gr *eruthros* = Go *rauþs*, ON *rauðr*, OE *read*, OHG *rót (red)*
- *gh > g* La *hostis* = Go *gasts*, ON *gestr*, OE *giest*, OHG *gast* (guest)
  or *> ʒ* La *vehere* = Go *gawigan*, ON *vega*, OE *wegan*, OHG *wegan* (to carry)

Verner's Law

During the early history of Proto-Germanic, some consonants further changed in circumstances where the vowel immediately before them was unstressed. This situation most commonly arose in the past tense of verbs. In the singular, the stress fell on the root syllable, but in the plural the stress was placed on the ending. Those consonants affected were *f* (changed to *ƀ*), *þ* (changed to *ð*), *h* (changed to *ʒ*), *s* (changed to *z*). Later changes have often obscured the original sounds in different ways in each Germanic language. The changes as seen in Old English (where *f* was usually pronounced *v* in the middle of a word), were as follows:

- *f > ƀ*   OE *ic cearf - we curfon* (I carved - we carved)
- *þ > ð*   OE *hit seaþ - hie sudon* (it boiled - they boiled)
- *h > ʒ*   OE *he sloh - hie slogon* (he struck - they struck)
- *hw > w*   OE *ic seah - we sawon* (I saw - we saw)
- *s > z*   OE *ic ceas - we curon* (I chose - we chose)

Initial stress accent

After a while, Germanic speakers began to place the stress always on the first or root syllable of words. This led to a greatly reduced emphasis on the pronunciation of endings, which became much reduced as a result. This process had only just begun in Gothic but had advanced much further by the time that the other Germanic languages were first written down. Examples are:

- PG *augón* - Go *augo* - ON *auga* - OE *eage* - OHG *ouga* (eye)
- PG *ahtau* - Go *ahtau* - ON *átta* - OE *eahta* - OHG *ahto* (eight)
- PG *ek beró* - Go *ik baira* - ON *ek ber* - OE *ic beru* - OHG *ih beru* (I bear)

Weak adjectives

Adjectives were given endings to agree with the noun they were describing. Hence, Old English *god mann* (a good person) but *gode menn* (good people). All Germanic languages used a second, different set of endings when the adjective occurred with the definite article. So, Old English had *se goda mann* (the good person) and *þa godan menn* (the good people). The original endings are termed strong and the newly developed endings are called weak. Examples are given below of the nominative masculine endings in the singular and plural for both strong and weak forms of the word 'good' in Table 17.

Language	Strong (sing. - plur.)	Weak (sing. – plur.)
Germanic	*góðaz - góðai*	*góðó – góðaniz*
Gothic	*goþs - godai*	*goda – godans*
Old Norse	*góðr - goeðir*	*goeði – goðu*
Old English	*gód - góde*	*góda – gódan*
Old High German	*guot - guote*	*guoto – guoton*

Table 17: The word *good* in various early Germanic languages

Weak past tense

Germanic languages developed classes of verbs that formed their past tenses by adding endings based on the consonant *ð*. These are termed weak verbs. The examples in Table 18 are translations of 'I hear' and 'I heard'.

Language	Present	Past
Germanic	*ek hausjó*	*ek hausiðón*
Gothic	*ik hausja*	*ik hausida*
Old Norse	*ek heyri*	*ek heyrða*
Old English	*ic hiere*	*ic hierde*
Old High German	*ih hóru*	*ih hórta*

Table 18: *I hear/heard* in various early Germanic languages

Appendix 5

Chronology of Anglo-Saxon Material Culture

The dominance of the culture-historical approach to archaeological investigation has led to the detailed analysis of artefact types and stylistic studies as the basis for chronology of the period in archaeology. Attempts to tie the chronologies into historically derived periods can sometimes yield circular argument with the dating of artefacts depending on historical dates, themselves supported by archaeological evidence as much as documents. It often seems that inordinate amounts of time have been spent debating the ethnic affiliation of artefact types and styles; debate rendered sterile in the absence of a proper understanding of the nature of ethnic identity and the symbolic role of material culture. Material culture does not equal a people even if aspects of material culture can be used by groups to signal their identity. Ethnic labels given to artefacts or styles must be treated with great care and used only with a good understanding of the significance of the label. Romano-British material culture developed along different lines to that of the Germanic peoples, stemming from both Roman artistic styles and native British artefact types and styles of ultimately Iron Age origin. This is not to say that Germanic and British styles can always be easily distinguished. We may find material culture that represents a fusion of styles and influences, such as the Quoit brooch style, or the use of red enamel in Anglo-Saxon metalwork. We may also find artefacts of British manufacture or artistic taste deposited in Germanic contexts, like the hanging bowls found on Anglo-Saxon sites in eastern Britain. Other artefacts of undoubted British origin are particular types of annular, penannular and disc brooches.

Artefacts were often a medium for artistic embellishment. The artistic style of this decoration has often been used as a way of dating artefacts, and sites, within the period. The interlaced animal and abstract ornament used as decoration on portable artefacts, survives today mainly in finds of jewellery and metalwork, but originally was most likely also used on woodwork, embroidery, painting and later in manuscripts. A summary knowledge of Germanic art styles as defined by modern scholars is useful (Speake 1980, Suzuki 2000).

Sösdala – stamped decoration and shallow chip carving with geometric and zoomorphic motifs, found on square-headed brooches, dating from the early 5th century.

Saxon – chip carved geometric and cast zoomorphic motifs, associated with equal arm brooches, derived from Roman military decoration and dating from c.375 to c.525.

Nydam – deep chip carving with some stamping, geometric and zoomorphic motifs, associated with square-headed brooches, belonging to the 5th century (c.400-475) and overlapping with the Sösdala style.

Style 1 – beginning in Jutland 475/500, greater emphasis on zoomorphic designs, adopted in Britain through Kent, continued in Britain into the 7th century in areas where style 2 had not yet been adopted.

Style 2 – beginning in Sweden c.550, shallower chip carving, use of cloisonné, niello and filigree, increasing linearity and abstraction, sinuous interlacing, adopted in Britain directly through East Anglia and through Kentish contacts with Jutland.

Many artefacts of the period no longer survive, being made of organic materials that have since decayed. What survives may be utilitarian or may have symbolic functions of varying extent and complexity. The most useful artefacts for chronological purposes are those whose form and decoration changed rapidly over time, those subject to changes in fashion and most used to symbolise status and identity. What follows is a very short and incomplete summary of the chronology of material culture in the south and east of Britain in the two hundred years after the end of Roman rule, taken largely from Lucy (2000), unless otherwise stated. References for each artefact type are placed in the chapter on sources.

Pottery

Pots were hand-made and probably mostly for simple domestic use in the kitchen and for storage. One specialised area of use was as funerary urns for holding the ashes of the dead. These form a large part of the archaeological record for the period. Pots have not been divided into clear types. However, datable features of the pottery are as follows, after Myres (1969) :

date	form	decoration
5th century	biconical, globular	broad and deep linear lines and grooves, corrugated, finger tipping, bosses (esp. *Buckelurnen*), standing arches
6th century	high shoulder	bosses, abundant use of stamps, pendant triangles and hanging arches, vertical lines
7th century	bag-shaped	random stamping

Brooches

Long brooches

These are based on a coiled spring underneath a head-plate with a pin catching behind a footplate, the two plates being joined by a bow. They are found mainly in parts of Britain that would later be termed Anglian or Jutish. Three kinds of long brooch may be distinguished: cruciform, short-long, square-headed.

Cruciform brooches

These have a head-plate with three arms, of vaguely cross-like shape. The footplate is an elongated and stylised animal head.

Type I   full, rounded knobs at the ends of the head-plate arms, 5th to early 6th centuries

Type II   half-rounded knobs, 5th to early 6th centuries

Type III   as type II but with scrolled nostrils on the animal heads, 6th century

Type IV   the footplate has lappets attached to the end of the animal head, middle to later 6th century

Type V   florid type (highly ornamented and elaborated), later 6th to early 7th centuries

An alternative classification by Mortimer in an unpublished thesis is:

Type A   small, with a simple footplate, circular top knobs, plain or simple decoration, early 5th century

Type B   expanded head-plate, flattened or semi-circular top knobs, simple animal heads

Type C   expanded footplate

Type D   lappets added to the footplate

Type Z   zoomorphic decoration

Square-headed brooches

These have a rectangular head-plate and a lozenge or diamond-shaped footplate.

Type A   a single footplate, later 5th century

Type B   a divided footplate, 6th century

Type C   a footplate that would normally be found on a cruciform brooch, 7th century

Hines placed these brooches into three phases rather than types.

Phase 1   small brooches, different to each other, c.500-520

Phase 2   larger and more alike, c.510-550

Phase 3   produced according to a more standardised design, c.530-570

There is a set of square-headed brooches found mainly in Kent (with a few found elsewhere), that form a different type. These are smaller than the others and can have an undivided foot, and sometimes a disc on the bow. The earliest examples may date from 480-500.

Small-long brooches

These are the plainer and simpler forms of bow brooch dress fastener. They have various cruciform or square heads and different styles of footplate. They have little decoration beyond some moulded ribs or simple stamped designs. They can be classified according to the style of head or footplate.

Trefoil   a square head with three round-topped arms

Cross Pattee   a head resembling a Maltese cross

Cross Potent   a similar head to the trefoil type but with flatter and wider arms

Square   a plain square head or one with two 'horns' at the top

Lozenge   a lozenge-shaped foot and various styles of head-plate

Round brooches

Round brooches have the pin and catch hidden under a single circular plate, or an open ring. The former types are found more often in southern areas of Britain, in areas later described as Saxon. Open ring types have a more general distribution and might well be of indigenous British origin.

Disc brooches

Circular brooches in bronze, cast in one piece and having incised or stamped decoration on the flat or domed surface. They date from the mid 5th to mid 6th centuries and were likely of Romano-British origin.

Saucer brooches

These are discs with an upstanding rim. The inside of the saucer thus created is decorated, either by a layer of decorated foil applied to the saucer, or by casting the brooch in a pre-carved mould. They date from the early fifth to the end of the 6th centuries. They were worn in pairs at the shoulders as fastening for women's dresses. Early forms have geometric decoration, later forms have stylised animals of Style 1 art.

Button brooches

These are much smaller types of saucer brooch, decorated with a human face or crouching animal design. They have been dated variously from the 5th, the later 5th to mid-6th centuries and to the middle and later 6th century.

Penannular brooches

Penannular brooches are an open ring with two ends leaving a gap, and a pin attached to the ring. They had an ancient origin in the pre-Roman iron age and represent continuing native British manufacture and influence. In Anglo-Saxon grave contexts, they date to the 6th century.

Annular brooches

These are complete open rings. The pin is attached at one side, extending across the open middle of the ring. Decoration is limited to incised lines or punched impressions. The ring itself can be either a broad or narrow band. They date from the late 5th century into the 7th century.

Swastika brooches

These are flat discs, cut through with open shapes leaving a swastika-like design joining the outer circle of the rim.

Quoit brooches

This is a style of brooch associated with the quoit brooch style of decoration (disc and penannular brooches may also have this decoration). The brooches take the form of an internal penannular brooch surrounded by a solid disc carrying the ornament. They are a display brooch of the 5th century, based on Romano-British models but incorporating elements of Germanic style decoration.

Keystone garnet brooches

With a distribution based on Kent, these are disc brooches with garnet settings within areas of animal ornament. There is a round garnet in the middle and other settings radiating out from this. They date from c.550 to c.630. The type would develop into plated and composite disc forms, lasting until the early 8th century.

Other brooches

There are various brooches that were probably made on the continent and either imported or brought over to Britain without developing a new source of manufacture in the island.

Tutulus brooches

A late 4th century type, resembling an elongated shield boss. These were old when brought over to Britain and deposited in the 5th century.

Supporting arm brooches

These have a wide, expanding head-plate but are otherwise quite simple in design and decoration.

Equal arm brooches

These have two equal trapezoidal or semi-circular plates either side of the bow, which can be plain or more usually have chip-carved decoration. They may well have developed from supporting arm brooches under the influence of late Roman military belt fittings. On the continent, most are found in the area between the Elbe and Weser rivers, and in Mecklenburg, dating between c375 and c.525. They were deposited in Britain between c.450 and c.550.

Radiate brooches

Five or seven knobs radiate from the top of a semi-circular headplate, and they have straight or expanded, lozenge-shaped foot plates. They may have been Frankish imports.

Bird brooches

Stylised and carved bird shapes. These were probably also Frankish imports.

Weapons

Weapons like the bow and arrow, the axe and the sword are only rarely found in the archaeological record. Swords especially were a high status artefact, as were the even rarer helmets. The commonest finds are of spearheads and shield bosses, outlined below.

Spearheads

Spearheads were perhaps the commonest of the weapons of the period. A few special types have been identified:

Type B	the blade having a dominant midrib, 7th century
Type C	leaf-shaped blade, 7th century
Type D	leaf-shaped blade, occurring at all periods
Types E, F	angular leaf-shaped blades, 7th century
Type G	long, sword-shaped blades, 7th century
Type H	angular with concave angles, 6th century
Types I – K	corrugated or asymmetrical cross sections, 6th century
Type L	like type H but corrugated, late 5th to early 6th centuries

Shields

The shields themselves were made of wood and so rarely survive. What is found is the shield boss, the iron cap in the middle of the shield that guarded the hand grip. Early bosses were carinated and belonged to the 5th, 6th and early 7th centuries, with carination becoming less pronounced until replaced by rounded forms (cone bosses) after c.650. The earliest forms of carinated boss were higher and more pointed than later forms, which tended to be lower and more rounded. The spike of these early forms was replaced by a flat button after the later 5th century.

Seaxes

These are one-edged knives, either short or long whose primary purpose may have been as hunting knives. The form of the blade is distinctive, Underwood (1999) listing several types from this period:

curved back and cutting edge	late 5th to early 8th centuries
straight back, curved edge	late 5th to late 7th centuries
angled back, curved cutting edgemid	6th to early 8th centuries
angled back, straight edge	late 6th to early 8th centuries
curved back, straight edge	early 7th to early 8th centuries

Other

Bracteates

These are golden or silver discs, mounted for wearing as amulets, made in Scandinavia and southern Britain from the 5th to early 7th centuries. Their form was derived from Roman medallions. As amulets they would have been meant to invoke divine protection and so are closely tied to the heathen Germanic religious beliefs. There are four types of iconography on bracteates.

A   carrying a human head, based on portraits of Roman Emperors (only a few in Britain)

B   with standing figure/s, based on Victory crowning a hero (only one known so far from Britain)

C   derived from the figure of the Emperor on horseback (mostly from East Anglia), 6th century

D   with Germanic animal ornament (mostly from East Anglia and Kent), c.475-550

Attempts to identify the figures shown on the bracteates with later Scandinavian gods and goddesses have not been entirely convincing.

Summary

A summary table of material culture may be produced (Table 19), although it represents a very crude scheme of the development of artefacts during the period and should be treated with great caution. The Table is divided into the two phases of migration and conquest.

Century	Brooches	Weapons	Other
PHASE 1			
early 5th	cruciform I small-long saucer tutulus supporting arm	spearheads D carinated shield boss straight, curved back knives	animal decorated buckles double sided combs
late 5th	cruciform I, II small-long saucer disc square-headed equal arm	spearheads D, L carinated shield boss straight, curved back knives	round, heart & kidney plate buckles double sided combs A & C bracteates
early 6th	cruciform I-III saucer disc square-headed 1-3 equal arm radiate bird	spearheads D, H-K, L carinated shield boss straight, curved back knives	scutiform pendants round, heart & kidney plate buckles oval, round, D-shaped buckles double sided combs D bracteates
PHASE 2			
late 6th	cruciform III-V saucer square-headed 3 keystone	spearheads D, H-K carinated shield boss straight, curved back knives	hanging bowls scutiform pendants triangular plate, small loop buckles double sided combs cowry shells
early 7th	cruciform V keystone disc	spearheads B-G hump back knives seaxes	hanging bowls gold disc pendants cabochon pendants triangular plate, small loop buckles single sided combs cowry shells

Table 19: Material culture in the migration period.

Appendix 6

Germanic and British Place Names

The evidence in Table 20 is presented in five main columns, showing the numbers of placements in each country.

A Names of early Germanic origin in *-ham, -ingaham, -ingas*. Other names are likely to be early as well, e.g. *-dun* and *-burne*, but these were also long-lived and not necessarily all of early date. It may well be that *-ingas* names were coined as late as the 7th century, and they are certainly not an indicator of the very earliest settlements.

B Names showing evidence of heathen Germanic religious belief or practice.

C Names showing the survival of British speaking populations into at least the 8th century, *Wala-, Bretta-, Cumbra-*.

D Names identified as Celtic in Coates et al. 2000.

E Names based on Latin (including *wic*-names) and borrowed into English early in the phase of settlement. These are possibly an indication of Germanic contact with immediate post-Roman populations.

Asterisks in columns B and D indicate provisional figures for counties which have not been fully surveyed for the names in question. The names are taken from Balkwill 1993, Cameron 1977, Coates et al. 2000, and Gelling 1978.

Other columns are headed Gm for Germanic and Br for British. These show how far the total of columns to the left exceed the notional average for each linguistic category: H = higher than expected, L = lower than expected.

High Germanic values are found in the south east - Essex, Kent, Surrey, Sussex - and the east coast - Lincoln, Norfolk, Suffolk. The East Riding of Yorkshire also belongs here, as does the heartland of the later Wessex - Hampshire and to a lesser extent Wiltshire. This coincides remarkably well with the distribution of the earliest Germanic cemeteries in Britain.

High British values occur where we might expect, in the north and west. From Northumberland and Cumberland to the West Riding and then Lancashire into the midlands of Cheshire, Derbyshire, Stafford and Shropshire, and southwards into Hereford, Worcester and Gloucester. High values also occur in Dorset, Somerset and Devon, and also in Hampshire and Wiltshire. One curious outlier is Middlesex. This county with Hertford and Buckingham is also an area of low Germanic values.

The counties in the table are arranged according to their possible location within the provinces of late Roman Britain. The existence of one of these provinces has been challenged, and the boundaries of the provinces are completely unknown. The arrangement in the table must therefore be regarded as highly speculative and represent my own feeling as to the likely boundaries. Other arrangements are equally possible. The table does not contain data for Anglo-Saxon areas now in Scotland, i.e. Lothian and the border shires of Berwick, Roxburgh, Selkirk and Peebles. It is unfortunate that place-name scholarship sticks to political boundaries that are irrelevant for the period.

Maxima Caesariensis shows a high proportion of early Germanic place-names, with only an inlier of low Germanic presence in the area north and north-west of London. The mixed origin of Wessex shows in the high incidence if both early Germanic and Celtic names in Hampshire and Wiltshire. Flavia Caesariensis is also an area of heavy Germanic settlement with East Anglia and Lincolnshire having very high proportions of place-names of early Germanic origin. The province has a generally low proportion of Celtic names. In contrast, Britannia Prima shows up as an area with a high concentration of Celtic place-names, as do Valentia and Northumberland. Britannia Secunda has a more mixed pattern. Apart from the old civitas of the Parisii, to become the East Riding, Celtic names have a high survival rate in the Pennine areas but seem to be less in evidence elsewhere. Names indicating early contact by Germanic settlers with Roman language and administration (column E) are highest in the areas which also have high concentrations of early Germanic names. The only exceptions are Hertford and Cambridge. The earliest areas to be settled on an official basis - Kent and Sussex - have by far the highest proportion of names in column E.

for key see p.219	A	B	Gm	C	D	Br	E
Maxima Caesariensis?							
Kent	28	6	H	2	10		11
Sussex	49	9*	H	1	9*		11
Surrey	15	10	H	3	7		3
Essex	33	8	H	3	4	L	5
Middlesex	3	2	L	1	25	H	2
Hertford	3	2	L	2	2	L	6
Hampshire	11	8	H		24	H	6
Wiltshire	3	11	H	2	28	H	6
Berkshire	8	2		1	8		3
Buckingham	1	1	L		7*	L	2
Oxford	6	4		1	5	L	1

for key see p.219	A	B	Gm	C	D	Br	E
Britannia Prima?							
Dorset	2		L		29*	H	2
Somerset	2	1	L		45*	H	2
Devon		1	L		67*	H	1
Warwick	2	5		1	7		1
Worcester	5	3		3	23*	H	
Gloucester	2	2	L	1	48	H	3
Hereford	2	1	L	1	25*	H	
Flavia Caesariensis?							
Bedford	4	2			2*	L	1
Cambridge	7	1		1	3	L	3
Huntingdon	4		L		3*	L	2
Suffolk	30	1	H	1	4*	L	5
Norfolk	62	1	H	2	9*		3
Lincoln	33	2	H	4	7*		3
Northampton	6	5		2	3	L	1
Rutland	2	1	L		1	L	
Leicester	2	1	L	3	4*	L	1
Britannia Secunda?							
Nottingham	7	2			5	L	
Derby		2	L	4	24	H	
E Riding	17		H		6*	L	1
N Riding	11	1		3	6*		2
W Riding	5	1		5	26	H	
Durham	2		L	1	5*	L	
Valentia?							
Shropshire	1		L	2	22*	H	
Stafford	1	3	L	2	21*	H	
Cheshire	5	4		4	25	H	
Lancashire	7			4	56*	H	
Cumberland	3		L	3	81	H	
Westmorland	1		L		10		
Outside Britannia							
Northumberland	9				21*	H	

Table 20: Incidence of place-names by county.

Appendix 7

Arthur

The figure of Arthur is probably the most contentious figure in British history. He has been a figure of European literature since the 12th century, a useful mythical figure for the projection of feudal ideals or Celtic nationalism, and a useful source of narrative for modern cinema. Historians are deeply divided as to whether he had any basis in reality. Opinions tend to be polarised and debate often emotive.

The later medieval Arthur of literature began life in the 12th century, in the skilful hands of Geoffrey of Monmouth, later Bishop of St. Asaph. Geoffrey was a canon of an Augustinian house in Oxford when he wrote his *Historia Regum Britanniae*, finishing it in 1136. He intended to provide a British (Welsh) history to rival and surpass that of the English. Arthur was the subject of only c.20% of the whole work. His tale was taken up by other writers who added various elements to the original. Wace in 1155 produced his *Roman de Brut* which included the idea of the round table. Chretien de Troyes wrote five stories of Arthur in the 1160s to 1180s and introduced the character of Lancelot along with Arthur's castle of Camelot. Robert de Boron added the search for the holy grail in his trilogy of the 1190s. An English writer, Laȝamon, produced a verse poem in English with a version of Arthur's story in c.1200. The Arthurian legends as we now know them were the work of Sir Thomas Malory who wrote *Le Morte d'Arthur* in 1470, published by the printer William Caxton in 1485.

Geoffrey was not the first writer to give literary form to Arthur. It is evident that Arthur was already a mythical and heroic figure in Welsh literature as early as the 9th century, e.g. *Y Trioedd, Preiddeu Annwn*. He was also present in early romances that would develop into the later medieval King Arthur, e.g. *Culhwch a Olwen*. Arthur occurs in various saints' lives, a few of which may be earlier than Geoffrey of Monmouth, e.g. *The Life of St. Cadoc* (c.1075). There are also incidental references in poems that may be very early, e.g. *Y Gododdin, Gereint fab Erbin*.

References to Arthur are quoted below from a variety of writers and works that have a bearing on Arthur's existence.

William of Malmesbury

William was librarian of Malmesbury Abbey and the most accomplished historian in England since Bede. He wrote his *Gesta Regum Anglorum* in 1125. There is nothing new about Arthur in this work, but William is scathing about current literary uses of Arthur. William was writing before Geoffrey of Monmouth published his work and therefore shows how Geoffrey was part of a wider Arthurian trend, not writing in isolation. The following extract is taken from the version of the *Gesta Regum Anglorum* edited by Stubbs (1887), the translation is from Stevenson (1854).

Sed, eo extincto, Britonum robur emarcuit, spes imminutae retro fluxere; et jam tunc profecto pessum issent, nisi Ambrosius, solus Romanorum superstes, qui post Wortigernum monarcha regni fuit, intumescentes barbaros eximia bellicosi Arturis opera pressisset. Hic est Artur de quo Britonum nugae hodieque delirant; dignus plane quem non fallaces somniarent fabulae, sed veraces praedicarent historiae, quippe qui labantem patriam diu sustinuerit, infractasque civium mentes ad bellum acuerit; postremo, in obsessione Badonici montis, fretus imagine Dominicae matris, quam armis suis insuerat, nongentos hostium solus adorsus incredibili caede profligarit.

... the British strength decayed; their hopes, becoming diminished, fled; and they would have soon perished altogether, had not Ambrosius, the sole survivor of the Romans, who became monarch after Vortigern, quelled the presumptuous barbarians by the powerful aid of warlike Arthur. This is that Arthur, of whom the Britons fondly fable even to the present day; a man worthy to be celebrated, not by idle fictions, but in authentic history. He, indeed, for a long time upheld the sinking state, and roused the broken spirit of his countrymen to war. Finally, at the siege of Mount Badon, relying on an image of the Virgin which he had affixed to his armour, he engaged nine hundred of the enemy single-handed, and dispersed them with incredible slaughter.

To find any historical Arthur we have to go behind Geoffrey and the literary references. The historical references are few and provide little that we can use to write a genuine history of Arthur.

Historia Brittonum *(A History of the Britons)*

This was a historical miscellany written in 829/30 and once attributed (wrongly) to a Welsh monk called Nennius. References to Arthur are found in chapter 56 (Morris 1980).

In illo tempore Saxones invalescebant in multitudine et crescebant in Brittannia. Mortuo autem Hengisto, Octha, filius ejus, transivit de sinistrali parte Brittanniae ad regnum Cantorum, et de ipso orti sunt reges Cantorum. Tunc Arthur pugnabat contra illos in illis diebus cum regibus Brittonum, sed ipse dux erat bellorum. Primum bellum fuit in ostium fluminis quod dicitur Glein. Secundum, et tertium, et quartum, et quintum super aliud flumen, quod dicitur Dubglas, et est in regione Linnuis. Sextum bellum super flumen quod vocatur Bassas. Septimum fuit bellum in silva Celidonis, id est Cat Coit Celidon. Octavum fuit bellum in castello Guinnion, in quo Arthur portavit imaginem sanctae Mariae perpetuae virginis super humeros suos, et pagani versi sunt in fugam in illo die, et caedes magna fuit super illos per virtutem Domini nostri Jesu Christi et per virtutem sanctae Mariae virginis genitricis ejus. Nonum bellum gestum est in urbe Legionis. Decimum gessit bellum in litore fluminis quod vocatur Tribruit. Undecimum factum est bellum in monte qui dicitur Agned. Duodecimum fuit bellum in monte Badonis, in quo corruerunt in uno die nongenti sexaginta viri de uno impetu Arthur; et nemo prostravit eos nisi ipse solus, et in omnibus bellis victor extitit.

At that time the English increased in numbers and grew in Britain. On Hengest's death, his son Octa came down from the north of Britain to the kingdom of Kent, and from him are sprung the kings of Kent. Then Arthur fought against them in those days, together with the kings of the British; but he was their leader in battle. The first battle was at the mouth of the river called Glein. The second, the third, the fourth and the fifth were on another river, called the Douglas, which is in the country called Lindsey. The sixth battle was on the river called Bassas. The seventh battle was in Celyddon Forest, that is the Battle of Coed Celyddon. The eighth battle was in Guinnion fort, and in it Arthur carried the image of the holy Mary, the everlasting virgin, on his shield, and the heathen were put to flight on that day, and there was a great slaughter upon them, through the power of our Lord Jesus Christ and the power of the holy Virgin Mary, his mother. The ninth battle was fought in the city of the Legion. The tenth battle was fought on the bank of the river called Tryfrwyd. The eleventh battle was on the hill called Agned. The twelfth battle was on Badon Hill and in it nine hundred and sixty men fell in one day, from a single charge of Arthur's, and no one laid them low save he alone; and he was victorious in all his campaigns.

Annales Cambriae *(The Welsh Annals)*

The Welsh Annals were written in Latin sometime between 954 and 977. They contain direct references to Arthur under two dates in the 6th century (Morris 1980). The dates themselves are not given but can be worked out from the known dates of other events in the sequence of years.

516 Bellum Badonis, in quo Arthur portavit crucem domini nostri Jhesu Christi tribus diebus et tribus noctibus in humeros suos et Brittones victores fuerunt.

The Battle of Badon, in which Arthur carried the cross of our lord Jesus Christ for three days and three nights on his shoulders and the Britons were the victors.

537 Gueith Camlann in qua Arthur et Medraut corruerunt, et mortalitas in Brittania et in Hibernia fuit.

The Battle of Camlann in which Arthur and Medrawd fell, and there was a plague in Britain and Ireland.

Genealogies

Royal and noble families used a very varied stock of names in the early medieval period. It was rare in Britain to find any one name being widely used. The name Arthur however crops up in four families in the 6th and 7th centuries. It has been suggested (Bromwich 1978) that this can only be due to the desire to commemorate a historical figure. Three of the four were born most likely around 575 or shortly thereafter.

Artur son of Aedan of Dal Riata (ruled 573-608) in what is now Argyll in Scotland (*Life of St Columba*). This Artur was killed in battle in 596.

Artur son of Conan (Aedan's son) of Dal Riata (genealogy in the *Senchus Fer nAlban*). This may be a misplacement of the Artur above.

Arthur son of Petr of Dyfed (*Harleian genealogies*). Petr was a grandson of the Vortipor mentioned by Gildas. Arthur would have been born c.570x600.

Artuir son of Bicoir the Briton, possibly of Strathclyde (*Annals of Tigernach*). Arthur is recorded as having killed King Mongan of Ulster in 625.

The main stumbling block in the way of accepting Arthur's actual existence as a historical figure has been his absence from the one documentary source that could have mentioned him, the *De excidio Britanniae* of Gildas. Arthur figures in the *Life of Gildas* written by Caradoc c.1130-50. Arthur's role in the life is as the killer of Gildas's brother Hueil, allowing Gildas to show his worth by forgiving Arthur and behaving as a true Christian towards his family's enemy. Caradoc probably knew Geoffrey of Monmouth since Geoffrey mentions him with respect. He also wrote a life of St Cadoc, in which Arthur also figures. Perhaps the most interesting reference to Gildas and Arthur is by Gerald of Wales (Giraldus Cambrensis). Gerald either records Welsh or Breton traditions, or elaborates the writings of Caradoc, to explain away the lack of mention of Arthur by Gildas.

Gerald of Wales

Gerald (c.1146-c.1223) was Archdeacon of Brecon and a failed claimant to the see of St. David's. Although largely of Norman origin he identified strongly with Wales and his maternal ancestry. It is in the second edition, finished in 1215, of his *Description of Wales* that his account of Gildas and Arthur appears. This extract is taken from the edition of Dimock (1868), with the translation of Thorpe (1978).

> De Gilda vero, qui adeo in gentem suam acriter invehitur, dicunt Britones, quod propter fratrem suum Albaniae principem, quem rex Arthurus occiderat, offensus haec scripsit. Unde et libros egregrios, quos de gestis Arthuri, et gentis suae laudibus, multos scripserat, audita fratris sui nece, omnes, ut asserunt, in mare projecit. Cuius rei causa, nihil de tanto principe in scriptis authenticis expressum invenies.

> The Britons maintain that Gildas criticised his own people so bitterly, he wrote as he did, because he was so infuriated by the fact that King Arthur had killed his own brother, who was a Scottish chieftain. When he heard the news of his brother's death, or so the Britons say, he threw into the sea a number of outstanding books which he had written in their praise and about Arthur's achievements. As a result you will find no book which gives an authentic account of that great prince.

There are various incidental references to Arthur in early literature, before the synthesis produced by Geoffrey of Monmouth. These may reflect traditions about a historical Arthur but most cannot really be trusted as historical sources. Only the most significant references are given below.

Y Gododdin

This is a poem about the Battle of Catterick between the Britons and the Angles, fought c.600. This survives in a manuscript of c.1250, which is thought to be a copy of an original manuscript written some time between 800 and 1100. The poem might have been handed down orally from a time close to the battle it describes. The reference to Arthur is only indirect. He is alluded to in a verse about a warrior named Gwawrddur (Jarman 1990) and seems to have been chosen to fit the rhyming structure of the poem.

> *Ef gwant tra thrichant echasaf,*
> *ef lladdai a perfedd ac eithaf,*
> *oedd gwiw ym mlaen llu llariaf,*
> *goddolai o haid meirch y gaeaf.*
> *Gochorai brain du ar fur caer*
> *cyn ni bai ef Arthur.*
> *Rhwng cyfnerthi yng nghlysur,*
> *yng nghynnor, gwernor Gwawrddur.*

He charged before 300 of the finest,
he cut down both centre and wing,
he excelled in the forefront of the noblest host,
he gave gifts of horses from the herd in winter.
He fed black ravens on the fortress rampart
though he was no Arthur.
Among the powerful ones in battle,
in the front rank, a palisade was Gwawrddur.

Gereint fab Erbin

This is a poem from the 13th century Black Book of Carmarthen (*Llyfr Du Caerfyrddin*). It may well have been a copy of a poem composed at the latest in the 10th century (and possibly much earlier) about the death of Gereint in an attack on Llongborth. Some would say it refers to King Gereint of Dumnonia, defeated by the West Saxons in 710. If so, the reference to Arthur would be a literary conceit reflecting Arthur's reputation in the 8th century. Others would say that Llongborth was Portchester and the attack took place c.500, and so reflects a genuine connection of Gereint with the historical Arthur. If this is true then it is perhaps significant that Arthur is referred to as Emperor, a term that would be anachronistic for any time later than the 6th century. The verse below is taken from Roberts (1978), with a translation amended from Morris (1975).

> *En llogporth y gueleise Arthur,*   In Llongborth I saw Arthur,
> *guir deur kymynint a dur,*   heroes who cut with steel,
> *ameraudur, llywiaudir llawur.*   The Emperor, ruler of our labour.

Y Trioedd Ynys Prydein *(The Triads of the Island of Britain)*

The Triads contain much early Welsh literary, mythical and historical material. The earliest manuscript belongs to the 13th century and may well be a copy of a 12th century manuscript. Bromwich (1978) has suggested that this in turn was based on material in oral circulation since the 9th century. There are 13 of the triads that mention Arthur but provide no evidence for any historical events he might have been associated with. Eight of these are later additions to the original triads, leaving five which may belong to the 9th century. These incorporate Arthur into mythical, literary narratives. Only three of them provide simple references to Arthur and these only provide the most general of allusions (Bromwich 1978).

2
Tri Hael Enys prydein
Nud Hael mab Senyllt,
Mordaf Hael mab Seruan,
Ryderch Hael mab Tudwal Tutclyt.
Ac Arthur ehun oedd haelach no'r tri.

Three Generous Men
Nudd the generous son of Senyllt,
Mordaf the generous son of Serwan,
Rhydderch the generous son of Tudwal Tudglyd.
But Arthur was himself more generous than the three.

12
Tri Overveird Enys Prydein
Arthur,
a Chatwallavn mab Catuan,
a Rahaut eil Morgant.

Three Frivolous Bards
Arthur,
and Cadwallon son of Cadfan,
and Rahawd son of Morgan.

20
Tri Ruduoavc Enys Prydein
Arthur,
a Run mab Beli,
a Morgant Mwynfawr.

Three Red Ravagers
Arthur,
and Rhun son of Beli,
and Morgan the wealthy.

Timeline: 406-634

The dating of events for most of the 5th and 6th centuries is fraught with difficulties. Faced with these, it is all to easy to give in to the counsel of despair uttered by Kemble in 1849 (Sims-Williams 1983: 41): "From what has preceded it will be inferred that I look upon the details of the German conquests in England as irrevocably lost to us". I regard this as unduly negative. We should make the attempt to construct a narrative of events for this period, albeit with a an open eye to the limits of probability. Few dates are provided by the rare early sources for the period and we rely on the reconstructions of later centuries. Most of the dates provided are unreliable in different degrees and careful detective work is needed to establish even an approximate chronology. Henry of Huntingdon in the 12th century, and Roger of Wendover in the 13th century, presented narratives of events tied to dates for the 5th and 6th centuries which are not found in surviving earlier sources. We have no means of judging whether their dates represent historical reality. This is also the case with many of the dates for events of this period written down in the Anglo-Saxon Chronicle in the late 9th century. It may be that intervals between events are more accurate than the dates themselves, and the intervals have been used to derive some of the dates below. Archaeology would tend to support an early 5th century arrival of Anglo-Saxons in England. This would agree with a starting point of 428, as in the *Historia Brittonum*, rather than the traditional starting date of 449 (taken from the Anglo-Saxon Chronicle and thence from Bede). I agree with the argument that Bede wrongly followed a mistake in Gildas to produce this 449 date. Accordingly, I use the 428 datum below for the calculation of many dates in the 5th century, with the proviso that its accuracy as the precise year of the first arrival of Germanic mercenaries is assumed rather than proven. Until 597 (the beginning of verifiable dates from Christian sources), and even for a while thereafter, the dates given below should be treated with extreme caution. The degree of difference in interpretation of the chronology and events of this period can be illustrated by difference between my scheme outlined below and that of Higham (1994) who would have Gildas writing in c.480 and the Saxon conquest of Britain taking place in the 440s with a Saxon overlord as tyrant of eastern Britain. Different authors will thus inevitably produce different schemes of dates and events, and I hesitantly offer my own scheme for comment and disapproval, conscious of the fact that I fly in the face of the words of Barbara Yorke (1993) when referring to early chronicles and genealogies - "but they should not be used, as they frequently have been, to construct a precisely dated narrative account of the foundation of kingdoms in the fifth and sixth centuries".

The nomenclature for dating events in this period is different to what we are used to today. There was no single internationally accepted calendar that followed a common era. Various forms of dating were used (Harrison 1976, Cheney 1981), which would lead to misunderstanding when copying information from one document using one system to another by a writer using a different system. It is no wonder that the same event can be referred to under different, often widely spaced, dates in different authorities. A common form of dating under the Roman Empire was by referring to the pair of consuls at Rome, changed every year. In this system, a year began on 1st January and years were counted from an era beginning with the founding of Rome, A.U.C. or *ab urbe condita* (equivalent to 753 BC). Dates could also be referred to the appropriate regnal year of the Emperor, a system officially laid down by Justinian in 537. Outside Rome, the regnal years of kings would be the appropriate framework. The Roman tax year, or Indiction, was also used for general dating. The indictions were a cycle of 15 years, beginning 1st September 312. This was made a compulsory part of official dating formulae by Justinian, also in 537. It was adopted by the Papacy from 584, and remained popular until the 8th century in England. The 6th century saw the widespread adoption of new Easter tables by the Christian church. The tables created by Victorius of Aquitaine in 457 were adopted in Gaul in 541. These were based on a era dating from the crucifixion, AP (*annus passionis*), equivalent to 28 AD, and contained lists of consuls to help correlate with conventional dating methods. New Easter tables were produced by Dionysius Exiguus beginning in 532 and based on an era dating from the birth of Christ, AD (*annus domini*). The Dionysian tables were adopted in 630 by the Papacy, and brought to Britain in the 660s. Although the tables began the year on 1st January, the more popular Christian beginning of the year was 25th December at this time. The use of AD dating based on Dionysius was made more popular by Bede, beginning with his *De Temporum Ratione* in 725. AD dating rapidly replaced indictional dates during the 8th century. Dionysius's tables were grouped into 19 year cycles. An event entered in the wrong group of tables would thus be dislocated by 19 years. The 5th and 6th centuries were thus a time of many changes in the reckoning of time. It is no wonder that the chronology of the period is so confused.

Roger of Wendover in the 13th century added some details to the narratives of the period which may come from sources now lost. Among these is a narrative of Vortigern, Ambrosius and Artorius (Arthur). This is largely derived from Geoffrey of Monmouth, and so likely to be a work of fiction. However, we have no way of checking independently how much Geoffrey embellished the truth and how much he incorporated oral traditions current in Wales or Brittany. His narrative certainly offers a convincing picture of events, seductively so. I prefer to believe that at least some of the picture presented (perhaps only a very small part) may have had a basis in reality, but we now have no way of knowing how much, or which events might have actually occurred. This 'legendary' information from Roger is given in italics. I leave the reader to judge and follow the sources for him or herself, and although events are treated here as historical they should be treated with the utmost suspicion. Dates as recorded in the Anglo-Saxon Chronicle (ASC) are given in brackets where relevant.

406   The usurpation of Marcus and then Gratianus in Britain.

407   Major Germanic invasions of Gaul led to Gratianus being replaced by a low ranking soldier, Constantinus III, who led an attempt to resist the Germanic invasions of Gaul, control Spain and become Emperor. Constantinus may have been a representative of a militant Christian faction opposed to the dominant pagan elite in Britain.

409/10   Under the impact of Saxon raids (409), Britain rebelled against the usurpation of Constantinus III but it proved impossible for Rome to send troops to Britain and the diocese was effectively granted independence, being told to look after its own defence by Emperor Honorius (410). This may have involved political dispute and strife, with vengeance being taken against opponents. Bishop Fastidius refers to magistrates being judged and executed by opponents at this time.

414?   A famine was recorded in Gaul in this year. Could it also have stuck Britain at the same time?

426?   The diocese was subjected to attack by Scots (then in Ireland) and Picts (from northern Britain).

428   It was decided to hire Germanic soldiers to help defend the diocese against the above attacks. The soldiers were led by Hengest with largely Jutish followers. 'Nennius' placed this in 428, while Bede placed it (probably incorrectly) between 449 and 455. It may be that other troops were hired in other parts of Britain. The tradition that Soemil the supposed ancestor of Ælle of Deira first separated Deira from Bernicia might be a garbled memory of troops being hired to guard York in the 420s/30s.

429   The first mission of Germanus (Bishop of Auxerre) and Lupus (Bishop of Troyes) against Pelagian heresy in the British church, in which Germanus became involved in military action against Saxon and Pictish raiders. *Hengest repelled a Pictish raid on the north and was given lands in Lindsey.*

430?   Hengest brought his son Octa to Britain with more mercenaries to defend the north from the Picts, married his daughter to Vortigern and received all of Kent in return. Was this to hold the Channel coast in opposition to possible Roman re-invasion after the consolidation of Imperial power in Gaul under Aetius?

431-32   A Christian mission by Palladius to Ireland may have been part of the British attempt to neutralise the Irish threat as a parallel strategy to the employment of Germanic soldiers. Palladius failed, but was followed in 432 by Patricius (Patrick) with greater success. (Some would place Patrick's mission a generation later in the 450s or 460s)

433?   The treaty between the Britons and Hengest broke down resulting in war. Vortigern's son Vortimer pushed Hengest back to Thanet after three battles - one by the Darenth, one at Episford and the third by the sea. The Anglo-Saxon Chronicle provided dates for battles in the war:

455 at Aylesford, 456 at Crayford, 465 at Wippedesfleot and at an unnamed site in 473. Using the same intervals these would be 434, 435, 444 and 452 if based on 428 instead of 449.

434   A Saxon attack took place on Ireland. Could this have been on behalf of the British by Saxons still loyal to Vortigern?

435   *The Germanic mercenaries under Hengest were expelled and returned to Germany.*

435/45 The second visit of Bishop Germanus of Auxerre and Severus, Bishop of Trier, to combat Pelagian heresy in the British church. Ellis 1993 places this visit in 446 as a diplomatic consequence of the British appeal to Aetius, see below. The tradition of enmity between Germanus and Vortigern might reflect opposition by Vortigern to the attempts to rely on an alliance with Imperial Gaul by the pro-Roman faction.

437   The Battle of Wallop between Vitalinus and Ambrosius. Ambrosius was traditionally portrayed as an opponent of Vortigern and this battle might well have been part of an internal British power struggle which resulted in his exile. *Roger of Wendover wrote that Ambrosius was later living in Brittany.*

439   The Irish annals record a second group of bishops being sent to Ireland to reinforce the work of Patrick.

440   *Hengest returned to Britain, engineering the murder of British leaders.*

441?   A Gaulish Chronicle noted that Britain had passed under Saxon control in 441, the meaning of which is uncertain, but must refer to some historical event. *Roger of Wendover noted that Vortigern was forced to cede lands in the eastern side of Britain to Hengest two years after the death of Vortimer (439), which would be in 441.* This could be the event recorded in the Gaulish Chronicle. 'Nennius' simply recorded that after the death of Vortimer, Hengest arranged the capture of Vortigern who was forced to cede Essex and Sussex.

444?   Leadership of the fight against the Saxons was assumed by Àmbrosius, the political opponent of Vortigern. *Roger of Wendover would place this event five years after the death of Vortimer. Roger wrote that Ambrosius succeeded in defeating and killing Vortigern the next year and then fought Hengest, Ælle (in Sussex) and Pascent, the son of Vortigern, before dying after a reign of 32 years (in 476).*

446   An unsuccessful appeal for military help was made to the Imperial Magister Militum Flavius Aetius in Gaul. This may represent the more pro-Roman policies of Ambrosius as opposed to the anti-Roman stance of Vortigern.

Apart from Hengest, the other major leader of the early phase of Anglo-Saxon settlement was Ælle of Sussex. Very little is known of him other than what is recorded in Anglo-Saxon Chronicle. Bede referred to him as the first of the Anglo-Saxon overlords, or Bretwaldas, and his importance must have been greater than we can now assess. If the later Kings of Kent were descended from Oisc, and he was only attached to Hengest by later genealogists, it may be that Ælle succeeded Hengest directly in command of Germanic settlers in the south east. He would then have authority over Kent as well as new settlers in Sussex. Oisc's position as King of Kent would then have occurred towards the end of Ælle's reign as a concession in old age, or revolt.

456?	Ælle and his sons arrived in Britain, attacking the Britons at Selsey Bill. The Anglo-Saxon Chronicle's date for Ælle's arrival was 477, 11 years before the death of Hengest. (Ælle's arrival may not have been an isolated event. The Gallic writer Sidonius described Saxon raids on Armorica, Brittany, c.455.)
464?	Ælle fought the Britons at *Mearcrædesburna* (ASC 485).
467?	'Nennius' has Hengest succeeded by his son - coming down from the north. *Roger of Wendover amplifies this by having Hengest executed after a major defeat by Ambrosius.* According to the Anglo-Saxon Chronicle it was Æsc (or Oisc) who succeeded Hengest in 488 (which would equal 467 if based on 428). Ælle succeeded Hengest as the leader of the Germanic settlers, *while Octa submitted to Ambrosius the following year.*
468	The Briton Riothamus (most likely from Britain but possibly from Brittany) led an army against the Goths under Euric on behalf of Emperor Anthemius (467-72). This may signify that a migration of Britons to Gaul had already begun, displaced by conditions in Britain (a British Bishop Mansuetus appeared at the Council of Tours in 461 who could have been based in Brittany).
470?	Ælle and Cissa took Pevensey from the Britons (ASC 491).
471	A Saxon raid on Ireland is recorded in the Annals of Innisfallen.
475?	*An attempt by Vortigern's son Pascent to invade was defeated by Ambrosius.*
476?	*On the death of Ambrosius the leadership of the Britons reputedly passed to his brother Uther, who defeated and killed Pascent, and inflicted a major defeat on Octa in the following year.*
488-91?	*A further war with Octa resulted in the defeat and death of Octa at Verulamium.*
493?	Roger of Wendover placed Ælle's death 37 years after his arrival (514 according to Roger).
495?	*Arthur succeeded his father Uther and led the fight against the English, but they brought over more men including kings from the continent.*

499? Arthur won a decisive victory over the Saxons at Badon Hill (*Bath according to Roger of Wendover who placed the battle just 4 years after Arthur's succession*). The event was dated by the Welsh Annals to 516, but most modern authors would place Badon in the 490s. Early sources do not name the leaders of the Germanic forces at Badon. *Geoffrey of Monmouth identifies them as Colgrin and his brother Baldulf. It is curious that Geoffrey's version of events has Colgrin reinforced by troops under one Cheldric, a Frankish name which would fit with a Frankish interest in Britain in the 6th century.*

500-02? *Arthur defeated Scots and Picts threatening Alclwyd (Strathclyde).*

511/21 A large number of Britons under Riwalos emigrated from Britain and settled in Brittany (could these be military active Britons displaced by the peace following Badon?). A British bishop was based in Spain, in Asturias, by 527. A British community continued to be recorded in the area until the later 7th century. These should represent another migration out of Britain during the 5th or early 6th century. *A curiosity of Geoffrey of Monmouth's narrative is that he has Arthur invading Gaul around 515/519; derived from a confused version of these events?*

520-21? The Welsh Annals record the death of Arthur and Medraut at the Battle of Camlann in 537. *An attempt by Medraut, Arthur's nephew, to seize power was ended by the Battle of Camlann where Medraut was killed. Roger of Wendover placed the Battle in 541, 25 years after Arthur's accession, and wrote that Arthur was wounded at the battle, and lived until the following year.*

With the death of Arthur, we have the last possible time of a post-Roman Britain-wide native political authority. The possibilities for Germanic settlement and political action must have been affected by this. The major new arrival of the early 6th century seems to have been the family of Cerdic. The dates given in the Anglo-Saxon Chronicle for this dynasty are now regarded as highly suspect and confused, and an alternative chronology has been worked out by David Dumville (DD), although I use my own preferred timescale below also based on reign lengths in the Anglo-Saxon Chronicle. The family of Cerdic may well have British origins. The tradition of their migration to Britain may be a fiction created later to align their origins with more undoubtedly Germanic royal houses. Twelfth century chroniclers noted the arrival of other Germanic settlers in the east of Britain in 527. The arrival of fresh settlers in the 520s would fit with the collapse of centralised British authority after the death of Arthur. Such an interpretation though would not be the case if the chronicle date of the event in 527 was a mistake for 515 as has been suggested by Davies (Scull 1992). The same chroniclers noted the origins of Essex also in 527, but the first King, Eorcenwine, is noted as dying in 587 after an unlikely reign of 60 years, which suggests that the beginning his reign has been misdated.

523?   Cerdic and Cynric arrived in Britain, attacking the Britons at *Cerdicesora* (ASC 494, DD 532). These may be local British leaders bidding for power in the vacuum left by Arthur's death.

527?   Germanic settlers arrived under various chieftains in East Anglia and Mercia. These were presumably invited in by local British rulers; perhaps a reversal of Arthurian policy.

529?   Cerdic and Cynric obtained the Kingdom of the West Saxons (*Gewisse*) (DD 538, ASC 500 or 519) and fought the Britons at *Cerdicesford*.

537?   Cerdic and Cynric won a major victory against the British king Natanleod (ASC 508). This might well be the same as the Battle of *Cerdicesleag* (ASC 527).

540?   Cerdic and Cynric took the Isle of Wight (ASC 530).

545?   Cynric succeeded Cerdic and reigned 26 years (DD 554, ASC 534). The Isle of Wight was given to Stuf and Wihtgar (Wihtgar died ASC 544).

It has been suggested that the 540s were a time of crisis. A major plague, comparable to the Black Death, was recorded by the Byzantine historian Procopius and had ravaged Europe and the Mediterranean. This began in Egypt in 541, reached Gaul by 543 and recurred over the next two decades. The Irish Annals of Innisfallen recorded a first plague, *mortalitas prima*, in 544 and a great plague, *mortalitas magna*, in 551, while the Annals of Ulster placed plagues in 545, 549 and 556 (Morris 1995, vol. 2). The Welsh Annals placed the death of Maelgwn of Gwynedd in 547 during an outbreak of plague. Morris thought that the plague had affected the Britons but not the Anglo-Saxons, allowing the latter to begin an advance against the Britons. More recently, the period 536-546 has been identified by Prof. Mike Baillie from tree ring evidence as a time of particularly harsh climatic conditions, brought about by meteorite or cometary impact (Baillie 2001). Crop failures and social and political dislocation might be an expected result of this. The Annals of Innisfallen placed a famine at 537, while the Annals of Ulster had famines at 536 and 539. There can be little doubt about the plague or the climatic downturn revealed in the tree rings. What is uncertain is what effect either of these might have had on the politics of the time. To be an important factor in relations between Britons and Anglo-Saxons, one would have to be less badly affected than the other by such calamities. Esmonde Cleary (1993) has doubted that plague was a factor in the period, and has also pointed out that historically documented plagues often cause reinforcement of the system under siege rather than its collapse. Plague and famine would have reduced the levels of population. The Germanic settlers might have had the advantage of being able to draw upon a reservoir of kin networks across the North Sea to replenish their numbers at a greater rate than the Britons. Whether this can account for the conquest of south-eastern Britain by the Anglo-Saxon royal families is a moot point since this seems to have taken place a generation later than the calamitous events of the 530s and 540s.

There is some evidence for Anglo-Saxon contacts outside Britain at around this time.

531   Saxons under Heaðugeat (Hadugat) returned to the continent to fight for Theuderic I of the Franks against the Thuringians in return for land.

548/53   Angles were included in a Frankish embassy to Constantinople.

550s   The Angles in Britain are recorded by the Byzantine historian Procopius as having engaged in a war with the continental Varni after a marriage alliance between them had been broken off, in favour of a Frankish alliance instead.

We begin to be on surer footing historically in the generation before the Augustinian mission to Kent. The chronology of the period has to be reconstructed from the later sources, with major amendments being needed to later writers' dating of events. The dating of events in Ceawlin's reign is particularly confused. The reconstruction offered below is merely my own interpretation of the dating evidence and should be treated with due caution. If right, it seems that there was a major expansion in Anglo-Saxon control of Britain around 570, seeing the founding of most of the later kingdoms, and the conquest of major areas from the native Britons. This is the same historical horizon that can be seen in most of the royal genealogies for the various Anglo-Saxon kingdoms. The events listed below are taken from the *Anglo-Saxon Chronicle* or the *Historia Brittonum* unless otherwise stated.

563?   Cynric began the expansion of Wessex, defeating the Britons at Salisbury (ASC 552).

567?   Cynric and Ceawlin fought the Britons at Barbury (ASC 556).

569   Ælle became Anglian King of Deira (ASC 560), based on the mid Yorkshire Wolds (RW). Soemil, 6 generations earlier, was the first to set up Deira as a separate area according to 'Nennius'.

?   Eorcenwine founded the Kingdom of Essex and died 587 (RW).

571   Wuffa founded the Kingdom of the East Angles (RW), although his father Wehha was first to rule according to 'Nennius'. Archaeology would place the centre of the kingdom in south east Suffolk.

571?   Ceawlin succeeded to Wessex (DD 581, ASC 560).

575?   Ida was the first king of Bernicia (see Appendix 3), reigning 12 years from Bamburgh. Outigern fought against the English in his time (ASC 547).

579?   Ceawlin and Cuða defeated Æþelberht of Kent (ASC 568).

580   Britons Gwrgi and Peredur of York died in battle (WA), after which York may have become part of Anglian Deira.

580?   Æþelberht, son of Eormenric of Kent, was married to the Frankish Princess Berhta, daughter of the late King Charibert of Paris.

582?   Cuþwulf defeated the Britons at *Bedcanford*, taking Limbury, Aylesbury, Benson and Eynsham (ASC 571). Sims-Williams (1983) would deny entries like this reflected 6th century reality rather being based on 9th century politics; a minimalist view which I find too rejectionist.

584   Ceawlin and Cuða fought the Britons at *Feþanleag*, Cuða being killed.

585   The Kingdom of Mercia was founded by Crioda (RW), based on the mid Trent and Soar valleys according to archaeology.

587?   Ida's successors were resisted by Urien, Rhydderch, Gwallaug and Morcant. Urien blockaded them in Lindisfarne but was killed at the instigation of Morcant. Þeodric (588-95?) fought vigorously against Urien and his sons. The Christian mission to Kent happened in the time of Friðuwald (595-601?). Sledda became King of the Essex, perhaps the first, or more likely succeeding Eorcenwine.

588?   Cuþwine and Ceawlin defeated the Britons at Dyrham and took Gloucester, Cirencester and Bath.

588?   Ceol (or Ceolric) became king of Wessex (DD 588, ASC 591) in opposition to Ceawlin, reigning 5 or 6 years.

589?   Ceawlin was expelled after a battle at Adam's Grave (ASC 592).

592   Æþelfrið began to reign in Bernicia. He united all of Northumbria under himself between 601 and 604, eliminating rival cousins in Bernicia and annexing Deira.

594   King Æþelberht of Kent (began to reign in 594 according to the Welsh Annals).

594?   Ceolwulf became king of Wessex (DD 594, ASC 597).

595?   A British force from Gododdin was defeated at the Battle of Catraeth (Catterick) sometime between the death of Urien and the Battle of *Degsastan*.

597   Arrival of a Papal mission in Kent under Augustine, linked with Pope Gregory and the Frankish Kings Þeudebert II (595-612) and Þeuderic II (595-613). This led later to the adoption of Christianity in Kent and Essex.

601-03   Bernicia was united by Æþelfrið (592-616). He defeated a Scottish army supporting a rival at the Battle of Degsastan (603).

602/04   A meeting between Augustine and British bishops failed to achieve British Christian submission to Canterbury.

604   Æþelfrið annexed Deira to create Northumbria.

613   Æþelfrið defeated a Welsh army at Chester (WA).

614   West Saxon expansion westwards into Devon was marked by the Battle of Bindon.

614   Bishop Justus of Rochester attended a synod organised by King Chlothar II (584-629) of the Franks at Paris.

616   Æþelfrið of Northumbria was killed by Rædwald of East Anglia at the Battle of the Idle. He was succeeded by Eadwine, who immediately annexed British Elmet (death of Ceredic 616 and Eadwine's accession 617 - WA).

616   The death of Æþelberht of Kent allowed a heathen reaction under his son King Eadbald.

621/24   Conversion of King Eadbald of Kent to Christianity.

624   Marriage alliance between Eadwine of Northumbria and Eadbald of Kent, leading to the adoption of Christianity in Northumbria in 627.

631   East Anglia became Christian under King Sigeberht, who had been in exile in Gaul.

633   Eadwine of Northumbria was killed at the Battle of Hatfield by an alliance between Cadwallon of Gwynedd and Penda of Mercia. His widow Æþelburg sent her children to Dagobert I (623-639) of the Franks for protection.

633-34   Cadwallon attempted to reverse the Anglian conquest of Northumbria, killing Eadwine's successors in Bernicia and Deira, Eanfrið and Osric, but was killed at the Battle of Heavenfield by Oswald (634-42) of Bernicia.

Continental events

The settlement of Britain was played out against the backdrop of events in Gaul, the growth of the Frankish state on the continent, and Roman Imperial ambitions. Indeed, the Frankish kings may have had a greater influence on events in Britain than the surviving sources reveal. A selection of key continental events is given below.

406   Invasion of Gaul across the Rhine by a coalition of Vandals, Alans and Suevi on 31 December, later followed by Alemanni and Burgundians.

407   The British usurper Constantinus III invaded Gaul and established his authority, then also took over Spain (408). His general Gerontius rebelled against him and besieged him in Arles. Both were defeated by an Imperial army under Constantius (411).

408   The Goths under Alaric besieged Rome and later Ravenna, but failed to get Imperial recognition and sacked Rome (410).

411   Constantinus III was captured and executed by Imperial forces.

412   Athaulf led the Goths into Gaul but was forced to retreat to Spain by 415. The Goths then subdued Spain for the Empire and received foederate status in Aquitaine (418).

413   The Burgundians were settled as foederates at Worms.

418   The Gallic diocesan council was reconvened at Arles, signifying that Roman rule had been stabilised over southern Gaul, and the Visigoths were settled as foederates on Roman soil at Toulouse.

422   Revolt of Vandals in Spain and Goths in Gaul, followed by a disputed succession on the death of Honorius (423), resulted in an Eastern Imperial victory in support of Valentinianus and the appointment of Aetius to Gaul (425).

427-30 Aetius restored Imperial rule over much of Gaul by subduing the Goths.

429-35 The Vandals conquered most of Africa.

433   Aetius became the real ruler of the west under Valentinianus.

435-36 Aetius defeated the Burgundians in Gaul, settling the remnant as foederati in Savoy (443).

437-39 Aetius contained the Goths and Bagaudae in Gaul, but the Suevi conquered most of Spain 438-48, and the Vandals conquered the remains of Roman Africa 439-42, being recognised as independent of the Empire.

451   Aetius defeated an invasion of Gaul by Attila and the Huns and various Germanic allies.

454   Aetius was murdered in a palace coup. Valentinianus III was then assassinated in favour of Maximus (455) who was killed during the sack of Rome by the Vandals, leaving the Magister Militum Ricimer as the real power in Rome.

461   The assassination of Emperor Majorian by Ricimer. Aegidius in Gaul refused to recognise Ricimer's appointment of Severus as his successor, and maintained an independent Roman state in northern Gaul. Aegidius died in 464, being succeeded by his son Syagrius.

463   Saxons under Odovacer were established at Angers, being dislodged only in 469.

c.470   The Franks were established as foederati in Belgica Secunda under Chilperic.

c.475   The Roman Emperors in Constantinople established diplomatic relations with native rulers in Britain.

481   Chlodovech King of the Franks, established the Franks as a major power by annexing the northern Gaulish kingdom of Syagrius 486, conquering the Alemanni 496-506, converting to Christianity 496, defeating the Goths and annexing Aquitaine 507. Chlodovech died in 511.

531   The Thuringians were annexed by Theuderic I (511-34), who also subjugated the Saxons around the same time.

532-34   Childebert and Chlothar I conquered Burgundy.

537   Provence was granted to the Franks by the Goths.

555/6   A Saxon revolt against Chlothar I was successful at first, but Frankish power was reasserted by 561.

558-61   The Franks were reunited under Chlothar I.

561   The Franks were divided into three parts on the death of Chlothar I: Austrasia, Neustria and Burgundy.

561/75   Chilperic I and Sigibert I campaigned against the Saxons. (Saxons raided Beauvais in 560 and Nantes in 571).

568   The Lombard invasion of Italy shattered Imperial ambitions in western Europe, and diplomatic links with native British rulers may have ended at around this time.

573-75   Major civil war between the kings of the Franks.

584   The death of Chilperic I left Neustria weakened under his son Chlothar II, facing a Burgundian/Austrasian alliance. There were Saxon raids on the Loire 584-90.

592   Austrasia and Burgundy were united under Childebert II.

600   Major defeat of Chlothar II by Theudebert and Theuderic (sons of Childebert II).

613   The Franks were reunited under Chlothar II - the peak of Merovingian power and influence under him and Dagobert I (629-39).

614   Chlothar II issued a constitution for the Franks dividing the kingdom permanently into Austrasia, Neustria and Burgundy, each with its own officials, and laying down that local counts were to be from the local aristocracy rather than royal officials.

623/29   An unsuccessful Saxon revolt against Dagobert I.

639   The death of Dagobert was followed by a defeat at the hands of the Thuringians, resulting in a major decline in Frankish power. The dominant political role passed to the palace mayors rather than the kings, e.g. the mayors of Neustria Erchinoald c.640-659, Ebroin 659-80.

Sources for the Period

The immediate post-Roman period is sometimes still referred to as 'the Dark Ages', a term that deserves to be relegated to the dustbin of scholarship. Sources for the period do exist, both historical and archaeological. They are admittedly fragmentary, sometimes contradictory and often of dubious factual content. Nevertheless, they exist and must be the starting point for all studies of the period. They can, when used together yield useful information; compared and contrasted with each other, with care taken about their context. Documentary sources for the period are scattered, partial and extremely variable in their purpose and reliability. On the other hand, archaeological remains are plentiful but capable of multiple interpretations. A growing trend in both history and archaeology has been to adopt a post-modernist attitude of self-criticism, ruthlessly analysing the database and inevitably finding it wanting. As noted by Yorke (1993), some archaeologists have been inclined to treat the period as essentially prehistoric. Some historians have been loath to accept documentary sources as in any sense reliable. However, the period is not prehistoric and to treat it only on the basis of the archaeological evidence would be wrong. Likewise, to use only documentary sources and ignore the wealth of archaeological material and approaches would likewise give an inadequate account of the period. To be selective is to run the risk of only using the sources that will bolster a particular argument or line of reasoning. While Dark (2000) may be willing to accept *Gildas*, the *Canu Taliesin* and *Y Gododdin*, but reject the *Anglo-Saxon Chronicle*, the *Historia Brittonum, Welsh Annals* and genealogies, others would compile a different list of what to accept and what to reject. For instance, Matthews (2001) has noted of Gildas's *De excidio Britanniae* that "there is virtually nothing in his work that can be shown to be historically accurate ...". Yorke (1993) felt that even Bede's knowledge of 5th and 6th century events was scant and not based on any reliable oral tradition. On the other hand, she accepted that the documentary evidence contains accounts of genuine events and persons. While we may accept that there is a chronological horizon for the accuracy of human memory in later written sources, this should not lead us to completely dismiss the partial and distorted evidence of myths and legends; it simply requires us to take greater care about their use.

Listed here are some key published references for the major historical and archaeological sources of information about the period. Excluded are works in other languages, e.g. German, and unpublished research, e.g. Ph.D. theses.

Documentary sources

Primary 5th and 6th century sources

Primary sources are few but varied, and can be confusing. A good starting point for an overview of the documentary sources is Morris 1995. They are listed here in chronological order.

Fastidius, Bishop, *Liber de vita Christiana* (c.411)

Evans, R F 1962 "Pelagius: Fastidus and the Pseudo-Augustinian De Vita Christiana", *Journal of Theological Studies* n.s. 13: 72-98

Muldowney, M S & M F McDonald (eds.) 1952 *The Fathers of the Church: treatises on various subjects.*

St. Patrick, *Confession and Letters* (mid 5th century)

Hood, A B E 1978 *St. Patrick: His Writings and Muirchu's "Life"*

anon., *Gallic Chronicles* (452 & 511)

Burgess, R W 1990 "The Dark Ages return to fifth-century Britain: the "restored" Gallic Chronicle exploded, *Britannia* 21: 185-95

Jones, M E & J Casey, 1991 "The Gallic Chronicle exploded?", *Britannia* 22: 212-15

Jones, M E & J Casey, 1988 "The Gallic Chronicle restored: a chronology for the Anglo-Saxon invasions and the end of Roman Britain, *Britannia* 19: 367-98

Muhlberger, S 1983 "The Gallic Chronicle of 452 and its authority for British events", *Britannia* 14: 23-33

Constantius of Lyon, *Life of St Germanus* (c.485)

Hoare, F R 1954 "Constantius, of Lyons, Life of St Germanus, Bishop of Auxerre", in *The Western Fathers*: 284-320

Thompson, E A 1984 *Saint Germanus of Auxerre and the end of Roman Britain* (Studies in Celtic History, 6)

Zosimus, *New History* (c.500)

Buchanan, J J (transcr. H T Davis) 1987 *Zosimus: Historia Nova*

Thompson, E A 1956 "Zosimus on the end of Roman Britain", *Antiquity* 30: 163-7

Gildas, *De Excidio et Conquestu Britanniae* (c.540, earliest MS 10th century)

Lapidge, M & D N Dumville, (eds.) 1984 *Gildas: new approaches*

Thompson, E A 1979 "Gildas and the History of Britain" *Britannia* 10: 203-26

Thompson, E A 1980 "Gildas and the History of Britain: corrigenda", *Britannia* 11: 344

Winterbottom, M 1978 *Gildas: The Ruin of Britain and other documents* (Arthurian Period Sources 7)

Procopius of Caesaria, *History of the Wars* (552)

Burn, A R 1955 "Procopius and the island of ghosts" *English Historical Review* 70: 258-61

Taliesin, *Canu Taliesin* (composed orally late 6th century, written down by the 10th century, earliest MS c.1275)

Williams Sir I (Trans. J E C Williams) 1968 *The Poems of Taliesin*

Pope Gregory, various letters (590-604)

Ewald, P & L M Hartmann, 1891-99 *Gregorii I Papae Registrum epistolarum*

Whitelock, D (ed.) 1955 English Historical Documents c.500-1042

Æþelberht, King of Kent, *Law code* (written 597 x 604/09, one MS 1122/24)

Attenborough, F L 1922 *The Laws of the Earliest English Kings*

Aneirin, *Y Gododdin* (composed orally c.600, written copies by the 9th century)

Jackson, K H 1969 *The Gododdin: the oldest Scottish poem*

Jarman, A O H 1990 *Aneirin: Y Gododdin: Britain's oldest heroic poem*

anon., *Tribal Hidage* (625/26?, earliest MS c.1025)

Davies, W & H Vierck, 1974 "The contexts of Tribal Hidage: social aggregates and settlement patterns", *Frühmittelalterliche Studien* 8: 223-93

Dumville, D N 1989 "The Tribal Hidage : an introduction to its texts and their history", in S Bassett (ed.) *The Origins of Anglo-Saxon Kingdoms*: 225-30, 286-7

Hart, C 1971 "The tribal hidage" *Transactions of the Royal Historical Society* 5th series, 21: 133-57

Rumble, A R 1996 "The Tribal Hidage: an annotated bibliography", in D Hill & A R Rumble (eds.) *The Defence of Wessex: the Burghal Hidage and Anglo-Saxon fortifications*: 182-88

Later sources

anon., *Life of Pope Gregory* (704 x 714)

Colgrave, B (ed.) 1968 *The Earliest Life of Gregory the Great by an anonymous monk of Whitby*

Bede (monk of Jarrow), *Historia Ecclesiastica Gentis Anglorum* (731)

Colgrave, B & R A B Mynors, 1969 *Bede's Ecclesiastical History of the English People*

Wallace-Hadrill, J M 1988 *Bede's Ecclesiastical History of the English People: a historical commentary*

anon., Anglo-Saxon genealogies (compiled c.770 onwards)

Dumville, D N 1976 "The Anglian collection of royal genealogies and regnal lists", *Anglo-Saxon England* 5: 23-50

anon. (trad. ascribed to Nennius), *Historia Brittonum* (c.829/30, earliest MS late 12th century)

Dumville, D N 1975 "Nennius and the Historia Brittonum", *Studia Celtica* 10: 78-95

Dumville, D N (ed.) 1985 *The Historia Brittonum 3: the 'Vatican' recension*

Jackson, K 1964 "On the northern British section in Nennius", in N K Chadwick (ed.) *Celt and Saxon: studies in the early British border*, 20-62

Morris, J 1980 *Nennius: British History and the Welsh Annals* (Arthurian Period Sources 8)

anon., *Anglo-Saxon Chronicle* (compiled 891, earliest copy c.900)

Bately, J 1986 *The Anglo-Saxon Chronicle, Volume 3: MS A*

Taylor, S 1983 *The Anglo-Saxon Chronicle, Volume 4: MS B*

Conner, P W 1996 *The Anglo-Saxon Chronicle 10: The Abingdon Chronicle (MS C)*

Cubbin, G P 1996 *The Anglo-Saxon Chronicle 6: MS D*

Irvine, S 2004 *The Anglo-Saxon Chronicle 7: MS E*

Baker, P 2000 *The Anglo-Saxon Chronicle 8*: MS F

anon., *Trioedd Ynys Prydein* (composed orally, written down c.900, completed c.1120, earliest MS 1250/75)

Bromwich, R 1991 *Trioedd Ynys Prydein: the Welsh triads*

anon., *Annales Cambriae* (c.970)

Ingram, J 1912 *The Annales Cambriae*

Morris, J 1980 *Nennius: British History and the Welsh Annals* (Arthurian Period Sources 8)

anon., Welsh genealogies (compiled c.975, earliest MS copy c.1100)

anon. 1963 *Bulletin of the Board of Celtic Studies* 20: 171-2

Bartrum, P C 1966 *Early Welsh Genealogical Tracts*

Bartrum, P C 1974 *Welsh Genealogies, A.D. 300-1400*

Miller, M 1975 "Historicity and the pedigrees of the Northcountrymen", *Bulletin of the Board of Celtic Studies* 26: 255-80

Geoffrey of Monmouth (Bishop of St Asaph's), *Historia Regum Britanniae* (1136)

Griscom, A 1929 *Geoffrey of Monmouth's Historia Regum Britanniae*

Thorpe, L 1966 *Geoffrey of Monmouth: The History of the Kings of Britain*

Wright, N (ed.) 1985 *The Historia regum Britannie of Geoffrey of Monmouth I: Bern, Burgerbibliothek, Ms 568*

Wright, N (ed.) 1985 *The Historia regum Britannie of Geoffrey of Monmouth II: The first variant version: a critical edition*

Crick, J C (ed.) 1989 *The Historia regum Britannie of Geoffrey of Monmouth III: A summary catalogue of the manuscripts*

Crick, J C (ed.) 1991 *The Historia regum Britannie of Geoffrey of Monmouth IV: Dissemination and reception in the later middle ages*

Wright, N (ed.) 1991 *The Historia regum Britannie of Geoffrey of Monmouth V: Gesta regum Britannie*

Henry (Archdeacon of Huntingdon), *Historia Anglorum* (written 1129-54)

Greenway, D 1996 *Henry, Archdeacon of Huntingdon: Historia Anglorum*

Roger of Wendover (monk of St Albans), *Flores Historiarum* (1231-34)

Coxe, H O 1841 *Rogeri de Wendover chronica, sive flores historiarum, Vol. 1: AD 447-1066*

Giles, J A 1849 *Roger of Wendover's Flowers of History, A.D. 447-1235*

Archaeological sources
This is only a selection of the abundant archaeological remains of the period.

Urban sites
Canterbury, Kent

Bennett, P 1989 "Canterbury", in V A Maxfield (ed.) *The Saxon Shore: a handbook*: 118-129

Brooks, D A 1988 "The case for continuity in fifth-century Canterbury re-examined", *Oxford Journal of Archaeology* 7: 99-114

Cirencester, Gloucestershire

Reece, R M & C Catling, 1975 *Cirencester: the development and buildings of a Cotswold town*

Wacher, J S 1976 "Late Roman developments", in A McWhirr (ed.) *Studies in the Archaeology and History of Cirencester*: 15-18

London, Middlesex

Marsden, P 1980 *Roman London*

Morris, J 1982 *Londinium: London in the Roman Empire*

Milne, G 1995 *The Port of Roman London*

Perring, D 1991 *Roman London*

St Albans, Hertfordshire

Branigan, K 1985 *The Catuvellauni*

Frere, S 1972-84 *Verulamium Excavations*

Silchester, Hampshire

Boon, G C 1974 *Silchester: the Roman town of Calleva*

Fulford, M G 1989 *The Silchester Amphitheatre: excavations of 1979-85*

Wroxeter, Shropshire

Barker, P 1997 *The Baths Basilica Wroxeter: excavations, 1960-90*

White, R H 2000 "Wroxeter and the transformation of late-Roman urbanism", in T R Slater (ed.) *Towns in Decline, AD 100-1600*: 96-119

White, R H & P Barker, 1998 *Wroxeter: life and death of a Roman city*

Rural settlements

Barton Court Farm, Oxfordshire

Miles, D 1986 *Archaeology at Barton Court Farm*, Council for British Archaeology Research Report 50

Bishopstone, Sussex

Thomas, G 2003 *Exploring the Origins and Development of an Anglo-Saxon Minster Settlement*

Cassington, Oxfordshire

Arthur, B V & E M Jope, 1962 "Early Saxon pottery kilns at Purwell Farm, Cassington, Oxfordshire", *Medieval Archaeology* 6: 1-14

Chalton, Hampshire

Addyman, P V, D Leigh, and M J Hughes, 1972 "Anglo-Saxon houses at Chalton, Hampshire", *Medieval Archaeology* 16: 13-31

Addyman, P V & D Leigh, 1973 "The Anglo-Saxon village at Chalton, Hampshire: second interim report", *Medieval Archaeology* 17: 1-25

Champion, T 1977 "Chalton", *Current Archaeology* 59: 364-9

Cowdery's Down, Hampshire

Millett, M & S James, 1983 "Excavations at Cowdery's Down, Basingstoke", *Archaeological Journal* 140: 151-279

Eynsham, Oxfordshire

Gray, M 1974 "The Saxon settlement at New Wintles, Eynsham, Oxfordshire", in T Rowley, (ed.) *Anglo-Saxon Settlement and the Landscape*, British Archaeological Reports 6: 78-86

Maxey, Northamptonshire

Addyman, P V 1964 "A Dark Age settlement at Maxey, Northants", *Medieval Archaeology* 8: 20-73

Mucking, Essex

Dixon, P 1993 *The Anglo-Saxon Settlement at Mucking: an interpretation*

Green, C J J 1988 *Excavations at Poundbury, Dorchester, Dorset 1966-1982, vol. 1: the settlements*

Hamerow, H 1988 *Mucking: the Anglo-Saxon Settlement*

Hamerow, H 1993 *Excavations at Mucking, Volume 2: The Anglo-Saxon Settlement*

Poundbury, Dorset

Jones, M U & W T Jones, 1975 "The crop mark sites at Mucking, Essex, England", in R Bruce-Mitford (ed.) *Recent Archaeological Excavations in Europe*: 133-187

Sutton Courtenay, Berkshire

Leeds, E T 1923 "A Saxon village near Sutton Courtenay, Berkshire", *Archaeologia* 72:147-92

Leeds, E T 1927 "A Saxon village near Sutton Courtenay, Berkshire", *Archaeologia* 76:59-79

Leeds, E T 1947 "A Saxon village near Sutton Courtenay, Berkshire", *Archaeologia* 92:79-93

Radford, C A R 1957 "The Saxon house: a review and some parallels", *Medieval Archaeology* 1: 27-38

West Heslerton, Yorkshire

Powlesland, D 1998 "The West Heslerton assessment", *Internet Archaeology* 5

West Stow, Suffolk

West, S 1985 *West Stow, the Anglo-Saxon Village*, East Anglian Archaeology Report 24

Wykeham, Yorkshire

Moore, J W 1966 "An Anglo-Saxon settlement at Wykeham, North Yorkshire", *Yorkshire Archaeological Journal* 41: 403-444

Military/royal sites

Aberffraw, Gwynedd

Edwards, N 1988 "Aberffraw", in N Edwards & A Lane (eds.) *Early Medieval Settlements in Wales, a.d. 400-1100*

White, R B 1979 "Excavations at Aberffraw, Anglesey, 1973 and 1974", *Bulletin of the Board of Celtic Studies* 28: 319-42

Dinas Powys

Alcock, L 1987 *Economy, Society and Warfare among the Britons and Saxons*

Dumbarton

Alcock, L 1987 *Economy, Society and Warfare among the Britons and Saxons*

Dunadd, Argyll

Christison, D & J Anderson, 1905 "Report on the Society's excavations of forts on the Poltalloch Estate, Argyll, in 1904-5", *Proceedings of the Society of Antiquaries of Scotland* 39: 259-322

Craw, J H 1930 "Excavations at Dunadd and at other sites on the Poltalloch Estates, Argyll", *Proceedings of the Society of Antiquaries of Scotland* 64: 111-146

Lane, A & E Campbell, 2000 *Dunadd: an early Dalriadic capital*

Hadrian's Wall, Cumbria and Northumberland

Breeze, D J & B Dobson, 1987 *Hadrian's Wall*

Portchester, Hampshire

Cunliffe, B 1976 *Excavations at Portchester Castle, vol. 2, Saxon*

South Cadbury, Somerset

Alcock, L 1972 *By South Cadbury that is Camelot*

Alcock, L 1972 "Excavations at Cadbury-Camelot, 1966-70", *Antiquity* 46: 29-38

Alcock, L 1982 "Cadbury-Camelot: a fifteen year perspective", *Proceedings of the British Academy* 68: 355-88

Tintagel, Cornwall

Dark, K R 1985 "The plan and interpretation of Tintagel", *Cambridge Medieval Celtic Studies* 9: 1-17

Radford, C A R 1939 *Tintagel Castle*

Thomas, C 1993 *Tintagel: Arthur and archaeology*

Yeavering, Northumberland

Hope-Taylor, B 1977 *Yeavering: an Anglo-British centre of early Northumbria*

Scull, C 1991 "Post Roman phase I at Yeavering: a reconsideration", *Medieval Archaeology* 35: 51-63

Churches and religious sites

Bath, Somerset

Cunliffe, B & P Davenport, 1985 *The Temple of Sulis Minerva at Bath, vol. 1: the site*

Canterbury St Martin, Kent

Micklethwaite, J T 1898 "Some further notes on Saxon churches", *Archaeological Journal* 55: 341-43

Routledge, C F 1897 "St Martin's church, Canterbury", *Archaeologia Cantiana* 22: 1-28

Taylor, H M & J 1965 *Anglo-Saxon Architecture, vol. I*: 143-145

Uley

Ellison, A 1980 *Excavations at West Hill Uley, 1977-1979: a native, Roman, and Christian ritual complex of the first millennium a.d.: second interim report*

Whithorn

Hill, P 1997 *Whithorn & St. Ninian: the excavation of a monastic town 1984-91*

Cemeteries

A general survey of cemeteries excavated up to 1964 is available in A Meaney 1964 *A Gazeteer of Early Anglo-Saxon Burials*. Only major cemeteries are listed below.

Bishopstone, Sussex

Thomas, G 2003 *Exploring the Origins and Development of an Anglo-Saxon Minster Settlement*

Caistor, Norfolk

Myres, J N L & B Green, 1973 *The Anglo-Saxon Cemeteries of Caistor-by-Norwich and Markshall, Norfolk*

Cambridge Girton

Hollingworth, E J & M M O'Reilly, 1925 *The Anglo-Saxon Cemetery at Girton College, Cambridge: a report based on the MS. notes of the excavations made by the late F.J.H. Jenkinson*

Cambridge St Johns

anon. 1888 *Cambridge Antiquarian Society Reports* 48: 111

anon. 1912 *Cambridge Antiquarian Society Communications* 16: 122-132

Cannington, Somerset

Rahtz, P, S Hirst, and S Wright, 2000 *Cannington Cemetery: excavations 1962-3 of prehistoric, Roman, post-Roman and later features at Cannington Park Quarry, near Bridgwater, Somerset*

Chessell Down, Isle of Wight

Arnold, C J 1982 *The Anglo-Saxon Cemeteries of the Isle of Wight*

Dover, Kent

Evison, V 1987 *Dover: the Buckland Anglo-Saxon Cemetery*

Finglesham, Kent

Chadwick, S E 1958 "The Anglo-Saxon cemetery at Finglesham, Kent: a reconsideration", *Medieval Archaeology* 2:1-71

Illington, Norfolk

Davison, A, B Green & W Milligan, 1993 *Illington: a study of a Breckland Parish and its Anglo-Saxon Cemetery*

Lackford, Suffolk

Lethbridge, T C 1951 *A Cemetery at Lackford, Suffolk*

Little Wilbraham, Cambridgeshire

Neville, R C 1852 *Saxon Obsequies Illustrated by Ornaments and Weapons Discovered by the Hon. R.C. Neville in a Cemetery near Little Wilbraham, Cambridgeshire During the Autumn of 1851*

Loveden Hill, Lincolnshire

Foster, C W 1926-27 "Excavation of an Anglian burial mound on Loveden Hill [Hough on the Hill, Lincs.]", *Reports of the Associated Architectural Societies* 38, 313-320

Markshall, Norfolk

Myres, J N L & B Green, 1973 *The Anglo-Saxon Cemeteries of Caistor-by-Norwich and Markshall, Norfolk*

Mucking, Essex

Hamerow, H 1993 *Excavations at Mucking, Volume 2: the Anglo-Saxon settlement*

Newark, Nottinghamshire

Kinsley, A G 1989 *The Anglo-Saxon Cemetery at Millgate, Newark-on-Trent, Nottinghamshire*

Norton on Tees, Durham

Sherlock, S J & M G Welch, 1992 *An Anglo-Saxon Cemetery at Norton, Cleveland*

Sancton, Yorkshire

Myres, J N L & W H Southern, 1973 *The Anglo-Saxon Cremation Cemetery at Sancton, East Yorkshire*

Reynolds, N 1979 *Investigations in the Anglo-Saxon Cemetery at Sancton, East Yorkshire, 1976-8*

South Elkington, Lincolnshire

Webster, G 1951 "An Anglo-Saxon urnfield at South Elkington, Louth, Lincolnshire", *Archaeological Journal* 108: 25–64

Spong Hill, Norfolk

Hills, C et al. 1977-95 *The Anglo-Saxon Cemetery at Spong Hill, North Elmham*, 8 vols

Sutton Hoo, Suffolk

Bruce-Mitford, R et al. 1975-83 *The Sutton Hoo Ship Burial*, 3 vols

Carver, M 1993 *Sutton Hoo: Research Committee Bulletins, 1983-1993*

Carver, M 1998 *Sutton Hoo: Burial Ground of Kings?*

Longworth, I H & I A Kinnes, 1980 *Sutton Hoo Excavations, 1966, 1968-70*

Wasperton, Warwickshire

Wise, P J 1991 "Wasperton", *Current Archaeology* 126: 256-9

West Heslerton, Yorkshire

Haughton, C & D Powlesland, 1999 *West Heslerton: the Anglian cemetery*

Runic inscriptions

General

Bammesberger, A (ed.) 1991 *Old English Runes and their Continental Background*

Elliott, R W V 1989 *Runes: an introduction*

Hines, J 1990 "The Runic Inscriptions of Early Anglo-Saxon England", in A Bammesberger, (ed.) 1990 *Britain 400-600: Language and History*: 437- 456

Looijenga, T 1997 *Runes around the North Sea and on the Continent AD 150-700* (available on the Internet at http://www.ub.rug.nl/eldoc/dis/arts/j.h.looijenga/)

Page, R I 1999 *An Introduction to English Runes*

Particular inscriptions

Caistor bone, Norfolk

Page, R I 1973 "The Runic inscription from N59", in J N L Myers & B Green *The Anglo-Saxon Cemeteries of Caistor-by-Norwich and Markshall, Norfolk*: 114-117

Chessel Down sword, Isle of Wight

Hawkes, S C & R I Page, 1967 "Swords and runes in south-east England", *Antiquaries Journal* 47: 11-18

Dover brooch, Kent

Evison, V I 1964 "The Dover rune brooch", *Antiquaries Journal* 44: 242-245

Gilton Pommel, Kent

Evison, V I 1967 "The Dover ring-sword and other sword-rings and beads", *Archaeologia* 101: 97-102

Harford Farm brooch, Norfolk

Hines, J 1991 "A new runic find from Norfolk", *Nytt om Runer* 6: 6-7

Loveden Hill urn, Lincolnshire

Elliott, R W V 1989 *Runes: an introduction*: 50-52

Sandwich Stone, Kent

Parsons, D 1994 "Sandwich: the oldest Scandinavian rune-stone in England?", in B Amrosiani & H Clarke (eds.) *Developments around the Baltic and the North Sea in the Viking Age*: 310-320

Sleaford brooch, Lincolnshire

Hines, J 1990 "The runic inscriptions of early Anglo-Saxon England", in Bammesberger, A (ed.) 1990 *Britain 400-600: Language and History*: 450

Watchfield fitting, Oxfordshire

Scull, C 1986 "A sixth-century grave containing a balance and weights from Watchfield, Oxfordshire, England", *Germania* 64: 105-138

Welbeck Hill bracteate, Lincolnshire

Hines, J 1990 "The runic inscriptions of early Anglo-Saxon England", in A Bammesberger, (ed.) 1990 *Britain 400-600: Language and History*: 445

West Heslerton brooch, Yorkshire

Haughton, C & D Powlesland, 1999 *West Heslerton: the Anglian Cemetery, vol. 2: catalogue of the Anglian graves and associated assemblages: 310–11*

Latin and Ogham inscriptions

Allen, J R & J Anderson, (eds.) 1903 *Early Christian Monuments of Scotland*

Dark, K R 1992 *The Inscribed Stones of Dyfed*

Nash-Williams, V E 1950 *The Early Christian Monuments of Wales*

Okasha, E 1993 *Corpus of Early Christian Inscribed Stones of Southwest Britain*

Pettigrew, T J 1954 "Ogham inscriptions", *British Archaeological Association* 17: 293-310

Radford, C A R 1975 *The Early Christian Inscriptions of Dumnonia*

Thomas, C 1993 *The Early Christian Inscriptions of Southern Scotland*

Thomas, C 1994 *And Shall These Mute Stones Speak? Post-Roman inscriptions in western Britain*

Artefact types

Long brooches

A useful overview of all brooch types can be found in Lucy (2000).

cruciform

Åberg, N 1926 The Anglo-Saxons in England

Leeds, E T & M Pocock, 1971 "A survey of Anglo-Saxon cruciform brooches of the florid type", *Medieval Archaeology* 15: 13-36

small-long

Leeds, E T 1945 "The distribution of the Angles and Saxons archaeologically considered", *Archaeologia* 91: 1-106

square-headed

Hines, J 1997 *A New Corpus of Early Anglo-Saxon Great Square-Headed Brooches*

Leeds, E T 1949 *A Corpus of Early Anglo-Saxon Great Square-Headed Brooches*

Kentish square-headed

Åberg, N 1926 *The Anglo-Saxons in England*

Leigh, D 1990 "Aspects of early brooch design and production", in E Southworth (ed.) *Anglo-Saxon Cemeteries: a reappraisal*

Round brooches

annular

Leeds, E T 1945 "The distribution of the Angles and Saxons archaeologically considered", *Archaeologia* 91: 1-106

disc

Dickinson, T 1979 "On the origin and chronology of the early Anglo-Saxon disc brooch", *Anglo-Saxon Studies in Archaeology and History* 1: 39-80

Leeds, E T 1945 "The distribution of the Angles and Saxons archaeologically considered", *Archaeologia* 91: 1-106

Kentish disc

Avent, R 1975 *Anglo-Saxon Garnet Inlaid Disc and Composite Brooches*

penannular

Fowler, E 1960 "The origins and development of the penannular brooch in Europe", *Proceedings of the Prehistoric Society* 26: 149-177

Fowler, E 1963 "Celtic metalwork of the fifth and sixth centuries A.D.", *Archaeological Journal* 120: 98-159

quoit brooches

Ager, B M 1985 "The smaller variants of the Anglo-Saxon quoit brooch", *Anglo-Saxon Studies in Archaeology and History* 4: 1-58

Leeds, E T 1945 "The distribution of the Angles and Saxons archaeologically considered", *Archaeologia* 91: 1-106

Suzuki, S 2000 *The Quoit Brooch Style and Anglo-Saxon Settlement*

saucer

Dickinson, T 1993 "Early Saxon saucer brooches: a preliminary overview", *Anglo-Saxon Studies in Archaeology and History* 6: 11-44

Evison, V I 1978 "Early Anglo-Saxon applied disc brooches, part 1: on the continent", *Antiquaries Journal* 58: 88-102

Evison, V I 1978 "Early Anglo-Saxon applied disc brooches. Part II: in England", *Antiquaries Journal* 58: 260-278

Other brooches

bird

Lucy, S 2000 *The Anglo-Saxon Way of Death*

button

Avent, R & V I Evison, 1982 "Anglo-Saxon button brooches", *Archaeologia* 107: 77-125

equal arm

Hines, J 1984 *The Scandinavian Character of England in the pre-Viking Age*

radiate

Åberg, N 1926 *The Anglo-Saxons in England*

supporting arm

Lucy, S 2000 *The Anglo-Saxon Way of Death*

swastika

Leeds, E T 1945 "The distribution of the Angles and Saxons archaeologically considered", *Archaeologia* 91: 1-106

tutulus

Lucy, S 2000 *The Anglo-Saxon Way of Death*

Pottery

Myers, J N L 1969 *Anglo-Saxon Pottery and the Settlement of England*

Myers, J N L 1977 *A Corpus of Pagan Anglo-Saxon Pottery*

Thomas, C (ed.) 1981 *A Provisional List of Imported Pottery in Post-Roman Western Britain and Ireland*

Weapons
knives

Evison, V I 1961 "The Saxon objects", in J Hurst "The kitchen area of Northolt Manor, Middlesex", *Medieval Archaeology* 5: 226-230

Evison, V I 1987 *Dover: the Buckland Anglo-Saxon cemetery*

shield bosses

Evison, V I 1963 "Sugar-loaf shield-bosses", *Antiquaries Journal* 48:231-246

Dickinson, T & H Härke, 1992 *Early Anglo-Saxon Shields*

spearheads

Swanton, M J 1973 *The Spearheads of the Anglo-Saxon Settlements*

Swanton, M J 1974 *A Corpus of Pagan Anglo-Saxon Spear Types*

swords

Bone, P 1989 "The development of Anglo-Saxon swords from the fifth to the eleventh century", in S C Hawkes (ed.) *Weapons and Warfare in Anglo-Saxon England*

Davidson, H R E 1962 *The Sword in Anglo-Saxon England*

Other
belt fittings

Hawkes, S C & G C Dunning, 1961 "Soldiers and settlers in Britain, fourth to fifth century: with a catalogue of animal-ornamented buckles and related belt-fittings", *Medieval Archaeology* 5: 1-70

bracteates

Gaimster, M 1992 "Scandinavian gold bracteates in England. Money and media in the Dark Ages", *Medieval Archaeology* 36: 1-28

buckles

Evison, V I 1968 "Quoit brooch style buckles", *Antiquaries Journal* 48: 231-246

Lucy, S 2000 *The Anglo-Saxon Way of Death*

glass vessels

Harden, D B 1972 "Ancient glass, III: post-Roman", *Archaeological Journal* 128: 78-117

hanging bowls

Brenan, J 1991 *Hanging Bowls and their Contexts: an archaeological survey of their socio-economic significance from the fifth to seventh centuries A.D.*

pendants

Geake, H 1997 *The Use of Grave-Goods in Conversion-Period England*

sleeve claps

Hines, J 1993 *Clasps, Hektespenner, Agraffen. Anglo-Scandinavian Clasps of Classes A-C of the 3rd to 6th Centuries A.D. Typology, Diffusion and Function.*

Maps

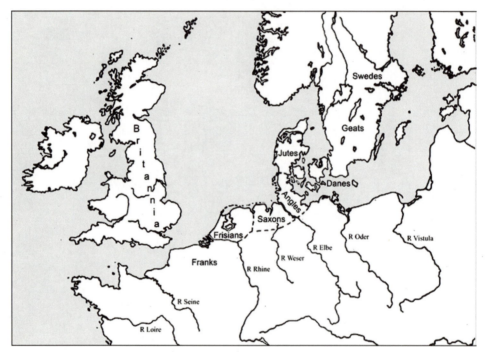

1. Europe

Læsø

Jylland

J
U
T
E
S

Fyn

Sjælland

DANES

Møn

Nord
Friesische
Inseln

Angeln

Lolland

Falster

ANGLES

Fehmarn

R. Eider

Ost Friesische Inseln

Wadden
Eilanden

R. Elbe

FRISIANS

SAXONS

R. Ems

R. Weser

R. Aller

FRANKS

2. Homelands

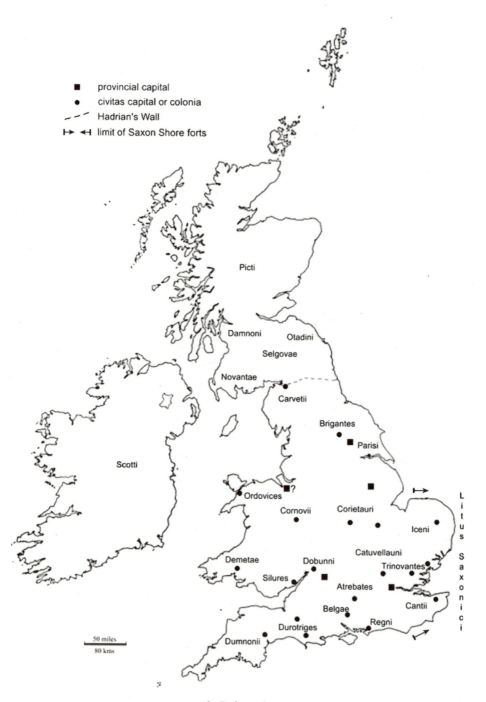

Legend

- ■ provincial capital
- ● civitas capital or colonia
- – · – Hadrian's Wall
- ↦ ⊣ limit of Saxon Shore forts

Picti

Damnoni   Otadini

Selgovae

Novantae

Carvetii

Brigantes

■ Parisi

Scotti

Ordovices   ■?

Cornovii   Corietauri

Iceni

Catuvellauni

Demetae   Dobunni

Trinovantes

Silures   ■

Atrebates

Cantii

Belgae

Regni

Durotriges

Dumnonii

Litus Saxonici

50 miles
80 kms

3. Britannia

British or Irish Kingdom

Germanic Ruled Kingdom

● 5th century Germanic cemetery

Picts

Gododdin

Dal
Riata

Alclwyd

Rheged

B
e
r
n
i
c
i
a

Deira

Ulaid

Elmet

Connachta

Mide

Gwynedd

Mercia

East
Anglia

Laigin

Powys

Mumu

Dyfed

Essex

Gewisse

Kent

Sussex

50 miles
80 kms

Devon

4. Kingdoms

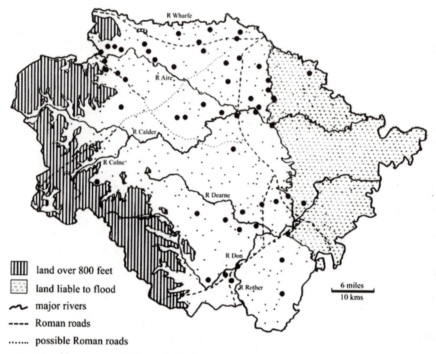

land over 800 feet
land liable to flood
major rivers
Roman roads
possible Roman roads
township names containing early Anglian elements

R Wharfe
R Aire
R Calder
R Colne
R Dearne
R Don
R Rother

6 miles
10 kms

5. Elmet

References

Abels, R P 1988 *Lordship and Military Obligation in Anglo-Saxon England*

Åberg, N 1926 *The Anglo-Saxons in England*

Ackroyd, P 2004 *Albion: origins of the English imagination*

Ager, B M 1985 "The smaller variants of the Anglo-Saxon quoit brooch", in *Anglo-Saxon Studies in Archaeology and History* 4: 1-58

Alcock, L 1971 *Arthur's Britain: history and archaeology AD 367-634*

Alcock, L 1981 "Quantity or quality: the Anglian graves of Bernicia", in V I Evison (ed.) *Angles, Saxons and Jutes: essays presented to J N L Myres*: 168-183

Alcock, L 1992 "Message from the dark side of the moon: western and northern Britain in the age of Sutton Hoo", in M O H Carver (ed.) *The Age of Sutton Hoo: the seventh century in north-western Europe*: 205-216

Allott, S 1974 *Alcuin of York*

Altet, X B i 1997 *Taschen's World Architecture: the Early Middle Ages, from late antiquity to A.D. 1000*

Amory, P 1997 *People and Community in Ostrogothic Italy*

Anthony, D 1997 "Prehistoric migration as social process", in J Chapman & H Hamerow (eds.) *Migrations and Invasions in Archaeological Explanation*: 21-32

Ardener, E 1989 "The construction of history: 'vestiges of creation'", in E Tonkin, M McDonald & M Chapman (eds.) *History and Ethnicity*: 22-33

Arnold, C J 1982 *The Anglo-Saxon Cemeteries of the Isle of Wight*

Arnold, C J 1984 *Roman Britain to Saxon England*

Arnold, C J 1988 "Territories and leadership: the frameworks for the study of emergent polities in early Anglo-Saxon southern England", in S T Driscoll & M R Nieke (eds.) 1988 *Power and Politics in Early Medieval Britain and Ireland*: 111-127

Arnold, C J 1997 *An Archaeology of the Early Anglo-Saxon Kingdoms*

Attenborough, F L 1922 *The Laws of the Earliest English Kings*

Auden, W H & P B Taylor, 1981 *Norse Poems*

Ausenda, G 1995 "The segmentary lineage in contemporary anthropology and among the Langobards", in G Ausenda (ed.) *After Empire: towards and ethnology of Europe's barbarians*: 15-50

Ausenda, G 1997 "Current issues and future directions in the study of the early Anglo-Saxon period", in J Hines (ed.) *The Anglo-Saxons from the Migration Period to the Eighth Century*: 411-450

Bailey, K 1989 "The Middle Saxons", in S Bassett (ed.) *The Origins of the Anglo-Saxon Kingdoms*: 108-122

Baillie, M 2001 "The AD 540 event", *Current Archaeology* 174: 266-269

Balandier, G 1986 "An anthropology of violence and war", *International Social Sciences Journal* 38(4): 499-511

Baldwin Brown, G 1903-15 *The Arts in Early England I-IV: Saxon art and industry in the pagan period*

Balkwill, C 1993 "Old English *wic* and the origin of the hundred", *Landscape History* 15: 5-12

Bammesberger, A (ed.) 1991 *Old English Runes and their Continental Background*

Bammesberger, A & A Wollmann (eds.) 1990 *Britain 400-600: language and history*

Barlow, F 1966 "The effects of the Norman Conquest" (reprinted in *The Norman Conquest and Beyond* 1983)

Barnes, J 1999 *England, England*

Barnwell, P S 1992 *Emperor, Prefects and Kings: the Roman West, 395-565*

Barnwell, P 1996 "*Hlafæta, ceorl, hid* and *scir*: Celtic, Roman or Germanic?", *Anglo-Saxon Studies in Archaeology and History* 9: 53-62

Barry, M 1964 "Traditional enumeration in the North Country", *Folk Life* 7: 75-91

Barth, F 1996 "Ethnic groups and boundaries", in J Hutchinson & A D Smith (eds.) *Ethnicity*: 75-83

Bartlett, R 1996 "Language and ethnicity in medieval Europe", in J Hutchinson & A D Smith (eds.) *Ethnicity*: 127-134

Bassett, S (ed.) 1989 *The Origins of Anglo-Saxon Kingdoms*

Bately, J 1986 *The Anglo-Saxon Chronicle, Volume 3: Ms A*

Battles, P 2000 "*Genesis A* and the Anglo-Saxon migration myth", *Anglo-Saxon England* 29: 43-66

Baucom, I 1999 *Out of Place: Englishness, empire and the locations of identity*

Biddle, M 1976 "Towns", in D M Wilson (ed.) *The Archaeology of Anglo-Saxon England*: 99-150

Branston, B 1957 *The Lost Gods of England*

Bremmer, R H 1990 "The nature of the evidence for a Frisian participation in the *Adventus Saxonum*", in A Bammesberger & A Wollmann (eds.), *Britain 400-600: language and history*: 353-371

Brøgger, A W & H Shetelig 1951 *The Viking Ships: their ancestry and evolution*

Bromwich, R 1978 *Trioedd Ynys Prydein*

Brooks, N 1971 "The development of military obligations in eigth- and ninth-century England", in P Clemoes & K Hughes (eds.) *England before the Conquest*: 69-84

Brooks, N 1989 "The creation and early structure of the kingdom of Kent", in S Bassett (ed.) *The Origins of the Anglo-Saxon Kingdoms*: 55-74

Brooks, N 1989 "The formation of the Mercian kingdom", in S Bassett (ed.) *The Origins of the Anglo-Saxon Kingdoms*: 159-170

Budd, P, A Millard, C Chenery, S Lucy & C Roberts 2004 "Investigating population movement by stable isotope analysis: a report from Britain", *Antiquity* 78: 127-141

Calhoun, C (ed.) 1994 *Social Theory and the Politics of Identity*

Cameron, K 1977 *English Place-Names*

Campbell, A 1977 *Old English Grammar*

Campbell, J 1971 "The first century of Christianity in England", in J Campbell (1986) *Essays on Anglo-Saxon History*: 49-67

Campbell, J, E John & P Wormald (eds.) 1982 *The Anglo-Saxons*

Capelli, C, N Redhead, J K Abernethy, F Gratrix, J F Wilson, T Moen, T Hervig, M Richards, M P H Stumpf, P A Underhill, P Bradshaw, A Shaha, M G Thomas, N Bradman & D B Goldstein 2003 "A Y chromosome census of the British Isles", *Current Biology* 13: 979-984

Carver, M O H 1989 "Kingship and material culture in early Anglo-Saxon East Anglia", in S Basset (ed.) *The Origins of Anglo-Saxon Kingdoms*: 141-158

Carver, M O H (ed.) 1992 *The Age of Sutton Hoo: the seventh century in north-western Europe*

Carver, M O H 1998 *Sutton Hoo: burial ground of kings?*

Case, H 1977 "The Beaker culture in Britain and Ireland", in R Mercer (ed.) *Beakers in Britain and Europe,* British Archaeologist Reports International Series 26: 71-101

Chadwick, H M 1905 *Studies on Anglo-Saxon Institutions*

Chadwick, H M 1907 *The Origin of the English Nation*

Chadwick, H M 1912 *The Heroic Age*

Chadwick, N 1970 *The Celts*

Chapman, J & H Hamerow (eds.) 1997 *Migrations and Invasions in Archaeological Explanation*, British Archaeological Reports International Series 664

Charles-Edwards, T (ed.) 2003 *After Rome,* Short Oxford History of the British Isles

References

Cheney, C R (ed.) 1981 *Handbook of Dates for Students of English History,* Royal Historical Society Handbook 4

Chibnall, M 1999 *The Debate on the Norman Conquest*

Chrysos, E 1997 "Conclusions: de foederati iterum", in W Pohl (ed.) *Kingdoms of the Empire*: 185-206

Clarke, D L 1970 *Beaker Pottery of Great Britain and Ireland*

Coates, R, A Breeze & D Horovitz 2000 *Celtic Voices, English Places*

Colgrave, B (ed.) 1927 *The Life of Bishop Wilfrid by Eddius Stephanus*

Colgrave, B (ed.) 1940 *Two Lives of Saint Cuthbert*

Colgrave, B (ed.) 1956 *Felix's Life of Saint Guthlac*

Colgrave, B (ed.) 1968 *The Earliest Life of Gregory the Great by an anonymous monk of Whitby*

Colgrave, B & R A B Mynors (eds.) 1969 *Bede's Ecclesiastical History of the English People*

Collingwood, R G & J N L Myres 1936 *Roman Britain and the English Settlements*

Collis, J R 1994 "Celtic fantasy", *British Archaeological News*, March 1994

Colls, R 2002 *Identity of England*

Connor, W 1996 "Beyond reason: the nature of the ethnonational bond", in J Hutchinson & A D Smith (eds.) *Ethnicity*: 69-75

Cramp, R 1988 "Northumbria: the archaeological evidence", in S T Driscoll & M R Nieke (eds.) *Power and Politics in Early Medieval Britain and Ireland*: 69-78

Dark, K R 1994 *Civitas to Kingdom: British political continuity 300-800*

Dark, K R 2000 *Britain and the End of the Roman Empire*

Davidson, H E 1993 *The Lost Beliefs of Northern Europe*

Davidson, H E & P Fisher (eds.) 1979 & 1980 *Saxon Grammaticus: The History of the Danes Books I-IX*

Davies, P 1998 *This England*

Davies, R R 1994 "The peoples of Britain and Ireland 1100-1400, 1. identities", *Transactions of the Royal Historical Society* 6th series, 4

Davies, W 1977 "Annals and the origin of Mercia", in A Dornier *Mercian Studies*: 17-29

Davies, W 1982 *Wales in the Early Middle Ages*

De Camp, D 1958 "The genesis of Old English: a new hypothesis", *Language* 34: 232-244

Derolez, R 1990 "Runic literacy among the Anglo-Saxons", in A Bammesberger & A Wollmann (eds.), *Britain 400-600: language and history*: 397-436

Dillon, M & N Chadwick 1967 *The Celtic Realms*

Dimock, J F 1868 *Giraldi Cambrensis Opera*, Rolls Series 21, vol. 6

Dixon, P H 1982 "How Saxon is the Saxon house?", in P J Drury (ed.) *Structural Reconstruction*, British Archaeological Reports 110: 275-287

Dixon, P H 1993 "The Anglo-Saxon settlement at Mucking: an interpretation", *Anglo-Saxon Studies in Archaeology and History* 6: 125-147

Dornier, A (ed.) 1977 *Mercian Studies*

Driscoll, S T & M R Nieke 1988 *Power and Politics in Early Medieval Britain and Ireland*

Drogin, M 1980 *Medieval calligraphy: its history and technique*

Duffy, M 2001 *England: the making of the myth from Stonehenge to Albert Square*

Dumville, D N 1976 "The Anglian collection of royal genealogies and regnal lists", *Anglo-Saxon England* 5: 23-50

Dumville, D N 1977 "Sub-Roman Britain: history and legend", *History* 62: 173-192

Dumville, D N 1979 "Kingship, genealogies and regnal lists", in P H Sawyer & I N Wood *Early Medieval Kingship*: 72-104

Dumville, D N 1985 "The West Saxon genealogical regnal list and the chronology of early Wessex", *Peritia* 4: 21-66

Dumville, D N 1989 "Essex, Middle Anglia and the expansion of Mercia in the south-east midlands", in S Bassett (ed.) *The Origins of the Anglo-Saxon Kingdoms*: 123-140

Dumville, D N 1989 "The origins of Northumbria", in S Bassett (ed.) 1989 *The Origins of Anglo-Saxon Kingdoms*: 213-222

Dumville, D N 1989 "The Tribal Hidage: an introduction to its texts and their history", in S Bassett (ed.) *The Origins of the Anglo-Saxon Kingdoms*: 225-230

Dumville, D N 1995 *The Anglo-Saxon Chronicle, Volume 1: Ms F*

Duncan, A A M 1984 "One English nation", in L Smith (ed.) *The Dark Ages*

Eagles , B 1989 "Lindsey", in S Bassett (ed.) *The Origins of Anglo-Saxon Kingdoms*: 202-212

Easthope, A 1998 *Englishness and National Culture*

Ekwall, E 1960 *The Concise Oxford Dictionary of English Place-names*

Eller, J & R Coughlan 1996 "The poverty of primordialism", in J Hutchinson & A D Smith (eds.) *Ethnicity*: 45-51

References

Elliot, R W V 1989 *Runes*

Ellis, P B 1993 *Celt and Saxon: the struggle for Britain AD410-937*

Enloe, C 1996 "Religion and ethnicity", in J Hutchinson & A D Smith (eds.) *Ethnicity*: 197-202

Eriksen, T H 1993 *Ethnicity and Nationalism: anthropological perspectives*

Esmonde Cleary, A S 1989 *The Ending of Roman Britain*

Esmonde Cleary, A S 1995 "Changing constraints on the landscape AD 400-600", in D Hooke & S Burnell (eds.) 1995 *Landscape and Settlement in Britain AD 400-1066*: 11-26

Esmonde Cleary, A S 1999 "Roman Britain: civil and rural society", in J Hunter & I Ralston (eds.) *The Archaeology of Britain*: 157-175

Evans, A C 1986 *The Sutton Hoo Ship Burial*

Evison, M P 2000 "All in the genes? Evaluating the biological evidence of contact and migration", in D M Hadley & J Richards (eds.) *Cultures in contact*: 277-294.

Evison, V I 1965 *The Fifth Century Invasions South of the Thames*

Falsetti, A B & R R Sokal 1993 "Genetic structure of human populations in the British Isles", *Annals of Human Biology* 20: 215–229

Fanning, S 1991 "Bede, *imperium*, and the bretwaldas", *Speculum* 66:1-26

Faulkner, N 2000 *The Decline and Fall of Roman Britain*

Faulkner, N 2002 "The debate about the end of Roman Britain: a review of evidence and methods", *Archaeological Journal* 159: 59-76

Faull, M L 1975 "The semantic development of Old English *Wealh*", *Leeds Studies in English* New Series 8: 20-44

Faull, M L & S A Moorhouse 1981 *West Yorkshire: an archaeological survey to AD 1500*

Finberg, H P R 1972 "The princes of the Hwicce", in *The Early Charters of the West Midlands*: 167-180

Finberg, H P R 1972 "The Princes of the Magonsæte", in *The Early Charters of the West Midlands*: 217-224

Fisher, G 1988 "Style and socio-political organisation: a preliminary study from early Anglo-Saxon England", in S T Driscoll & M R Nieke (eds.) *Power and Politics in Early Medieval Britain and Ireland*: 145-161

Fishman, J 1996 "Ethnicity as being, doing and knowing", in J Hutchinson & A D Smith (eds.) *Ethnicity*: 63-69

Fletcher, E 1980 "The influence of Merovingian Gaul on Northumbria in the seventh century", *Medieval Archaeology* 24: 69-86

Foot, S 1996 "The making of Angelcynn: English identity before the Norman conquest", *Transactions of the Royal Historical Society* 6.6: 25-49

Fowler, P J 1977 "Agriculture and rural settlement", in D M Wilson *The Archaeology of Anglo-Saxon England*: 23-48

Fox, K 2004 *Watching the English*

Frazer, W O & A Tyrrell 2000 *Social Identity in Early Medieval Britain*

Frere, S 1967 *Britannia*

Gamble, C 2001 *Archaeology: the basics*

Gardner, K S 2002 "How was the west won?", *Council for British Archaeology South West* 8: 22-24

Garmonsway, G N 1954 *The Anglo-Saxon Chronicle*

Geertz, C 1996 "Primordial ties", in J Hutchinson & A D Smith (eds.) *Ethnicity*: 40-45

Gelling, M 1978 *Signposts to the Past: place-names and the history of England*

Gelling, M 1984 *Place-Names in the Landscape*

Gelling, M 1988 "Towards a chronology for English place-names", in D Hooke (ed.) *Anglo-Saxon Settlements*: 59-76

Gelling, M 1989 "The early history of western Mercia", in S Bassett (ed.) *The Origins of the Anglo-Saxon Kingdoms*: 184-201

Gelling, M 1993 "Why aren't we speaking Welsh?", *Anglo-Saxon Studies in Archaeology and History* 6: 51-56

Glasswell, S 2002 *The Earliest English: living and dying in Anglo-Saxon England*

Godden, M 1991 "Biblical literature: the Old Testament", in M Godden & M Lapidge (eds.) *The Cambridge Companion to Old English Literature*: 206-226

Godfrey, J 1962 *The Church in Anglo-Saxon England*

Goodier, A 1984 "The formation of boundaries in Anglo-Saxon England: a statistical study", *Medieval Archaeology* 28: 1-21

Green, D H 1995 "The rise of Germania in the light of linguistic evidence", in G Ausenda (ed.) *After Empire: towards and ethnology of Europe's barbarians*: 143-162

Greenfield, S B 1975 "The Finn episode and its parallel", in J F Tuso (ed.) *Beowulf*: 86-88

Greenway, D (ed.) 1996 *Henry of Huntingdon, Historia Anglorum: the history of the English people*

Grimond, J 1978 *The Common Welfare*

Halsall, G 1992 "Social change around AD 600: an Austrasian perspective", in M O H Carver (ed.) *The Age of Sutton Hoo: the seventh century in north-western Europe*: 265-278

Hamerow, H 1997 "Migration theory and the Anglo-Saxon identity crisis", in J Chapman & H Hamerow (eds.) *Migrations and Invasions in archaeological explanations*: 33-44

Hamerow, H 2003 *Early Medieval Settlements: the archaeology of rural communities in north-west Europe 400-900*

Hamp, E P 1982 '*Lloegr*: the Welsh name for England', *Cambridge Medieval Celtic Studies* 4: 83-85

Härke, H 1990 "'Warrior graves'? The background of the Anglo-Saxon weapon burial rite", *Past & Present* 126: 22-43

Härke, H 1992 "Changing symbols in a changing society: the Anglo-Saxon weapon burial rite in the seventh century", in M O H Carver (ed.) *The Age of Sutton Hoo: the seventh century in north-western Europe*: 149-166

Härke, H 1997 "Early Anglo-Saxon social structure", in J Hines (ed.) *The Anglo-Saxons from the Migration Period to the Eighth Century*: 125-170

Harris, A 2003 *Byzantium, Britain and the West: the archaeology of cultural identity AD 400-650*

Harrison, K 1976 *The Framework of Anglo-Saxon History to A.D.900*

Harrison, R J 1980 *The Beaker Folk*

Hart, C 1977 "The kingdom of Mercia", in A Dornier *Mercian Studies*: 43-61

Haseler, S 1996 *The English Tribe. Identity, nation and Europe*

Haselhoff, G 1974 "Salin's Style I", *Medieval Archaeology* 18: 1-15

Hawkes, S C & G C Dunning 1962 "Soldiers and settlers in Britain, fourth to fifth century: with a catalogue of animal-ornamented buckles and related belt-fittings", *Medieval Archaeology* 5: 1-70

Haywood, J 1999 *Dark Age Naval Power: reassessment of Frankish & Anglo-Saxon seafaring activity*

Hedeager, L 1992 "Kingdoms, ethnicity and material culture: Denmark in a European perspective", in M O H Carver (ed.) *The Age of Sutton Hoo: the seventh century in north-western Europe*: 279-300

Heather, P J 1997 "*Foedera* and *foederati* of the fourth century", in W Pohl (ed.) *Kingdoms of the Empire*: 57-74

Hendry, J 1999 *An Introduction to Social Anthropology: other people's worlds*

Henig, M 2002 "Roman Britons after AD 410", *British Archaeology* 68: 8-11

Herbert, K 1993 *Spellcraft: Old English heroic legends*

Higham, N 1992 *Rome, Britain and the Anglo-Saxons*

Higham, N 1993 *The Kingdom of Northumbria AD 350-1100*

Higham, N 1994 *The English Conquest: Gildas and Britain in the fifth century*

Higham, N 1995 *An English Empire: Bede and the early Anglo-Saxon kings*

Higham, N 1997 *The Convert Kings: power and religious affiliation in early Anglo-Saxon England*

Higham, N 2000 "King Edwin of the Deiri: rhetoric and the reality of power in early England", in H Geake & J Kenny (eds.) *Early Deira: archaeological studies of the East Riding in the fourth to ninth centuries AD*: 41-49

Hills, C 1978 "The archaeology of Anglo-Saxon England in the pagan period: a review", *Anglo-Saxon England* 8: 297-329

Hills, C 1990 "Roman Britain to Anglo-Saxon England", *History Today* 40, 10: 46-52

Hills, C 1999 "Early historic Britain", in J Hunter & I Ralston (eds.) *The Archaeology of Britain*: 176-193

Hills, C 2003 *Origins of the English*

Hines, J 1984 *The Scandinavian Character of Anglian England in the pre-Viking Period*, British Archaeological Reports British Series 124

Hines, J 1990a "Philology, archaeology and the adventus Saxonum vel Anglorum", in A Bammesberger & A Wollmann (eds.), *Britain 400-600: language and history*: 17-36

Hines, J 1990b "The runic inscriptions of early Anglo-Saxon England", in A Bammesberger & A Wollmann (eds.), *Britain 400-600: language and history*: 437-455

Hines, J 1991 "Some observations on the runic inscriptions of early Anglo-Saxon England", in A Bammesberger (ed.), *Old English Runes and their Continental Background*: 61-83

Hines, J 1992 "The Scandinavian character of Anglian England: an update", in M O H Carver (ed.) *The Age of Sutton Hoo: the seventh century in north-western Europe*: 315-330

Hines, J 1994 "The becoming of the English: identity, material culture and language in early Anglo-Saxon England", *Anglo-Saxon Studies in Archaeology and History* 7: 49-59

Hines, J 1995 "Cultural change and social organisation in early Anglo-Saxon England", in G Ausenda (ed.) *After Empire: towards and ethnology of Europe's barbarians*: 75-93

Hines, J 1996 "Britain after Rome: between multiculturalism and monoculturalism", in P S Graves-Brown, S Jones & C Gamble (eds.) *Cultural Identity and Archaeology*: 256-270

Hines, J 1997 *A New Corpus of Anglo-Saxon Great Square-Headed Brooches*

Hines, J (ed.) 1997 *The Anglo-Saxons from the Migration Period to the Eighth Century*

Hines, J 1997 "Religion, the limits of knowledge", in J Hines (ed.) *The Anglo-Saxons from the Migration Period to the Eighth Century*: 375-410

Hines, J 2003 "Society, community, and identity", in T Charles-Edwards (ed.) *After Rome*: 61-102

Hinton, D A 1990 *Archaeology, Economy and Society: England from the fifth to the fifteenth century*

Hitchens, C 2003 *That Blessed Plot, That Enigmatic Isle*

Hodder, I 1982 *Symbols in Action*

Hodges, R 1983 *Mohammed, Charlemagne and the Origins of Europe*

Hodges, R 1989 *Dark Age Economics: the origins of towns and trade AD 600-1000*

Hollander, L M (ed.) 1962 *The Poetic Edda*

Holt, J C 1997 *Colonial England 1066-1215*

Hooke, D 1985 *The Anglo-Saxon Landscape: the kingdom of the Hwicce*

Hooke, D 1995 "Introduction", in D Hooke & S Burnell (eds.) *Landscape and Settlement in Britain AD 400-1066*: 1-10

Hooke, D 1997 "The Anglo-Saxons in England in the seventh and eighth centuries: aspects of location in space", in J Hines (ed.) *The Anglo-Saxons from the migration period to the eighth century*: 65-99

Hooke, D & S Burnell (eds.) 1995 *Landscape and Settlement in Britain AD 400-1066*

Houts, E van 1999 *Memory and Gender in Medieval Europe 900-1200*

Horowitz, D 1996 "Symbolic politics and ethnic status", in J Hutchinson & A D Smith (eds.) *Ethnicity*: 285-291

Howe, N 1989 *Migration and Mythmaking in Anglo-Saxon England*

Hutchinson, J & A D Smith (eds.) 1996 *Ethnicity*

Inker, P 2000 "Technology as active material culture: the Quoit-brooch style", *Medieval Archaeology* 44: 25-52

Jackson, K H 1953 *Language and History in Early Britain*

Jackson, K H 1969 *The Gododdin: the oldest Scottish poem*

James, E 1988 *The Franks*

References

James, E 1989 "The origins of the barbarian kingdoms: the continental evidence", in S Bassett (ed.) *The Origins of the Anglo-Saxon Kingdoms*: 40-52

Jarman, A O H 1990 *Aneirin: Y Gododdin*

Jenkins, R 1997 *Rethinking Ethnicity: arguments and explorations*

John, E 1964 *Land Tenure in Early England*

John, E 1966 *Orbis Britanniae*

John, E 1996 *Reassessing Anglo-Saxon England*

Johnson, M 1999 *Archaeological Theory: an introduction*

Johnson, S 1980 *Later Roman Britain*

Jones, A H M 1964 *The Later Roman Empire 284-602: a social, economic and administrative survey*

Jones, B & D Mattingly 1990 *An Atlas of Roman Britain*

Jones, E 1998 *The English Nation: the great myth*

Jones, G R J 1975 "Early territorial organization in Gwynedd and Elmet", *Northern History* 10: 3-27

Jones, G R J 1979 "Multiple estates and early settlement", in P H Sawyer (ed.) *English Medieval Settlement*: 9-34

Jones, M E & J Casey 1991 "The Gallic Chronicle exploded?", *Britannia* 22: 212-215

Jones, M E 1996 *The End of Roman Britain*

Jones, S 1997 *The Archaeology of Ethnicity: constructing identities in the past and present*

Kapelle, W E 1979 *The Norman Conquest of the North: the region and its transformation*

Kirby, D P 1977 "Welsh bards and the border", in A Dornier *Mercian Studies*: 31-42

Kirby, D P 1991 *The Earliest English Kings*

Knight, J K 1999 *The End of Antiquity: archaeology, society and religion AD 235-700*

Krapp, G P 1931 *The Junius Manuscript*, Anglo-Saxon Poetic Records I

Kumar, K 2003 *The Making of English National Identity*

Kylie, E 1924 *The English Correspondence of Saint Boniface*

Lamb, H H 1995 *Climate, History and the Modern World*

Lancaster, L 1958 "Kinship in Anglo-Saxon society", *British Journal of Sociology* 9: 230-250, 359-377

Langford, P 2000 *Englishness Identified*

Lapidge, M 1991 "The saintly life in Anglo-Saxon England", in M Godden & M Lapidge (eds.) *The Cambridge Companion to Old English Literature*: 243-263

Lass, R 1987 *The Shape of English: structure and history*

Lass, R 1994 *Old English: a historical linguistic companion*

Leeds, E T 1913 *The Archaeology of the Anglo-Saxon Settlements*

Leeds, E T 1936 *Early Anglo-Saxon Art and Archaeology*

Linsell, T (ed.) 2000 *Our Englishness*

Linsell, T 2000 "Nations, nationalism and nationalists", in T Linsell (ed.) *Our Englishness*: 49-73

Liuzza, R M 1994 *The Old English Version of the Gospels*, Early English Text Society 304

Loveluck, C 2002 "The Romano-British to Anglo-Saxon transition – social transformations from the late Roman to early medieval period in northern England, AD 400-700", in C Brooks, R Daniels & A Harding *Past, Present and Future: The Archaeology of Northern England*: 127-148

Loyn, H R 1962 *Anglo-Saxon England and the Norman Conquest*

Lucy, S 2000 *The Anglo-Saxon Way of Death: burial rites in early England*

MacCana, P 1983 *Celtic Mythology*

Mallory, J P 1989 *In Search of the Indo-Europeans*

Malone, K (ed.) 1977 *Deor*, Exeter Medieval English Texts

Matless, D 1998 *Landscape and Englishness*

Matthews, K J 2001 "From Roman to Saxon: the late fourth to seventh centuries A.D. in Cornovia", *West Midlands Archaeology* 44: 17-25

Mattingly, H & S A Handford (eds.) 1970 *Tacitus: the Agricola and the Germania*

Metcalf, D M 1977 "Monetary affairs in Mercia in the time of Æthelbald", in A Dornier *Mercian Studies*: 87-106

Mierow, C C 1915 *The Gothic History of Jordanes*

Moreland, J 2000 "Ethnicity, power and the English", in W O Frazer & A Tyrrell *Social Identity in Early Medieval Britain*: 23-51

Morgan, L H 1877 *Ancient Society: or researches in the lines of human progress from savagery, through barbarism to civilization*

Morris, J 1975 *The Age of Arthur*

Morris, J 1980 *Nennius: British History and the Welsh Annals*, Arthurian Period Sources 8

Morris, J 1995 *Arthurian Period Sources* (6 vols.)

Morris, R 1989 *Churches in the Landscape*

Murray, A C 1983 *Germanic Kinship Structure*, Pontifical Institute of Mediaeval Studies, Studies and Texts 65

Myres, J N L 1969 *Anglo-Saxon Pottery and the Settlement of England*

Myres, J N L 1970 *The Angles, the Saxons and the Jutes*, the Raleigh Lecture on History, the British Academy

Myres, J N L 1977 *A Corpus of Anglo-Saxon Pottery of the Pagan Period*

Myres, J N L 1989 *The English Settlements*

Nash, M 1996 "The core elements of ethnicity", in J Hutchinson & A D Smith (eds.) *Ethnicity*: 24-28

Newman, J 1992 "The late Roman and Anglo-Saxon settlement pattern in the Sandlings of Suffolk", in M O H Carver (ed.) *The Age of Sutton Hoo: the seventh century in north-western Europe*: 25-38

Newton, S 1992 "Beowulf and the East Anglian royal pedigree", in M O H Carver (ed.) *The Age of Sutton Hoo: the seventh century in north-western Europe*: 65-74

Ó Corráin, D 1998 "Creating the past: the early Irish genealogical tradition", *Peritia* 12: 177-208

Orchard, A 1997 *Dictionary of Norse Myth and Legend*

Owen, G R 1981 *Rites and Religions of the Anglo-Saxons*

Padel, O J 1985 *Cornish place-name elements*, English Place-name Society, vols. 56, 57

Page, R I 1987 *Runes*

Page, R I 1995 *Runes and Runic Inscriptions*

Parker, C 1990 *The English Historical Tradition since 1850*

Paxman, J 1999 *The English: portrait of a people*

Pehrson, R N 1971 "Bilateral kin groups", in J Goody *Kinship: selected readings*

Pennar, M 1988 *Taliesin Poems*

Plummer, C 1896 *Venerabilis Bedae Opera Historica*

Pohl, W (ed.) 1997 *Kingdoms of the Empire*

Pohl, W 1997 "Ethnic names and identities in the British Isles: a comparative perspective", in J Hines (ed.) *The Anglo-Saxons from the Migration Period to the Eighth Century*: 7-40

Pohl, B W 1998 "Telling the difference: signs of ethnic identity", in B W Pohl & H Reimitz (eds.) *Strategies of Distinction: the construction of ethnic communities, 300-800*: 17-69

Powlesland, D 1997 "Early Anglo-Saxon settlements, structures, form and layout", in J, Hines (ed.) *The Anglo-Saxons from the Migration Period to the Eighth Century*: 101-124

Pretty, K 1989 "Defining the Magonsæte", in S Bassett (ed.) *The Origins of the Anglo-Saxon Kingdoms*: 171-183

Previté-Orton, C W 1952 *The Shorter Cambridge Medieval History, Volume 1: the later Roman Empire to the twelfth century*

Pryor, F 2004 *Britain AD*

Rahtz, P 1977 "The archaeology of west Mercian towns", in A Dornier *Mercian Studies*: 107-129

Reece, R 1980 "Town and country: the end of Roman Britain", *World Archaeology* 12.1: 77-92

Reynolds, S 1985 "What do we mean by 'Anglo-Saxon' and 'Anglo-Saxons'?", *Journal of British Studies* 24: 395-414

Richards, J D 1988 "Style and symbol: explaining variability in Anglo-Saxon cremation burials", in S T Driscoll & M R Nieke (eds.) *Power and Politics in Early Medieval Britain and Ireland*: 145-161

Richards, J D 1992 "Anglo-Saxon symbolism", in M O H Carver (ed.) *The Age of Sutton Hoo: the seventh century in north-western Europe*: 131-148

Richards, J D 1995 "An archaeology of Anglo-Saxon England", in G Ausenda (ed.) *After Empire: towards and ethnology of Europe's barbarians*: 51-74

Rieck, F 1997 *Recent Excavations at Nydam: the Danish National Museum's Nydam project 1989-1997*

Roberts, B F 1978 "Rhai o gerddi ymddiddan Llyfr Du Caerfyrddin", in R Bromwich & R B Jones *Astudiathau ar yr Hengerdd* (*Studies in Old Welsh Poetry*): 281-325

Rose, P & A Preston-Jones 1995 "Changes in the Cornish countryside AD 400-100", in D Hooke & S Burnell (eds.) *Landscape and Settlement in Britain AD 400-1066*: 51-68

Sawyer, P H (ed.) 1979 *English Medieval Settlement*

Scheff, T 1994 "Emotions and identity: a theory of ethnic nationalism", in C Calhoun (ed.) *Social theory and the politics of identity*: 277-303

Scruton, R 2001 *England: an elegy*

Scull, C J 1992 "Before Sutton Hoo: structure of power and society in early East Anglia", in M O H Carver (ed.) *The Age of Sutton Hoo: the seventh century in north-western Europe*: 3-24

Scull , C J 1993 "Archaeology, early Anglo-Saxon society and the origins of early Anglo-Saxon kingdoms", *Anglo-Saxon Studies in Archaeology and History* 6: 65-82

Serjeantson, M S 1935 *A History of Foreign Words in English*

Sermon, R 2001 "Britons and Saxons in Gloucestershire: migration or assimilation?", *CBA South West Journal* 7: 37-40

Shennan, S (ed.) 1989 *Archaeological Approaches to Cultural Identity*

Sims-Williams, P 1983 "The settlement of England in Bede and the Chronicle", *Anglo-Saxon England* 12: 1-41

Smith, A D 1986 *The Ethnic Origins of Nations*

Smith, A D 1996 "Chosen peoples", in J Hutchinson & A D Smith (eds.) *Ethnicity*: 189-197

Smith, A D 1999 *Myths and Memories of the Nation*

Smith, A D 2000 *The Nation in History: historiographical debates about ethnicity and nationalism*

Smith, A H 1961-63 *The Place-Names of the West Riding of Yorkshire*

Smith, G 1996 *The English Companion. An idiosyncratic A-Z of England and Englishness*

Smyth, A P (ed.) 1998 *Medieval Europeans*

Snyder, C A 1998 *An Age of Tyrants: Britain and the Britons A.D. 400-600*

Sowell, T 1998 *Conquests and Cultures*

Speake, G 1980 *Anglo-Saxon Animal Art and Its Germanic Background*

Stafford, P 1985 *The East Midlands in the Early Middle Ages*

Stenton, F M 1971 (1st ed. 1943) *Anglo-Saxon England*

Stevenson, J 1854 *William of Malmesbury: The History of the Kings of England*, Church Historians of England 3, part 1

Stevenson, J 1992 "Christianity in sixth- and seventh-century Southumbria", in M O H Carver (ed.) *The Age of Sutton Hoo: the seventh century in north-western Europe*: 175-184

Stubbs, W 1887 *Willelmi Malmesbiriensis Monachi: De Gestis Regum Anglorum. Libri Quinque*, Rolls Series 90, vol. 1.

Suzuki, S 2000 *The Quoit Brooch Style and Anglo-Saxon Settlement*

Swift, E 2000 *The End of the Western Roman Empire*

Szarmach, P E & J T Rosenthal (eds.) 1997 *The Preservation and Transmission of Anglo-Saxon Culture*

Talbot, C H 1954 *The Anglo-Saxon Missionaries in Germany*

Taylor, C M 1992 "Elmet: boundaries and Celtic survival in the post-Roman period", *Medieval History* 2: 111-129

Taylor, S 1983 *The Anglo-Saxon Chronicle, Volume 4: Ms B*

Thomas, J 1996 *Time, Culture and Identity: an interpretive archaeology*

Thorpe, B 1861 *The Anglo-Saxon Chronicle*, Rolls Series 23

Thorpe, L 1966 *Geoffrey of Monmouth: The History of the Kings of Britain*

Thorpe, L 1978 *Gerald of Wales: The Journey through Wales and the Description of Wales*

Todd, M 1992 *The Early Germans*

Todd, M 2000 *Migrants and Invaders: the movement of peoples in the ancient world*

Tolkein, J R R (ed. A Bliss) 1982 *Finn and Hengest: the fragment and the episode*

Tonkin, E, M McDonald & M Chapman (eds.) 1989 *History and Ethnicity*

Trudgill, P 2000 *Sociolinguistics: an introduction to language and society*

Upex, S 2002 "Landscape continuity and fossilization of Roman fields into Saxon and medieval landscapes", *Archaeological Journal* 159: 77-108

Vamsittart, P 1998 *In Memory of England. A novelist's view of history.*

Vince, A (ed.) 1993 *Pre-Viking Lindsey*

Walker, I W 2000 *Mercia and the Making of England*

Waring, G 1861 *The Lindisfarne and Rushworth Gospels, part II*, Surtees Society 39

Weale, M E, D A Weiss, R F Jager, N Bradman & M G Thomas 2002 "Y chromosome evidence for Anglo-Saxon mass migration", *Molecular Biology & Evolution* 19: 1008-1021

Weber, M 1996 "The origins of ethnic groups", in J Hutchinson & A D Smith (eds.) *Ethnicity*: 35-40

Webster, L & M Brown (eds.) 1997 *The Transformation of the Roman World AD 400-900*

Weight, R 2002 *Patriots*

Welch, M 1992 *Anglo-Saxon England*

Whitelock, D 1952 *The Beginnings of English Society*

Whitelock, D (ed.) 1955 *English Historical Documents c.500-1042*

Williams Sir I (trans. C Williams) 1968 *The Poems of Taliesin*

Williamson, T 1986 "Parish boundaries and early fields: continuity and discontinuity", *Journal of Historical Geography* 12: 241-248

Wilson, D 1992 *Anglo-Saxon Paganism*

Wilson, D M (ed.) 1976 *The Archaeology of Anglo-Saxon England*

Wilson, J F, DA Weiss, M Richards, M G Thomas, N Bradman & D B Goldstein 2001 "Genetic evidence for different male and female roles during cultural transitions in the British Isles", *Proceedings of the National Academy of Sciences* 98, 9: 5078-5083

Wilson, R M 1970 *The Lost Literature of Medieval England*

Winterbottom, M 1978 *Gildas: The Ruin of Britain and other documents,* Arthurian Period Sources 7

Wirth, G 1997 "Rome and its Germanic partners in the fourth century", in W Pohl (ed.) *Kingdoms of the Empire*: 13-55

Wolff, P 1971 *Western Languages AD 100-1500*

Wolfram, H (trans. T Dunlap) 1990 *History of the Goths*

Wolfram, H (trans. T Dunlap) 1997 *The Roman Empire and Its Germanic Peoples*

Wood, I 1992 "Frankish hegemony in England", in M O H Carver (ed.) *The Age of Sutton Hoo: the seventh century in north-western Europe*: 235-241

Wood, I 1994 *The Merovingian Kingdoms 450-751*

Wood, I 1997 "Before and after the migration to Britain", in J Hines (ed.) *The Anglo-Saxons from the Migration Period to the Eighth Century*: 41-64

Wood, M 1999 *Domesday: a search for the roots of England*

Wood, M 2000 *In Search of England*

Wood, P N 1996 "On the little British kingdom of Craven", *Northern History* 32: 1-20

Woolf, A 2000 "Community, identity and kingship in early England", W O Frazer & A Tyrrell (eds.) *Social Identity in Early Medieval Britain*: 91-109

Wormald, P 1983 "Bede, the Bretwaldas and the origins of the Gens Anglorum", in P Wormald (ed.) *Ideal and Reality in Frankish and Anglo-Saxon Society*: 99-129

Wormald, P 1994 "Engla lond: the making of an allegiance", *Journal of Historical Sociology* 7: 10-15

Wormald, P 1995 "The making of England", *History Today* Feb: 26-32

Wormald, P 1999 *The Making of English Law: King Alfred to the twelfth century*

Wrenn, C L (ed.) 1973 *Beowulf with the Finnesburg Fragment*

Yorke, B 1985 'The kingdom of the East Saxons', *Anglo-Saxon England* 14: 1-36

Yorke, B 1990 *Kings and Kingdoms of Early Anglo-Saxon England*

Yorke, B 1993 "Fact or fiction? The written evidence for the fifth and sixth centuries AD", *Anglo-Saxon Studies in Archaeology and History* 6: 45-50

Yorke, B 1995 *Wessex in the Early Middle Ages*

Yorke, B 2000 "Political and ethnic identity: a case study of Anglo-Saxon practice", in W O Frazer & A Tyrrell (eds.) *Social Identity in Early Medieval Britain*: 53-89

Zaluckyj, S 2001 *Mercia: the Anglo-Saxon kingdom of central England*

Zettersten, A (ed.) 1979 *Waldere*, Old and Middle English Texts

Index

Words beginning Æ are included under A. Words beginning Ð are under T.

Some of our other titles

The English Warrior from earliest times to 1066
Stephen Pollington

This is not intended to be a bald listing of the battles and campaigns from the Anglo-Saxon Chronicle and other sources, but rather it is an attempt to get below the surface of Anglo-Saxon warriorhood and to investigate the rites, social attitudes, mentality and mythology of the warfare of those times.

> "An under-the-skin study of the role, rights, duties, psyche and rituals of the Anglo-Saxon warrior. The author combines original translations from Norse and Old English primary sources with archaeological and linguistic evidence for an in-depth look at the warrior, his weapons, tactics and logistics.
>
> A very refreshing, innovative and well-written piece of scholarship that illuminates a neglected period of English history"
>
> *Time Team Booklists* - Channel 4 Television

Revised Edition

An already highly acclaimed book has been made even better by the inclusion of additional information and illustrations.

£16.95   ISBN 1–898281–42–4   245 x 170mm   over 50 illustrations   304 pages hardback

The Mead Hall The feasting tradition in Anglo-Saxon England
Stephen Pollington

This new study takes a broad look at the subject of halls and feasting in Anglo-Saxon England. The idea of the communal meal was very important among nobles and yeomen, warriors, farmers churchmen and laity. One of the aims of the book is to show that there was not just one 'feast' but two main types: the informal social occasion *gebeorscipe* and the formal, ritual gathering *symbel*.

Using the evidence of Old English texts - mainly the epic *Beowulf* and the *Anglo-Saxon Chronicles*, Stephen Pollington shows that the idea of feasting remained central to early English social traditions long after the physical reality had declined in importance.

The words of the poets and saga-writers are supported by a wealth of archaeological data dealing with halls, settlement layouts and magnificent feasting gear found in many early Anglo-Saxon graves.

Three appendices cover:

- Hall-themes in Old English verse;
- Old English and translated texts;
- The structure and origins of the warband.

£14.95 ISBN 1-898281-30-0   9 ¾ x 6 ¾ inches   248 x 170mm   288 pages   hardback

First Steps in Old English

An easy to follow language course for the beginner

Stephen Pollington

A complete, well presented and easy to use Old English language course that contains all the exercises and texts needed to learn Old English. This course has been designed to be of help to a wide range of students, from those who are teaching themselves at home, to undergraduates who are learning Old English as part of their English degree course. The author is aware that some individuals have difficulty with grammar. To help overcome this and other difficulties, he has adopted a step-by-step approach that enables students of differing abilities to advance at their own pace. The course includes practice and translation exercises.

There is a glossary of the words used in the course, and 16 Old English texts, including the Battle of Brunanburh and Battle of Maldon.

£16.95 ISBN 1-898281-38-6 10" x 6½" (245 x 170mm) 256 pages

Ærgeweorc Old English Verse and Prose

read by Stephen Pollington

This audiotape cassette can be used with *First Steps in Old English* or just listened to for the sheer pleasure of hearing Old English spoken well.

Tracks: 1. Deor. 2. Beowulf – The Funeral of Scyld Scefing. 3. Engla Tocyme (The Arrival of the English). 4. Ines Domas. Two Extracts from the Laws of King Ine. 5. Deniga Hergung (The Danes' Harrying) Anglo-Saxon Chronicle Entry AD997. 6. Durham 7. The Ordeal (Be ðon ðe ordales weddigaþ) 8. Wið Dweorh (Against a Dwarf) 9. Wið Wennum (Against Wens) 10. Wið Wæterælfadle (Against Waterelf Sickness) 11. The Nine Herbs Charm 12. Læcedomas (Leechdoms) 13. Beowulf's Greeting 14. The Battle of Brunanburh 15. Blacmon – by Adrian Pilgrim.

£7.50 ISBN 1–898281–20–3 C40 audiotape

Wordcraft: Concise English/Old English Dictionary and Thesaurus

Stephen Pollington

This book provides Old English equivalents to the commoner modern words in both dictionary and thesaurus formats. The Thesaurus presents vocabulary relevant to a wide range of individual topics in alphabetical lists, thus making it easily accessible to those with specific areas of interest. Each thematic listing is encoded for cross-reference from the Dictionary. The two sections will be of invaluable assistance to students of the language, as well as to those with either a general or a specific interest in the Anglo-Saxon period.

£9.95 A5 ISBN 1–898281–02–5 256pp

An Introduction to the Old English Language and its Literature

Stephen Pollington

The purpose of this general introduction to Old English is not to deal with the teaching of Old English but to dispel some misconceptions about the language and to give an outline of its structure and its literature. Some basic knowledge of these is essential to an understanding of the early period of English history and the present form of the language.

£4.95 A5 ISBN 1–898281–06–8 48pp

A Guide to Late Anglo-Saxon England

From Alfred to Eadgar II 871–1074

Donald Henson

This guide has been prepared with the aim of providing the general readers with both an overview of the period and a wealth of background information. Facts and figures are presented in a way that makes this a useful reference handbook.

Contents include: The Origins of England; Physical Geography; Human Geography; English Society; Government and Politics; The Church; Language and Literature; Personal Names; Effects of the Norman Conquest. All of the kings from Alfred to Eadgar II are dealt with separately and there is a chronicle of events for each of their reigns. There are also maps, family trees and extensive appendices.

£9.95 ISBN 1–898281–21–1 9½" x 6¾"/245 x 170mm, 6 maps & 3 family trees 208 pages

The English Elite in 1066 - Gone but not forgotten

Donald Henson

The people listed in this book formed the topmost section of the ruling elite in 1066. It includes all those who held office between the death of Eadward III (January 1066) and the abdication of Eadgar II (December 1066). There are 455 individuals in the main entries and these have been divided according to their office or position.

The following information is listed where available:

What is known of their life;

Their landed wealth;

The early sources in which information about the individual can be found

Modern references that give details about his or her life.

In addition to the biographical details, there is a wealth of background information about English society and government. A series of appendices provide detailed information about particular topics or groups of people.

£16.95 ISBN 1–898281–26–2 245 x 170mm / 10 x 7 inches   paperback   272 pages

Tastes of Anglo-Saxon England

Mary Savelli

These easy to follow recipes will enable you to enjoy a mix of ingredients and flavours that were widely known in Anglo-Saxon England but are rarely experienced today. In addition to the 46 recipes, there is background information about households and cooking techniques.

£4.95 ISBN 1-898281-28-9 A5 80 pages

Anglo-Saxon Food & Drink

Production, Processing, Distribution, and Consumption

Ann Hagen

Food production for home consumption was the basis of economic activity throughout the Anglo-Saxon period. Used as payment and a medium of trade, food was the basis of the Anglo-Saxons' system of finance and administration.

Information from various sources has been brought together in order to build up a picture of how food was grown, conserved, distributed, prepared and eaten during the period from the beginning of the 5th century to the 11th century. Many people will find it fascinating for the views it gives of an important aspect of Anglo-Saxon life and culture. In addition to Anglo-Saxon England the Celtic west of Britain is also covered.

This edition combines earlier titles – *A Handbook of Anglo-Saxon Food* and *A Second Handbook of Anglo-Saxon Food & Drink*.

Extensive index.

£25   10" x 7" (250 x 175mm)   ISBN 1–898281–41-6   Hardback 512pp

English Heroic Legends

Kathleen Herbert

The author has taken the skeletons of ancient Germanic legends about great kings, queens and heroes, and put flesh on them. Kathleen Herbert's extensive knowledge of the period is reflected in the wealth of detail she brings to these tales of adventure, passion, bloodshed and magic.

The book is in two parts. First are the stories that originate deep in the past, yet because they have not been hackneyed, they are still strange and enchanting. After that there is a selection of the source material, with information about where it can be found and some discussion about how it can be used.

£9-95   A5   ISBN 0–9516209–9–1   292pp

Peace-Weavers and Shield-Maidens: Women in Early English Society

Kathleen Herbert

The recorded history of the English people did not start in 1066 as popularly believed but one-thousand years earlier. The Roman historian Cornelius Tacitus noted in *Germania*, published in the year 98, that the English (Latin *Anglii*), who lived in the southern part of the Jutland peninsula, were members of an alliance of Goddess-worshippers. The author has taken that as an appropriate opening to an account of the earliest Englishwomen, the part they played in the making of England, what they did in peace and war, the impressions they left in Britain and on the continent, how they were recorded in the chronicles, how they come alive in heroic verse and riddles.

£4.95   A5   ISBN 1–898281–11–4   64pp

Dark Age Naval Power

A Reassessment of Frankish and Anglo-Saxon Seafaring Activity

John Haywood

In the first edition of this work, published in 1991, John Haywood argued that the capabilities of the pre-Viking Germanic seafarers had been greatly underestimated. Since that time, his reassessment of Frankish and Anglo-Saxon shipbuilding and seafaring has been widely praised and accepted.

In this second edition, some sections of the book have been revised and updated to include information gained from excavations and sea trials with sailing replicas of early ships. The new evidence supports the author's argument that early Germanic shipbuilding and seafaring skills were far more advanced than previously thought. It also supports the view that Viking ships and seaborne activities were not as revolutionary as is commonly believed.

> 'The book remains a historical study of the first order. It is required reading for our seminar on medieval seafaring at Texas A & M University and is essential reading for anyone interested in the subject.'
>
> F. H. Van Doorninck, *The American Neptune*

£16.95 ISBN 1-898281-43-2 approx. 10 x 6½ inches (245 x 170 mm) Hardback 224 pages

English Martial Arts

Terry Brown

Little is known about the very early history of English martial arts but it is likely that methods, techniques and principles were passed on from one generation to the next for centuries. By the sixteenth century English martial artists had their own governing body which controlled its members in much the same way as do modern-day martial arts organisations. It is apparent from contemporary evidence that the Company of Maisters taught and practised a fighting system that ranks as high in terms of effectiveness and pedigree as any in the world.

In the first part of the book the author investigates the weapons, history and development of the English fighting system and looks at some of the attitudes, beliefs and social pressures that helped mould it.

Part two deals with English fighting techniques drawn from books and manuscripts that recorded the system at various stages in its history. In other words, all of the methods and techniques shown in this book are authentic and have not been created by the author. The theories that underlie the system are explained in a chapter on *The Principles of True Fighting*. All of the techniques covered are illustrated with photographs and accompanied by instructions. Techniques included are for bare-fist fighting, broadsword, quarterstaff, bill, sword and buckler, sword and dagger.

Experienced martial artists, irrespective of the style they practice, will recognise that the techniques and methods of this system are based on principles that are as valid as those underlying the system that they practice.

The author, who has been a martial artist for twenty-eight years, has recently re-formed the Company of Maisters of Defence, a medieval English martial arts organization.

£16.95 ISBN 1–898281–29-7 10 x 6½ inches - 245 x 170 mm 220 photographs 240 pages

Latest Titles

Anglo-Saxon Attitudes – A short introduction to Anglo-Saxonism
J.A. Hilton

This is not a book about the Anglo-Saxons, but a book about books about Anglo-Saxons. It describes the academic discipline of Anglo-Saxonism; the methods of study used; the underlying assumptions; and the uses to which it has been put.

Methods and motives have changed over time but right from the start there have been constant themes: English patriotism and English freedom.

£6.95   A5   ISBN 1–898281–39-4   9 ¾ x 6 ¾ inches   245 x 170mm   Hardback 64 pages

The Origins of the Anglo-Saxons
Donald Henson

This book has come about through a growing frustration with scholarly analysis and debate about the beginnings of Anglo-Saxon England. Much of what has been written is excellent, yet unsatisfactory. One reason for this is that scholars often have only a vague acquaintance with fields outside their own specialism. The result is a partial examination of the evidence and an incomplete understanding or explanation of the period.

The growth and increasing dominance of archaeological evidence for the period has been accompanied by an unhealthy enthusiasm for models of social change imported from prehistory. Put simply, many archaeologists have developed a complete unwillingness to consider movements of population as a factor in social, economic or political change. All change becomes a result of indigenous development, and all historically recorded migrations become merely the movement of a few hundred aristocrats or soldiers. The author does not find this credible.

£19.95   ISBN 1–898281–40-2   9 ¾ x 6 ¾ inches   245 x 170mm   Hardback 304 pages

A Departed Music – Readings in Old English Poetry
Walter Nash

The *readings* of this book take the form of passages of translation from some Old English poems. The author paraphrases their content and discuses their place and significance in the history of poetic art in Old English society and culture.

The authors knowledge, enthusiasm and love of his subject help make this an excellent introduction to the subject for students and the general reader.

£16.95   ISBN 1–898281–37-8   9 ¾ x 6 ¾ inches   245 x 170mm   Hardback 240 pages

English Sea Power 871-1100 AD
John Pullen-Appleby

This work examines the largely untold story of English sea power during the period 871 to 1100. It was an age when English kings deployed warships first against Scandinavian invaders and later in support of Continental allies.

The author has gathered together information about the appearance of warships and how they were financed, crewed, and deployed.

Price £14.95   ISBN 1–898281–31-9   9 ¾ x 6 ¾ inches   245 x 170mm   Hardback 114 pages

Anglo-Saxon Riddles

Translated by John Porter

Here you will find ingenious characters who speak their names in riddles, and meet a one-eyed garlic seller, a bookworm, an iceberg, an oyster, the sun and moon and a host of others from the everyday life and imagination of the Anglo-Saxons. Their sense of the awesome power of creation goes hand in hand with a frank delight in obscenity, a fascination with disguise and with the mysterious processes by which the natural world is turned to human use. This edition contains **all 95 riddles of the Exeter Book in both Old English and Modern English.**

£4.95   A5   ISBN 1–898281–13–0   144 pages

Tolkien's *Mythology for England*

A Guide to Middle-Earth

Edmund Wainwright

Tolkien set out to create a mythology for England and the English but the popularity of his books and the recent films has spread across the English-speaking world and beyond.

You will find here an outline of Tolkien's life and work. The main part of the book consists of an alphabetical subject entry which will help you gain a greater understanding of Tolkien's Middle-Earth, the creatures that inhabit it, and the languages they spoke. It will also give an insight into a culture and way-of-life that extolled values which are as valid today as they were over 1,000 years ago.

This book focuses on *The Lord of the Rings* and shows how Tolkien's knowledge of Anglo-Saxon and Norse literature and history helped shape its plot and characters.

£9-95 ISBN 1-898281-36-X approx. 10 x 6½ inches (245 x 170 mm) Hardback 128 pages

Anglo-Saxon Books

Tel. 0845 430 4200 Fax. 0845 430 4201   email: enq@asbooks.co.uk

Please check availability and prices on our web site at www.asbooks.co.uk

See website for postal address.

Payment may be made by Visa / Mastercard or by a cheque drawn on a UK bank in sterling.

UK deliveries add 10% up to a maximum of £2·50

Europe – including **Republic of Ireland** – add 10% plus £1 – all orders are sent airmail

North America add 10% surface delivery, 30% airmail

Elsewhere add 10% surface delivery, 40% airmail

Overseas surface delivery 6 – 10 weeks; airmail 6 – 14 days

Most titles can be obtained through North American bookstores.

Organisations

Þa Engliscan Gesiðas

Þa Engliscan Gesiðas (The English Companions) is a historical and cultural society exclusively devoted to Anglo-Saxon history. Its aims are to bridge the gap between scholars and non-experts, and to bring together all those with an interest in the Anglo-Saxon period, its language, culture and traditions, so as to promote a wider interest in, and knowledge of all things Anglo-Saxon. The Fellowship publishes a journal, *Wiðowinde,* which helps members to keep in touch with current thinking on topics from art and archaeology to heathenism and Early English Christianity. The Fellowship enables like-minded people to keep in contact by publicising conferences, courses and meetings which might be of interest to its members.

For further details see www.tha-engliscan-gesithas.org.uk or write to: The Membership Secretary, Þa Engliscan Gesiðas, BM Box 4336, London, WC1N 3XX England.

Regia Anglorum

Regia Anglorum was founded to accurately re-create the life of the British people as it was around the time of the Norman Conquest. Our work has a strong educational slant. We consider authenticity to be of prime importance and prefer, where possible, to work from archaeological materials. Approximately twenty-five per cent of our members, of over 500 people, are archaeologists or historians.

The Society has a large working Living History Exhibit, teaching and exhibiting more than twenty crafts in an authentic environment. We own a forty-foot wooden ship replica of a type that would have been a common sight in Northern European waters around the turn of the first millennium AD. Battle re-enactment is another aspect of our activities, often involving 200 or more warriors.

For further information see www.regia.org or contact: K. J. Siddorn, 9 Durleigh Close, Headley Park, Bristol BS13 7NQ, England, e-mail: kim_siddorn@compuserve.com

The Sutton Hoo Society

Our aims and objectives focus on promoting research and education relating to the Anglo Saxon Royal cemetery at Sutton Hoo, Suffolk in the UK. The Society publishes a newsletter SAXON twice a year, which keeps members up to date with society activities, carries resumes of lectures and visits, and reports progress on research and publication associated with the site. If you would like to join the Society please see website: www.suttonhoo.org

Wuffing Education

Wuffing Education provides those interested in the history, archaeology, literature and culture of the Anglo-Saxons with the chance to meet experts and fellow enthusiasts for a whole day of in-depth seminars and discussions. Day Schools take place at the historic Tranmer House overlooking the burial mounds of Sutton Hoo in Suffolk.

For details of programme of events contact:-
Wuffing Education, 4 Hilly Fields, Woodbridge, Suffolk IP12 4DX
email education@wuffings.co.uk website www.wuffings.co.uk
Tel. 01394 383908 or 01728 688749

Places to visit

Bede's World at Jarrow

Bede's world tells the remarkable story of the life and times of the Venerable Bede, 673–735 AD. Visitors can explore the origins of early medieval Northumbria and Bede's life and achievements through his own writings and the excavations of the monasteries at Jarrow and other sites.

Location – 10 miles from Newcastle upon Tyne, off the A19 near the southern entrance to the River Tyne tunnel. Bus services 526 & 527

Bede's World, Church Bank, Jarrow, Tyne and Wear, NE32 3DY

Tel. 0191 489 2106; Fax: 0191 428 2361; website: www.bedesworld.co.uk

Sutton Hoo near Woodbridge, Suffolk

Sutton Hoo is a group of low burial mounds overlooking the River Deben in south-east Suffolk. Excavations in 1939 brought to light the richest burial ever discovered in Britain – an Anglo-Saxon ship containing a magnificent treasure which has become one of the principal attractions of the British Museum. The mound from which the treasure was dug is thought to be the grave of Rædwald, an early English king who died in 624/5 AD.

This National Trust site has an excellent visitor centre, which includes a reconstruction of the burial chamber and its grave goods. Some original objects as well as replicas of the treasure are on display.

2 miles east of Woodbridge on B1083   Tel. 01394 389700

West Stow Anglo-Saxon Village

An early Anglo-Saxon Settlement reconstructed on the site where it was excavated consisting of timber and thatch hall, houses and workshop. There is also a museum containing objects found during the excavation of the site. Open all year 10am–4.15pm (except Yuletide). Special provision for school parties. A teachers' resource pack is available. Costumed events are held at weekends, especially Easter Sunday and August Bank Holiday Monday. Craft courses are organised.

For further details see www.stedmunds.co.uk/west_stow.html or contact:

The Visitor Centre, West Stow Country Park, Icklingham Road, West Stow,

Bury St Edmunds, Suffolk IP28 6HG   Tel. 01284 728718